"Copan and Flannagan address the arguments of the atheists who use divine violence in the Bible to undermine belief and confidence in God. Not only are they adept at biblical interpretation and philosophy as they effectively counter this challenge, but they also write in a deeply compelling way that will appeal to both students and laypeople."

—**Tremper Longman III**, Robert H. Gundry Professor of Biblical Studies, Westmont College

"In their wide-ranging book, Copan and Flannagan go beyond standard treatments of Old Testament warfare; they incorporate biblical, theological, philosophical, ethical, legal, and historical perspectives on a much-debated but often-misunderstood topic. This volume makes important strides forward in laying out a case for the coherence of divine command theory in connection with these Yahweh-war texts."

—**William Lane Craig**, research professor of philosophy, Talbot School of Theology

"This is a very lucid and helpful discussion of this troubling topic."

—**Gordon Wenham**, professor of Old Testament, Trinity College Bristol

"This brave, hard-nosed, and wide-ranging study constitutes a serious attempt at facing all the varied aspects of a question that troubles so many people. Well done!"

—**John Goldingay**, David Allan Hubbard Professor of Old Testament, Fuller Theological Seminary

"As a full-scale follow-up to the excellent popular treatment of the topic in *Is God a Moral Monster?*, this book provides the most thorough and comprehensive treatment of the problem of violence in the Old Testament that I have encountered. The authors tackle the aggressive charges of the new atheists, as well as other equally sceptical but less strident critics of 'the God of the Old Testament.' And they do so with a blend of careful biblical exegesis and incisive moral argumentation. The book reaches deep, but remains readable, and the summaries at the end of every chapter are a great help in following the case as it is steadily built up. All of us who, in teaching or preaching the Old Testament, are constantly bombarded with 'But what about the Canaanites?' will be very grateful for these rich resources for a well-informed, gracious, and biblically faithful reply."

—**Christopher J. H. Wright**, International Ministries Director, Langham Partnership; author of *Old Testament Ethics for the People of God* and *The God I Don't Understand*

"Does your god order you to slaughter your enemies? Did God's command to the Israelites to kill the Canaanites set a pattern for human behaviour? Do Joshua's wars justify the Crusades? Does the Bible promote violence against dissenters and opponents, as the Qur'an does? Reading the Bible as a modern book leads to false conclusions, the authors show clearly. Comparing writings from Assyria, Babylonia, Egypt, and the Hittites with biblical texts, they demonstrate the common use of exaggerated language—so that 'all' may not mean 'every single person,' for example—bringing clearer understanding of God's apparently genocidal commands about the Canaanites. Carefully argued, with clear examples and helpful summaries, these chapters give Christians sound bases for defending and sharing their faith in the God of love, justice, and forgiveness. This is an instructive and very welcome antidote to much current thought."

—**Alan Millard**, Rankin Professor Emeritus of Hebrew
and Ancient Semitic Languages, University of Liverpool

DID GOD REALLY COMMAND GENOCIDE?

COMING TO TERMS WITH THE JUSTICE OF GOD

Paul Copan and Matthew Flannagan

BakerBooks

a division of Baker Publishing Group
Grand Rapids, Michigan

© 2014 by Paul Copan and Matthew Flannagan

Published by Baker Books
a division of Baker Publishing Group
P.O. Box 6287, Grand Rapids, MI 49516-6287
www.bakerbooks.com

Printed in the United States of America

Library of Congress Cataloging-in-Publication Data
Copan, Paul.
    Did God really command genocide? : coming to terms with the justice of God / Paul Copan and Matthew Flannagan.
        pages cm
    Includes bibliographical references and index.
    ISBN 978-0-8010-1622-6 (pbk. : alk. paper)
    1. Ethnicity in the Bible. 2. Genocide—Biblical teaching. 3. Genocide—Religious aspects—Christianity. 4. Violence in the Bible. 5. Theodicy. 6. God (Christianity)—Righteousness—Biblical teaching. 7. God (Christianity)—Love—Biblical teaching. I. Title.
BS1199.E8C66 2014
239—dc23   2014022539

14   15   16   17   18   19   20   7   6   5   4   3   2   1

From Paul

For my dear daughter Kristen Copan:
an old soul with a spunky spirit,
philomathean mind, and servant's heart—
a great blessing from the Lord

From Matthew

For Madeleine Jane Flannagan,
whose patience and support enabled this project to be completed

Contents

Introduction: The New Atheism and the Old Testament   9

Part 1: Genocide Texts and the Problem of Scriptural Authority

1. The Problem Clarified: An Atheistic Philosophical Argument   17
2. What Does It Mean to Say the Bible Is the Word of God?   23
3. The God of the Old Testament versus the God of the New?   37

Part 2: Occasional Commands, Hyperbolic Texts, and Genocidal Massacres

4. Does the Bible Command *Us* to Kill Innocent Human Beings?   53
5. Does the Bible Portray the Canaanites as Innocent?   61
6. Thrusting Out, Driving Out, and Dispossessing the Canaanites—Not Annihilating Them   76
7. The Question of Genocide and the Hyperbolic Interpretation of Joshua   84
8. Genocide and an Argument for "Hagiographic Hyperbole"   94
9. Objections from the Biblical Text to the Hyperbolic Interpretation   109
10. Legal and Theological Objections concerning Genocide   125

Part 3: Is It Always Wrong to Kill Innocent People?

11. Divine Command Theory: Preliminary Considerations   141
12. The Divine Command Theory of Obligation: What It Is—and Is Not   148

13. Arbitrary Divine Commands? The Euthyphro Dilemma   159
14. Other Euthyphro-Related Objections   171
15. Can One Coherently Claim That God Commanded the Killing of Innocents?   186
16. Can One Rationally Believe God Commands a Violation of Innocent Human Beings?   194
17. Is It Rational to Believe God Commanded the Killing of Innocents?   210
18. What If Someone Claimed God Commanded Killing the Innocent Today?   233
19. The Role of Miracles and the Command to Kill Canaanites   246

Part 4: Religion and Violence

20. Does Religion Cause Violence?   259
21. Are Yahweh Wars in the Old Testament Just like Islamic Jihad?   276
22. Did Old Testament War Texts Inspire the Crusades?   288
23. Turning the Other Cheek, Pacifism, and Just War   299

Afterword   317
Notes   319

Introduction

THE NEW ATHEISM AND THE OLD TESTAMENT

The world's leading atheist, Oxford University's Richard Dawkins, has engaged in a good deal of name-calling. The object of his scorn? Yahweh, the God of the Old Testament. "The God of the Old Testament is arguably the most unpleasant character in all fiction: jealous and proud of it; a petty, unjust, unforgiving control-freak; a vindictive, bloodthirsty ethnic cleanser; a misogynistic, homophobic, racist, infanticidal, genocidal, filicidal, pestilential, megalomaniacal, sadomasochistic, capriciously malevolent bully."[1]

Now, it has long been known that Dawkins and other "New Atheists" use rhetorical smokescreens and "village atheist" tactics—marked by aggressiveness, intolerance, and sophomoric argumentation—not endorsed by other atheists in the academy, and Dawkins has admitted that his own theory of atheism is contradicted by the realities of everyday life.[2]

And despite well-informed, credible attempts to correct Dawkins's definition of "faith," he brazenly continues to define it as belief *immune* to all evidence and inquiry—a characterization no Christian theologian worthy of the name would accept. And even though modern science was established by Bible-believing theists, Dawkins perpetuates the myth that "faith" is opposed to "science."

Loads of scholars have responded to the caricatures, rhetoric, and sometimes downright silliness of the New Atheists.[3] In fact, the philosopher of science Michael Ruse, an atheist himself, declares that Dawkins's *God Delusion* book "makes me embarrassed to be an atheist."[4]

9

That said, what about Dawkins's claim that the God of the Old Testament is *genocidal* and a *bloodthirsty ethnic cleanser?* Is he correct when he calls Joshua's destruction of Jericho an example of Israel's "ethnic cleansing" in which "bloodthirsty massacres" were carried out with "xenophobic relish"? Are these events "morally indistinguishable from Hitler's invasion of Poland" or "Saddam Hussein's massacres of the Kurds and the Marsh Arabs"?[5]

Here, a number of people, including Christians, think that Dawkins may have a point. After all, Christians typically accept that the Bible, being the Word of God, is trustworthy in all it affirms. In particular, they insist on its authority for faith and morals. Yet a perennial challenge to such a stance is a series of jarring passages in the Old Testament using language such as "leave alive nothing that breathes," "utterly destroy," and "no survivor was left." This appears to teach that God has commanded genocide, which the *Oxford English Dictionary* defines as "the deliberate and systematic extermination of an ethnic or national group."[6] But surely genocide, and the divine command to "utterly destroy" (NASB) is morally wrong. It would seem, therefore, that the Bible teaches serious moral error.

The Current Discussion in Philosophy and Biblical Studies

If you read contemporary philosophical critiques of theism, theological ethics, and the moral argument for God's existence, you will eventually encounter biblical references in which God purportedly commands genocide. In a debate on God's existence with Christian philosopher Alvin Plantinga, atheist philosopher Michael Tooley states that "although I am an atheist, I should very much like it to be the case that I am mistaken in that God, as I have defined him, exists."[7] However, "the God of Roman Catholicism or Protestant Fundamentalism, or of Islam I would not welcome, for it would mean that the world, while not the worst imaginable, would be very bad indeed." One reason he gives for this conclusion is "Yahweh's command to Saul to kill all the Amalekites,"[8] and he cites 1 Samuel 15:3: "Now go, attack the Amalekites and totally destroy all that belongs to them. Do not spare them; put to death men and women, children and infants, cattle and sheep, camels and donkeys."

Similarly, in his book *Morality without God*, Walter Sinnott-Armstrong opens a chapter on divine commands and ethics (see discussion in chaps. 11–14 of this book) with a citation of Joshua 10:40: "So Joshua defeated the whole land, . . . he left none remaining, but utterly destroyed all that breathed, as the LORD God of Israel commanded him."[9] Another atheist philosopher, Louise Antony, wonders what people would say if God commanded genocide today "as he does in 1 Samuel 15:1–3."[10] Such comments are reflective of the rising tide of atheists—including the New Atheists—who are writing books and articles using biblical proof texts in an attempt to show that the biblical God commands genocide.

In 2009, the philosophy of religion journal *Philosophia Christi* devoted an entire issue to the question "Did God Mandate Genocide?"[11] The same year the Center for Philosophy of Religion at the University of Notre Dame hosted a conference on ethical questions raised by the Abrahamic God in the Hebrew Scriptures,[12] where skeptics and believers alike debated whether some of Yahweh's commands were morally justifiable; the skeptics claimed that God commanded the killing of Canaanite noncombatants as a genocide. The Society of Biblical Literature in 2009 and 2010 hosted panel sessions on such issues. And we are seeing scholars devoting increased attention to these topics with book titles such as *God Behaving Badly, Is God a Moral Monster?, Holy War in the Bible, The God I Don't Understand, Disturbing Divine Behavior, The Violence of Scripture, Seriously Dangerous Religion*, and the like.[13] Clearly this classic question of violence in Scripture is an issue that is not going away.

Contents of the Book

Because of the enduring nature of this topic, our book is dedicated to discussing and responding to the question of whether God really commanded genocide. We examine what we take to be the critic's strongest arguments and address those concerns by offering a coherent and wide-ranging response—biblically, theologically, philosophically, ethically, and legally. And in light of our previous work in this area and discussions about this topic, we examine related topics that inevitably emerge in open forums, online discussions, and personal conversations.[14]

Though most of the book will be readily accessible, there are a few places involving more technically difficult philosophical discussion about the nature of divine-human authorship of Scripture as well as divine commands. We have provided extensive summaries at the end of each chapter that will assist the uninitiated reader in navigating through these portions. And since we provide a summary of the key points at the end of each chapter, we'll only briefly review the book's contents here.

The book is broken up into four parts. Part 1 ("Genocide Texts and the Problem of Scriptural Authority") addresses what the problem actually is and how critics typically formulate their arguments against the God of the Bible, who commands killing Canaanites—which seems to give Bible believers

precedent for engaging in similar acts of aggression (chap. 1). In light of a
God who reveals his will and sometimes issues harsh commands, we address
the topic of what it means to say that the Bible is the Word of God and that
both God and humans are its authors (chap. 2). Another matter related to
biblical authority concerns the matchup between the characteristics of God
in the Old Testament and God as described in the New, looking at the work
of Old Testament scholars Eric Seibert and Peter Enns in particular (chap. 3).

In part 2 ("Occasional Commands, Hyperbolic Texts, and Genocidal Massacres"), we address the matter of occasional—or particular, uniquely issued—
commands. In chapter 4, we discuss the question, does the Bible actually command *us* to kill innocent people? We move from there to the matter of whether
the Canaanites could be described as "innocent" (chap. 5).

Then we move to questions of how to understand the commands to "utterly destroy" and "leave alive nothing that breathes." We see these commands
as hyperbolic (using exaggerated language), which is evident both in ancient
Near Eastern war texts and when comparing biblical texts with each other.
For example, the Bible uses the language of "driving out" and "dispossessing" the Canaanites, and the Bible does not claim that God commanded the
virtual extermination of everyone in Canaan—that is, genocide. And where
we are told of the "utter destruction" of Canaanites or other groups, the Bible
indicates that they continue to exist in large numbers (chaps. 6 through 8).

We move from there to address critics' objections to interpreting the relevant
biblical texts hyperbolically (chap. 9). In chapter 10, we respond to the *legal*
objection that even displacement of a people is technically genocide. We look
at legal precedent of recent international law/human rights cases—particularly
the horrors of the former Yugoslavia—to show that the "genocide" charge is
misguided. Additionally, this chapter examines certain theological objections
to the hyperbolic interpretation—slippery slopes, false analogies, and the like.

Part 3 ("Is It Always Wrong to Kill Innocent People?") takes us into the
realm of theology, ethics, and philosophy. We present a basic understanding
of what is called "divine command theory"—that human obligations are
grounded in and constituted by the commands of a good, just God who may
issue occasional difficult commands (e.g., to kill Canaanites) to achieve a
greater good. Unfortunately, many critics treat divine commands as arbitrary
and utterly unconnected to the good, wise character of the God who issues
them. For example, they reveal their mistaken understanding of divine command theory by raising such nonsensical questions as, "What if God commanded something intrinsically evil?" This is like asking, "What would it
be like if square circles existed?" We discuss these and other such objections
in chapters 12 and 13.

Plato's Euthyphro objection is commonly raised in the context of divine commands. Are God's commands—and thus, our duties—merely *arbitrary*? That is, could God simply command us to do the opposite of what he does? Or is the very concept of goodness *empty*? If what God commands is our duty, then this means that God has no moral obligations. So how can God be good if he has no moral obligations? We respond to an array of Euthyphro-related questions as they have a bearing on divine commands to kill human beings (chaps. 13 and 14).

While some claim that God could never command killing that involves noncombatants, a wide range of ethical systems recognize that this is not absolute. A case of supreme emergency may override generally binding moral principles—for example, deceiving Nazis to save Jewish lives. Those who assume that our confidence in the trustworthiness of difficult divine commands in Scripture must always be overridden by generally accepted moral principles are making some questionable assumptions; we argue that the grounds the biblical theist has for thinking a good, wise God issued these unique commands are *stronger* than the grounds for thinking that killing the innocent is always wrong. In chapters 15 and 16, we explore these and other challenges about difficult divine commands—including moral intuitions about bludgeoning babies, the morally corrupting effects of killing, rationalizing genocide, and the like.

Chapter 17 further engages biblical texts on commands to kill Canaanites, Midianites, and Amalekites, responding to various philosophical criticisms along the way. We argue that the biblical theist has adequate grounds for thinking that God, on these unique occasions, issued such an exemption to the general rule against killing. Then in the next two chapters, we address the question of why we *shouldn't* believe some claimant today (say, a fictitious Texas governor) who insists that God "told" him to "utterly destroy" some criminal sect in his state—and also the matter of why we *should* believe that God truly commanded Moses and Joshua to kill Canaanites. In chapter 18, we look at criteria for prophetic authenticity, and in chapter 19, we expound on the place of abundant miraculous validation as the backdrop for these difficult commands.

In part 4 ("Religion and Violence"), we look at topics that typically emerge in the context of warfare in the Old Testament. In chapter 20, we explore the question, does religion cause violence? Then in chapter 21, we compare Old Testament warfare and Islamic jihad, which are often lumped together while ignoring important distinctions. The next chapter briefly examines the myth that the text of Joshua inspired the Crusades—as well as other myths related to the Crusades. And finally, we look at questions related to Jesus's words about "resisting evil" and "turning the other cheek," as well as issues concerning pacifism and just war. We see the Old Testament Yahweh wars as unique events in salvation history and not a model for modern warfare. We recognize that Christians disagree on just war–pacifism questions, but we find a just war position morally justifiable and less problematic than pacifism.

A Word of Thanks

We are grateful to IVP Academic and to B&H Academic for permission to revise and expand on material previously published with them—particularly Paul Copan and Matthew Flannagan, "The Ethics of 'Holy War' for Christian Morality and Theology" in *Holy War in the Bible: Christian Morality and an Old Testament Problem*, edited by Jeremy Evans, Heath Thomas, and Paul Copan (Downers Grove, IL: IVP Academic, 2013); Matthew Flannagan and Paul Copan, "Does the Bible Condone Genocide?," in *In Defense of the Bible: A Comprehensive Apologetic for the Authority of Scripture*, edited by Steven Cowan and Terry Wilder (Nashville: B&H Academic, 2012); and Matthew Flannagan, "Did God Command the Genocide of the Canaanites?," in *Come Let Us Reason: New Essays in Christian Apologetics*, edited by Paul Copan and William Lane Craig (Nashville: B&H Academic, 2012). Thanks also to the journal *Dialogue* (UK), which granted permission for revision of Matthew Flannagan, "Defending Divine Commands," *Dialogue* 37 (November 2011).

In addition, we would like to heartily thank Kurt Jaros and David J. Clark for their generous help in reviewing the manuscript and making many helpful comments. We are grateful to Robert Hosack at Baker for his friendship and for his support of this book idea. Thanks also to James Korsmo and the other Baker editors for their careful work on this book. And we are grateful to our families for their unstinting support and encouragement throughout this endeavor.

PART 1

GENOCIDE TEXTS AND THE PROBLEM OF SCRIPTURAL AUTHORITY

1

The Problem Clarified

AN ATHEISTIC PHILOSOPHICAL ARGUMENT

In this chapter, we'll look at the argument of the philosopher Raymond Bradley, who does as good a job as any critic on this topic.[1] He asserts that a "logical quandary" arises for any theist who believes that the Bible is "a reliable guide to what we should and should not do."[2] To show this, he lays out an argument, which assumes the following moral principle, which we'll call the *Crucial Moral Principle*:

> *It is morally wrong to deliberately and mercilessly slaughter men, women, and children who are innocent of any serious wrongdoing.*[3]

To negatively illustrate this principle, Bradley cites a series of Old Testament passages to "show" God apparently does issue commands to kill innocent women and children. He refers to the book of Joshua here:

> Consider the case in which God commands Joshua to slaughter virtually every inhabitant of the land of Canaan. The story commences in chapter 6 of the book of Joshua, telling how the hero and his army conquer the ancient city of Jericho where they "utterly destroyed everything in the city, both man and woman, young and old." Then, in chapters 7 through 12, it treats us to a chilling chronicle of the thirty-one kingdoms, and all the cities therein, that fell victim to Joshua's, and God's, genocidal policies. Time and again we read the phrases

"he utterly destroyed every person who was in it," "he left no survivor," and "there was no one left who breathed."[4]

What, then, is the quandary for the Bible-believing theist? Bradley asserts that this theist cannot, without contradiction, believe all four of the following affirmations:

1 Any act that God commands us to perform is morally permissible.
2 The Bible reveals to us many of the acts that God commands us to perform.
3 It is morally impermissible for anyone to commit acts that violate the Crucial Moral Principle.
4 The Bible tells us that God commands us to perform acts that violate the Crucial Moral Principle.[5]

Bradley states that the Crucial Moral Principle is universal and exceptionless: it holds true "for all persons, places, and times."[6] By "God," Bradley means a "robust supernatural being"[7] who is "omnipotent, omniscient, and morally perfect."[8] And the Bible "reveals to us many of the acts that God commands us to perform."[9] Of course, here Bradley is assuming that the Bible *accurately* records these commands. Some scholars would argue that the Bible *inaccurately* records God's acts or commands; therefore the affirmation, "The Bible inaccurately records God's acts or commands," could then be compatible with 1, 3, and 4.

However, Bradley makes it clear that he has a robust view of biblical authority in mind. He assumes that "the Holy Scriptures of the Old and New Testaments are the revealed Word of God."[10] Bradley cites Christian philosopher Alvin Plantinga for support: "Scripture is inerrant: the Lord makes no mistakes; what he proposes for our belief is what we ought to believe."[11] Bradley cites these as typifying the view he tries to criticize—a position he refers to as *biblical theism*. This suggests that the argument should be rephrased as follows:

1   Any act that God commands us to perform is morally permissible.
2' God is the author of the Bible.
3   It is morally impermissible for anyone to commit acts that violate the Crucial Moral Principle.
4' The author of the Bible commands us to perform acts that violate the Crucial Moral Principle.

Bradley points out that all four of these statements, taken together, are inconsistent. The biblical theist, however, is committed to 1 and 2'—that what God, the author of the Bible, commands us is morally permissible and that God is the author of the Bible. So the biblical theist must reject *either* 3 (that it is morally wrong to violate the Crucial Moral Principle [slaughtering innocent people]) *or* 4′ (that the Bible's author commands us to violate that Crucial Moral Principle). However, Bradley argues that the biblical theist can't reject 3 or 4′ without being inconsistent. To do so is either to deny what the Bible clearly says or to endorse moral absurdities. We will argue against Bradley's claim in this book. In fact, we argue that the biblical theist can defensibly reject *both* 3 and 4′—that it is always morally impermissible to mercilessly slaughter innocent people and that the divine author of Scripture commands us to do this.

Initial Clarifications: Human and Divine Authors of Scripture

Before proceeding to assess Bradley's argument, an important ambiguity needs to be ironed out from 2′—which affirms that God is the author of the Bible. Traditional Christian teaching, however, accepts that the Bible has multiple authors. Each book of the Bible has a human author; the Pauline Epistles, for example, are attributed to Paul or an amanuensis (secretary) writing on his behalf. Jews have traditionally accepted that Moses in some sense authored (or perhaps, to some degree, edited) the first five books of the Old Testament and that David wrote some of the Psalms.

At the same time, biblical theists accept that the primary author of Scripture is God (or 2′). Bradley refers to Plantinga as a prime example of a biblical theist. Plantinga himself affirms that "an assumption of the enterprise [of traditional biblical commentary] is that the principal author of the Bible—the entire Bible—is God himself (according to Calvin, God the Holy Spirit). Of course each of the books of the Bible has a human author or authors as well; still, the principal author is God."[12]

This, however, leads to an immediate issue with premise 4′—namely, "The author of the Bible commands us to perform acts that violate the Crucial Moral Principle": does Bradley mean the *human* author(s) of the books in question, or the *divine* author?

Initially, one might contend that the answer is obvious. Bradley is an atheist. So he obviously cannot mean that the divine author of Scripture commands us to kill innocent people since there is, in his view, no such divine author at all. But this response would be much too quick. Bradley's argument is what philosophers call a *reductio ad absurdum* of biblical theism—an argument that attempts to reduce, in this case, biblical theism to absurdity. Though he is not a biblical theist, he assumes this stance "for the sake of argument" to show that obvious absurdities or contradictions flow from accepting this position. Bradley argues that biblical theists *must* accept all four of the statements above—1, 2′, 3, and 4′—but that they *cannot* accept them without logical contradiction. So a "logical quandary arises" for any *theist* who believes that the Bible is "a reliable guide to what we should and should not do."[13]

A problem surfaces: if we assume that the *human author* of Scripture commands us to perform acts that violate the Crucial Moral Principle, then this undermines Bradley's argument. Let's rework things to show how this is so:

1 Any act that God commands us to perform is morally permissible.
2′ God is the (*primary*) author of the Bible.
3 It is morally impermissible for anyone to commit acts that violate the Crucial Moral Principle.
4″ The *secondary* human author of the Bible commands us to perform acts that violate the Crucial Moral Principle.

Notice that these four truth claims (propositions) are consistent and don't involve any contradiction whatsoever. To get a contradiction, we have to add a further premise: *God's role as primary author entails that whatever the secondary human author of the Bible affirms or commands, God likewise affirms or commands.* But this argument therefore must assume a particular understanding of the relationship between divine and human authors of Scripture so that whatever the human author says or affirms is identical with what God says or affirms.

But this understanding of the relationship between divine and human authors is implausible. It would be silly to say that whatever the human author says or affirms is identical to what God says or affirms. Consider this affirmation by Paul: "Paul, a servant of Jesus Christ, called to be an apostle, set apart for the gospel of God" (Rom. 1:1 NRSV). Even if God is the primary author of Scripture, God is not saying his name is Paul or that God is an apostle. Or in David's famous psalm of repentance, he says, "Against you, you only, have I sinned and done what is evil in your sight; so you are right in your verdict" (Ps. 51:4). Surely this psalm is not affirming that God is a sinner! While these human authors of Scripture affirm, respectively, the status of being an apostle and a sinner, God is obviously not affirming this.

Equally important, this relationship between divine and human authors is rejected by many biblical theists—including Plantinga, whom Bradley cites as a paradigmatic example of a biblical theist. As we saw above, Plantinga understands scriptural inerrancy as based on the fact that *God* makes no mistakes, and what the divine author, God, "proposes for our belief" with the text is what we "ought to believe."

Plantinga clarifies his position (in a different article in the same issue of the journal we cited above, where he replies to Ernan McMullin):

> I think *he* thinks what is decisive here is what the *human author(s)* of the text in question had in mind. If that *is* what he means, I am obliged to disagree with him. In order to understand Scripture, we must know who its author and audience is [*sic*]. As to the latter, it is the Christian church over the ages; as to the former, as Aquinas and Calvin agree, the principle and primary author of Scripture is the Lord. (Of course this doesn't imply any kind of crude dictation theory.) What we really need to know, therefore, is what *he* intends to teach in the text in question. This may very well be what the human author had in mind in writing that text; but of course it needn't be. It might be that the Lord proposes to teach us (coming where we do in the whole history of his interactions with his children) something that hadn't occurred to the person or persons actually composing the text in question. I would concur with those Christians, for example, who see various Old Testament passages (Isaiah and elsewhere) as really referring to Christ, the second person of the Trinity, and making assertions about him; it is unlikely, however, that the original author intended to make assertions about the second person of the Trinity. What the original authors had in mind will ordinarily be of importance, but it will not necessarily settle the issue as to how to understand the text in question.[14]

Later in his book *Warranted Christian Belief* (published in 2000), Plantinga revisits this topic. There he distinguishes two different types of scriptural scholarship. The first is *historical biblical criticism*, which sets aside "theological assumptions or presuppositions";[15] this approach attempts to discern what "the human author" of a given book or passage intended to assert.[16] The second is *traditional biblical commentary*; this approach assumes that "the principal author of the Bible is God" and seeks to understand "what it is that the Lord intends to teach in that passage."[17]

Likewise, the Christian philosopher William Lane Craig, who takes a similar view, offers further clarification. He also rejects the *dictation* theory of biblical inspiration—the view that God dictated the Bible to human authors, who simply wrote it down word-for-word. Craig argues: "There are also elements in Scripture that express the emotions and anxieties and the depression of the human authors, and it seems implausible to attribute those to God's dictation. These seem rather to be genuine human emotions that are being expressed."[18] An example he gives are the so-called imprecatory (or prayer-curse) psalms. Psalm 137 is a psalm written while in exile in Babylon: "By the rivers of Babylon we sat and wept when we remembered Zion. There on the poplars we hung our harps, for there our captors asked us for songs" (vv. 1–2). The psalm ends with a startling statement: "Daughter Babylon, doomed to destruction, happy is the one who repays you according to what you have done to us. Happy is the one who seizes your infants and dashes them against the rocks" (vv. 8–9). Craig argues that this runs contrary to what Jesus said about loving our enemies, concluding that it is "hard to think of this as something that is dictated by God rather than a genuine expression of the Psalmist's anger and indignation of those who opposed God."[19]

Craig not only rejects a dictation theory of biblical inspiration, but he thinks that what humans affirm is not necessarily what God affirms. That is, God *allows* human authors of Scripture to express unrestrained emotion, even though God, the divine author, would not approve.[20] Such a psalm reminds us about honestly expressing our emotions, such as rage or despair, in our prayers about where we should look for justice. And while psalmists may utilize hyperbole and strong speech in the midst of their white-hot rage, they are expressing the very biblical desire for justice to be done—that God repay people according to their deeds, as the martyrs do in Revelation 6:9–10.[21] However the believer approaches such psalms, Craig's approach nicely illustrates how God's being the author of the Bible does not mean he endorses everything that the human author expresses.

We have laid out a standard philosophical argument against the biblical God and author of Scripture, who allegedly commands genocide and thus violates the "inviolable" Crucial Moral Principle. To help clarify Bradley's argument, we have also differentiated between divine and human authors in order to avoid some implausible—indeed nonsensical—conclusions.

Summary

• The Crucial Moral Principle affirms that deliberately taking innocent human life is always and everywhere morally wrong.

• And, the argument (by Raymond Bradley) goes, God, the author of Scripture, commands people—even us today—to perform such acts.

• The Bible's authors are both divine and human, though God is the primary author.

• However, it would be silly to say that whatever the human author says or affirms is identical to what God says or affirms (e.g., human emotions expressed in the Psalms, "Paul, a servant of God . . .").

• Human biblical authors were not God's typewriters nor were their words being dictated by God.

2

What Does It Mean to Say the Bible Is the Word of God?

Recent Philosophical Discussion

We've seen that Christian philosophers like Alvin Plantinga and William Lane Craig reject the notion that God expresses everything that the human authors of Scripture express. And they reject this idea while affirming that God is, in fact, the divine author of those same Scriptures. But this raises the question: *How exactly do these and many other biblical theists understand the relationship between divine and human authorship?* Or, going beyond this, what are the *most promising* ways of understanding this relationship? If Bradley's argument is to carry any weight, it should be directed at a rigorous, philosophically informed perspective on this—not just some Sunday school caricature.

The Appropriation Model of Craig and Wolterstorff

William Lane Craig has advocated a philosophically nuanced view of biblical inspiration.[1] He affirms that Scripture is inspired by God in such a way that God is the primary author. In addition, he says that "inspiration is a property of the written text, not the mode of its production."[2] His view takes for granted that the omniscient God knows what any human author would freely write when placed in certain circumstances. For example, "God knows under just what circumstances Paul would, for example, freely write his letter to the Romans. By creating Paul in those circumstances, God can bring it about that Romans is just the message He wants to convey to us."[3] So divine and human authorship are simultaneously affirmed: Paul can write Romans out of his own free, intellectual creativity and theological understanding while God is responsible for the text as well.

Some might raise the objection, What makes the Bible different from other books since, say, the atheist Christopher Hitchens's book *God Is Not Great* could be divinely inspired along the same lines? After all, didn't God know what Hitchens would freely write given a set of particular circumstances and sovereignly bring about this best-selling, atheism-promoting outcome? What makes the Bible different? Craig argues this way:

> The essential difference lies in God's attitude toward what is written. In the one case, God wills to communicate via the author His message to us. He intends that the letter to the Romans be His Word to us. Romans is therefore a case of *appropriated* or *delegated* speech, much as a boss makes a letter composed by his secretary his own by affixing his signature to it. By contrast, God merely allows Hitchens to write what he does without endorsing its truth or adopting it as His own. God lets Hitchens put forth his falsehoods because in His providence Hitchens' books have their part to play in God's overall plan for human history. But God does not see Hitchens' books as His Word to us, to be trusted and obeyed. Therein lies the essential difference between the Bible and every other literary product of free human activity.[4]

For Craig, what makes the Bible God's Word, then, is not just that God providentially brings it about that Paul wrote Romans the way he did. Rather, it is that God in his providence *appropriated* the biblical text as his own speech, and he *delegated* the biblical authors to speak on his behalf—which may have included the possibility that Paul was prompted by the Holy Spirit to write. Given this basic understanding from Craig, we can explore more fully what is meant by divine authorship and delegated speech. Here we move to the work of Nicholas Wolterstorff.

The Appropriation Model and Speech Act Theory

Wolterstorff gives an account of what this divinely delegated and appropriated speech looks like.[5] He builds on the work of other thinkers (J. L. Austin and John Searle) to apply "speech act theory" to divine authorship. What is speech act theory? Basically, it states that *speech is an action one performs* (or more precisely, the product of a number of actions one performs). Wolterstorff distinguishes three types of action that one performs in speaking:

- *Locutionary act*: This is simply uttering sounds or transcribing words. Let's say Brittany says to Noah, "Shut the door." Brittany performs the locutionary act of uttering the relevant English sentence; her vocal apparatus projects sound waves in the direction of Noah.
- *Illocutionary act*: This action one does *by way of performing a locutionary act*. This involves actions such as asserting, declaring, warning, promising, or commanding. So Brittany does much more than project sound waves; she also *performs* the illocutionary act by actually *commanding* Noah to shut the door.
- *Perlocutionary act*: The action associated with the intention to bring about some effect *by way of* the illocutionary act. This act involves changing someone's thinking or actions by inspiring, persuading, or deterring. So through Brittany's persuasive commanding, Noah actually gets up to shut the door.

There are distinctions here. One can utter words ("The cat sat on the mat") without issuing a command or warning (e.g., "Avoid stepping on the cat"); that is, one can perform a locutionary act without it being an illocutionary one. And one doesn't have to use vocal utterances either (locutionary acts): one may command (illocutionary act) simply by using body language (pointing toward the door), sign language, or Morse code.

Given such distinctions from speech act theory, Wolterstorff offers an understanding about how we can sensibly claim that God speaks. To say "God speaks" is simply to say that God performs a particular illocutionary act. To say the Bible is God's Word, therefore, is to say that God uses the biblical text and its authors to perform illocutionary acts of commanding, asserting, promising, and so on. Because God is infallible and supremely authoritative, the speech acts he performs are authoritative: what he asserts we are to believe; what he commands we are to obey; and his promises are completely trustworthy.

Double Agency Discourse

How then does God perform illocutionary acts through the writings of human authors? And how do we understand how these authors are delegated or appropriated by God in such a way that it's not necessarily the case that what they affirm God also affirms?

The key to answering these questions is that of *double agency discourse*. That is, one person or personal being (in this case, God) performs some illocutionary action by way of another (in this case, human) person performing a locutionary or illocutionary action through his writing. A simple example would be the case of a secretary. Consider a secretary who drafts a letter and has it signed by the manager. The locutionary act is performed by the secretary, who may *not* have been performing any illocutionary act at all. However, in signing it, the manager performs an illocutionary act with the text the secretary composed.

In other cases, a person may perform an illocutionary act by way of another person who is likewise performing an illocutionary act. Wolterstorff offers two important categories. The first has to do with *delegated* or *deputized* speech. Here a person is deputized or commissioned to speak in the name of another or on their behalf. For example, an ambassador is commissioned to speak on behalf of a nation. Another example is Person A giving Person B the power of attorney to represent Person A in legal matters and make decisions for Person A. In both the ambassador and power of attorney examples, *one person is able to speak on behalf of another in such a way that that speech can legitimately be called someone else's speech.* An ambassador addressing another country's head of state speaks on behalf of the nation he or she represents. The message, whether in the ambassador's own words or not, is taken to be the message of his or her nation.

Likewise, an attorney may speak on behalf of a client. A lawyer may write up an affidavit for a client and file it. Then, provided that the testimony is properly sworn, the client is held to have affirmed its contents and, if the contents are false, can be held liable for perjury.

Wolterstorff also stresses the category of *appropriation*. Here, instead of performing some delegated or deputized action, one *appropriates* another's discourse for one's own purposes. We commonly do this in our writing or speech. For example, we may quote another person to illustrate a point ("In the words of . . ."); we may quote another person *approvingly* ("We agree with Wolterstorff, who writes . . ."); or we may simply, after hearing another speak, say something like: "I agree with his comments," or "He speaks for me." In this case, no prior commissioning is needed. One simply takes a bit of discourse and appropriates it—makes it one's own.

Wolterstorff suggests that the model of *delegation* best fits the model of the prophetic and apostolic writings. These are examples of *deputized* speech, where someone is commissioned by God to speak on his behalf to a particular audience. The prophets give deputized divine speech to ancient Israel on certain historical occasions. The apostles deliver messages on God's behalf to particular churches in particular places and times (for example, Paul's Letters to first-century churches in Rome and Corinth).

However, Wolterstorff suggests that the Bible as the Word of God to us today is best understood in terms of God's *appropriating* various illocutionary acts as his own. In Wolterstorff's words, "All that is necessary for the whole [Bible] to be God's book is that the human discourse it contains have been appropriated by God, as one single book, for God's discourse."[6] Here we appropriate (!) Wolterstorff's affirmation that "an eminently plausible construal of the process whereby these books found their way into a single canonical text, would be that by way of that process of canonization, God was authorizing these books as together constituting a single volume of divine discourse."[7]

This is what Craig means when he claims that Paul's Epistle to the Romans is *appropriated* or *delegated* speech. As an apostle, Paul had been commissioned by God to preach and teach on behalf of Jesus to largely gentile communities. Hence, his writing to Rome was a form of *delegated* speech on God's behalf. Later when these writings were incorporated into a single biblical canon, God was *appropriating* this book alongside various others as his speech.

This explains how one can affirm that the Bible is God's Word and that God is the primary author of Scripture without affirming that God dictated it. It also explains how the Bible can simultaneously be the Word of God and the words of humans. So when a head of state *commissions* an ambassador to speak on her behalf (or when someone is given power of attorney), that person doesn't become a mere mouthpiece. Rather, that representative chooses his own words—words that reflect his personality, character, and knowledge (or perhaps lack of it)—even if they are not the precise words the head of state (or the client) herself would have chosen. And when someone *appropriates* another's writing, that appropriated discourse retains its character; had you written it yourself, it might have come out very differently. Similarly, biblical interpretation can take into account all the particularities and styles of the human writers and still interpret what God said by that.

The appropriation model also explains how one can accept that the Bible is God's Word without claiming that God necessarily affirms exactly what the human author affirms. Usually when someone appropriates the illocutionary act of another, one affirms exactly what the writer or speaker affirms. But this isn't always the case. Sometimes a person can appropriate what a speaker says in a new context and say something quite different than what the original speaker did. The philosopher Richard Swinburne offers this example:

> The most familiar modern secular example of this [kind of appropriation] is where one author puts a number of his previously published papers together into

one volume, and adds a preface explaining that while he republishes the papers in the form in which they were originally published, he now wishes some of them to be understood with certain qualifications; or, more radically, that he does not now agree with the argument of some of the earlier papers but republishes them in order to show what is wrong with them. In such a context the author is not expressing the views contained in the papers, but rather quoting them; and the meaning of the whole is what the author says it is in the preface, with the qualifications which he makes there—even if that was not the meaning of the papers as originally published.[8]

This position appears to be much like William Lane Craig's view on Psalm 137, an imprecatory psalm: the original human author was using the psalm to express rage and hatred, but this was incorporated into a larger collection of psalms that served as a prayer book for God's people—even though God does not endorse everything expressed therein. That is, God is not always affirming what the human author affirms.

Bradley's Argument Clarified

With this backdrop we can now return to Raymond Bradley's (revised) argument that we discussed in the previous chapter. Bradley maintains that the biblical theist who believes God exists and that the Bible is God's authoritative Word is committed to four inconsistent affirmations.

1 Any act that God commands us to perform is morally permissible.
2′ God is the author of the Bible.
3 It is morally impermissible for anyone to commit acts that violate the Crucial Moral Principle.
4′ The author of the Bible commands us to perform acts that violate the Crucial Moral Principle.

Earlier we discussed how Bradley left his argument open to criticism for failing to distinguish between the divine (primary) author of Scripture and the human (secondary) authors of Scripture. That said, Bradley has affirmed that in "his holy scripture God, proposes for our belief" that he commanded us to violate the Crucial Moral Principle.[9] His claim is that the biblical theist is committed to interpreting Scripture in such a way that God commands us to kill innocent men, women, and children. He also contends that no biblical theist can rationally deny that the killing of innocent men, women, and children is always wrong. That is, the biblical theist must reject *either* 3 (that it is morally wrong to violate the Crucial Moral Principle [killing innocent people]) *or* 4′ (that God commands us to violate that Crucial Moral Principle). But Bradley asserts the biblical theist can't reject 3 or 4′ without being inconsistent.

Inerrancy: What Is at Stake?

Before examining this claim, it is worth reflecting on what is and is not at stake here. Central to this argument is the claim that a biblical theist is committed to 4′, the claim that the *divine* author of Scripture commands acts that violate the Crucial Moral Principle. We noted above that it is possible, and in some cases plausible, that what God says by way of appropriating the biblical text as his Word is not the same as what the human author of the text states.

Wolterstorff argues that this is a general feature of how one interprets appropriated discourse. He offers the "fundamental principle" for the interpreter that, "the interpreter takes the stance and content of my appropriating discourse to be that of your appropriated discourse, *unless there is good reason to do otherwise.*"[10] Now if Person A appropriates Person B's words in such a way that, based on the probability of evidence, it is highly unlikely that Person B's intentions are being expressed, then it is fair to conclude that Person A has not properly appropriated them. When it comes to God, however, there is no debate: "God does not unwittingly say things God never intended to say, nor does God misunderstand the discourse God appropriates!"[11]

So determining what *God* says within the biblical text involves a two-stage process. In doing so, we are operating with the "fundamental principle": "the interpreter takes the stance and content of my appropriating discourse to be that of your appropriated discourse, *unless there is good reason to do otherwise.*" *The first step is to work out what illocutionary act the human author performed when he authored the text—that is, discerning what the human author is saying.* (Recall that illocutionary acts are such things as asserting, declaring, warning, promising, or commanding.)

Once we've worked out what the human author was saying, *the second step involves ascertaining whether we have good reason to think God was saying something different than the human author in appropriating his text.* This second step involves reading the different human authors in the Bible together as a single literary unit—an important point to note in chapters 7 and 8. Wolterstorff gives an everyday example of how this works. He asks us to suppose that someone remarks: "You'll get what I want to say if you take what Ruth said just now along with what Michelle said." So to discern the appropriating discourse, we need to consider those two appropriated pieces of discourse together as a unit.[12] Likewise, "to discern what God is saying by way of the Bible, we have to take these sixty-six or so biblical books *together*."[13]

In addition to *reading the human authors together*, Wolterstorff argues, *we also assume certain theological beliefs*—that God does not utter falsehoods, that he is morally good, that he has purposes for speaking, and so on. All of these are background information when discerning whether God was most likely appropriating the human discourse to affirm some proposition. Now some people may object to this idea of God's character informing the discernment process. But just a little reflection on human communication suggests that background assumptions about an author's character and purposes often play a crucial role in communication. Suppose for example that you are standing in front of your refrigerator, and you say to those present, "There's no milk." Now if your hearers ("interpreters") focus just on the sentence itself and ignore other factors, like your good character, or even the context in which you say it, the statement could sound very much like there is no milk anywhere. But this would not be a sensible interpretation of your statement—especially if milk is available at a convenience store up the street. The sensible interpreter would take you to be saying there is no milk *in the refrigerator*. Part of the reason for such an interpretation is that they have information about you: you are standing in front of the refrigerator; your friends know you to be a trustworthy person; and, what's more, you wouldn't have the slightest reason for speaking deceptively about such mundane matters. Character, context, and likely purposes in making an utterance are all factors that make for a sensible interpretation. Proper interpretation requires more than simply paying attention to words.

When we read the biblical authors together (who contribute to the larger canonical and literary unit), we take into account background beliefs about what illocutionary acts (e.g., commands, warnings) God is likely (or not likely) to perform. Then what is plausible to attribute to the divine author will (or will not) be identical with what one attributes to the human authors. In light of the established historical practice of biblical interpretation, Wolterstorff suggests five ways in which the illocutionary act of the *divine* biblical author may differ from the illocutionary act of the *human* author(s).

First is the rhetoric-conceptual structure of Scripture texts. As we've already noted, what we typically attribute to humans will obviously differ from what we can plausibly attribute to God, such as when biblical authors refer to themselves in the first person ("I," "me") and God in the second ("you") or third person ("he," "him"). We looked at the example of Paul as an apostle and David as a sinner against God. In such instances, what God says must differ from what the human author says—though of course what one does attribute to God must be plausibly anchored by the text.[14]

Second is the distinction between the point the human author affirms within the text, what he is teaching, and the way the human author makes the point. Craig offers a helpful example:

> Nobody thinks that when Jesus says that the mustard seed is the smallest of all seeds (Mark 4.31) this is an error, even though there are smaller seeds than mustard seeds. Why? Because Jesus is not teaching botany; he is trying to teach a lesson about the Kingdom of God, and the illustration is incidental to this lesson. Defenders of inerrancy claim that the Bible is authoritative and inerrant in *all that it teaches* or *all that it means to affirm*. This raises the huge question as to what the authors of Scripture intend to affirm or teach.[15]

Craig's point here is that Jesus's comment taken literally contains a falsehood (i.e., that the mustard seed is the smallest of all seeds). We are inclined to see hyperbole here and so do not think that Jesus taught that the mustard seed is literally the smallest of seeds; if we supposed he did, then his statement would be false. Nevertheless, as Craig correctly notes, this is irrelevant because even if the author of Mark's Gospel believed mustard seeds were the smallest of all seeds, this passage is not intended to teach us about botany but about the growth of God's kingdom. The saying about the mustard seed is simply a way of illustrating the point Jesus is trying to teach. What is actually being taught as true is what is at stake when it comes to biblical authority—not the details of how it is expressed.

The third way in which the divine and human illocutionary acts may differ is where the human author is affirming something *literally*, but the divine author is taken to be appropriating what the human author says in a nonliteral fashion. One example is allegorical interpretations of the Song of Solomon, which have been widely adopted throughout church history. Whereas the human author was originally writing love poems about a man and a woman, many theologians have understood God to be making an allegory about Christ and the church. Some may disagree that such an allegorical interpretation has the backing of Scripture. But another biblical example might better illustrate this point: In Ephesians 5:31–32, Paul is reflecting on Genesis 2:24, where a man leaves his father and mother, cleaves to his wife, and the two become one flesh. Rather than marriage at creation informing Christ's relationship to the church, Paul puts it the other way around: he views the mystery of Christ's relationship to the church as informing and modeling what human marriages are to be like.

A fourth way is what Wolterstorff calls *transitive discourse*—when we perform one illocutionary action we perform another—"by saying one thing we say another thing."[16] In telling King David a story about a rich man taking a poor man's lamb, the prophet Nathan accused him of stealing another man's wife.[17] By telling a parable about a Samaritan, Jesus commanded his hearers to love their neighbors and showed them how to do so in a basic, practical way. Similarly, biblical narratives about Israel's history fit this category: "most of those who have interpreted these stories as part of divinely appropriated discourse have believed that God appropriated them to make a point." And this is so even if the human authors did not tell these stories to make this point.[18]

A fifth way of distinguishing is in recognizing the difference between a *general* principle and its *specific* application for a particular time and place. A good illustration is found in Deuteronomy 22:8: "When you build a new house, make a parapet around your roof so that you may not bring the guilt of bloodshed on your house if someone falls from the roof." The original author commanded Israelites to build fences around their roofs. Yet no contemporary commentator takes God to be teaching us today to build fences around roofs.

In the context of ancient Israel, one can understand the rationale: people lived in houses with flat roofs, and the roof was often a place where people entertained guests. In that context, failure to have a fence or railing around one's roof meant that when people gathered together on the roof, there was a real danger that someone, maybe even a small child, could fall off the edge and die; hence the law of God required that one secure the roof in this way. Because of the likelihood of such a danger in ancient Israel, those who built houses had a duty to put in place protections against this risk.

In twenty-first-century Auckland, New Zealand, or West Palm Beach, Florida, however, failure to put a fence around one's roof is unlikely to make one liable to a wrongful death lawsuit. Instead, we typically have slanted roofs; so we don't entertain on the roof and almost never venture to get on our roofs. In our particular settings, we just don't have family members and small children running around on rooftops.

Despite this, however, it does not follow that God is *not* commanding or teaching something important for us today in these texts. While the human author was issuing a specific command, God uses this as an example or an illustration of a general principle that can be applied to our context in different ways. We might apply it, for instance, by installing railings for stairways or balconies in our homes to prevent injury or even death. The point here is that what God says with the text might be a more general point, while the human author had something more specific in mind. What the human author issued as a specific command in a particular context, God appropriates to illustrate a more general principle.

These guidelines help us see the alternatives more clearly: if biblical the-ists consider a text in which the human author seems to attribute to God a command that they have a good reason to think God would not command, then they must (1) interpret the text to say that God is saying something else in appropriating the human author's text; or (2) perhaps conclude that they have misunderstood the text and do not know what God is saying; or as some interpreters have done, (3) conclude that God did not appropriate the text in question. The option chosen will depend on the evidence for and against each option—understanding the text in its context, the meanings of the words, and theological and moral judgments about what God is likely to have said.

If a biblical theist concludes that the human author commanded some immoral action, it doesn't automatically follow that biblical theists must conclude that God commanded this, nor does it require that theists give up their belief in biblical authority. To get to either of these conclusions, one needs to show that options 1 and 2 are ruled out by the evidence.[19] However, it is the *divine* issuing of these commands that is connected to inerrancy:[20] This point is often missed, as some writers move too quickly from the claim that the human author affirmed a falsehood to a denial of inerrancy. William Lane Craig, probably the most prominent defender of the Christian faith today, has written:

> The problem, it seems to me, is that if God could not have issued such a command, then the biblical stories must be false. Either the incidents never really happened but are just Israeli folklore; or else, if they did, then Israel, carried away in a fit of nationalistic fervor, thinking that God was on their side, claimed that God had commanded them to commit these atrocities, when in fact He had not. In other words, this problem is really an objection to biblical inerrancy.
>
> In fact, ironically, many Old Testament critics are skeptical that the events of the conquest of Canaan ever occurred. They take these stories to be part of the legends of the founding of Israel, akin to the myths of Romulus and Remus and the founding of Rome. For such critics the problem of God's issuing such a command evaporates.
>
> Now that puts the issue in quite a different perspective! The question of biblical inerrancy is an important one, but it's not like the existence of God or the deity of Christ! If we Christians can't find a good answer to the question before us and are, moreover, persuaded that such a command is inconsistent with God's nature, then we'll have to give up biblical inerrancy.[21]

Craig here contends that if one concludes both that the human authors attributed a particular command to God and that a loving and just God could not or did not issue such commands, then one will have to give up the doctrine of biblical inerrancy. For reasons spelled out above, however, it's not clear that this follows. Nor is it that Craig's own views on inspiration and authority commit him to this conclusion. It would follow only if, in addition to reaching these conclusions, one also found that options 1 and 2 are ruled out by the evidence. Determining whether or not this is the case would require argumentation beyond simply noting that the human authors affirmed that God commanded the killing of innocent people and that a loving and just God would not command this.

That said, we agree that one need not hold biblical inerrancy to make a strong case for God's existence, for the historicity of Jesus's bodily resurrection, or that moral obligations are rooted in God's nature and will. Our only point here is that even biblical inerrancy is not threatened as readily as Craig suggests without some further argument.

Conclusion: What the Critic Needs to Do

In this chapter, we have tried to grasp the true nature of the problem generated for the Christian believer by Scripture's so-called "genocide" texts. In so doing we have examined a representative argument—one offered by Raymond Bradley—that fairly sums up the problem. We have stated that in order for this argument to be plausible, and for it not to involve attacking a mere caricature (what's called a "straw man" argument), the argument should be reformulated to give it greater clarity and precision.

Biblical theists are people who affirm both that a loving and just God exists and that the Bible is the authoritative Word of God. They are committed to the following four propositions:

1 Any act that God commands us to perform is morally permissible.
2′ God is the author of the Bible.
3 It is morally impermissible for anyone to commit acts that violate the Crucial Moral Principle, which says, "It is morally wrong to deliberately and mercilessly slaughter men, women, and children who are innocent of any serious wrongdoing."
4‴ The divine author of the Bible uses the text to perform the speech act of commanding us to perform acts that violate the Crucial Moral Principle.

As we've seen, Bradley claims that biblical theists *cannot*—but yet *must*—hold to all four of these statements. The statements are logically incompatible.

We've noted our disagreement as well. We would dispute that biblical theists are committed to 3 and 4′ (the "author of the Bible commands . . .")—or 3 and 4″ (the "*secondary* human author of the Bible commands . . ."), or 3 and 4‴ (the "divine author . . ."). So Bradley and his like-minded critics would have to show that biblical theists are committed to interpreting the biblical text in a certain way—that the divine author of Scripture is using the text to perform the speech act of commanding us to commit acts that violate the Crucial Moral Principle. The critics must show that this understanding of the biblical text is the only plausible or defensible one available to biblical theists, and in part 2, we disagree that the critics have successfully shown this.

Second, the critics must show that biblical theists must accept that it is always wrong to kill innocent people—or, at best, that it was wrong in the circumstances where God is recorded as issuing these "genocide" commands in Scripture. In part 3, we argue that attempts to establish this point fail as well. We will point out there that biblical theists who hold to a divine command theory of ethics—not the crude version of this theory that is so often misunderstood and abused by critics—can defensibly claim that it is permissible to kill innocent human beings in rare circumstances without being committed to absurd moral and philosophical implications.

Before we do this, however, in the next chapter we will examine one influential attempt to resolve this problem by drawing a sharp distinction between the Old and New Testaments recently proposed by Eric Seibert and Peter Enns.

Summary

- What is the *most promising* way of understanding the relationship between the divine and human authors of Scripture?

- If Bradley's argument is to carry any weight, it should be directed at a rigorous, philosophically informed perspective on this—not just some Sunday school caricature.

- The human writers of Scripture can write out of their own free, intellectual creativity and theological understanding while God brings it about that the biblical books are the message God desires to convey to us.

- God *appropriates* the human writers' work as his own speech, delegating the biblical authors to speak on his behalf. So the human writers' work becomes God's word to us, and it is to be trusted and obeyed—unlike other literary works.

- We can apply speech act theory (i.e., speech is an action one performs) to the discussion of our understanding of divine speech.

- One can simply *utter or transcribe words* (*locutionary* act); one can *perform* a locutionary act (*illocutionary* act—warning, promising, commanding); one can intend a speech act to bring about some effect (*perlocutionary* act).

- To say God speaks is to say God performs a particular illocutionary act—that is, God uses the biblical text and its authors to perform illocutionary acts of commanding, asserting, promising, and so on. These divine speech acts are authoritative and trustworthy and ought to be obeyed.

• *Double agency discourse* has to do with *delegated* or *deputized* speech—the human author is commissioned to speak on behalf of God in what he writes. Also, God *appropriates* this human speech for his own purposes (e.g., when we write, we quote others and indicate that we agree with the person or that the person speaks for us).

• So in the Bible (God's Word), God appropriates the writing of a human being with the writer's own personality, character, and writing style.

• With this in mind, we can come back to the argument articulated by Raymond Bradley, who failed to distinguish between the divine (primary) and human (secondary) authors of Scripture.

• When interpreting appropriated discourse, we must ask what the text is actually saying and then determine whether we have good reason to think God, in appropriating the text, was saying something different than the human author.

• This approach assumes a knowledge of certain theological beliefs (e.g., God is trustworthy, morally good). It also acknowledges that some texts, if taken literally, become falsehoods (e.g., the mustard seed is not *literally* the smallest of all seeds). Furthermore, we should distinguish between a general principle (e.g., making buildings safe) and its application in context-specific texts (e.g., putting parapets around the roof of ancient Near Eastern homes).

• The critic would have to show that biblical theists are committed to interpreting the biblical text in a certain way (that the divine author is using the text to command us to commit acts that violate the Crucial Moral Principle).

• The critic must also show that biblical theists must accept that it is always wrong to kill innocent people.

3

The God of the Old Testament versus the God of the New?

Marcion's Deity

The name "Marcion" is not well loved by orthodox Christians. Whereas early Christians such as Origen (185–253/4) allegorized troubling Old Testament passages, Marcion (born ca. 100) took such passages straightforwardly. *And* he rejected these passages as well as the "lesser" Creator God of the Jews—the God of justice and wrath—portrayed within them. In light of his belief that Jesus revealed the good and supreme God, Marcion formed his own anti-Judaistic canon of a revised Luke (the *Euangelikon*) and ten of Paul's Letters (the *Apostolikon*). According to Marcion, the God of the Old Testament is much different than the God of the New.

This is a common criticism today as well. The killing of the Canaanites, plagues and other divine judgments, imprecatory (prayer-curse) psalms, and harsh laws in the Old Testament seem to be of a different spirit than the "loving, nonviolent Jesus" of the New Testament. To many, the options are either choosing the vengeful and violent God of the Old Testament or the loving God and Father of Jesus Christ in the New. So if those are the options, who wants to side with the Old Testament God? *Is* the God of the Old Testament somehow different from the God of the New? Does Jesus—along with the

New Testament writers—attempt to distance himself from the God portrayed in the Old Testament?

Certain Christian scholars today seem to make this strong distinction. For example, French scholar René Girard asserts: "In the Old Testament we never arrive at a conception of the deity that is entirely foreign to violence. . . . Only the texts of the Gospels manage to achieve what the Old Testament leaves incomplete."[1] Fallen human cultures may glorify war or even give it the stamp of the divine—even in the Old Testament—but the New Testament makes clear that the one true God is removed from all violence.

The late biblical scholar Peter Craigie (a Mennonite) considered war "a form of evil human activity"—although with ancient Israel God participates in it as "the Warrior" both to judge and redeem.[2] Regardless, war is "never less than unmitigated evil and its frequent mention in the Old Testament does not elevate its character. It is . . . a form of evil human activity through which God in his sovereignty may work out his purposes of judgment and redemption."[3]

Christians who adopt this line of reasoning assume a wide gap between the worldview of ancient Israelites and the teaching of Jesus (and our own modern way of thinking). For example, Thomas Mann's commentary on Deuteronomy claims Israel held to a primitive worldview in which they believed God was responsible for sending rain in blessing or for withdrawing it as punishment for Israel's disobedience (Deut. 11:10–17; 28:12, 23–24); such divine curses also included human illness, crop blights, or insect infestations (Amos 7:1–3). We enlightened moderns recognize that God is not responsible for weather patterns or any physical ills that befall humans.[4]

Shades of Marcion?

A couple of Christian Old Testament scholars have been called Marcionites by others in the Christian community—most notably Peter Enns and Eric Seibert. Is this a fair charge? Both repudiate it. For example, Peter Enns blogs about this accusation, "Is Peter Enns a Marcionite?" He writes:

> The New Testament leaves behind the violent, tribal, insider-outsider, rhetoric of a significant portion of the Old Testament. Instead, the character of the people of God—now made up of Jew and Gentile—is dominated by such behaviors as faith in Christ working itself out in love, self-sacrifice, praying for one's enemies and persecutors. You know, Jesus 101.[5]

He later adds: "I don't think the Gospel permits, condones, or supports the rhetoric of tribal violence in the Old Testament. But this does not mean I believe the Old and New Testaments give us different Gods. They give us, rather, different portrayals of God." So, Enns asserts, the claim that he is a Marcionite is tantamount to saying that he was born on Mars.

Eric Seibert, who teaches Old Testament at Messiah College, has written *The Violence of Scripture: Overcoming the Old Testament's Troubling Legacy* (2012), which builds on his earlier work, *Disturbing Divine Behavior* (2009).[6] He summarizes his approach to Scripture at Peter Enns's blog site in the post "When the Good Book Is Bad":

> To put it bluntly: **not everything in the "good book" is either good, or good for us.** I realize this may sound blasphemous to some people and flies in the face of everything they have been taught to believe about the Bible. When the Church grandly proclaims the Bible to be the Word of God, it gives the impression that the words of Scripture are above critique and beyond reproach. We are taught to read, revere, and embrace the Bible. We are *not* taught to challenge its values, ethics, or portrayals of God.[7]

Again, both of these authors repudiate Marcionism. They reject the notion that there are two distinct Gods in view; they claim that the testaments *portray* God differently. They don't jettison the entire Old Testament as Scripture, but they urge us to read these violent texts carefully and critically. They appreciate the Old Testament text, and they seek to understand its tensions and the "subversive" texts that undermine or challenge what appears to be divinely approved violence. Unlike Marcion, they do not recoil from things Judaistic such as kosher laws or temple ceremonies. That said, some of the things we read by them don't square with Scripture's own emphasis and pronouncements. So perhaps we could explore some of these concerns in this chapter.

Like Enns, who states that the two Testaments give us "different portrayals of God," Seibert rejects the idea that the one true God is actually behind violent commands. Moreover, the real God is not behind bringing temporal judgment on human beings. No, this is not the one true God (the "actual God"), but rather a literary representation (the "textual God").[8] And even though these violent texts are technically "God's Word," they have nothing to do with God's character, who is nonviolent and loving. Although Bible readers have taken these harsh texts as giving a clear portrayal of God as the "actual God," these texts have repeatedly misled Jesus's followers into committing all kinds of horrendous acts in his name.

Seibert and Enns claim that their interpretive frame of reference is Jesus of Nazareth—and how could any right-thinking believer disagree? While appealing to Jesus is praiseworthy, we are presented with a limited picture of Jesus—and one that ignores authoritative affirmations by New Testament writers and speakers about Yahweh and his actions in the Old Testament. Seibert notes that "virtuous violence" in Old Testament texts has been used to justify colonialism, ethnic violence, and the abuse of women: "The Old Testament *itself* is part of the problem."[9] This is due largely to the fact that the Old Testament text absorbs much of the biblical writers' own ancient Near Eastern values and beliefs. These include ethnocentrism and patriarchy—not to mention temporal judgments threatened by the prophets or allegedly divine acts of destruction such as Noah's flood or the rain of brimstone on Sodom. These don't reflect the character of a compassionate, merciful God.[10]

What is violence? Seibert defines this as "*physical, emotional, or psychological harm done to a person by an individual (or individuals), institution, or structure that results in injury, oppression, or death.*"[11] What's more, violence has nothing to do with God's character. Seibert's solution, as we noted above, is to distinguish between the *textual* God (the author's literary representation) and the *actual* God (the living reality)—especially in the Old Testament, where the gap between them is often very wide. In Seibert's estimation, the Old Testament makes assumptions about God that "people of faith today should no longer accept."[12] For example, God doesn't cause a nation to win (or lose) battles; rather, this depends on troop size, sophistication of weapons, and the like. To guide us in interpreting Old Testament texts, we should look to the nonviolent, enemy-loving Jesus, whose example and teachings reveal the character of God perfectly. We should think of God's judgment as *eschatological* (at the end of all things) and not *temporal* (within history as we know it). And that end-times judgment (perhaps "final irreversible destruction") need not be construed as inherently violent.[13]

Seibert thus urges us to read the Bible carefully, conversantly, and critically—not compliantly.[14] He gives specific guidance for reading the Old Testament nonviolently: read actively (not passively); question (don't just listen to) texts; ethically critique (don't uncritically approve) violent texts. We engage in ethical critique by carefully following the rule of love (reading for the love of God and others); committing to justice (setting things right); and having a consistent ethic of life (valuing all people). In critiquing, we should consider the Old Testament's multiple "voices," some of which challenge "virtuous violence." For instance, consider how the Canaanite Rahab appears more like an Israelite than the Israelite Achan, who appears more like a Canaanite. Recognizing this will prevent us from pitting "bad" Canaanites against "good" Israelites. Another strategy is to read *with* the victims and their families ("Didn't Goliath have a family, for whom he cared?"). And we should read Scripture *from the margins*, from the outsider's point of view ("How would *Canaanites* have viewed Israel's entrance into *their* land?"). In all of this, we should transcend the Old Testament's violence by looking at the character of God in Christ.

As Seibert moves through his *Violence of Scripture* book, he applies these guidelines and offers specific strategies for dealing with violent texts, particularly when it comes to warfare and the treatment of women. For example, we should *name* the violence—calling the killing of the Canaanites "genocide." We should also recognize the bias of Israel's one-sided war stories and develop compassion for Israel's enemies.[15] Warfare harms everyone: it leaves in its wake widows and orphans, and it encourages revenge.[16]

The God of Jesus *Is* the God of Moses

Is the "severe," "harsh," and "violent" God portrayed in the Old Testament the God and Father of our Lord Jesus Christ? Do scholars like Seibert, Enns, Girard, and others accurately represent the Old Testament's portrayal of the God of Moses and Joshua? Do they perhaps downplay the New Testament's portrayals of God that resemble the Old Testament? A few responses are in order.

First, *it is true that we should think more deeply about difficult, ethically troubling Old Testament passages rather than gloss over them.* Scholars such as Christopher Wright, Gordon Wenham, David Lamb, and John Goldingay have done an admirable job of honestly wrestling with them. And both of us authors have been tackling these topics as part of an ongoing project. While we may disagree with the conclusions and methodology of certain scholars, we truly appreciate their desire to grapple with these texts that perplex and trouble many. And we *should* be distressed by professing Christians' abuse of Scripture, using such texts to justify the subjugation of women, the horrors of the slave trade, and the oppression of people groups. Yet despite the "Christian" distortion of Scripture across the centuries, let us not forget about the moral gains brought about by, yes, Bible-reading Christians in Western civilization and Western (especially Protestant) missionaries who brought many democratizing gains, moral reforms, and protection of indigenous peoples from colonial powers. Other gains include democracy, literacy, human rights, women's rights, civil rights, abolition of slavery, and so on.[17]

Second, *Seibert's negative comment that the church "grandly proclaims" the Bible to be God's Word is rather unfair.* After all, Jesus himself "grandly proclaims" this as well—down to the "smallest letter or stroke" (Matt. 5:18; cf. John 10:35). Likewise, Paul insists that *all* Scripture is inspired by God and is profitable (2 Tim. 3:16). Ironically, while Seibert claims that Jesus is the hermeneutical key to his ethic, he does not actually adopt Jesus's own attitude toward Scripture. This point becomes quite apparent in the appendix to his *Disturbing Divine Behavior*, where he views divine inspiration of the Old Testament as "general" rather than "comprehensive"—certainly not the "smallest letter or stroke" variety.

Third, *we must be careful not to appeal to Jesus's authority selectively*. In Old Testament prophetic fashion, Jesus regularly engages in denouncements and threats of judgments—*both* temporal and final. He routinely pronounces temporal judgment on Jerusalem; this judgment would come by Rome in AD 70. He also assumes Sodom, Tyre, and Sidon had been *divinely* and *violently* judged, which serves as a springboard for condemning his unbelieving contemporaries in Bethsaida, Chorazin, and Capernaum (Matt. 11:21–24; cf. 10:15). Notice these warnings of judgment immediately precede Jesus's own self-description as gentle and humble in heart (11:28–30)! Jesus likewise takes for granted divine and violent judgment in Noah's day (Matt. 24:37–39). And in a symbolic act, an enraged Jesus makes a whip to drive out moneychangers from the temple and prevents people from even entering the temple (John 2:15; cf. Mark 11:15–17). Does this not have a touch of the kind of "violence" Seibert and Enns would consider un-Christlike? What of Jesus's indictment of stumbling blocks who should have a millstone tied around their neck to be drowned (Matt. 18:6)? He threatens the "wretched" vine-growers (Israel's leaders) with temporal judgment (Matt. 21:41; Mark 12:9). Jesus likewise declares he will "make war" on the Nicolaitans "with the sword of My mouth," and he will throw the false prophetess "Jezebel" onto a "bed of sickness" and bring "pestilence" upon her followers (Rev. 2:16, 20–23 NASB). Jesus clearly believes in the appropriateness of temporal divine punishment and the Mosaic death penalty (Matt. 15:4).

Furthermore, Jesus takes for granted the general theological outlook of the Old Testament. For example, just as the "Old Testament God" was sovereign over the weather, Jesus himself (and contra Mann) affirmed that his heavenly Father "causes His sun to rise" and "sends rain" on the good and wicked alike (Matt. 5:45 NASB). Also, he reminds Pilate that any authority Rome may have has been bestowed by God and thus is not a matter of having larger armies and better military strategies (John 19:10–11). While we see Jesus acknowledging that the hardness of human hearts meant that certain less-than-ideal conditions were permitted by God (e.g., Matt. 19:8), he saw himself as standing in the line of prophets whose theological perspective he shared, including belief in a holy God who brings violent temporal judgments on nations—including Israel by Rome in AD 70—and who consigns evildoers to "Gehenna."

Fourth, *we must not pit Jesus's teaching (or a certain understanding of it) against the affirmations elsewhere in the New Testament,* appealing to a "nonviolent" Jesus but ignoring not only his assumptions about violent judgments but also other strong, authoritative voices in the New Testament. Paul refers to severe temporal punishments on Israel as an example to us—some Israelites laid low; others destroyed by serpents, others by "the destroyer" (1 Cor. 10 NASB). He refers to the judgment of sickness and even death because of the abuse of the Lord's Table (1 Cor. 11:30). Stephen matter-of-factly mentions nations dispossessed by Joshua (Acts 7:45 NASB: "the nations whom *God* drove out"). Paul likewise affirms that "He [God] had destroyed seven nations" of Canaan (Acts 13:19 NASB). The author of Hebrews speaks of the faith of those who "conquered kingdoms," "became mighty in war," and "put foreign armies to flight" (11:33–34 NASB). He also commends Noah and Abraham for their faith (11:7, 17)—which included violent activity. And what about temporal judgments—and the final judgment—on unbelievers mentioned throughout Revelation? The "nonviolent Jesus" is portrayed as sitting on a "white horse," and "in righteousness He judges and wages war" (19:11 NASB). He is "clothed with a robe dipped in blood" so that he may "strike down the nations, and He will rule them with a rod of iron; and He treads the wine press of the fierce wrath of God, the Almighty" (vv. 13, 15 NASB). This sounds very much like the language of the God of the Old Testament (Isa. 63:2–6). Though Revelation is highly symbolic, we see Jesus himself engaging in acts of seemingly violent final judgment there; we must be careful about treating such texts wholly symbolically. For one thing, Jesus promises the false prophetess Jezebel, "I will throw her on a bed of sickness, and those who commit adultery with her into great tribulation, unless they repent. And I will kill her children with pestilence, and all the churches will know that I am He who searches the minds and hearts" (Rev. 2:22–23 NASB)—an act of temporal judgment. And Jesus himself (Matt. 24:37–51), as well as Peter (2 Peter 3:1–13), compares the violent end-times judgment with that of the temporal violent judgment of Noah's flood. And Jesus uses fierce language to depict the severity of this end-times judgment in a parable of a master who returns to an evil, inattentive slave and "will cut him in pieces" (Matt. 24:51 NASB; Luke 12:46; cf. Mark 12:9; Luke 20:16). Enns considers the command to "utterly destroy" the Canaanites to be at odds with "Christian theology" as well as "Jesus' teachings about how to treat sinners and enemies, which do not rest comfortably with God's order to slaughter men, women, and children."[18] Enns takes the command regarding the Canaanites literally rather than (as we argue later) hyperbolically, but that would still be irrelevant to Enns and Seibert.

The problem for both Enns and Seibert is that *Jesus and the New Testament writers don't actually read the Old Testament "in a nonviolent way."* On the contrary, we see very clear pronouncements (or descriptions) of divine judgment and wrath both by Jesus and the New Testament authors, and none of them shrink from portrayals of God in the Old Testament. Furthermore, to downplay or even deny the historicity of a number of Old Testament events and clear statements by Jesus because of their connection to divine wrath is to skew the biblical portrayal of Jesus, who affirms such texts (Noah's flood; Mosaic capital punishment; the destruction of Sodom, Gomorrah, Tyre, and Sidon). To explain away some clear connections between God and violent actions in the Old and New Testaments by questioning their historicity is problematic; once we say that in only a "few cases" are historical events essential to our faith, this goes against general biblical assumptions of the historicity of, say, divine temporal judgments and the presumption of New Testament authors and Jesus himself that these events were historical.[19]

To impose a nonviolent or pacifistic grid on the words and actions of God/Jesus requires significant hermeneutical gymnastics—an approach that creates an interpretive straitjacket. To proclaim an absolute pacifism and a rejection of any association between God and violent action requires dismissing or ignoring Jesus's own authoritative statements, vast tracts of Scripture pertaining to divine judgment—such as the prophetic books—and the book of Revelation, which heavily cites those prophetic books. Doing so also ignores sections of Scripture where force—even lethal force—is warranted. These include God's ordaining the minister of the state to bear "the sword" (Rom. 13:4 NASB) or Paul's benefiting from military force when his life is under threat (Acts 23). What about Peter, through whom God's Spirit struck down Ananias and Sapphira, who had lied to God (Acts 5)? What of Paul, through whom God struck Elymas blind (Acts 13)? And when the Eleven sought a replacement for Judas Iscariot, were they ignoring Jesus's words about loving enemies when they cited *two* imprecatory psalms to support their actions? Their scriptural support is, "let his homestead be made desolate, and let no one dwell in it," and "let another take his office" (Acts 1:20 NASB; cf. Pss. 69:25; 109:8). Not only did Paul use such imprecatory language when he called Elymas, "you son of the devil" (Acts 13:10), as well as John when he refers to "the children of the devil" (1 John 3:10 NASB), but Jesus *himself* declared that his opponents' "father" is "the devil" (John 8:44). Should these be included in the "violent texts" of Scripture?

Paul expressed a prayer of justice concerning Alexander the coppersmith who did him much harm: "the Lord will repay him according to his deeds" (2 Tim. 4:14 NASB). Paul said that those who refuse to "love the Lord" are "accursed" (1 Cor. 16:22 NASB)—as are those who teach a false gospel (Gal. 1:8–9). He even wished that those troubling Judaizers would go the whole way and mutilate themselves (Gal. 5:12). He called them "dogs" (Phil. 3:2 NASB)—outsiders to the covenant. Jesus uses similar language about those who despise the sacred things of God, calling them "dogs" and "swine" (Matt. 7:6 NASB)—in the very Sermon on the Mount where Jesus speaks of loving enemies! Later in Matthew, Jesus has very harsh words for those who oppose him and attribute his works to Satan (Matt. 23)—even though he prays for their forgiveness at the cross (Luke 23:34).

When God's enemies are justly punished, the New Testament writers echo the rejoicing of their Old Testament counterparts: "Rejoice over her [Babylon], O heaven, and you saints and apostles and prophets, because God has pronounced judgment for you against her" (Rev. 18:20 NASB; cf. Pss. 96:10–13; 97:7–9; 98:7–9; 99:4–5). These expressions of satisfaction—even joy—at divine wrath and judgment are justified: "They deserve it" (Rev. 16:6 NASB).[20] This does not oppose Jesus's call to love and pray for our enemies—indeed, to desire their salvation. Yet John Stott puts this in context: "We cannot desire their salvation in defiance of their own unwillingness to receive it. This is the heart of the matter."[21] Stott continues: "We should earnestly desire the salvation of sinners if they would repent and equally, earnestly desire their (and our) destruction if they (or we) will not."[22] Here again we see very strong continuity between the two Testaments.

"Behold then the kindness and the severity of God" (Rom. 11:22 NASB). Yes, we must read the Scriptures discerningly, but we must take care to avoid an undiscerning selectivity that ignores the very stance of the New Testament and Jesus himself. We see in Scripture with abundant clarity God's *kindness*, but we must not deny God's *severity*; to essentially dismiss as misrepresentation many violent judgment texts attributed to God/Jesus is to leave a massive explanatory hole. Even the chief Old Testament text describing the God of Israel as "compassionate and gracious, slow to anger, and abounding in lovingkindness and truth" (Exod. 34:6 NASB) is immediately followed by, "He will by no means leave the guilty unpunished" (v. 7; cf. Exod. 20:6). The prophet Habakkuk pleads with God in light of pending judgment on Judah: "In wrath remember mercy" (3:2 NASB). The message of Jesus clearly emphasizes divine mercy, but it acknowledges divine wrath.

John Goldingay offers his assessment:

> Many modern people don't like the way the book [of Joshua] portrays Joshua's leading Israel in killing many Canaanites, but there is no indication that the New Testament shares this modern unease. The New Testament pictures Joshua as

a great hero (see Hebrews 11) and portrays God's violent dispossession of the Canaanites as part of the achievement of God's purpose in salvation (see Acts 7). If there is a contradiction between loving your enemies and being peacemakers, on one hand, and Joshua's undertaking this task at God's command, on the other, the New Testament does not see it.[23]

Yes, there are differences in God's dealings with his people under the old and new covenants—for example, capital punishment was commanded or permitted for certain actions in ancient Israel as opposed to excommunication of the immoral person from the New Testament church (1 Cor. 5). Also, God permits inferior moral conditions in the Old Testament that the New Testament notes (e.g., Matt. 19:8). However, Jesus and his earliest followers take for granted the same unchanging character of the God of the Hebrew Scriptures. To assume that Jesus rejected divine temporal judgment in the Old Testament Scriptures runs contrary to Jesus's own assumption of the historicity of these events, his own wrathful pronouncements, and his strong identification with the Old Testament worldview. So we should carefully study and qualify the nature of violence in Scripture, but we must not do violence *to* Scripture in the process.

Summary

- The ancient writer Marcion repudiated the Old Testament as coming from the "lesser" Creator God of the Jews.

- We must not create a chasm between the harsh, wrathful, war-commanding God of the Old Testament and the loving, compassionate, nonviolent God spoken of by Jesus.

- Those who sharply distinguish here tend to argue that God doesn't send judgments like famine or crop failure on people (this reflected the biblical authors' ancient Near Eastern worldview), nor could he command warfare or bring about harsh judgments.

- We should avoid a strong distinction between "the textual God" (the author's literary representation) and "the actual God" (the living divine reality) in the name of the flawed, restrictive assumption that the true God never utilized violence in judgment. This is not borne out by reading the words of Jesus himself or the rest of the New Testament witness.

- Such thinkers take the nonviolent, enemy-loving Jesus as their reference point to show us God's character. They admonish us to read the Old Testament nonviolently and from the outsider's point of view (e.g., didn't Goliath have a family whom he loved and for whom he was responsible?). We should also *name* the violence—for example, calling the killing of the Canaanites "genocide."

- True, we should think more deeply about difficult, ethically troubling Old Testament passages rather than glossing over them. We should speak out against the misuse of biblical texts.

- Despite the misreading of biblical texts over the centuries, let us remember the great moral gains brought about by Bible-reading Christians in Western civilization. These gains include democracy, literacy, human rights, women's rights, civil rights, abolition of slavery, and much more.

- Yes, the church "grandly proclaims" the Bible to be God's Word, but Jesus does this too down to the "smallest letter or stroke" (Matt. 5:18 NASB; cf. John 10:35; cf. Paul as well: 2 Tim. 3:16). Clearly, simply making this pronouncement does not automatically make one susceptible to misusing Scripture!

- We must avoid a selective appeal to Jesus's authority. After all, Jesus does denounce Jerusalem, Bethsaida, Chorazin, and Capernaum and acknowledge Mosaic capital punishment (Matt. 15:4), and he assumes that Sodom, Tyre, and Sidon had been divinely judged in history (Matt. 11:21–24; cf. 10:15).

- Jesus makes a whip to drive out moneychangers from the temple (John 2:15; cf. Mark 11:15–17). He speaks in violent terms of those who are stumbling blocks (Matt. 18:6) as well as the "wretched" vine-growers—Israel's leadership (Matt. 21:41; Mark 12:9). In Revelation, Jesus makes threats of severe temporal judgment on "Jezebel" and her followers (Rev. 2:16, 21–23—a sickbed, great tribulation, and the death of "her children with pestilence"). He speaks in a parable of an evil slave, and the returning master (representing *God*) who will "cut him in pieces" (Matt. 24:51 NASB; Luke 12:46).

- Jesus also embraces the general theological outlook of the Old Testament—that the heavenly Father "causes His sun to rise" and "sends rain" on the good and wicked alike (Matt. 5:45 NASB). He also affirms that military strength and strategy don't guarantee

victory since authority has been bestowed by God (John 19:10–11).

- We should not neglect the message of the rest of the New Testament—including Paul and others affirming severe divine temporal punishments on Israel (1 Cor. 10) and even divine judgment in their own day (1 Cor. 11:30). They affirm warfare against the Canaanites and other battles (Acts 7:45; 13:19; Heb. 11:33, 34), and Noah (who was delivered in judgment) and Abraham (who offered up Isaac) are commended for their faith (Heb. 11:7, 17).

- It seems that Jesus and the New Testament writers don't actually read the Old Testament the way Seibert and Enns think they should.

- The grid of pacifism/nonviolence seems to go against other affirmations in the New Testament (Rom. 13:4; Acts 23:12–35, where Paul appeals to the Roman military for protection from harm). Beyond this, Jesus himself uses strong language against his enemies (Matt. 7:6; John 8:44), as do the apostles (Acts 13:10; Gal. 1:8–9; 5:12; Phil. 3:2; 1 John. 3:10). The apostles invoke imprecatory psalms (Acts 1:20; cf. Pss. 69:25; 109:8). Ananias and Sapphira are struck dead (Acts 5:1–5), and Elymas is struck blind (Acts 13)—both by God. Paul and the martyred saints have expectations of justice against wrongs done (2 Tim. 4:14; Rev. 6:9–10). These themes reflect both the *kindness* and *severity* of God (Rom. 11:22).

PART 2

OCCASIONAL COMMANDS, HYPERBOLIC TEXTS, AND GENOCIDAL MASSACRES

Before we proceed to chapter 4, we want to review where we've already been to set a context for our discussion in the next several chapters. In chapter 1, we explored a representative version of the argument we address in this book set forth by atheist philosopher Raymond Bradley. He presented what we have called the Crucial Moral Principle: *It is morally wrong to deliberately and mercilessly slaughter men, women, and children who are innocent of any serious wrongdoing.* He claimed that a "biblical theist" is rationally committed to the following four (revised) propositions—but, alas, propositions that are inconsistent:

1 Any act that God commands us to perform is morally permissible.
2' God is the author of the Bible.
3 It is morally impermissible for anyone to commit acts that violate the Crucial Moral Principle.

4‴ The divine author of the Bible uses the text to perform the speech act of commanding us to perform acts that violate the Crucial Moral Principle.

Bradley points out that these propositions, 1–4‴, are inconsistent. Central to this argument is the claim that a biblical theist is commited to 4‴: *the divine author of Scripture uses the biblical text to command us to kill innocent people.* Bradley argues that the biblical theist is committed to violating this Crucial Moral Principle about the wrongness of slaughtering innocents. How so? Because to deny it flies "in the face of facts ascertainable by anyone who takes the care to read: objective facts about what the Bible actually says." In chapter 1 we cited Bradley, who claims that God commanded Joshua to exterminate virtually every Canaanite, adding that in Joshua 7–12 we read the "chilling chronicle" of God's "genocidal policies." Bradley makes three points about what is affirmed in these texts.

First, Bradley asserts that the book of Joshua records the Israelites carrying out the "slaughter" of "virtually every man, woman and child in Canaan" at God's command. He describes God as *commanding genocide.* Here, of course, Bradley is representative of many critics. Edwin Curley, for example, refers to the same commands in the book of Joshua and maintains they describe "a genocidal command" wherein "complete extermination is prescribed."[1] Theologian Randal Rauser and atheist philosopher Wes Morriston alike contend that in these passages God commands genocide.[2] As we have seen, Old Testament scholar Eric Seibert asserts that the "textual God" of the Old Testament (though not the "actual God") commands genocide. We could add atheist philosophers such as Louise Antony and Evan Fales as well.[3] The list goes on.

Second, Bradley contends that the author portrays the Canaanites as *innocent* people. Remember that the Crucial Moral Principle states that it is "morally wrong to deliberately and mercilessly slaughter men, women, and children who are innocent of any serious wrongdoing." The picture he paints is of slaughtered innocent people who have committed no fault, done no wrong, and violated no one's rights. Antony makes a similar claim: "Sometimes, [in the text] there's not even a pretext that the doomed people are morally at fault: The only 'crime' committed by the Canaanites was living in a land God wanted for his people."[4] Peter Millican similarly talks about God "annihilating six nations merely for being in the wrong place."[5] Morriston argues the biblical narratives are analogous to the United States using the vast military power at its disposal "to obliterate . . . the nation of Iran."[6]

Third, from chapter 1 onwards, we have cited Bradley's assertion: "The Bible tells us that God commands us to perform acts that violate [the Crucial Moral Principle]."[7] This suggests he understands the divine author of Scripture to be using the text to issue commands to its readers to kill innocent human beings. Bradley is not alone in phrasing the problem in this way. Christopher Hitchens, for example, claims the Bible constitutes a warrant for ethnic cleansing and indiscriminate massacre. The only reason we are not "bound" by these commands, he contends, is because it was put together "by crude, uncultured human animals."[8] He insinuates that if the Bible is the Word of God, we are required to follow these ancient commandments. But if it is not, one can defensibly claim we are not bound to follow them.

Before addressing each of these claims, it is worth remembering a qualification we mentioned in chapter 1. Bradley's argument contends that a biblical theist is committed to the claim that the *divine* author of Scripture commands acts that violate the Crucial Moral Principle. We also pointed out that it is possible, and in some cases plausible, that what God says by way of appropriating the biblical text as his Word is not the same as what the human author of the text states. Consequently, even if biblical theists believe that a statement or command is part of inspired Scripture, it does not automatically follow that they must conclude that God approved or commanded this—nor does it necessarily require giving up their belief in biblical authority.

Despite this, however, we remain unconvinced that the texts Bradley cites are successful even in showing that the human author of the Bible affirms that God commands us to perform acts that violate the Crucial Moral Principle. This is because we contend that the three claims he and others make about the text are inaccurate and a distortion of what the authors of these texts actually affirm.

We will address each of these claims below in reverse order. We argue, first, that these texts do not command us today to kill innocent people; second, that the text does not in fact portray the Canaanites as, in general, innocent of any serious wrongdoing; and, finally, that the text does not paint a picture of genocide, or of God commanding the extermination of virtually every inhabitant of Canaan. This last point will take us on to chapters 7, 8, and 9, where we defend the claim that the language of "he utterly destroyed every person who was in it," "he left no survivor," and "there was no one left who breathed" is hyperbolic; it is not being used by the author to affirm literally that Israelites killed every single Canaanite at God's command. Then in chapter 10, we look at legal and theological objections concerning the charge of genocide.

4

Does the Bible Command *Us* to Kill Innocent Human Beings?

W e've seen that Raymond Bradley maintains that the book of Joshua records the Israelites carrying out the "slaughter" of "virtually every man, woman and child in Canaan" at God's command. Hence, the divine author of the Bible commands *us* to perform acts that violate the Crucial Moral Principle.

The basis for this claim, however, is dubious. Even if we grant Bradley's interpretation of these commands as involving genocide (a claim we dispute throughout part 2), his conclusion does not follow. These texts state that God commanded *Joshua* to carry out the slaughter of innocent people, but that by itself is insufficient to conclude that the text mediates a command *to us* to carry out those practices. Richard Mouw makes the point: "We must also insist that not all commandments which are found in the Bible are to be obeyed by contemporary Christians. For example, God commanded Abram to leave Ur of the Chaldees, and commanded Jonah to preach in Nineveh; it would be silly to suppose that it is part of every Christian's duty to obey these commandments."[1] The examples of Jonah and Abraham are instructive here. The book of Genesis makes reference to a command God issued to Abraham. But the author of the text is not using the text to command *us* to leave Ur of the Chaldees (notwithstanding the dictum that to Ur is human). Rather the author uses the text to narrate God giving Abram a command. Of course doing so serves an important normative function in Genesis: Abraham is held up as an example of a man of faith, and we can model his faith by trusting the promises God gives to us. So one can plausibly see the author as endorsing Abraham's actions as a model of faith, but nothing in the text is intended to communicate a command to the reader to leave Ur of the Chaldees. The commands narrated are understood as *occasional* commands—that is, given to a particular person for a particular occasion and not to be understood as general commands issued to all people everywhere. And as we note in chapters 18 and 20, certain particular divine commands may be misused by subsequent generations of "Bible believers," but such a flawed application is the result of a failure to appreciate the uniqueness of these commands in the flow of salvation history portrayed in Scripture.

Of course there are other commands narrated in Scripture which are not understood to be merely occasional commands. In 1 Corinthians 7, Paul refers back to Jesus's teaching on divorce in Matthew 5 and 19, which refer to the intended permanence of marriage and to sexual immorality as grounds for divorce (v. 10: "not I, but the Lord" NASB). But Jesus does not deal with a situation Paul had to face—namely, gentile unbelievers abandoning newly converted spouses (v. 12: "I say, not the Lord" NASB): "the wife should not leave her husband (but if she does leave, she must remain unmarried, or else be reconciled to her husband), and . . . the husband should not divorce his wife (vv. 10c–11). Now in one sense this is an occasional command, in that Paul is writing a letter to the church in Corinth to address specific problems that the congregation faced. However, in this text, Paul is applying to the Corinthian congregation a command or imperative that is considered to be applicable to all human beings. In Jesus's teaching, which Paul cites, divorce was implicitly condemned in the garden of Eden (cf. Gen. 2:24), and hence the norms of fidelity in question are applicable to the whole human race. The point then is this: the mere fact that a command is recorded in the scriptural narrative is *by itself* insufficient to establish that it is a command to us. To determine this, one needs to examine carefully the context of the command, the writer's reason for articulating it, the command's wider context in the biblical narrative, and so on.

This is complicated by the fact that, in addition to occasional and general commands, a good number of commands narrated in the Pentateuch record divine commands given not to specific individuals but to Israel's leaders or to specific groups within Israel. For example, God commands Moses to strike a rock (Exod. 17:6), and he expects the Levites to carry the ark of the covenant following specific protocols (Deut. 10:8; cf. Exod. 25:14).

Alan Donagan makes the general observation: "While the whole Torah [i.e., the law of Moses] does not purport to be binding on all mankind, *part of it does*. Even in biblical times, the Jews had come to distinguish from mere heathens those gentiles who recognized that part of the Mosaic Halachah [the Jewish Talmud's laws and their interpretation] which applies to gentiles and Jews alike."[2] Jewish exegesis distinguishes between what the rabbis called the Noahide law (Gen. 9) and the Mosaic law. The former are the commands God addresses to all humankind, Jew and gentile alike. Jewish tradition teaches that these laws were first given during the time of Adam for Adam and all of his descendants and then again to Noah. The Mosaic law, on the other hand, is a covenant between God and Israel. However, as the Jews are obviously a subset of all people, various Noahide laws are repeated in the Mosaic law—even though Israel is given a body of other laws that are binding on them in virtue of their special calling as a nation. A good example is seen in the contrast between laws prohibiting Israel from eating certain types of meat that are deemed unclean and the prohibitions against sexual immorality.

Take the laws regarding clean and unclean food. These laws appear in Leviticus 11 and Deuteronomy 14. Now, Deuteronomy 14 begins with a reminder to Israel: "Out of all the peoples on the face of the earth, the Lord has chosen you to be his treasured possession. Do not eat any detestable thing" (vv. 2–3). This is followed by a list of animals declared unclean and thus prohibited in Israel's diet. Immediately after prohibiting the eating of such animals, the text states, "You may give it to the foreigner residing in any of your towns, and they may eat it, or you may sell it to any other foreigner. But you are a people holy to the Lord your God" (v. 21). The text makes clear that these prohibited animals can be sold to gentiles, who may eat them; the Jews, however, are to refrain from eating them because of their special covenant relationship with God: "Out of all the peoples on the face of the earth. . . ." If one reads the earlier sections of the Pentateuch, such as Genesis 9, it teaches that gentiles have been permitted by God to eat any animal. Hence, the kosher laws are not addressed to gentiles and do not expound a command that God had given to all human beings prior to Sinai.

Or consider Amos 1–2, where we see how gentile nations surrounding Israel are condemned for basic moral violations—breaking treaties, delivering vulnerable refugees into the hands of their enemies, ripping open pregnant women to expand national borders. They are not divinely judged merely for failing to circumcise boys or to eat only kosher foods.

This kind of distinction is further supported by the fact that, later in the New Testament, the apostles at the Council of Jerusalem (Acts 15) and Paul in his Letter to the Galatians confirm this interpretation and hold that gentile believers are not required by God to follow Israel's food laws.

This is in stark contrast to the laws laid down in Leviticus 18. This passage opens with God telling Moses to "speak to the Israelites and say to them:

'I am the LORD your God. You must not do as they do in Egypt, where you used to live, and you must not do as they do in the land of Canaan, where I am bringing you. Do not follow their practices'" (vv. 1–3). God then issues a series of commands to refrain from certain sexual practices such as incest (vv. 6–16), bigamy (v. 18), homosexual conduct (v. 22), adultery (v. 20), and bestiality (v. 23), as well as a command to refrain from infant sacrifice (v. 21). God then goes on to state,

> Do not defile yourselves in any of these ways, because this is how the nations that I am going to drive out before you became defiled. Even the land was defiled; so I punished it for its sin, and the land vomited out its inhabitants. But you must keep my decrees and my laws. The native-born and the foreigners residing among you must not do any of these detestable things, for all these things were done by the people who lived in the land before you, and the land became defiled. And if you defile the land, it will vomit you out as it vomited out the nations that were before you. (vv. 24–28)

Here Israel is commanded to refrain from various practices that gentiles engage in, and the reason given is that it is wrong for gentiles to do such things. God explicitly states that he condemned gentiles who did these things prior to the giving of the Mosaic law and that Israel was simply being held to the same standard as gentiles. The conclusion is that no one is to engage in these practices, whether an Israelite ("native") or a gentile ("aliens living among you").

When one turns to the New Testament, the biblical writers recognize general moral duties for both the people of God and for pagans. Paul, for example, excommunicates a congregant in Corinth for incest—"a kind that even pagans do not tolerate" (1 Cor. 5:1). And for those who fail to care for their own family members, they are "worse than an unbeliever" (1 Tim. 5:8). And Paul rejects homosexual practices in Romans 1 as being contrary to the natural order of creation—a point he makes elsewhere in his epistles, using the very language of Leviticus 18[3] to express his objection to such acts (1 Cor. 6:9–10; 1 Tim. 1:9–11).[4]

We have good biblical reasoning for thinking this distinction between demands on all people and demands on believers is sound.[5] However, to defend it further would go beyond the scope of this book. Instead, we will argue that a careful examination of the commands to which Bradley refers suggests two things: first, these commands were given specifically to Israel in a particular historical context and not to all peoples everywhere; second, even when occasional commands were given to Israel in specific circumstances, we should understand that these are not general rules to be applied in future situations.

In this respect they are like God's command to Abram to leave Ur. Such are commands to specific persons to carry out specific actions in the founding of Israel as a nation, not a command to all people for all times.

Was the Command to All the Nations or Just to Israel?

An examination of the command to "destroy" or "drive out the Canaanites" in their historical and literary context makes it clear that this is a command specifically given to Israel in virtue of the special covenant God made with that nation as his chosen people. Deuteronomy 7 records that God commanded Israel to "totally destroy" the Canaanite nations, to "make no treaty with them, and show them no mercy" (v. 2). The text gives a specific historical context:

> For you are a people holy to the LORD your God. The LORD your God has chosen you out of all the peoples on the face of the earth to be his people, his treasured possession. The LORD did not set his affection on you and choose you because you were more numerous than other peoples, for you were the fewest of all peoples. But it was because the LORD loved you and kept the oath he swore to your ancestors that he brought you out with a mighty hand and redeemed you from the land of slavery, from the power of Pharaoh king of Egypt. (vv. 6–8)

The command to Israel to destroy the Canaanite nations, according to the biblical text, is tied to Israel's special status as a nation chosen by God to be a treasured possession—a status rooted in his covenant with Abraham and the patriarchs. On the face of it, this is not a general command to all people, Israelite and gentile. Other nations were not chosen in this way as parties to this covenant or as key players in the unfolding of God's special redemptive-historical activity.

The same point is made in Deuteronomy 9:5: "It is not because of your righteousness or your integrity that you are going in to take possession of their land; but on account of the wickedness of these nations, the LORD your God will drive them out before you, to accomplish what he swore to your fathers, to Abraham, Isaac and Jacob." Israel's dispossessing the Canaanite nations is tied to the specific historical purposes God bestowed on this nation, anchored in the various covenants with Abraham, Isaac, and Jacob. God's purposes were for Israel to live in the land so that eventually God's promised redemption of the world would be achieved, though this would mean dispossessing the Canaanites. No other country in history was set apart for this purpose or party to this covenant.

Moreover, unlike the laws on adultery, rape, inhospitality, sexual immorality, homicide, or violence, there is no precedent before the giving of the Torah to

Moses of God commanding gentiles to "dispossess" other nations. Nor is such a command said to be binding on the Christian believers in the New Testament, nor is the directive to "drive out" other peoples given to the nations of today's world. In fact, as we have noted in the oracles given to the nations by Amos, one finds they explicitly condemn the killing of noncombatants in war. Gaza and Tyre are condemned for taking captive whole communities and selling them into slavery (1:6, 9); Edom is condemned for stifling compassion against his brother Israel by pursuing him to the death (1:11). Ammon is condemned "because he ripped open the pregnant women of Gilead in order to extend his borders" (1:13). In other words, Ammon killed women and children in an aggressive war of conquest and is condemned accordingly.

Was the Command to "Utterly Destroy" an Occasional Command?

Not only is the command given to Israel, but it occurs in the narrative as an occasional command. This is perhaps clearest in Deuteronomy 20:10–18, which is worth quoting at length:

> [10]When you march up to attack a city, make its people an offer of peace. [11]If they accept and open their gates, all the people in it shall be subject to forced labor and shall work for you. [12]If they refuse to make peace and they engage you in battle, lay siege to that city. [13]When the LORD your God delivers it into your hand, *put to the sword all the men in it* [*'et kol zekurah lepiy hareb*]. [14]As for the women, the children, the livestock and everything else in the city, you may take these as plunder for yourselves. And you may use the plunder the LORD your God gives you from your enemies. [15]This is how you are to treat all the cities that are at a distance from you and do not belong to the nations nearby. [16]However [*raq*], in the cities of the nations the LORD your God is giving you as an inheritance, do not leave alive anything that breathes. [17]Completely destroy them—the Hittites, Amorites, Canaanites, Perizzites, Hivites and Jebusites—as the LORD your God has commanded you. [18]Otherwise, they will teach you to follow all the detestable things they do in worshiping their gods, and you will sin against the LORD your God.

The New International Version (NIV) translates "put to the sword [*zekurah*, from the Hebrew verb *nakah*]" (v. 13) as a command (the imperative of the imperfect verb). However, Old Testament scholar Joe Sprinkle argues that identical or similar parallels to this verse should be understood as a *permissive* use of this (imperfect) verb. That is, the verse *permits* the killing of the men. Thus verses 12–13 would be rendered this way: "Now if it [the city] is unwilling to make peace with you, but instead makes war with you, then you are *permitted* to besiege it. Now when YHWH your God gives it into your hand, then you *may* kill any of its men with the edge of the sword."[6]

Immediately following these verses, a particle (*raq*)—which the NIV translates "As for"—comes at the beginning of verse 14: "*As for* the women, the children, the livestock and everything else in the city . . ." This particle, Sprinkle notes, typically qualifies or restricts a previous statement. The previous clause in verse 13 indicates what can be done to the "men/males," and the following *raq* clause qualifies and clarifies that such a rule does not apply to women, children, and spoil.[7] Verses 13–14 therefore express the principle of noncombatant immunity. *If* a city refuses terms of peace, one can permissibly kill the men.[8] For those who will be engaging in the combat, however, this permission does not extend to women, children, and spoil; one is prohibited from killing them.

What is significant for our purposes is that the command to totally destroy the Canaanites in verses 16–17 is explicitly stated to be an exception to this normal rule. The particle *raq* ("As for" or "However") suggests an exception to what has gone before. This passage comes in the context of laws about warfare with nations that are "at a distance from you" and do not belong to "the nations nearby." That is, these are cities outside the Promised Land; they are not found within the territory of the seven nations occupying Canaan. Of course, once Israel gained occupation of the Promised Land, *every* other nation, by definition, would be "far away"; the dispossessed seven nations would not belong to "the nations nearby."

Now in the ancient Near Eastern world in which warfare was the chief means of national survival, the instructions in verses 13–14 give general guidance for Israel in battle. These are the rules, writes Sprinkle, "that governed war outside the land of promise and that were meant to govern all war once Israel occupied the land."[9] So the command to "completely destroy" the Canaanites, then, is an exception to the normal rules of warfare mentioned in verses 13–14, a divinely mandated exception that was unique and unrepeatable.

The command to "completely destroy" the Canaanites, then, isn't presented as a general command for how all nations are to conduct war in general; in fact, it's not even a general command for how Israel is to typically conduct warfare. Rather, this is an exception to the normal rules, which is applied only to the nations occupying the land God had promised Israel through the patriarchs at the time of entry into Canaan.

In fact, the law of Moses *prohibited* Israel from conquering other neighboring nations such as Moab, Ammon, and Edom (Deut. 2:4, 9, 19; 23:7); this is precisely because these nations did not live in the land God had given Israel, and God had not given the land these people occupied to the nation of Israel for the sake of achieving his redemptive purposes.[10]

Summary

- Contrary to Bradley and others, not all commands in the Bible are to be obeyed by contemporary Christians (God does not command us to leave our home country as Abram did). These are *occasional* commands—for certain persons in a particular time at a particular place; they are not binding on all peoples at all times.

- There are enduring, binding commands in Scripture as well. Yet the commands of the entire law of Moses were not intended to be binding on *all* human beings (e.g., kosher food laws); only a portion of them are binding. See the Noahide laws of Gen. 9, which were intended for all people (cf. the moral law assumed in Amos 1–2; 1 Cor. 5:1; 1 Tim. 1:9–11).

- Leviticus 18 lists moral violations of which the Canaanites were guilty and therefore were to be "vomited out" of the land; Israel was not to repeat these actions—bestiality, adultery, incest, ritual prostitution, and the like. Of course, infant sacrifice was an act of gross wickedness.

- The command to "utterly destroy" is clearly directed to Israel, not to all the nations or Christians (cf. Deut. 7:1–8). God's commands to Israel are often connected to his unfolding historical purposes for them.

- The command to "utterly destroy" the Canaanites is an *occasional* command. Deuteronomy 20 gives warfare instructions to Israel about the Canaanite cities/citadels ("the nations nearby") and about those "far away."

- The command to "utterly destroy" only applies to the Canaanites as Israel enters the land. Once Israel takes the land, then this is no longer relevant. All the other nations would be "far away."

- Israel was *prohibited* from attacking neighboring nations such as Moab, Ammon, and Edom (Deut. 2:4, 9, 19; 23:7)—nations that did not live in the land God had given to Israel.

5

Does the Bible Portray
the Canaanites as Innocent?

In the previous section, we saw that the command to exterminate the Canaanites was an *occasional* command; that is, it was not an application of a general rule relevant to all people throughout history. Rather, in one particular campaign, theocratic national Israel, by virtue of its unique covenantal status, was authorized to make an exception to the general principles governing warfare.

Let's come back to Raymond Bradley's Crucial Moral Principle: "It is morally wrong to deliberately and mercilessly slaughter men, women, and children who are innocent of any serious wrongdoing." *At best*, Bradley's argument shows that at one point in history God commanded Joshua to violate the Crucial Moral Principle by issuing a command to exterminate every single Canaanite man, woman, and child in the land he had given his people. What should be clear, however, is that God does *not* command *us* to violate the Crucial Moral Principle.

However, even this more limited conclusion is not as straightforward an inference from the text as Bradley thinks. Merciless slaughter is not how the biblical text portrays the situation. While it may be plausible to suggest that some Canaanite individuals, particularly Canaanite children, are innocent of any crime, the Bible does not portray the Canaanites in general as innocent of any serious wrongdoing. Three features of the narrative make this plain.

Feature 1: Israel's Legal Ownership of Canaan

First, the text indicates that the Canaanites are occupying land of which Israel has legal ownership—and without the consent of the owner. This was seen in the passages we examined in the previous chapter. Deuteronomy 20 limits the command to "completely destroy" the Canaanites in "cities of the nations the LORD your God is giving you as an inheritance" (v. 16–17). It was limited to the nations occupying land to which Israel had divinely granted legal title. The same point is made in Exodus 13:5, where Moses emphasizes that "the land of the Canaanites, Hittites, Amorites, Hivites and Jebusites" was the land which *the Lord* "swore to your ancestors to give you."

Similarly, as we have seen above, in the narrative God *prohibited* Israel from conquering other neighboring nations such as Moab, Ammon, and Edom (cf. Deut. 2:4, 9, 19; 23:7) because these peoples—*not* the Israelites—had legitimate title to their lands. God tells Israel not to provoke Edom to war, "for I will not give you any of their land, not even enough to put your foot on. *I have given Esau the hill country of Seir as his own.* You are to pay them in silver for the food you eat and the water you drink" (2:5–6). Likewise, they are commanded not to attack Moab because "I will not give you any part of their land. I have *given Ar to the descendants of Lot as a possession*" (v. 9). Similarly, God says this of Ammon: "for I will not give you possession of any land belonging to the Ammonites. *I have given it as a possession to the descendants of Lot*" (v. 19). Unlike these nations, the Canaanites are squatters on Israel's land; hence, Israel has a right to "drive them out" or "dispossess them" in a way in which they do *not* have a right to drive out others (e.g., Exod. 23:28; Deut. 11:23).

Israel's title—and hence legal right—to the land the Canaanites possess forms a central theme of the narrative. The account of the entrance into Canaan in the book of Joshua comes after a long narrative that begins in the book of Genesis. In the book of Genesis, after the protohistory of the creation, fall, flood, Babel, and so on, the story of Israel's history proper begins in Genesis 12 with Abram being called by God to leave Ur of the Chaldeans to go to an unknown land. This land is later identified as Canaan. Abram was given several promises that would ultimately lead to the renewal of all nations on earth. The text states: "The LORD had said to Abram, 'Go from your country, your people and your father's household to the land I will show you. I will make you into a great nation and I will bless you; I will make your name great, and you will be a blessing'" (vv. 1–2).[1] God tells Abram that he will be the father of an entire nation—one that will have its own country and land. Whereas arrogant builders of Babel attempt to "make for [them]selves a name [*shem*]" (11:4 NASB), God tells Abram, "I will make your name [*shem*] great" (12:2).

The point is that Abram was given this land as a means to bless the whole world and reverse the curse of Babel.[2] Abram and his descendants are promised a land for the purpose of carrying out this task. David Lamb notes, "The gift of the land was one of the primary ways Yahweh planned to bless Israel, and it was through this land that God would work his ultimate purposes to bless and call all nations to himself."[3] Christopher Wright makes the same point: "God declared to Abraham that his purpose in calling him was that all nations on the earth would find blessing. This is repeated six times in Genesis and is clearly a central dimension of Israel's election. . . . Israel was to be the means of blessing to the nations."[4]

This promise was reiterated and elaborated in several other encounters between God and Abram. In the next chapter, Abram and Lot had reached Canaan, and Abram had amassed considerable wealth. Disagreement over land and resources led to "quarreling . . . between Abram's herders and Lot's" (13:7). Abram diplomatically solved the dispute by allowing Lot to take his pick of the land, promising that his men would go elsewhere: "Lot *looked around* and saw that the whole plain of the Jordan toward Zoar was well watered, like the garden of the LORD [an allusion to Eden], like the land of Egypt. . . . So Lot chose for himself the whole plain of the Jordan and set out toward the east" (vv. 10–11). Despite having been promised the land of Canaan in Genesis 12, Abram rather generously gave it to Lot. In response, God told Abram: "*Lift up* [Hebrew verb *nasa'*] *your eyes and look* [Hebrew verb *ra'ah*] from the place where you are, northward and southward and eastward and westward; for all the land which you see, I will give it to you and to your descendants forever. . . . Arise, walk about the land through its length and breadth; for I will give it to you" (vv. 14–17 NASB). Gary Anderson notes that "walking across a piece of territory in such a fashion has often been understood as the legal custom of formally taking possession"; hence, in this passage, by divine decree, Abram gains legal possession of Canaan.[5] The same Hebrew verbs "lift up" (*nasa'*) and "look" (*ra'ah*) make a deliberate contrast to the greedy conduct of Abram's nephew Lot a few verses earlier (v. 10). Anderson notes: "Abraham only receives the land of Canaan as an *eternal* patrimony after he has shown himself willing to part with its most valuable acreage. The making of a great name is predicated on an act of generosity rather than legal entitlement."[6] Because of his generosity and willingness to share the land with others, Abram and his offspring were given *eternal* title to the land.[7]

Israel's title to the land is reiterated several times in the proceeding narrative. In Genesis 17:8, God makes a covenant with Abraham and his descendants: "The whole land of Canaan . . . I will give as an everlasting possession to you and your descendants after you." If, as the psalmist contends, the "earth is the LORD's, and everything in it" (Ps. 24:1), and the Creator promises a portion of that earth—the land of Canaan—to Abraham and his descendants, then they are the rightful owners of that land. God makes a similar promise to Abraham's son Isaac: "For to you and your descendants I will give all these lands and will confirm the oath I swore to your father Abraham" (Gen. 26:3). Subsequently, God appears to Jacob in a dream at Bethel and promises: "I am the LORD, the God of your father Abraham and the God of Isaac. I will give you and your descendants the land on which you are lying" (28:13).

Not only is the land promised to Abraham and his descendants, but Genesis emphasizes how the patriarchs began to legally occupy this land in their lifetime. In chapter 23, Abraham purchases a field in Machpelah from Ephron the Hittite. Note the text's emphasis:

> Ephron's field in Machpelah near Mamre—both the field and the cave in it, and all the trees within the borders of the field—was deeded to Abraham as his property in the presence of all the Hittites who had come to the gate of the city. . . . So the field and the cave in it were deeded to Abraham by the Hittites as a burial site. (vv. 17–20)

The reference to a burial site is significant; in the ancient Near East acquiring a burial plot was a sign of permanent occupation. Acquiring a burial plot for oneself and one's descendants signified that one was staying permanently. Later, Jacob purchased a plot of land in Shechem: "For a hundred pieces of silver, he bought from the sons of Hamor, the father of Shechem, the plot of ground where he pitched his tent. There he set up an altar and called it El Elohe Israel" (33:19–20). And when Jacob relocates to Egypt, it is explicitly temporary and based on the understanding that he and his descendants will return.

So the commands occur in the context of the Canaanites living on land that Israel's ancestors had lived on, owned property in, and to which they had legal title for the purpose of establishing a community through which salvation would be brought to the world. Hence, as the commands occur in the biblical narrative, the Canaanites are, strictly speaking, *trespassers*. Moreover, the book of Joshua portrays the Canaanites as aware of this fact. Rahab tells the Hebrew spies in Jericho: "I know that the LORD has given you this land and that a great fear of you has fallen on us, so that all who live in this country are melting in fear because of you. We have heard how the LORD dried up the water of the Red Sea for you when you came out of Egypt" (2:9–10).

The narrative then stresses that for over a generation the Canaanites were aware of the miracles God had performed in Egypt that showed he was the superior deity and that he had given the land to Israel. Similarly, the men of

Gibeon tell Joshua they were "clearly told how the LORD your God had commanded his servant Moses to give [Israel] the whole land" (9:24).

Hence, when Israel is commanded to attack these nations, they are not, as far as the narrator is concerned, conquering or attacking an innocent nation and stealing their land; rather, Israel is repossessing land that already belongs to them and evicting people who are trespassing on it and refusing to leave.

At this point some will protest that this all assumes the narrative is accurate. They will object that history is written by the winners who rationalize their own behavior. One cannot trust the biblical accounts of Canaanite practices because the authors of this text engaged in unjustified extermination of the peoples in question.

Several things can be said in response to this. In the context of our discussion, this objection is obviously circular: it assumes that the Bible is not trustworthy because it commands extermination. This, however, is precisely the conclusion the argument is supposed to establish. To assume one is unreliable in interpreting the text and then using that interpretation to argue against its reliability is to assume what one wants to prove. Moreover, it also fails to address the issue being discussed in this section. The question being asked in this section is whether a person who accepts the Bible as the Word of God, and hence as authoritative, is committed to holding that God commands the killing of innocent people. The critic may point out that believers are mistaken for accepting the Bible as authoritative, but this still does not answer the question of how one should interpret the command *if* it is assumed that the command is authoritative.

An objector might press the point further by asking, What if the Israelites were in the land, and another group attacked them claiming divine justification for doing so? Or what if *any* nation were attacked by another nation with the justification that God (or "the gods") had given them this land in the past? The problem with such scenarios is at least twofold. First, *they implicitly deny the historicity of authoritative, though challenging and perplexing, divinely mandated events*; these questions wrongly assume there is no God who forcefully speaks, commands, and judges or who makes covenants with and grants land to particular individuals or groups in the flow of human history. Second, *such questions ignore the entirety of the biblical narrative*. One cannot assess the morality of the Old Testament without leaving a faithful, good God embedded within the biblical story to make sense of such commands. To remove a fully wise, good, and just God from the Canaanite warfare accounts in Scripture ("What if some foreign army invaded *your* country?") and then attack that narrative would be to gut and destabilize it. We can't fairly remove key characters like Gandalf from the plot line of *The Lord of the Rings* ("What gives *that* wizard the authority to lead 'the Fellowship of the Ring' through such dangerous places?") without distorting the coherence and purpose of the story. To treat Gandalf as nonessential is to empty the story of its meaning.[8]

Feature 2: Israelite Refugees and the Sins of the Amorites

Despite having legal title to the land, Abram and his descendants could not take immediate occupation of the land. In Genesis 15, we read that "the word of the Lord came to Abram in a vision" (v. 1 NASB). Abram's response was, "You have given me no children; so a servant in my household will be my heir" (v. 3). God's answer was emphatic: "This man will not be your heir, but a son who is your own flesh and blood will be your heir" (v. 4). The text continues: "He took him outside and said, 'Look up at the sky and count the stars—if indeed you can count them.' Then he said to him, 'So shall your offspring be'" (v. 5). And this is followed by an important dialogue between God and Abram. God tells Abram, "I am the LORD, who brought you out of Ur of the Chaldeans to give you this land to take possession of it" (v. 7). Abram asks, "Sovereign Lord, how can I know that I will gain possession of it?" (v. 8). In response God enters into a covenant ritual with Abram and states:

> Know for certain that for four hundred years your descendants will be strangers in a country not their own and that they will be enslaved and mistreated there. But I will punish the nation they serve as slaves, and afterward they will come out with great possessions. You, however, will go to your ancestors in peace and be buried at a good old age. In the fourth generation your descendants will come back here, for the sin of the Amorites has not yet reached its full measure. (vv. 13–16)

Two things are noteworthy here. First, the nation of Israel will gain possession of the land only *after* they have been oppressed in Egypt for several generations. It is only after Israel returns to its proper homeland out of Egyptian oppression that they will finally possess the land. Lamb observes that "unlike Assyria and Moab, which were expanding their own borders to enrich their own kingdoms," the biblical narrative presents Israelites as "refugees who had experienced hundreds of years of oppression in a foreign land and needed a place to live"; they were "attempting to gain a homeland."[9]

Second, in spite of having a legal title and a divinely approved claim on the land, Abram and his descendants could not take immediate and total occupation of the land. They had to wait until the "sin of the Amorites" had "reached its full measure" (v. 16). Christopher Wright, an Old Testament scholar, notes that this passage "seems to say that the nature of Amorite/Canaanite society in Abraham's day was not yet so wicked as to justify God acting in such a comprehensive judgment upon it."[10] Anderson notes, "Even if the land of Canaan will become part of the eternal patrimony of the descendants of Abraham it is not a land that God can simply hand over at will. The rights of the citizens who presently reside upon it must be respected. God will not evict them until their immoral ways justify such a punishment."[11] So simply owning the land is insufficient to drive the inhabitants out with force. This, according to the narrative, had to be conjoined with generations of unrepentant wrongdoing on the part of the occupiers.

This point is seen in another episode in the Genesis narrative. Genesis 34 records how Shechem, a Hivite prince living in the land, "defiles" Dinah, Jacob's daughter. This is something which in the eyes of the biblical author is "an outrageous thing in Israel . . . a thing that should not be done" (v. 7). Jacob's sons were angered that Shechem had treated their sister "like a prostitute" (v. 31). Simeon and Levi attacked the city and "killed all the males," and the other brothers plundered the city (v. 25, 27 NRSV). The Hivites are one of the seven people groups God commands Israel to "drive out" and "totally destroy" in the book of Deuteronomy. Here, they are said to be living in the land God has promised Israel. Yet despite this, Jacob's sons are explicitly condemned for this activity. In the closing section of Genesis 34, Jacob rebukes Levi and Simeon because of this conduct.

Hence, during the days of the patriarchs, Abraham's offspring were *forbidden* to engage in violence against the Canaanite nations occupying the land. It is only centuries later when the sin of the Amorites has "reached its full measure" that Israel is authorized to do so. The suggestion is that, even when Canaan occupied land to which Israel had legal title, the inhabitants could not simply be evicted on a whim. It was only when certain immoral practices had been culturally entrenched in the Canaanites for centuries without repentance that Israel would be permitted to drive them out.

Centuries later, we read in the Pentateuch, Israel is divinely authorized to take the land because the Amorite iniquity was finally complete. Deuteronomy states that Israel could drive out the nations on account of their "wickedness" (9:4–5 NASB). The wickedness referred to is not trivial. The most exhaustive list of the kinds of wickedness comes from Leviticus 18. It chronicles incest, adultery, bestiality, ritual prostitution, and homosexual acts; and, most significantly, Deuteronomy 12:29–31 singles out child sacrifice as particularly abhorrent.[12] We find a repeated polemic against ritual infant sacrifice in the Prophets, Psalms, and historical books.[13] And though some claim that God permitted infant sacrifice to him but not other deities, this claim reads too much into certain ambiguous texts.[14]

It is worth noting that most of these practices are illegal today, even in modern Western nations, and no religious group that practiced incest, ritual prostitution, bestiality, or human sacrifice would be tolerated even in contemporary liberal societies with freedom of religion laws. Moreover in many jurisdictions, such as various states of the United States, adults who engage in human sacrifice could face the death penalty. Hence the practices in question are serious crimes—not trivial practices of mere personal preference.

Feature 3: Corrupting Influences and the Risk of Assimilation

The biblical text shows concern not just with the existence of these practices, which were also practiced by Israel's neighbors, but repeatedly warns of the corrupting influence of these practices on the embryonic Israelite nation in the land of Canaan. Deuteronomy 20 warns that if the Israelites follow the practice of taking captives and integrating them into the Israelite community, "they will teach you to follow all the detestable things they do in worshiping their gods, and you will sin against the LORD your God" (v. 18). If the Israelites intermarry with the Canaanite population, God says the Canaanites "will turn your children away from following me to serve other gods" (Deut. 7:4). Indeed, they will be "a snare" (v. 16 NASB). Exodus is explicit: "Do not let them live in your land or they will cause you to sin against me, because the worship of their gods will certainly be a snare to you" (23:33). Similarly, "Be careful not to make a treaty with those who live in the land; for when they prostitute themselves to their gods and sacrifice to them, they will invite you and you will eat their sacrifices. And when you choose some of their daughters as wives for your sons and those daughters prostitute themselves to their gods, they will lead your sons to do the same" (34:15–16). And here a lesser-noted feature of the text is worth mentioning; on the face of it there is an inconsistency in the narrative. In Deuteronomy 20:16–18, Israel is warned if they don't totally destroy the Canaanites, they will be led astray. However, in our discussion of verses 10–15 in the previous chapter, we noted that Israelites were permitted to marry inhabitants from the cities outside Israel's borders; these inhabitants were from the cities "at a distance from you and [who] do not belong to the [seven Canaanite] nations nearby." Yet the inhabitants of these other cities themselves worshiped idols. So why are only the Canaanites singled out?

Two things can be said in response to this. One is that the concern in Deuteronomy 20 is not just that Israel will be led to worship other gods, but that "they will teach you to follow all the detestable things they do in worshiping their gods," that is, practices of prostitution, human sacrifice, incest, and so on done in worship. But more importantly, the biblical text emphasizes that the Canaanites dramatically outnumbered the Israelites (4:38; 7:1, 8; 9:1). Hence, if the minority Israelites lived in the land side by side with the Canaanites, freely intermingling amongst them, they risked being assimilated into the majority culture in which immoral—indeed, criminal—practices were entrenched.

One therefore needs to appreciate the very different contexts that are contrasted between 20:10–15 (the cities that are "at a distance") and verses 16–18 ("the cities of the nations the LORD your God is giving you as an inheritance"). In the latter situation, Israel has entered the Promised Land where seven other, more numerous nations live and engage in practices Israel cannot directly control. In that context, a policy of allowing marriage is likely to lead to cultural, moral, and theological assimilation. In the former scenario (cities "at a distance"), verses 10–15 present Israel's standing policy for all future wars in general once Israel has gained control of the Promised Land. In this setting, the seven nations have been driven out, and a soldier from Israel marries a woman from a nation far away. In this context, it is more likely that the woman who will now leave her home and live within Israel will be assimilated into Israel's culture, not the soldier into the foreign woman's culture. Furthermore, the law makes a gracious provision for such a transfer and assimilation (21:10–14); the rape of foreign women—or any sexual intimacy outside marriage—was prohibited (cf. 22:14, where virginity before marriage is treated with great seriousness in Israel). The main concern, then, is that the small embryonic Israelite nation, which is called to be the people of God and the vehicle through which God will redeem the world, will be assimilated into the corrupt religious practices of the surrounding nations living in the land.

To establish and sustain Israel's own national identity and mission to be a channel of blessing to the entire world is no trivial matter. Indeed, the Hebrew Scriptures take seriously this life-and-death struggle for Israel's own national and spiritual integrity. In fact, we could rightly argue that anything threatening to tear apart the moral and spiritual fabric of Israel could be compared to acts of treason in our own day. When the American citizen John Walker Lindh left his country to join the Taliban to fight against Americans in Afghanistan, this was rightly seen as an act of treason. Or in the previous century, the Americans John and Ethel Rosenberg were executed (in 1950) for supplying nuclear secrets to the Soviet Union—a serious threat to the security and integrity of the United States. Or consider someone who makes sensitive, classified US government documents available on the internet, giving away military secrets and thus undermining American national security. We readily understand the serious threat of treason that could undermine the well-being of a nation.

Prior to the Enlightenment (1650–1800), no serious attempt was made to separate the sacred and the secular, or religion and the state. Of course, it is impossible to compartmentalize these; there is no metaphysics-free worldview, no neutral philosophy of life. All worldviews reflect a deep heart commitment of one sort or another. In a pre-Enlightenment setting, a threat against the *state* was a threat against *religion*—and vice versa. And whatever undermined a nation's identity or integrity was taken seriously. So whether in ancient Near Eastern Israel or in today's nation-states, a common feature is the reality and need of shaping a coherent or cohesive society around a common primary loyalty. As Rob Barrett argues, "Each [of these settings, whether ancient or modern] demands that primary loyalty and threatens with destruction any who prove disloyal to the disadvantage of the rest of the society."[15]

So, contrary to Bradley, the Bible does not portray the Canaanites in general as innocent of any serious wrongdoing. The text portrays the Canaanites as people trespassing on land owned by Israel—land given them as a base for their mission to bring blessing and ultimately salvation for the world. The Canaanites had been using it for centuries without repentance to engage in serious, morally abhorrent criminal practices. The Bible also portrays the situation as one where Israel, being the minority, could not use the land for the purpose for which it was given them without being assimilated into the majority culture with its pervasive criminal practices. If the Israelites lived in their midst and freely intermingled among the Canaanites, Israel's own identity, integrity, calling, and destiny would be undermined—a scenario comparable to treason. It is in that context that God issues the occasional command exempting them from the normal rules governing warfare involving noncombatant immunity.

Finally, there are hints in the text that Canaanites who rejected these kinds of practices were to be spared and could live in the land amongst the Israelite community. We will provide three examples below.

Rahab

An obvious example is Rahab, the Canaanite tavern-keeper, who is explicitly exempted from death at the hands of the Israelites. Atheist philosopher Wes Morriston sets aside the question of what the two Israelite spies were doing in Rahab's home in Jericho (Josh. 2), and he asserts that Rahab was more prudent than pious in asserting her allegiance to Yahweh, the God of the Israelites: "Her 'fear of Yahweh' is the most ordinary kind of fear, and she is willing to betray her entire city in order to save her own skin, and that of the rest of her family."[16] But this reading of the Rahab story is questionable.

First, contrary to Morriston's insinuation, the text does not claim the Israelite spies slept with Rahab. Old Testament scholar Richard Hess notes, "The text carefully avoids implying a sexual liaison between the spies and their hostess. . . . If the intention was to imply sexual relations, there would be no intermediate term such as, *the house of*," when Samson visited a prostitute and 'went to spend the night with her' (Judg. 16:1)."[17] Hess adds that "the last verb in the verse, *stayed there*, is not used for sexual relations without the occurance of the preposition 'with' followed by designation of a partner."[18] Furthermore, Rahab was the tavern-keeper (who also happened to be a harlot), and taverns in ancient Near Eastern cities were public places where travelers could, among other things, learn about the features of these cities; so these Israelite spies could discover the practical and military dispositions of the area and could solicit a possible "fifth column" of support.[19]

Second, contrary to Morriston, the text does suggest that Rahab embraces Yahweh as her own, as explicitly stated in Joshua 2:11. Douglas Earl notes that this is a "confession par excellence."[20] He explains the very wording of this confession is found in only two other places in the Old Testament: Moses's confession in Deuteronomy 4:39 and Solomon's confession in 1 Kings 8:23.[21] Rahab states that she and the whole country of Canaan had heard of God's miraculous signs and wonders in the exodus and know that God has given the land to the Israelites. In response to these signs, she confesses, "For the LORD your God is God in heaven above and on the earth below" (Josh. 2:11).

Moreover, Earl observes that the prominent position the story of Rahab has in the narrative confirms this reading. Just prior to the battle of Jericho, Joshua encountered an angel who identifies himself as the commander of the Lord's army. When Joshua asks the angel if he is on Israel's side or the side of the Canaanites, the response is that the angel is not on either side. He is on the side of the Lord (5:13–15). Then in the following chapter, the Canaanite Rahab displays strong faith in God and is saved from destruction. But by contrast, the Israelite Achan disobeys God's command and is destroyed. Earl notes several obvious parallels between the accounts of Rahab and Achan. Rahab *hides* (*taman*, 2:6) the spies—also called *messengers* (*malakim*)—sent by Joshua, an action leading to her escaping from destruction (6:25). Achan *hides* (*taman*, 7:21) the contraband from Joshua which the messengers (*malakim*, 7:22) from Joshua discover, leading to Achan's destruction. The juxtaposing of these episodes with their similar language and linguistic parallels leads many commentators to conclude that the author here is making an explicit point: it is faithfulness to God's commands—not one's ethnicity—that makes one a true Israelite. And it is *disobedience*—not ethnicity—that makes one subject to destruction.[22]

Perhaps most significantly, the Bible itself interprets Rahab's story this way. The book of Hebrews states: "By faith the prostitute Rahab, because she welcomed the spies, was not killed with those who were disobedient" (11:31). Rahab was a Canaanite, yet she was spared because she was not like those who are disobedient, but rather responded in faith. The author of Joshua emphasizes that Rahab "lives among the Israelites to this day" (Josh. 6:25),[23] and Matthew lists her as an ancestor of both David and Jesus the Messiah (Matt. 1:5).

Caleb

Caleb is another example who stands out against the backdrop of the majority Israelite community. He expressed full confidence that God would fulfill his promises, and he wholeheartedly obeyed. God responded: "Because my servant Caleb has a different spirit and follows me wholeheartedly, I will bring him into the land he went to, and his descendants will inherit it" (Num. 14:24). God's promise to Caleb would be fulfilled, as Joshua 14:14 indicates: Caleb and his family were given a share in the inheritance. What many readers fail to notice is this: Caleb, though from the tribe of Judah, has a *Canaanite* background! The text refers to him as "Caleb the son of Jephunneh the Kenizzite" (Num. 32:12; Josh. 14:6, 14). Who were the Kenizzites? They were one of the seven nations in Canaan and were listed along with the Hittites and the Perizzites who lived on the land God would be giving to Abram (Gen. 15:18–20). These were the peoples God commanded Israel to "utterly destroy." Yet Caleb the Kennizite was one of the few in the nation of Israel to see the Promised Land because "he followed the LORD wholeheartedly." These two examples suggest that any Canaanite who turned from the detestable practices mentioned would not be killed; obedience to God, not ethnicity or national identity, appears to be the issue.[24]

Shechemites

This protection based on obedience to God is further borne out by the fact that other Canaanites (i.e., the Shechemites) are included in Israel's renewal ceremony mentioned at the end of Joshua 8: "All Israel with their elders and officers and their judges were standing on both sides of the ark . . . the stranger [*ger*] as well as the native" (v. 33 NASB). At Shechem, those who heard the Law being read included not only "the assembly of Israel" but also "the strangers who were living among them" (vv. 33, 35). Sprinkle notes, "Joshua 8:30–35 narrates a covenant renewal ceremony at Shechem despite the fact that Shechem was a major power during the Late Bronze Age as the fourteenth century B.C. El Amarna tablets from Egypt indicate. This suggested to [John] Bright that Shechem was absorbed into Israel rather than being conquered, and so the covenant renewal ceremony was on the occasion of additional people being added to the covenant."[25]

So the Canaanites are not in general portrayed as innocent. They are trespassing on land belonging to Israel and have engaged in practices such as human sacrifice for centuries without repentance. Their numerical and cultural dominance meant Israel could not live in the land alongside them without being absorbed into a culture engaging in abhorrent practices; yet the text suggests that Canaanites who turned from these practices could be spared. So the picture painted by Raymond Bradley and other previously mentioned critics is misleading.

At one point atheist philosopher Louise Antony appears to concede this. She grants that "various apologists" have argued that the Canaanites were "morally corrupt." She then responds: "But this hardly distinguishes them from the Israelites themselves, about whom God is constantly fuming and whom he is constantly threatening to destroy."[26]

This is an odd comeback for two reasons. First, this commits the *tu quoque* ("you too") logical fallacy; it is a kind of "red herring" argument—a distraction technique that evades the truth of the criticism by charging that the critic himself ("you too") is guilty of the same thing. So even if the Israelites behaved very much like the Canaanites, it doesn't follow from the narrative that the Canaanites didn't act in this way. And so when Antony claims that if the Israelites would do things the Canaanites did and thus the only "crime" committed by the Canaanites must have been that they were "living in a land God wanted for his people,"[27] she is making a false statement. The Canaanites did in fact engage in morally corrupt—indeed, criminal—practices, and Israel's copying their practices (which God *also* judged) do not diminish the fact that the Canaanites were worthy of divine judgment in their own right.

Second, Antony's charge fails to note what is actually taught in the text— namely, that Israel's occupation of the land was *conditional*. God gave Israel the land for a specific purpose: to bless all the nations of the world. A condition of them occupying the land was entering into a covenant involving promises not to engage in the corrupt practices of the Canaanites; if they were to breach this covenant, they, like the Canaanites, would lose possession of the land. As we will see in the next chapter, the very language of "utterly destroy [*haram*]" could be applied equally to Israel.[28] The catalog of sins mentioned in Leviticus 18 finishes with this command:

Do not defile yourselves in any of these ways, because this is how the nations that I am going to drive out before you became defiled. Even the land was defiled; so I punished it for its sin, and the land vomited out its inhabitants. But you must keep my decrees and my laws. The native-born and the foreigners residing among you must not do any of these detestable things, for all these things were done by the people who lived in the land before you, and the land became defiled. And if you defile the land, it will vomit you out as it vomited out the nations that were before you. (vv. 24–28)

If one pays attention to the remaining narrative, one will see that it documents (throughout Deuteronomistic history and the Prophets) how Israel did not obey the terms of the covenant. Centuries after the exodus, the Israelites were exiled and dispossessed of the land. The biblical narrative makes it clear that Israel's possession of Canaan *was* subject to the same conditions as the Canaanites' possession had been. Just as Israel waited over four hundred years for the sins of the Amorites to be full before they could occupy the land, so too God tolerated Israel's continual and repeated violations of the covenant in their engaging in these practices for several centuries before sending both Israel and later Judah into exile.

Summary

- In one particular campaign, theocratic national Israel, in virtue of its unique covenantal status, was authorized to make an exception to the general principles governing warfare.

- At best, all that critics like Bradley can show is that *at one point in history* God commanded Joshua to violate the Crucial Moral Principle to "utterly destroy" the Canaanites.

- However, God does *not* command *us* to violate the Crucial Moral Principle.

- Israel had legal title to the land of Canaan based on the promise God had made to the patriarchs (Deut. 20:16). The Canaanites were essentially trespassers or squatters (Josh. 2:9–11).

- The ultimate goal of Abraham's calling was to bring blessing to the nations, and this promise includes permanent possession of the land (which, as Scripture progresses, expands into possession of the new heaven and new earth by God's people).

- Our point takes for granted that God is central to the biblical narrative, that he acts in history, reveals himself to people, and makes promises to them. To remove God from the narrative is to gut the narrative of its very coherence.

- Some may argue: "Well, what if another nation claimed God told *them* to attack the Israelites?" However, we are only assuming and defending the view that God commanded Israel to "utterly destroy" the Canaanites and how to interpret this command *if* it is God's Word.

- Israel had to wait many generations—including having to endure slavery in Egypt—before it could take possession of the land because the Canaanites were not yet sufficiently wicked to judge (Gen. 15:16). The Canaanites certainly would reach this point.

- Also, the Israelites were refugees who had faced hundreds of years of oppression and now needed a place in which to live.

- So simply owning the land is insufficient to drive out the inhabitants with force. According to the narrative, ownership had to be conjoined with generations of unrepentant wrongdoing on the part of the occupiers.

- During the days of the patriarchs, Abraham's people were *forbidden* to engage in violence against the Canaanite nations occupying the land.

- The kinds of wicked acts (Deut. 9:4–5) the Canaanites engaged in were not trivial: incest, adultery, bestiality, ritual prostitution, homosexual acts, and most significantly, child sacrifice (Lev. 18; Deut. 12:29–31). Most of these acts are illegal, even in modern Western nations. Any group practicing these actions would not be tolerated even in contemporary liberal societies, and in some jurisdictions, violators would be sentenced to death.

- Israel also faced the danger of corrupting influences and the risk of assimilation (Deut. 7:4; 20:18; etc.).

- The Canaanites were more numerous than Israel (Deut. 4:38; 7:1, 8; 9:1), and if Israel lived side by side with them, they risked being influenced by corrupt Canaanite practices over which they had no control. They were not to freely intermarry with the Canaanites under such conditions (Deut. 7:1–7).

- Once they had driven the Canaanites out of the land, the Israelites could intermarry women from nations "far away" (Deut. 21:10–14); in this setting, the woman could make a break with her past and be assimilated into Israel by marriage. (Rape of foreign and Israelite women was prohibited, and virginity was the presumed state in which to enter marriage [Deut. 22:14].)

- Israel was to establish its own national identity and preserve its spiritual and moral character so it could be a blessing to the nations. Anything that could tear apart the fabric of its national identity and integrity would be tantamount to treason—again, no trivial matter. (We recognize this in our nation-states today.) Whatever threatens the destruction of Israel's calling and integrity should be taken with utter seriousness.

- In the context of fighting other nations once Israel was established in the land, it was to operate by the normal rules of noncombatant immunity. The command to drive out the Canaanites was an *occasional* command that could involve noncombatant immunity. We also see hints that those with a Canaanite background could be incorporated into Israel (cf. Rahab, Caleb, the Shechemites).

- Some raise the objection that Rahab (in Josh. 2) acted out of convenience in siding with Israel. But the text is emphasizing Rahab's obedience—and her taking great risk in doing so.

- Israel's own occupation of the land was *conditional*; Israel too would be "utterly destroyed" if it engaged in the defiling practices of the Canaanites (Lev. 18:25–28). Indeed, later the Israelites *would be* judged—removed from the land through exile—because they violated the terms of the covenant.

6

Thrusting Out, Driving Out, and Dispossessing the Canaanites— Not Annihilating Them

Not only are the inhabitants of Canaan not typically portrayed as generally innocent, but the Bible does not unequivocally state that God commanded Israel to *exterminate* every single Canaanite man, woman, and child in the Promised Land. The dominant language used in Scripture is not of extermination but of "driving out" and "thrusting out" the Canaanites. In Exodus 23, God states he will "wipe out" the seven nations. However, the elaboration follows immediately:

> I will send my terror ahead of you and throw into confusion every nation you encounter. I will make all your enemies turn their backs and run. I will send the hornet ahead of you to drive the Hivites, Canaanites and Hittites out of your way. But I will not drive them out in a single year, because the land would become desolate and the wild animals too numerous for you. Little by little I will drive them out before you, until you have increased enough to take possession of the land. I will establish your borders from the Red Sea to the Mediterranean Sea, and from the desert to the Euphrates River. I will give into your hands the people who live in the land, and you will drive them out before you. (vv. 27–31)

The picture here is of God driving out the Canaanites. In this text God says he will "send the hornet" ahead of the Israelites causing the inhabitants to flee and be driven out *before* Israel arrives to fight them. Some have suggested the "hornet" here refers to the armies of Pharaoh—a picture of the Egyptian army's campaign that will drive out most of the inhabitants before Israel arrives. However, the context suggests otherwise. The statement, "I will send the hornet ahead of you to drive the Hivites, Canaanites and Hittites out of your way" parallels the promise that God makes: "I will send my terror ahead of you and throw into confusion every nation you encounter." The hornet, then, is probably a metaphor for terror and confusion.

The book of Joshua confirms this picture. Rahab tells the Israelites that when the Jericohites learned of God's miracles at the time of the exodus, they felt "a great fear" (Josh. 2:9). Similarly, the spies reported that all the people were melting away in fear (v. 24). Later the men of Gibeon state that they had heard "all that [God] did in Egypt," about Israel's victories, and how God had commanded Moses to wipe out all the inhabitants, so they "feared for our lives" (9:9–11, 24). The picture then is that the message of Israel's coming had reached the Canaanites well before Israel arrived. This awareness brought about fear and confusion resulting in people fleeing and leaving before Israel even arrived.[1]

Moreover, this is described as a gradual process. The Canaanites will be driven out little by little. The same picture is described in Exodus: "I will send an angel before you and drive out the Canaanites, Amorites, Hittites, Perizzites, Hivites and Jebusites" (33:2). A similar picture occurs in Leviticus 18:

> Do not defile yourselves in any of these ways, because this is how the nations that I am going to drive out before you became defiled. Even the land was defiled; so I punished it for its sin, and the land vomited out its inhabitants. But you must keep my decrees and my laws. The native-born and the foreigners residing among you must not do any of these detestable things, for all these things were done by the people who lived in the land before you, and the land became defiled. And if you defile the land, it will vomit you out as it vomited out the nations that were before you. (vv. 24–28)

Here the nations (it is anticipated) will be driven out, and the image is of the land vomiting them out—a picture of expulsion. This point is made even more clearly by the parallel in verse 28: if Israel defiles the land in the same way as the Canaanites, then the land "will vomit [them] out as it vomited out the nations." When it violated the covenant, Israel would be exiled; Assyria destroyed the northern kingdom of Israel in 722 BC, and the Babylonians did the same to the southern kingdom of Judah in 587/6 BC. Israel's being "vomited out" into exile is something any post-exilic reader of the final canon would immediately recognize. The same point is repeated two chapters later in 20:22–23: "Keep all my decrees and laws and follow them, so that the land where I am bringing you to live may not vomit you out. You must not live according to the customs of the nations I am going to *drive out* before you."

The book of Numbers paints a similar picture: "After Moses had sent spies to Jazer, the Israelites captured its surrounding settlements and *drove out* the Amorites who were there" (21:32). Then in chapter 33, God commands Moses:

> Speak to the Israelites and say to them: "When you cross the Jordan into Canaan, *drive out all* the inhabitants of the land before you. Destroy all their carved images and their cast idols, and demolish all their high places. Take possession of the land and settle in it. . . . But if you do not *drive out* the inhabitants of the land, those you allow to remain will become barbs in your eyes and thorns in your sides. They will give you trouble in the land where you will live. And then I will do to you what I plan to do to them." (51–56)

When we look at the book of Deuteronomy, the picture of *driving out* predominates. God "brought [Israel] out of Egypt . . . to *drive out* before you nations greater and stronger than you and to bring you into their land to give it to you for your inheritance, as it is today" (4:37–38). Moses commands Israel: "Do what is right and good in the LORD's sight, so that it may go well with you and you may go in and take over the good land the LORD promised on oath to your ancestors, *thrusting out* all your enemies before you, as the LORD said" (6:18–19). In perhaps the most cited passage by critics, God commands Israel to "destroy" the seven nations "totally" and to "make no treaty with them, and show them no mercy" (7:2). Even in this passage, however, the predominant picture is not that Israel is to exterminate every man, woman, and child in Canaan but rather to drive them out. The whole context is as follows:

> When the LORD your God brings you into the land you are entering to possess and drives out before you many nations—the Hittites, Girgashites, Amorites, Canaanites, Perizzites, Hivites and Jebusites, seven nations larger and stronger than you—and when the LORD your God has delivered them over to you and you have defeated them, then you must destroy them totally. Make no treaty with them, and show them no mercy. Do not intermarry with them. Do not give your daughters to their sons or take their daughters for your sons, for they will turn your children away from following me to serve other gods, and the LORD's anger will burn against you and will quickly destroy you. This is what you are

to do to them: Break down their altars, smash their sacred stones, cut down their Asherah poles and burn their idols in the fire. (vv. 1–5)

The command to "totally destroy" the seven nations occurs in a context that clearly states God has *already* driven out the seven nations before Israel. In context, then, "them" can only refer to those Canaanites who have not fled but remain in the land after the military defeat. Moreover, Deuteronomy 7 goes on to state:

> "These nations are stronger than we are. How can we drive them out?" But do not be afraid of them; remember well what the LORD your God did to Pharaoh and to all Egypt. You saw with your own eyes the great trials, the signs and wonders, the mighty hand and outstretched arm, with which the LORD your God brought you out. The LORD your God will do the same to all the peoples you now fear. (vv. 17–19)

Here the driving out of the Canaanites is portrayed as analogous to the way God brought Israel out of Egypt. The text continues:

> Moreover, the LORD your God will send the hornet among them until even the survivors who hide from you have perished. Do not be terrified by them, for the LORD your God, who is among you, is a great and awesome God. The LORD your God will drive out those nations before you, little by little. You will not be allowed to eliminate them all at once, or the wild animals will multiply around you. But the LORD your God will deliver them over to you, throwing them into great confusion until they are destroyed. (vv. 20–23)

Here the imagery of God sending the hornet is again used. In Exodus 23:28, God promised to send the hornet before the Israelites arrive in the land so that the population flees. Here God states he will send the same confusion and fear amongst those who *survive* the military attack and remain in the land. Moreover, the text states explicitly that he "will drive out those nations before you, little by little," which suggests not a rapid genocidal conquest, but a long struggle during which the Canaanites and Israelites would coexist while the former were gradually driven out (see further discussion on this in chap. 17).

The *destroy* language, then, cannot in context refer to every single man, woman, and child in Canaan. The language of "destruction" stands right alongside language of "driving out" and "dispossessing" these seven nations. Large numbers are driven out of the land before Israel arrives, and many survive and remain in hiding after Israel has "totally destroyed them." Moreover, the Canaanite nations will remain to be "driven out" little by little over time.

Deuteronomy 9 states that Israel will cross the Jordan and *"dispossess* nations greater and stronger" than they (v. 1). The text goes on to state twice that it is "on account of the wickedness of these nations that the LORD is going to *drive them out* before you" (vv. 4–5). In chapter 11, God says that he will *"drive out* all these nations before you, and you will *dispossess* nations larger and stronger than you" (v. 23). Several chapters later, Moses lists a series of occultic practices, reminding Israel that "because of these same detestable practices the LORD your God will *drive out* those nations before you" (18:12). He repeats the point two verses later: "The nations you will *dispossess* listen to those who practice sorcery or divination" (18:14). In the next chapter, Moses declares: "When the LORD your God has destroyed the nations whose land he is giving you, and when you have driven them out and settled in their towns and houses . . ." (19:1). Here, destroying the nations is understood in terms of *driving them out* and settling in their towns and houses.

The text therefore continually and repeatedly states that the Canaanites will not be exterminated in the sense that the Israelites are to kill every single man, woman, and child in Canaan. Rather, it states they are to be driven out. As we have noted, the language of "destroy" or "annihilate" is typically in a context of gradually driving out the nations—or of nations fleeing before the battle is joined. "Driving out" or "dispossessing" is different from "wiping out" or "destroying." If you state that you had driven an intruder from your house, no one would assume the intruder was dead in your living room. Similarly, if you say you had killed an intruder, one would not normally think this meant the intruder had been "driven out." The Hebrew text confirms this; the same language of "driving out" and "casting out" is used elsewhere to refer to Adam and Eve being driven from Eden (Gen. 3:24), Cain being "driven" into the wilderness (Gen. 4:14 NASB), and David being "driven out" by Saul (1 Sam. 26:19). In fact, the same language of "drive out" is used of Israel being driven out of Egypt by Pharaoh.[2] In all of these cases, the meaning precludes literal extermination. How is this to be explained? Here we quote a summary of the data:

- These words group into two categories: dispossession versus destruction. "Dispossession" would include words like *drive out, dispossess, take over possession of, thrust out, send away* (33 occurrences). "Destruction" words would include *annihilate, destroy, perish,* and *eliminate* (11 occurrences). The Dispossession words would indicate that the population "ran away"— migrated out of the Land prior to any encounter with the Israelites; Destruction words would indicate the consequences for those who stayed behind.
- What then is the mix of these two sets of words? **The "Dispossession" words outnumber the "Destruction" words by 3-to-1!** This would indicate that

the dominant "intended effect" was for the peoples in the [Promised] Land *to migrate somewhere else*. So, consider Deut. 12.29[–30]: "The LORD your God will cut off before you the nations you are about to invade and dispossess. But *when you have driven them out and settled in their land*, and after they have been destroyed before you, be careful not to be ensnared by inquiring about their gods, saying, "How do these nations serve their gods? We will do the same.""[3]

Defending Biblical Genocide?

Several others have come to the same conclusion—namely, that Israel's chief responsibility was to dispossess or drive out the Canaanites rather than kill them. Consider, for example, the Christian philosopher William Lane Craig who is often—mistakenly in our view—said to be a defender of biblical genocide. Craig writes: "I've come to appreciate that the object of God's command to the Israelis was not the slaughter of the Canaanites, as is often imagined. The command rather was primarily *to drive them out of the land*. The judgment upon these Canaanite kingdoms was to dispossess them of their land and thus destroy them as kingdoms."[4] Elsewhere Craig reiterates the same point.

> I have come to appreciate as a result of a closer reading of the biblical text that God's command to Israel was not primarily to exterminate the Canaanites but *to drive them out of the land*. It was the land that was (and remains today!) paramount in the minds of these Ancient Near Eastern peoples. The Canaanite tribal kingdoms which occupied the land were to be destroyed as nation states, not as individuals. The judgment of God upon these tribal groups, which had become so incredibly debauched by that time, is that they were being divested of their land. Canaan was being given over to Israel, whom God had now brought out of Egypt. *If the Canaanite tribes, seeing the armies of Israel, had simply chosen to flee, no one would have been killed at all*. There was no command to pursue and hunt down the Canaanite peoples.
>
> It is therefore completely misleading to characterize God's command to Israel as a command to commit genocide. Rather it was first and foremost a command to drive the tribes out of the land and to occupy it. Only those who remained behind were to be utterly exterminated.[5]

Richard Dawkins has sarcastically responded to Craig's assessment by saying, "So, apparently it was the Canaanites' own fault for not running away. Right."[6] But sarcastic jibes do not constitute valid rebuttals of the interpretation being proposed, especially when the jibes misrepresent the position they are attacking. Craig is not arguing that the Canaanites deserved genocide because they refused to leave. The conclusion he draws from the fact that the Canaanites fled is that this wasn't genocide. The purpose of the command was not to exterminate all or even most Canaanites in existence. It was to drive them out. Craig, in fact, makes it clear in the very next line—which, interestingly, Dawkins snips just before he makes his sarcastic jab—that Craig believes it is probable that most people did flee. (This is an observation backed up by numerous texts cited above stating that God would drive out large numbers of the inhabitants before Israel arrived.) Based on these facts, Craig points out that what the Bible describes is not genocide. Indeed, he offers other arguments for the conclusion that it is not unjustified.

Old Testament scholar Joe Sprinkle offers a similar reading of the biblical material: "If Israel had continued to conduct war strictly and successfully according to the rules of *ḥērem* ['utter destruction'], including the total destruction of populations that those rules demanded, the natural reaction of the native Canaanite population would have been to flee for their lives."[7] Sprinkle adds that the result would be that "most Canaanites would have survived as refugees outside the [promised] land."[8]

What then are we to make of the passages that Bradley cites from Joshua 6–12 that record that Joshua "utterly destroyed everything in the city, both man and woman, young and old," that "he utterly destroyed every person who was in it," "he left no survivor," and "there was no one left who breathed"? Bradley is correct that if these chapters are read in isolation from the rest of the narrative and in a straightforward, literal way, they appear to affirm that Israel slaughtered every inhabitant in the land of Canaan. There are, however, good reasons why these passages should not be read in a straightforward, literal way. It is to this issue that we turn in the next chapter.

Summary

- The biblical command to "utterly destroy" cannot refer to anything like "absolute extermination" since there are an even greater number of commands or descriptions related to "dispossession" or "driving out" the Canaanites (Exod. 23:27–31; Num. 21:32; 33:51–56; Deut. 7:17–23).

- The expectation is that the Canaanites would be driven out *gradually*.

- The fear of Israel and Israel's God would go ahead of Israel resulting in confusion and terror (Josh. 2:9, 24; 9:24).

- Israel would be "vomited out" or "driven out" of the land just like the other nations if it disobeyed God (Lev. 20:22–23).

- Exodus 23:27–31 uses the image of the "hornet" driving out Canaanites. A large number of them will flee, while others who survive military attack will remain in the land and be driven out little by little, suggesting a long struggle and a coexistence of Canaanites and Israelites.

- The biblical text repeatedly states that the Canaanites will *not* be exterminated but will be driven out (Deut. 9:1; 11:23; 18:12, 14; 19:2). "Driving out" or "dispossessing" is different from "wiping out" or "destroying." Israel itself was driven out of Egypt by Pharaoh (Exod. 6:1).

- If the Canaanites had chosen to flee from the land, none of them would have been killed at all. Most of them in all likelihood did flee.

- Texts using the "utterly destroy" language should not be read in a straightforward, literal way.

7

The Question of Genocide and the Hyperbolic Interpretation of Joshua

arlier, we noted philosopher Raymond Bradley's quoting from Joshua 6–12, in which we read that Joshua "utterly destroyed everything in the city, both man and woman, young and old," that "he utterly destroyed every person who was in it," "he left no survivor," and "there was no one left who breathed." We have cited Bradley's assessment of Israel's/God's "genocidal policies."[1] We've also noted that thinkers such as philosopher Walter Sinnott-Armstrong and zoologist Richard Dawkins cite Joshua to make the same argument.[2] Bradley, Sinnott-Armstrong, and Dawkins do have a point when they say that if we read such verses in isolation from the rest of the narrative and do so in a straightforward, literal way, it appears that Israel committed genocide at God's command, slaughtering every last inhabitant of the land of Canaan.

There are, however, good reasons why these passages should not be read in a straightforward, literal way. Nicholas Wolterstorff, who taught philosophical theology at Yale, puts forward two strong arguments for rejecting the kind of literalistic reading that Bradley and his atheistic comrades-in-arms promote. First, it's quite implausible that those who authorized the final form of the text were affirming that all Canaanites were exterminated at God's command. Second, the accounts that appear to say otherwise are utilizing extensive hyperbole and are not intended to be taken literally. In this chapter and the next, we'll develop and defend these arguments. If Wolterstorff's arguments are correct—and there are a number of biblical scholars who take this view—then the author(s) of the biblical text aren't affirming that God commanded genocide.

An Argument against Literalism

Wolterstorff's first argument rejects a literalistic reading of these Joshua texts: "A careful reading of the text in its literary context makes it implausible to interpret it as claiming that Yahweh ordered extermination."[3] What is this literary context? "Joshua as we have it today was intended as a component in the larger sequence consisting of Deuteronomy, Joshua, Judges, 1 and 2 Samuel, and 1 and 2 Kings. . . . I propose that we interpret the book of Joshua as a component within this larger sequence—in particular, that we interpret it as preceded by Deuteronomy and succeeded by Judges."[4] Jews and Christians accept the final form of Joshua as part of a sequence in a larger canonical arrangement. When reading it this way, certain features of the narrative become apparent. The first feature is that *a tension exists between early chapters of Joshua and the opening chapters of Judges, which is the literary sequel to Joshua.* Joshua 6–11 summarizes several battles and concludes with, "So Joshua took the entire land, just as the LORD had directed Moses, and he gave it as an inheritance to Israel according to their tribal divisions. Then the land had rest from war" (11:23). Scholars readily agree that Judges is literarily linked to Joshua.[5] Yet the early chapters of Judges, which, incidentally, *repeat* the death and burial of Joshua, show a different picture:

> After the death of Joshua, the Israelites inquired of the LORD, "Who shall go up first for us against the Canaanites, to fight against them?" The LORD said, "Judah shall go up. I hereby give the land into his hand." Judah said to his brother Simeon, "Come up with me into the territory allotted to me, that we may fight against the Canaanites; then I too will go with you into the territory allotted to you." So Simeon went with him. Then Judah went up and the LORD gave the Canaanites and the Perizzites into their hand; and they defeated ten thousand of them at Bezek. (Judg. 1:1–4)

On the surface Joshua appears to affirm that *all* the land was conquered, yet Judges proceeds on the assumption that it has not been and still needs to be.

Similarly, Joshua 10–11 appears to state that Joshua exterminated *all* the Canaanites in the land. Repeatedly, the text states that Joshua left "no survivors" and "destroyed everything that breathed" in "the entire land" and "put all the inhabitants to the sword." Alongside these general claims, the book of Joshua identifies several specific places and cities where Joshua exterminated "everyone" and left no survivors. These include Hebron (10:36), Debir (10:38), the hill country, the Negev, and the western foothills (10:40).

In contrast, the first chapter of Judges affirms eight times that the Israelites had failed to conquer the land or the cities; they could not drive the inhabitants out. The narrator states that the Canaanites lived in the Negev, in the hill country (v. 9), in Debir (v. 11), in Hebron (v. 10), and in the western foothills (v. 9). Moreover, they did so in such numbers and strength that they had to be driven out by force with great difficulty. These are the same cities noted in Joshua 10, which claims all inhabitants had been annihilated with no remaining survivors. The opening section of Judges finishes with the angel of the Lord at Bokim rebuking them for failing to drive out the inhabitants of these areas (Judg. 2:1–5).[6] And further along in the text, the affirmation that Joshua did not destroy all the Canaanites in the land becomes even more explicit: "I will no longer drive out before them any of the nations that Joshua left when he died"; the text continues: "The LORD had left those nations, not driving them out at once, and had not handed them over to Joshua" (vv. 21, 23 NRSV). Contrast this with the sweeping affirmation made in Joshua 11:23: "So Joshua took the whole land, according to all that the LORD had spoken to Moses, and Joshua gave it for an inheritance to Israel according to their divisions by their tribes. Thus the land had rest from war" (NASB).

We see other passages that seem to suggest extermination—only to be told shortly afterward that nothing of the sort happened:[7]

"Extermination"	"No Extermination"
Josh. 10:20a: "It came about when Joshua and the sons of Israel had finished slaying them with a very great slaughter until they were destroyed. . ." (NASB).	Josh. 10:20b: ". . . and the survivors who remained of them had entered the fortified cities" (NASB).
Josh. 10:39: "every person" in Debir was "utterly destroyed" (NASB).	Josh. 11:21: Later Joshua "utterly destroyed" Anakites in Debir (NASB).
Josh. 11:21: The Anakites were "cut off" and "utterly destroyed" in Hebron—as well as from Debir, Anab, and "all the hill country of Judah." There were "no Anakim left in the land of the sons of Israel" (v. 22 NASB).	Josh. 15:13–14: Caleb "drove out" the Anakites from Hebron; cf. Judg. 1:20, where Caleb "drove out" the Anakites from Hebron (NASB).

"Extermination"	"No Extermination"
Judg. 1:8: "Then the sons of Judah fought against Jerusalem and captured it and struck it with the edge of the sword and set the city on fire" (NASB).	Judg. 1:21: "But the sons of Benjamin did not drive out the Jebusites who lived in Jerusalem; so the Jebusites have lived with the sons of Benjamin in Jerusalem to this day" (NASB).
Josh. 11:23: "So Joshua took the whole land, according to all that the LORD had spoken to Moses, and Joshua gave it for an inheritance to Israel according to their divisions by their tribes. Thus the land had rest from war" (NASB).	Judg. 2:21, 23: "I also will no longer drive out before them any of the nations which Joshua left when he died. . . . So the LORD allowed those nations to remain, not driving them out quickly; and He did not give them into the hand of Joshua" (NASB).

At the end of the book, Joshua refers to "these nations . . . which remain among you" (23:7 NASB), and he warns against clinging to "the rest of these nations" (v. 12 NASB).

So, on the surface, Joshua appears to affirm that these cities were conquered and their inhabitants completely exterminated. Judges proceeds, however, on the assumption that they are yet to be conquered and the Canaanites still live there in significant numbers, although Joshua gives indications of this as well. Yet Joshua and Judges sit side by side in the biblical canon, the latter being a continuation of the narrative of the former. Old Testament scholar John Goldingay makes this observation: "While Joshua does speak of Israel's utterly destroying the Canaanites, even these accounts can give a misleading impression. When a city is in danger of falling, people do not simply wait there to be killed; they get out. . . . That may be one reason why peoples that have been annihilated have no trouble reappearing later in the story; after Judah puts Jerusalem to the sword, its occupants are still living there 'to this day' (Judg. 1:8, 21)."[8]

Finally, the account of what God commanded differs in the two narratives. Joshua states: "He left no survivors. He totally destroyed all who breathed, *just as the LORD, the God of Israel, had commanded*" (Josh. 10:40) and "exterminating them without mercy, as *the LORD had commanded Moses*" (11:20). However, when this command is retroactively referred to in Judges 2:1, there is no mention of genocide or annihilation. Instead we read of how God had promised to drive them out and of God's commands not to make treaties with the Canaanites but to destroy their shrines. This silence is significant in the context. If God had commanded genocide, then it is odd that only instructions concerning treaties and shrines were mentioned (a theme we also see in Deut. 7:1–6). So there are obvious tensions between a surface reading of Joshua and Judges (a sequel to Joshua). However, these tensions do not merely occur between Joshua and Judges. The same tension occurs *within* the book of Joshua itself. Chapter 11 finishes in this manner: "So Joshua took the entire land, just as the LORD had directed Moses, and he gave it as an inheritance to Israel according to their tribal divisions. Then the land had rest from war" (v. 23). Note that the conquered region is the *same land* that is later divided among the Israelite tribes.

However, when the text turns to giving an account of these tribal divisions only a chapter (or so) later, God says, "You are now very old, and there are still very large areas of land to be taken over" (13:1). Then, in the next five chapters, it is stressed repeatedly that the land was not yet conquered, and the Canaanites were, in fact, not literally wiped out. As we have seen, when we examine the allotment given to Judah, we see Caleb asking permission to drive the Anakim from the hill countries (14:12), describing how he has to defeat the Anakim living in Hebron, and, after this, marching against the people "living in Debir" (15:13–19).

Similarly, it is evident with several of the other allotments that the people still had to drive out Canaanites entrenched in the area and were not always successful in doing so. We read, for example, that the Ephraimites and Manassites "did not dislodge the Canaanites living in Gezer; to this day the Canaanites live among the people of Ephraim" (16:10). Similarly, chapter 17 states, "Yet the Manassites were not able to occupy these towns, for the Canaanites were determined to live in that region. However, when the Israelites grew stronger, they subjected the Canaanites to forced labor but did not drive them out completely" (vv. 12–13). We read that "when the territory of the Danites was lost to them, they went up and attacked Leshem, took it, put it to the sword and occupied it. They settled in Leshem and named it Dan after their ancestor" (19:47). Here we see the same land said to be subdued and conquered by Joshua in battles where he exterminated and left alive nothing that breathed. This land was yet to be occupied by the tribes of Israel and was still occupied by Canaanites, who were often heavily armed and deeply entrenched (17:16–18).

So a surface reading of the passages that Bradley and Sinnott-Armstrong cite not only seems to contradict Judges, but also the preceding chapters of the book of Joshua itself.

Biblical scholar Brevard Childs notes the apparent contradiction:

> Critical scholars have long since pointed out the tension—it is usually called a contradiction—in the portrayal of the conquest of the land. On the one hand, the conquest is pictured in the main source of Josh. 1–12 as a unified assault against the inhabitants of the land under the leadership of Joshua which succeeded in conquering the entire land (11.23; 18.1; 22.43). On the other hand,

there is a conflicting view of the conquest represented by Judges 1 and its parallels in Joshua (15.13–19, 63; 16.10; 17.11–13; 19.47) which appears to picture the conquest as undertaken by individual tribes, extending over a long period beyond the age of Joshua, and unsuccessful in driving out the Canaanites from much of the land.[9]

More recently, Kenneth Kitchen has taken issue with Childs's picture of Joshua 1–12. He notes that, when one takes into account the rhetorical flourishes common to ancient Near Eastern war accounts of this sort,[10] a careful reading of Joshua 1–12 makes it clear that it does not portray Israel as actually occupying or conquering the areas mentioned. Kitchen notes that after crossing the Jordan, the Israelites set up camp in Gilgal "on the east border of Jericho" (Josh. 4:19). He points out that after every battle in the next six chapters, the text explicitly states *that they returned to Gilgal*:

> The conflict with Canaanite city-state rulers in the southern part of Canaan is worth close observation. After the battle for Gibeon, we see the Hebrews advance upon six towns in order, attacking and capturing them, killing their local kings and such of the inhabitants as had not gotten clear, and *moving on, not holding on to these places*. Twice over (10:15, 43), it is clearly stated that their strike force *returned to base camp at Gilgal*. So there was no sweeping takeover and occupation of this region at this point. And *no* total destruction of the towns attacked.[11]

Kitchen continues:

> What happened in the south was repeated up north. Hazor was both leader and famed center for the north Canaanite kinglets. Thus, as in the south, the Hebrew force defeated the opposition; captured their towns, killed rulers and less mobile inhabitants, and symbolically burned Hazor, and Hazor only,[12] to emphasize its end to its local supremacy. Again Israel did *not* attempt to immediately hold on to Galilee; they remained *based at Gilgal* (cf. 14:6).[13]

Kitchen notes that "the first indication of a *real* move in occupation outward beyond Gilgal comes in 18:4." This is "after the first allotment (14–17) of lands-to-be-occupied had been made," and as we saw above, the Israelites did not find occupying these allotments easy. He concludes, "These campaigns were essentially *disabling raids*: they were not territorial conquests with instant Hebrew occupation. The text is very clear about this."[14]

Joshua as we have it today, then, occurs in a literary context in which the language of "killing all who breathed," "putting all inhabitants to the sword,"

and "leaving no survivors" is followed up by a narrative that affirms straightforwardly that the Canaanites were not literally wiped out or exterminated
in this manner. Moreover the text of Joshua itself mixes and juxtaposes these
two pictures of the entrance into Canaan. If one reads the whole narrative as
a sequence, these are not subtle contrasts; they are, in Wolterstorff's words,
"flamboyant" ones.

It is worth emphasizing how "flamboyant" these tensions are. Joshua 6–11
rhythmically and repeatedly emphasizes that Joshua "put all the inhabitants
to the sword" and "left no survivors." It additionally spells out specific places
this occurred. The section finishes in this manner: "So Joshua took the entire
land, just as the LORD had directed Moses, and he gave it as an inheritance
to Israel according to their tribal divisions. Then the land had rest from war"
(11:23). Yet, at the same time, after every battle it is stressed that Israel *returned
to base camp at Gilgal*. So there was no sweeping takeover and occupation of
this region at that point.

Then, in the next five chapters, it is stressed repeatedly that the land was
not yet conquered, and the Canaanites were, in fact, not literally wiped out.
Furthermore, the very same regions were still occupied by the Canaanites
who remained heavily armed and deeply entrenched in the cities. This is then
followed by the opening chapters of Judges, which *affirm eight times* (in a
single chapter) that the Israelites had failed to conquer the land or the cities
and had failed to drive the inhabitants out. As we noted earlier, the account
finishes with the angel of the Lord at Bokim rebuking them for failing to drive
the inhabitants out. While one might contend a human author could make
an editorial error, it is unlikely that an intelligent editor or arranger would
have missed something this blatant. Wolterstorff concludes: "Those whose
occupation it is to try to determine the origins of these writings will suggest
that the editors had contradictory records, oral traditions, and so forth to
work with. No doubt this is correct. But those who edited the final version of
these writings into one sequence were not mindless; they could see, as well
as you and I can see, the tensions and contradictions—surface or real—that
I have pointed to. So what is going on?"[15] Wolterstorff's point is that regardless of what sources or strata of tradition are alleged to be behind the final
form of Joshua, those who edited the final version of these writings into one
sequence would have been well aware of the obvious tensions in the passages
mentioned above. Moreover, they were not mindless or stupid. Consequently,
it is unlikely, when read in this context, that those who authorized the final
form of Joshua were using the text to assert literally that Joshua carried out an
extermination of all the inhabitants of Canaan at God's command. Evidently,
something else is going on.

The Use of Sources and Not-So-Intelligent Editors

Some critics have objected that this argument from Wolterstorff relies on the uninformed claim that if an editor put two contradictory sources together, the editor was either truly intellectually challenged or not affirming both in a literal sense. These critics object that Wolterstorff offers an utterly false dichotomy. Consider, though, what the objector is implying by this "false dichotomy" charge. The critic suggests that the final editors of the text could be affirming *both* that Israel killed every single person in Canaan *and* that Israel did not do this, which, of course, makes no sense.

To back up their claim that the final editors are including blatantly contradictory materials, critics may appeal to influential positions proposed from within the camp of "source criticism." The argument states that the ancient editors weren't bothered by such contradictions in the way we moderns are. The ancient editors' *literary* modus operandi—which included political or aesthetic considerations—was to faithfully preserve the source material despite its obviously contradictory nature when taken *literally*. Consider the *political* motivation: different groups of people with divergent traditions came together as one group, and so the traditions were woven together not for the sake of consistency but to reflect the unity of the group. The goal was to preserve the distinctiveness of the material and also to unite the people. Ancient editors cared about the material not because they thought it was "inerrant" but because it reflected the different traditions of the various peoples within that group.

Or maybe an editor would take a well-known tradition that was also subversive to establishment orthodoxy; he might add elements to it in order to make it conform to the official position. Ecclesiastes could be an example here, where the message of "the Teacher" contradicts long-standing orthodoxy, but a later editor deliberately contradicts its message by adding passages to subvert the original message (Eccles. 12:9–14).

The problem is that even if it is correct that genuine contradictions exist in the text, this charge fails to show that Wolterstorff's argument relies on a false dichotomy. For one thing, the editor isn't assuming that both affirmations—say, extermination and nonextermination—are literally true. The editor preserves them to show unity, which doesn't counter Wolterstorff's assumption; in fact, Wolterstorff would readily affirm this. The editor clearly has something else in mind in preserving statements that affirm both extermination and nonextermination.

What about the even clearer example of Ecclesiastes, in which we find two "voices"; there is the cynical "Preacher/Teacher" *and* the godly editor, who in the end exhorts the reader to "fear God and keep His commandments"

(12:9–14 NASB). The final editor is not assuming both positions are true. He repudiates the voice of the Preacher, who did say some provocative and even wise things (vv. 9–11). But the second voice stands to affirm a hope-filled stance that is quite distinct from the Preacher's message of cynicism, emptiness, and despair.[16]

How indeed could Wolterstorff argue that even a half-intelligent editor would knowingly affirm *both* that Joshua exterminated every person in Canaan *and* that after he did so, abundant numbers of Canaanites were still alive? Ancient standards of accuracy or aesthetics are relevant here. Whatever differences they had from us, it is clear that ancient Near Easterners knew that if an enemy left absolutely no survivor in a city, then the people of that city were dead. It doesn't make sense to affirm otherwise.[17]

Wolterstorff's first argument, therefore, appears sound. When the passages Bradley cites are read in context, it seems quite implausible to affirm that the final editor and arranger of Joshua was using this text to assert that absolute (or something approximating) extermination took place at God's command. Something else is going on.

Summary

• We must not read the "utterly destroy" texts in isolation from the rest of the biblical narrative, as other texts make clear that not all the Canaanites were anywhere near destroyed. These biblical texts are using extensive hyperbole or exaggeration.

• The biblical writers and final editors/arrangers of the biblical canon were not mindless in placing both extermination and nonextermination texts alongside each other. Joshua appears in a larger sequence consisting of Deuteronomy, Joshua, Judges, 1 and 2 Samuel, and 1 and 2 Kings, and we should interpret Joshua in light of this arrangement.

• A tension exists between early chapters of Joshua and the opening chapters of Judges, which is the literary sequel to Joshua. While the book of Joshua at points indicates that Joshua "left no survivors," Judges 1–2 indicates that many Canaanites remained entrenched in the land "to this day." The book of Joshua refers to "these nations . . . which remain among you" (23:7 NASB) and "the rest of these nations" (v. 12 NASB).

• We are also told that Joshua had utterly destroyed the inhabitants "just as *the* LORD *had commanded Moses*" (Josh. 11:20 NASB), which means that Moses's use of "utterly destroy" in Deuteronomy 7 and 20 must also have been hyperbolic language.

• We also see texts where Israel is commanded to "utterly destroy," yet thereafter told not to make treaties with them (Deut. 7:1–6). This assumes a nonliteral reading of the command to "leave alive nothing that breathes."

• Even within Joshua, we have texts that indicate utter destruction, yet those same places still have inhabitants.

• Also, Joshua 1–12 indicates that the Israelites set up base camp at Gilgal east of Jericho, made forays into Canaan cities, and then returned to Gilgal. The attacks on Canaanite cities were more like *disabling raids*, not utter destruction.

• Judges *affirms eight times* in a single chapter that the Israelites had failed to conquer the land or the cities, and had failed to drive the inhabitants out. We cannot affirm *both* utter destruction and abundant survivors in a literal fashion; this leads to contradiction.

• Some will claim that different sources are being used (for literary or political motivations) to explain these differences. Even so, this doesn't disprove the point, and ancient writers knew the difference between literal extermination and plenty of survivors. And if we understand that this exaggerated language is part of ancient Near Eastern war rhetoric, then any charge of contradiction disappears (see the next chapter for a continuation of this discussion).

8

Genocide and an Argument for "Hagiographic Hyperbole"

If those who edited the final version of these writings into one sequence were not using the text to affirm that genocide occurred at God's command, what then *is* going on? This brings us to Wolterstorff's second line of argument. He uses the term *hagiography* ("holy writing")—which refers to certain idealized, sometimes exaggerated accounts of events. In the United States, for example, we have a hagiography of the Pilgrims interacting with noble savages, Washington chopping down a cherry tree, and Washington crossing the Delaware—events that may reflect historical realities but are "sanitized" or "air-brushed" to remove any defect, messiness, or nuance. These might have the benefit of teaching a moral lesson, and the storytelling is not intended to tell us exactly what occurred historically. Some literary liberties are being taken.

Nicholas Wolterstorff suggests that *hagiography*—though properly clarified and qualified—serves as a helpful way of looking at Joshua's exploits:

> The book of Joshua has to be read as a theologically oriented narration, stylized and hyperbolic at important points, of Israel's early skirmishes in the promised land, with the story of these battles being framed by descriptions of two great ritualized events. The story as a whole celebrates Joshua as the great leader of his people, faithful to Yahweh, worthy successor of Moses. If we strip the word "hagiography" of its negative connotations, we can call it a hagiographic account of Joshua's exploits. The book is not to be read as claiming that Joshua

conquered the entire promised land, nor is it to be read as claiming that Joshua exterminated with the edge of the sword the entire population of all the cities on the command of Yahweh to do so. The candor of the opening chapter of Judges, and of Yahweh's declaration to Joshua in his old age that "very much of the land still remains to be possessed," are closer to a literal statement of how things actually went.[1]

Wolterstorff alludes to several features and literary figures of speech in the text to support this view. He notes that the early chapters of Judges, by and large, read like "down-to-earth history." However, he continues, anyone carefully reading the book of Joshua will recognize in it certain stylistic renderings— "formulaic phrasings" and "formulaic convention[s]"[2]—and stylized language like "utterly destroy," "put to the edge of the sword," "leave alive nothing that breathes," and "man and woman, young and old," as well as "the highly ritualized character of some of the major events described."[3] "The book is framed by its opening narration of the ritualized crossing of the Jordan and by its closing narration of the equally ritualized ceremony of blessing and cursing that took place at Shechem; and the conquest narrative begins with the ritualized destruction of Jericho."[4] A related ritualistic feature is "the mysterious sacral category of *being devoted to destruction*."[5] However, the most significant is the use of formulaic language:

> Anyone who reads the book of Joshua in one sitting cannot fail to be struck by the prominent employment of formulaic phrasings. . . . Far more important is the formulaic clause, "struck down all the inhabitants with the edge of the sword."
>
> The first time one reads that Joshua struck down all the inhabitants of a city with the edge of the sword, namely, in the story of the conquest of Jericho (6:21), one makes nothing of it. But the phrasing—or close variants thereon—gets repeated, seven times in close succession in chapter 10, two more times in chapter 11, and several times in other chapters. The repetition makes it unmistakable that we are dealing here with a formulaic literary convention.[6]

So while the accounts in Judges appear as "down-to-earth history," the passages in Joshua referring to "leaving alive none that breathes" and "putting all inhabitants to the sword" appear in contexts full of ritualistic, stylized, formulaic language. It therefore looks like something other than a mere literal description of what occurred. In light of these facts, Wolterstorff argues that Judges should be taken literally whereas Joshua is hagiographic history, a highly stylized, exaggerated account of the events designed to teach theological and moral points rather than to describe in detail what *literally* happened.

Ancient Near Eastern Conquest Accounts

Wolterstorff's thesis has been substantially confirmed in a study he cites in a footnote. In a comprehensive comparative study of ancient Near Eastern conquest accounts, Lawson Younger Jr. documents that Joshua employs the same stylistic, rhetorical, and literary conventions of other war reports of the same period.[7] Three conclusions of Younger's research are pertinent.

The first is that comparisons between the book of Joshua and other ancient Near Eastern conquest accounts demonstrate some important stylistic parallels. According to Ziony Zevit, "when the composition and rhetoric of the Joshua narratives in chapters 9–12 are compared to the conventions of writing about conquests in Egyptian, Hittite, Akkadian, Moabite, and Aramaic texts, they are revealed to be very similar."[8] Younger notes similarities in the preface, structure, and even the way the treaty with the Gibeonites is recorded in Joshua and various ancient Near Eastern accounts.[9] Joshua follows this convention in describing numerous battles occurring in a single day or within a single campaign.[10] Like Joshua, ancient Near Eastern accounts also repeatedly make reference to the enemy "melting with fear."[11] Even the way post-battle pursuits are set out and described shows similarities with comparable pursuits in ancient Near Eastern literature.[12] Commenting on the structure of the campaigns mentioned in Joshua 9–12, Egyptologist Kenneth Kitchen reminds us:

> This kind of report profile is familiar to readers of ancient Near Eastern military reports, not least in the second millennium. Most striking is the example of the campaign annals of Tuthmosis III of Egypt in his Years 22–42 (ca. 1458–1438). . . . The pharaoh there gives a very full account of his initial victory at Megiddo, by contrast with the far more summary and stylized reports of the ensuing sixteen subsequent campaigns. *Just like Joshua* against up to seven kings in south Canaan and four-plus up north . . .[13]

He adds, "The Ten Year Annals of the Hittite king Mursil II (later fourteenth century) are also instructive. *Exactly like the 'prefaces' in the two Joshua war reports* (10:1–4; 11:1–5), detailing hostility by a number of foreign rulers against Joshua and Israel as the reason for the wars, so in his annals Mursil II gives us a long "preface" on the hostility of neighboring rulers and people groups that lead to his campaigns."[14] Kitchen offers other examples. He observes that the same formulaic style found in Joshua is also used in two of the Amarna letters—a correspondence written in Akkadian between Egyptian administrators in Canaan and Amurru and two particular pharaohs, Amenhotep III and Akhenaten (fifteenth and fourteenth centuries BC).[15] Similarly, before his major campaigns, "Joshua is commissioned by YHWH not to fear (cf. 5:13–15; 10:8; 11:6). So also by Ptah and Amun were Merenptah in Egypt, and Tuthmosis IV long before him; and likewise Mursil II of the Hittites by his gods (Ten-Year Annals, etc.), all in the second millennium, besides such kings as Assurbanipal of Assyria down to the seventh century."[16]

Second, Younger also notes that such accounts are "figurative" and utilize what he calls a "transmission code": a common, frequently stylized, stereotyped, and frequently hyperbolic way of recording history.[17] The literary motif of divine intervention is an example. Both The 10 Year Annals of Mursil (also known as "Mursili") and Sargon's Letter to the God record a divine intervention where the god sends hailstones on the enemy.[18] Tuthmosis III has a similar story regarding a meteor—or what appears to have been a meteor shower.[19] Younger observes that these accounts are very similar to parallel accounts in Joshua 10 where God rains hailstones on Israel's enemies. Similarly, Younger points out that in many ancient Near Eastern texts, "one can discern a literary technique in which a deity is implored to maintain daylight long enough for there to be a victory,"[20] which has obvious parallels to Joshua 10:13–14. The numbers of armies and enemy casualities are rhetorically exaggerated. The fact that similar events are narrated in multiple different accounts suggests they are "a notable ingredient of the transmission code for conquest accounts"[21]—that is, they are part of the common hyperbolic rhetoric of warfare rather than descriptions of what actually occurred.

Third and most significantly for this discussion, part of this "transmission code" is that victories are narrated in an exaggerated hyperbolic fashion in terms of total conquest, complete annihilation, and destruction of the enemy, killing *everyone*, leaving *no* survivors, etc. Kitchen offers illuminating examples:

> The type of rhetoric in question was a regular feature of military reports in the second and first millennia, as others have made very clear. . . . In the later fifteenth century Tuthmosis III could boast "the numerous army of Mitanni, was overthrown within the hour, annihilated totally, like those (now) non-existent"[22]— whereas, in fact, the forces of Mitanni lived to fight many another day, in the fifteenth and fourteenth centuries. Some centuries later, about 840/830, Mesha king of Moab could boast that "Israel has utterly perished for always"—a rather premature judgment at that date, by over a century! And so on, ad libitum. It is in this frame of reference that the Joshua rhetoric must also be understood.[23]

Younger offers numerous other examples. Merneptah's Stele (thirteenth century BC) describes a skirmish with Israel as follows, "Yanoam is nonexistent; Israel is wasted, his seed is not."[24] Here a skirmish in which Egypt prevailed is described in terms of the total annihilation of Israel. Sennacherib uses similar hyperbole, "The soldiers of Hirimme, dangerous enemies, I cut down with the sword; and not one escaped."[25] Mursil(i) II records making "Mt. Asharpaya empty (of humanity)" and the "mountains of Tarikarimu empty (of humanity)."[26] Mesha (whom Kitchen cited as stating "Israel has utterly perished for always")[27] describes victories in terms of his fighting against a town, taking it, and then killing *all* the inhabitants of the town.[28] Similarly, *The Bulletin of Ramses II*, a historical narrative of Egyptian military campaigns into Syria, narrates Egypt's considerably-less-than-decisive victory at the battle of Kadesh with the following rhetoric: "He took no note of the *millions* of foreigners; he regarded them as *chaff*. . . . His majesty slew the *entire force* of the wretched Foe from Hatti, together with his great chiefs and all his brothers, as well as *all* the chiefs of *all* the countries that had come with him, their infantry and their chariotry falling on their faces one upon the other. His majesty slaughtered and slew them in their places . . ; and his majesty was *alone, none other with him.*"[29] Numerous other examples could be provided. The hyperbolic use of language similar to that in Joshua is strikingly evident. Though instances could be multiplied, but the point is that such accounts contain extensive hyperbole and are not intended to be taken as literal descriptions of what occurred.

Rhetorical Function and Ideology

Some critics will disagree with this hyperbolic interpretation of Joshua, but we should consider the point of hyperbole itself in such contexts. One conclusion Younger draws from his study is that the transmission code employed in Joshua 9–12 reflects the same imperialistic ideology as other ancient Near Eastern conquest accounts. This ideology means "victory must be described in black and white terms since there is only a 'them' vs. 'us' relationship."[30] Such rhetoric was used to inspire fear and obedience in those subjects who heard it.[31] If the reader only heard such rhetoric as exaggeration, then the rhetoric would not have had the effect it was intended to have.

This inference is mistaken, firstly, because it is false that hyperbolic rhetoric must be taken literally in order to inspire fear and obedience. Suppose a boxer before a boxing match states that he is going to murder his opponent and make his children orphans. This sort of rhetoric is designed to inspire fear and intimidate. Does it follow that it is intended to be taken literally? Similarly, school bullies tell potential victims that if they "narc" on them, the bullies will "kill them and smash their heads in." Do the victims have to believe they will *literally* be killed and have their heads *actually* smashed in to get the message?

Secondly, this objection fails to grasp the *reasons* Younger proffers for Joshua 9–12 reflecting the same imperialistic ideology as other ancient Near Eastern conquest accounts. Younger states: "Can one conclude that since the text of Joshua 9–12 manifests the same transmission code as other texts of ancient Near Eastern history writing, it is the product of the same underlying ideology? The indications from this study seem to point to an affirmative answer."[32] Younger concludes that Joshua 9–12 has the same ideology as other ancient Near Eastern accounts because it uses the same rhetorical transmission code—a code Younger documents as containing "extensive use of hyperbole."[33] He concludes: "Israelite ideology had certain similarities with the 'Imperialistic' ideologies of the ancient Near East," which included "a similar view of the enemy, the calculated terror, *the high use of hyperbole . . . and the use of stereotyped syntagms* [linguistic units in ordered words/phrases like "utterly destroyed"] *to transmit the high-redundance message of the ideology.*"[34]

Younger is clear on his meaning of *hyperbole*—namely, using "exaggerated terms for the purpose of emphasis and/or heightened effect," adding that "more is said than is literally meant." In fact, even when Younger talks of how victory must be described "in black and white terms," he cites an example of the "figurative aspect" of such accounts and part of the "extensive use of hyperbole."[35]

Consequently, the critic cannot cite Younger's conclusions (about Joshua reflecting the same imperialistic ideology as other ancient Near Eastern conquest accounts) as evidence that the rhetoric in these texts was intended to be taken literally. The whole reason Younger concludes that these texts reflect this ideology is because they follow the same rhetorical conventions common to such accounts, conventions that were not meant to be taken literally.

Younger's study shows quite conclusively that Joshua is written in accord with the rhetoric and conventions of ancient Near Eastern conquest accounts. Such accounts narrate history in a highly rhetorical, stereotyped, figurative fashion and utilize substantial hyperbole, narrating battles in terms of total annihilation of everyone. To read these accounts as though the author were literally affirming that total extermination had taken place is simply to misread them. Younger states, "It is evident that the syntagms . . . ('they completely destroyed it and everyone in it,' 'he left no survivors'), etc. are to be understood as hyperbole. Just like other ancient Near Eastern conquest accounts, the biblical narrative utilizes hyperbolic, stereotyped syntagms to build up the account."[36] Younger suggests this misreading has led scholars like Brevard Childs to mistakenly see contradictions between Joshua and the early chapters of the book of Judges. "Thus when the figurative nature of the account is considered there are really no grounds for concluding that Judges 1 presents a different view of the conquest from that of Joshua or that it must be an older account."[37] And Kitchen states that Old Testament scholars have read into the book of Joshua "*a whole myth of their own making*, to the effect that the book of Joshua presents a sweeping, total conquest *and occupation* of Canaan by Joshua, which can then be falsely pitted against the narratives in Judges."[38] This myth is "based on the failure to recognize and understand ancient use of rhetorical summations. The 'alls' are qualified in the Hebrew narrative itself."[39]

Biblical Hyperbole

Several other considerations can be added to bolster this point. One is the fact that such hyperbolic language is clearly being used within the book of Joshua itself, which we noted earlier. In Joshua 10:20 (NASB), for example, we are told that Joshua and the sons of Israel had been "slaying them with a very great slaughter, until they were destroyed." Immediately, however, the text affirms that the "survivors who remained of them had entered the fortified cities." In this context, the language of total destruction is clearly hyperbolic.

A similar phenomenon seems to occur in the account of the battle of Ai. After Joshua's troops feign a retreat, the text states that "*all* the men of Ai" are pressed to chase them (Josh. 8:16). "Not a man remained in Ai or Bethel who did not go after Israel. They left the city open and went in pursuit of Israel" (v. 17). Joshua lures the pursuers into a trap "so that they were caught in the middle, with Israelites on both sides. Israel cut them down, *leaving them neither survivors nor fugitives*" (v. 22). Then, after noting the capture of Ai's military ruler (v. 23), the text immediately states: "When Israel had finished killing all the men of Ai in the fields and in the wilderness where they had chased them, and when every one of them had been put to the sword . . ." (v. 24). Taken literally, this is patently absurd. If there were no survivors or fugitives, whom were the Israelites chasing?

The account of the battle of Ai ends with the summary, "Twelve thousand men and women fell that day—all the people of Ai" (v. 25), yet earlier in the same account it says, "Not all the army will have to go up against Ai. Send two or three thousand men to take it and do not weary the whole army, for only a few people live there" (7:3). The text also describes Israel being routed when the men of Ai "killed about thirty-six of them" (v. 5). Clearly the casualty figures cannot be literally correct here. However, they are quite consistent with the conclusions drawn by Daniel Fouts that exaggerated numbers are common forms of hyperbole in ancient Near Eastern battle accounts.[40] Archaeology suggests smaller numbers as well. Old Testament scholar Richard Hess notes that as with the "city [*'ir*]" of Ai or other "cities" raided by the Israelites, Jericho was not a population center but a small, strategic military settlement or citadel. It was led by a commander or "king [*melek*]," also housing religious and political personnel. Jericho probably held a hundred or fewer men. This is why all of Israel could circle it seven times and then do battle against it on the same day![41]

Even if the numbers are not hyperbolic, matters seem complicated by the Hebrew term *'eleph*, commonly rendered "thousand." A possible interpretation is that these numbers may not be as high as our translations indicate. This term can also mean "unit," "troop," or "squad," without specifying the exact number.[42] However, the massive numbers in biblical war texts fit quite nicely within the genre of ancient Near Eastern war texts with many examples of extraordinarily high numbers; thus we consider the hyperbolic numbers to be more plausible.

Similar hyperbole occurs in other biblical books, using the same phraseology we find in Joshua of "utterly destroying [*haram*]" populations "with the sword." First Chronicles 4:41 states: "They attacked [*nakah*] the Hamites in their dwellings and also the Meunites who were there and completely destroyed [*haram*] them." But only a few verses later, we read that *the survivors* fled to Amalek where they were later all "destroyed [*nakah*]" a second time (v. 43 NASB)!

Later in 2 Chronicles 36:16–17, the author narrates the fall of Jerusalem: "But they mocked God's messengers, despised his words and scoffed at his prophets until the wrath of the LORD was aroused against his people and there was no remedy. He brought up against them the king of the Babylonians, who killed their young men with the sword in the sanctuary, and did not spare young men or young women, the elderly or the infirm. God gave them all into the hands of Nebuchadnezzar." Only a few verses later, however, the narrator states, "He carried into exile to Babylon the remnant, who escaped from the sword, and they became servants to him and his successors until the kingdom of Persia came to power" (v. 20).

Similarly, compare verse 19: "They [the Babylonians] set fire to God's temple and broke down the wall of Jerusalem; they burned *all* the palaces and destroyed *everything* of value there." With verse 18, "He [king Nebuchadnezzar of Babylon] carried to Babylon *all* the articles from the temple of God, both large and small, and the treasures of the LORD's temple and the treasures of the king and his officials." Taken literally this is absurd. How could they carry off all the treasure from the palaces and temple if everything of value had been destroyed? But this was not intended to be taken literally. This account was written to a post-exilic audience who knew full well that not every one of the Judahites had been killed. They, as the descendants of the survivors, knew that Judah had been exiled and was later restored under Cyrus: a fact pointed out only a few verses later (cf. vv. 21–23).

One finds the same language of killing all inhabitants with the sword also used hyperbolically in Judges. Judges 1:8 states, "The men of Judah attacked Jerusalem also and took it. They put the city to the sword and set it on fire." A few verses later, however, the text states: "The Benjamites, however, did not drive out the Jebusites, who were living in Jerusalem; to this day the Jebusites live there with the Benjamites" (v. 21).

Similar language is used hyperbolically in the prophetic writings. In the context of the Babylonian invasion and Judah's exile (sixth century BC), God said he would "lay waste the towns of Judah so no one can live there" (Jer. 9:11). Indeed, God said, "I will completely destroy them and make them an object of horror and scorn, and an everlasting ruin" (25:9). Note that this is the same verb (*haram*) used for "utterly destroying" the Canaanites. In Jeremiah, God threatened to "stretch out My hand against you and destroy you" (15:6 NASB; cf. Ezek. 5:16)—to bring "disaster" against Judah (Jer. 6:19). However, the biblical text suggests that while Judah's political and religious structures were ruined or disabled, and that Judahites died in the conflict, the "urban elite" were deported to Babylon while many "poor of the land" remained behind.[43] Similarly, in Isaiah God says, "I consigned Jacob to destruction [*herem*] and Israel to scorn" (43:28). Then in the very next verse (44:1), God tells "Jacob," whom he has "chosen," that God will restore his people and bring them out of exile under a new covenant in which he will pour out his Spirit upon them.

As a final example, consider the "covenant curses" of Deuteronomy 28. Verse 20 warns: "The LORD will send on you curses, confusion and rebuke in everything you put your hand to, until you are destroyed and come to sudden ruin." But this is followed by the threat that "the LORD will plague you with diseases until he has destroyed you from the land" (v. 21). And once again we see the language of still further destruction: "The LORD will turn the rain of your country into dust and powder; it will come down from the skies until you are destroyed. . . . All these curses will come on you. They will pursue you and overtake you until you are destroyed" (v. 24, 45).

But the text goes on to state that though Israel has been "destroyed," they will face further perils in exile: "Then the LORD will scatter you among all nations, from one end of the earth to the other. There you will worship other gods—gods of wood and stone, which neither you nor your ancestors have known. . . . There the LORD will give you an anxious mind, eyes weary with longing, and a despairing heart. You will live in constant suspense, filled with dread both night and day, never sure of your life" (vv. 64–66). Those who were said to be destroyed are alive in exile.

The same kind of language used to describe the fate of the Canaanites is frequently used hyperbolically throughout the Bible. In all these cases, the language of destroying "all" is seen to be qualified by the fact that a significant number (in fact) fled, escaped, and survived. Kitchen notes that in ancient rhetorical summaries of this sort, "the 'alls' are qualified by the Hebrew narrative itself. In 10:20 we learn that Joshua and his forces massively slew their foes 'until they were finished off'. . . , but in the same breath the text states that 'the remnant that survived got away into their defended towns.' Thus the absolute wording is immediately qualified by exceptions—'the quick and the dead,' as one might say of pedestrians trying to cross our busy highways!"[44]

Preliminary Conclusions

When we study the evidence, three things emerge. First, Joshua 1–11 occurs in a context where the so-called genocidal language of exterminating all and leaving no survivors occurs alongside a narrative that affirms matter-of-factly that large numbers of people were not killed and many survived. Second, as Wolterstorff comments, "Those who edited the final version of these writings into one sequence were not mindless,"[45] and so it is unlikely they intended to affirm both these pictures as literally true. The biblical author clearly has something else in mind. Third, while Judges reads more like "down-to-earth history" (though not without mention of both destruction and many survivors [e.g., 1:8, 21]), a careful reading of Joshua reveals it to be full of ritualistic, stylized accounts and formulaic language. This third point is supported by research into ancient Near Eastern conquest accounts. Such studies show the following:

1 Such accounts are highly hyperbolic, hagiographic, and figurative, and follow a common transmission code;

2 Comparisons between these accounts and the early chapters of Joshua suggest Joshua is written according to the same literary conventions and transmission code;

3 Part of this transmission code is to hyperbolically portray a victory in absolute terms of totally destroying the enemy or in terms of miraculous divine intervention: "such statements are rhetoric indicative of military victory,"[46] not literal descriptions of what occurred;

4 The same language and phraseology has a well-attested hyperbolic use in Joshua and elsewhere throughout Scripture.

Taken together, these points give persuasive reasons for thinking that one should interpret the extermination language in Joshua 1–12 as offering a highly figurative and hyperbolic account of what occurred. It seems sensible to conclude that the language of "leaving alive nothing that breathes," "leaving no survivors," and "put[ting] all inhabitants to the sword" is not meant to be taken literally.

After comparing the figures of speech and rhetoric used in numerous Hittite, Assyrian, and Egyptian conquest accounts with those of Joshua, Younger concludes, "The syntagms (. . .'they completely destroyed everyone in it') and (. . .'he left no survivors') are obvious hyperbole. This is also true for these: (. . .'Not sparing anyone who breathed'), and (. . .'until they exterminated them'). That these are figurative is clear from numerous ancient Near Eastern texts."[47] (See such hyperbole in Mark 1:5: Is *all* Judea/Jerusalem emptied?)

Three Implications

We should read Joshua in its "literary context" as a component in the larger sequence, preceded by Deuteronomy and followed by Judges, 1 and 2 Samuel, and 1 and 2 Kings. (This portion of the Hebrew canon is "Ruth-less"; Ruth appears later in the "Writings" section.) This reading of Joshua forces a "back-interpretation" of Deuteronomy. As Wolterstorff notes, "If 'struck down all the inhabitants with the edge of the sword' is a literary convention when used to describe Joshua's exploits, then it is likewise a literary convention when similar words are used by Moses in his instructions to Israel in general and to Joshua in particular."[48] We think Wolterstorff is correct here: seeing Joshua in its broader canonical context forces a back-interpretation of Moses's commands in Deuteronomy for the following three reasons.

Implication 1: A comparison of similar phraseology in Deuteronomy and Joshua suggests hyperbole.

First, Deuteronomy 7:2 states: "When the LORD your God delivers them before you and you defeat them, then you shall utterly destroy them" (NASB). Similarly, 20:16–17 commands: "Do not leave alive anything that breathes. Completely destroy them." In Joshua 10, one sees the formulaic language of "and the Lord gave [the city]" and he/they "struck it and its king with the edge of the sword" until "there was no one remaining" (NRSV). The chapter is summarized with the phrase, "So Joshua defeated the whole land . . . ; he left no one remaining, but utterly destroyed all that breathed" (v. 40 NRSV). The similar phraseology is evident.

Implication 2: The author of Joshua understood Moses's command as hyperbolic.

Second, the book of Joshua clearly, explicitly, and repeatedly identifies what Joshua did in these chapters with the command that Moses had given regarding the Canaanites in Deuteronomy. Joshua's "utter destruction" of the Canaanites is exactly what "Moses the servant of the LORD had commanded":

- "Joshua captured all the cities of these kings, and all their kings, and he struck them with the edge of the sword, and utterly destroyed them; just as Moses the servant of the LORD had commanded" (Josh. 11:12 NASB).

- "All the spoil of these cities and the cattle, the sons of Israel took as their plunder; but they struck every man with the edge of the sword, until they had destroyed them. They left no one who breathed. Just as the LORD had commanded Moses his servant, so Moses commanded Joshua, and so Joshua did; he left nothing undone of all that the LORD had commanded Moses" (vv. 14–15 NASB).

- ". . . that he might destroy them, just as the LORD had commanded Moses" (v. 20 NASB).

Joshua's comprehensive language echoes Moses's sweeping commands to "consume" and "utterly destroy" the Canaanites, to not "leave alive anything that breathes." Scripture clearly indicates that Joshua fulfilled Moses's charge to him. So *if* Joshua did just as Moses commanded, and *if* Joshua's described destruction was really massive hyperbole common in ancient Near Eastern warfare language (and familiar to Moses), *then* clearly Moses himself did not intend a literal, comprehensive Canaanite destruction.

Some object that a hyperbolic interpretation does not fit the context of Deuteronomy 20, which draws a contrast between "cities that are at a distance" (v. 15), where the Israelites are prohibited from killing "the women, the children, the livestock" (v. 14), and "the cities of the nations the LORD your God is giving you as an inheritance," where they are to totally destroy them ("do not leave alive anything that breathes," v. 16). This contrast is indeed in the text. However, it fails to show that the language is not hyperbolic; one could grant a hyperbolic reading and concur with Kitchen that "the 'alls' are qualified in the Hebrew narrative itself" and allow exceptions, for "the remnant that survived got away into their defended towns."[49] If the text describes disabling raids where they killed all those who had not cleared out, one would still have the contrast in question.

The contrast would be between (1) what one does in cities at a distance to those less mobile inhabitants who did not leave the theater of battle before

Israel arrived, and (2) what one does to the same group of people in "the cities of the nations the Lord your God is giving you as an inheritance." Nor is this interpretation stretched; it is pretty obvious in Deuteronomy 20 when it states, "As for the women, the children, the livestock and everything else in the city, you may take these as plunder for yourselves. And you may use the plunder the LORD your God gives you from your enemies. This is how you are to treat all the cities that are at a distance from you and do not belong to the nations nearby" (vv. 14–15). This passage can only be referring to those inhabitants of the city that have not "gotten clear" (have not left); it wouldn't refer to the possibly significant number who had fled, escaped, or been driven out before the army arrived. Obviously, you can only take as plunder livestock that remain in the city; you cannot take as plunder livestock that have escaped to some other city or country that you don't occupy. And beyond this, these "cities" themselves, as we have already noted, were not population centers but strategic military, political, and religious centers.[50] And the attacks against them were *disabling raids*, as Israel would return from raids to their base camp at Gilgal.

Implication 3: Comparing Deuteronomy, Joshua, and Judges suggests a hyperbolic interpretation.

A final point on this is the crucial issue of whether a hyperbolic interpretation is more plausible than a literal one, even if a literal interpretation fits Deuteronomy 20 better. Above, we have argued that a literal interpretation puts Joshua 6–11 at odds with Judges 1–2 and the later chapters of Joshua. It would be strange to reject a hyperbolic interpretation because one passage in Deuteronomy 20 does not cohere with it and instead embrace a literal interpretation, which creates an even greater incoherence in the text. This point is reinforced by Deuteronomy 7. Notice that immediately after the command to "utterly destroy" the Canaanites (v. 2a NASB), the text takes for granted that Canaanites will be nearby. And the chief emphasis is not on the destruction of the Canaanites; rather, it is on destroying Canaanite altars and images—in addition to avoiding the Canaanites' abhorrent moral practices that flowed from their theology:

> You shall make no covenant with them and show no favor to them. Furthermore, you shall not intermarry with them; you shall not give your daughters to their sons, nor shall you take their daughters for your sons. For they will turn your sons away from following Me to serve other gods; then the anger of the LORD will be kindled against you and He will quickly destroy you. But thus you shall do to them: you shall tear down their altars, and smash their sacred pillars, and hew down their Asherim, and burn their graven images with fire. (vv. 2b–5 NASB)

Younger comments on the focus of the "utter destruction" (*hērem*):

The *hērem* was not designed by God to eliminate the Canaanite culture per se but to eliminate the Canaanite religious influence. While it may be readily recognized that it is difficult in many instances to separate the two, there is nonetheless a distinction. The Israelite *hērem* commandments had close links to the issues of idolatry and the breaking of the second commandment (Exod. 22:20 . . . ; Deut. 7:26; 13:16–18 . . .). That this is the case in [the first introduction] of Judges (1:1–2:5) is reinforced by Yahweh's confrontation of the nation in 2:1–5, where it is their failure on the religious front that is of primary concern.

In other words, the *hērem* was not concerned with the eradication of Canaanite clothing fashions, pottery styles, music, diet, and other types of particular cultural preferences. But it was deeply concerned with the eradication of the Canaanite religion: its gods/idols, altars, rituals, divinatory practices, uses of magic, and so on.[51]

Because the accounts are highly hyperbolic, one cannot draw the conclusion that the author uses them to assert that the Israelites were literally commanded to exterminate every man, woman, and child in Canaan. Wolterstorff writes:

So what was the writer asserting—assuming he did not intend it as pure fiction, which I very much doubt? Not at all easy to tell. When a high school basketball player says his team slaughtered the other team last night, what is he asserting? Not easy to tell. That they scored a decisive victory? Maybe. But suppose they barely eked out a win. Was he then lying? Maybe not. Maybe he was speaking with a wink-of-the-eye hyperbole.[52]

In the same way, when one realizes that Joshua is hagiographic and highly hyperbolic in its narration of what occurred, the best one can conclude from the accounts of "killing everyone that breathed" is that "Israel scored a decisive victory and once you recognize the presence of hyperbole it is not even clear how decisive the victories were. Joshua did not conquer all the cities in the land, nor did he slaughter all the inhabitants in the cities that he did conquer. The book of Joshua does not say that he did."[53] As we continue in this book, we'll build on some of this chapter's themes and explore some of their implications.

Summary

- We could call Joshua's account *hagiographic* (though properly clarified); it is an idealized or "sanitized" account of Joshua's military exploits.

- This hagiography in Joshua—though anchored in historical events—utilizes stylized language like "utterly destroy," "put to the edge of the sword," "leave alive nothing that breathes," and "man and woman, young and old" to strongly suggest this. By contrast, Judges is more like "down-to-earth history."
- This kind of language is found not only in biblical war texts, but it was common in ancient Near Eastern war texts as well. Comparing accounts of conquests such as in Egyptian, Hittite, Moabite, Akkadian, and Aramaic texts with Joshua's composition and narrative in chapters 9–12 reveals striking similarities—battles in a single day, the enemy "melting with fear," etc.
- In such accounts, a certain "transmission code" is used—a highly stylized, stereotyped, and usually hyperbolic way of recording history.
- As part of this "transmission code," the language used is exaggerated, referring to total conquest, utter annihilation, leaving no survivors.
- Joshua uses the same us-versus-them rhetoric as ancient Near Eastern accounts using black-and-white language—in the genre of ancient imperialistic ideology. This kind of rhetoric was used to inspire fear and obedience in those who heard it—like a boxer who says he's going to "kill" his opponent.
- In this style of stereotypical language, more is *said* than is *meant*. The "alls" in such texts do not literally mean "all" (e.g., in the battle of Ai—"all the men of Ai"—in Joshua 8). So there is no need to pit Joshua against Judges 1–2 as contradictory sources placed into the same canon.
- The massive military troop numbers (and of those who die in battle) are far too high and are thus most plausibly part of the ancient Near Eastern exaggeration motif. (Some have explained these numbers differently: the word '*eleph*—usually translated "thousand"—could simply mean "unit," "troop," or "squad" and therefore the actual number is much lower. We find this less likely.)
- Archaeology suggests smaller numbers as well (Jericho probably held a hundred or

fewer men). The "cities" of Canaan raided by Israel were not population centers but small, strategic military settlements or citadels.
- We see similar language elsewhere throughout the Old Testament (e.g., 1 Chron. 4:41–43: "completely destroyed" yet *survivors* fled and were "destroyed" a second time!). Jeremiah 25:9 uses the language of God's utterly destroying (*haram*) Judah—yet the end of the book makes clear that Judah, though devastated, is far from annihilated (cf. Deut. 28:20–24, 64–66; Isa. 43:28).
- As we read Joshua in its broader canonical context, we see the exaggerations can properly be "read back" (or back-interpreted) into the instructions to Moses in Deuteronomy 7 and 20. After all, Joshua did "just as Moses the servant of the LORD had commanded" (Josh. 11:12, 14–15, 20 NASB). So if Joshua did not literally "utterly destroy" yet did exactly as Moses commanded, then Moses must have been using the hyperbolic language so common in ancient Near Eastern texts.
- Some object that hyperbole doesn't fit Deuteronomy 20 because of the distinction between "cities that are at a distance"—where Israel is prohibited from killing "the women, the children, the livestock" (v. 14)—and "the cities of the nations the LORD your God is giving you as an inheritance," which are to be totally destroyed (v. 16). However, this still doesn't show that the language isn't hyperbolic. We see throughout Deuteronomy and Joshua that the "alls" are qualified, allowing plenty of room for many survivors.
- The contrast would be between (1) what one does in cities at a distance to those less mobile inhabitants who did not leave the theater of battle before Israel arrived, and (2) what one does to the same group of people in "the cities of the nations the Lord your God is giving you as an inheritance."
- Deuteronomy 7:1–5 makes clear that "utter destruction" (*herem*) was not intended to eliminate all Canaanites or even Canaanite culture per se (clothing, food, etc.) but to prevent the Canaanite religious and moral practices from damaging Israel's spiritual and moral integrity.

9

Objections from the Biblical Text to the Hyperbolic Interpretation

I n the previous chapter, we argued that the biblical affirmations such as "they completely destroyed it and everyone in it," "he left no survivors," and "leave alive nothing that breathes" are to be understood as hyperbolic—as exaggerations rather than literal statements that Joshua killed every single man, woman, and child in southern and northern Canaan at God's command.

Critics of the morality of the Old Testament have been less than impressed with this interpretation. They have raised several objections to a hyperbolic reading of Joshua in particular. Here we'll focus on the most prominent objections. In the next chapter, we look at various legal and philosophical objections.

An Objection about 1 Samuel 15 and Judges 1

To an early suggestion by one of us (Paul) that the genocidal language is hyperbolic, philosopher Wes Morriston responds: "It is quite a stretch to imagine that a God who said all should be destroyed would be displeased if all were destroyed."[1] Morriston offers two lines of argument from the Bible: the first from 1 Samuel 15 and the second from texts like Judges 1.

1 Samuel 15: Saul and the Amalekites

Morriston's first line of argument cites 1 Samuel 15:10–11 (NASB): "Then the word of the LORD came to Samuel, saying, 'I regret that I have made Saul king, for he has turned back from following Me and has not carried out My commands.'"[2] To understand what Morriston is driving at, some context is necessary. Earlier in this chapter, King Saul had been commanded to "strike Amalek and utterly destroy all that he has, and do not spare him; but put to death both man and woman, child and infant, ox and sheep, camel and donkey" (v. 3 NASB). So Saul mustered an army of 210,000 soldiers (v. 4) and "defeated the Amalekites, from Havilah as you go to Shur" (v. 7 NASB). Saul's army "utterly destroyed all the peple with the edge of the sword" (v. 8 NASB). However, he destroyed only the livestock that were despised and weak. He spared Agag the Amalekite king and the best sheep and cattle (v. 9). So the passage Morriston cites recounts God's response to Saul's actions. Because Saul did not follow God's instructions but instead "rushed upon the spoil" (v. 19 NASB), God regretted making him king.

Morriston appears to be arguing that Saul was rejected for not taking the command literally. If the command had been hyperbolic, then Saul's behavior would have been compatible with what was commanded; hence, he would not have been condemned.

This, however, is false. Suppose the language in 1 Samuel 15 of "totally destroying" the Amakelites is not a literal description of genocide. As Kenneth Kitchen argues, a hyperbolic summary is being used to describe "*disabling raids*" in which Israel killed rulers and less mobile inhabitants "that had not gotten clear."[3] "The 'alls' in the text are qualified"; such texts allow exceptions: "the remnant that survived got away into their defended towns."[4] Even on this interpretation, Saul's actions of sparing the best sheep would still violate God's command. Any livestock the Israelites captured would have been livestock that *escaping, surviving Amalekites*—those who had "gotten clear"—*did not take with them*, which were part of the livestock Saul was commanded to destroy![5] God's recorded response in the text is, therefore, compatible with either a literal *or* hyperbolic reading of the command. If Morriston maintains this particular passage should be read literally, he needs to point to some other feature of the text to substantiate this.

That said, a literal reading of this passage is *not* compatible with other features of the text. To see this, one needs to consider the fact that the text states quite clearly that with the exception of Agag, whom Saul spares, *the command to destroy the Amalekite people was carried out*. We see this when we compare the wording of the command in verse 3 with verses 7–9. Verse 3 reads: "strike [*nakah*] Amalek [the Amalekites] and utterly destroy [*haram*] all that he has, and do not spare [*hamal*] him; but put to death both man and woman, child and infant, ox and sheep, camel and donkey" (NASB). Then verses 7–9 go on to affirm that Saul has indeed done this:

So Saul defeated [*nakah*] the Amalekites, from Havilah as you go to Shur, which is east of Egypt. He captured Agag the king of the Amalekites alive, and *utterly destroyed [haram] all the people with the edge of the sword.* But Saul and the people spared [*hamal*] Agag and the best of the sheep, the oxen, the fatlings, the lambs, and all that was good, and were not willing to destroy them utterly [*haram*]; but everything despised and worthless, that they utterly destroyed. (NASB)

The language of "defeated" (or "struck") and "utterly destroyed" as well as the reference to "sparing" livestock is identical to the language of the earlier command in 15:3.

As the text continues, it takes for granted that Saul had "utterly destroyed" the Amalekites—a point that we show cannot be taken literally in light of the latter chapters of 1 Samuel. Note that the point of Saul's disobedience is not that he hadn't "utterly destroyed" the Amalekites. The problem of disobedience is in two areas: (1) primarily, that Saul preserved animals left behind that he should have destroyed; and (2) secondarily, that Saul allowed the Amalekite king, Agag—apparently something of a trophy and credit to Saul's own superior kingship—to remain alive. Of these two matters of disobedience, the theme of the livestock is the focal point in the remainder of the chapter:

[10]Then the word of the LORD came to Samuel, saying, [11]"I regret that I have made Saul king, for he has turned back from following Me and has not carried out My commands." And Samuel was distressed and cried out to the LORD all night. [12]Samuel rose early in the morning to meet Saul; and it was told Samuel, saying, "Saul came to Carmel, and behold, he set up a monument for himself, then turned and proceeded on down to Gilgal." [13]Samuel came to Saul, and Saul said to him, "Blessed are you of the LORD! I have carried out the command of the LORD." [14]But Samuel said, "What then is this bleating of the sheep in my ears, and the lowing of the oxen which I hear?" [15]Saul said, "They have brought them from the Amalekites, for the people spared the best of the sheep and oxen, to sacrifice to the LORD your God; but the rest we have utterly destroyed." [16]Then Samuel said to Saul, "Wait, and let me tell you what the LORD said to me last night." And he said to him, "Speak!"

[17]Samuel said, "Is it not true, though you were little in your own eyes, you were made the head of the tribes of Israel? And the LORD anointed you king over Israel, [18]and the LORD sent you on a mission, and said, 'Go and utterly destroy the sinners, the Amalekites, and fight against them until they are exterminated.' [19]Why then did you not obey the voice of the LORD, but rushed upon the spoil and did what was evil in the sight of the LORD?"

[20]Then Saul said to Samuel, "I did obey the voice of the LORD, and went on the mission on which the LORD sent me, and have brought back Agag the king of

Amalek, and have utterly destroyed the Amalekites. [21]But the people took some of the spoil, sheep and oxen, the choicest of the things devoted to destruction, to sacrifice to the LORD your God at Gilgal." [22]Samuel said,

> "Has the LORD as much delight in burnt offerings and sacrifices
> As in obeying the voice of the LORD?
> Behold, to obey is better than sacrifice,
> And to heed than the fat of rams.
> [23]For rebellion is as the sin of divination,
> And insubordination is as iniquity and idolatry.
> Because you have rejected the word of the LORD,
> He has also rejected you from being king."

[24]Then Saul said to Samuel, "I have sinned; I have indeed transgressed the command of the LORD and your words, because I feared the people and listened to their voice." (1 Sam. 15:10–24 NASB)

As we noted, except for keeping the Amalekite king Agag alive, *Saul accomplished his military objectives of "utterly destroying" the Amalekites.* Not only does the narrator affirm that Saul utterly destroyed the Amalekites (vv. 7–9), Saul states this emphatically: "I did obey the voice of the LORD, and went on the mission on which the LORD sent me, and have brought back Agag the king of Amalek, and have utterly destroyed the Amalekites" (v. 20).

Given this, it seems implausible that we should interpret the command in verse 3 as *literal* but the fulfilment, just four verses later, as *hyperbolic.* No, the text requires that the command and fulfilment be read in the same sense. Hence, *if the command is literal as Morriston contends, the text must be affirming that all the Amalekites were annihilated.* Only Agag and some livestock survived.

The key area of failure, however, had to do with preserving the livestock that had been left behind rather than destroying them. First, the prophet Samuel challenges Saul about his incomplete obedience by focusing on the animals: "What then is this bleating of the sheep in my ears, and the lowing of the oxen which I hear?" (v. 14). Second, Saul responds to the charge of disobedience by blaming the people for keeping the animals: "for the people spared the best of the sheep and oxen, to sacrifice to the LORD your God; but the rest we have utterly destroyed" (v. 15). Third, Samuel rebukes Saul by saying God had given him a command ("Go and utterly destroy the sinners, the Amalekites" [v. 18]), which Saul does, but Saul "did . . . not obey the voice of the LORD"; instead he "rushed upon the spoil and did what was evil in the sight of the LORD" (v. 19). Fourth, Saul once again blames the people for his failure in leadership:

"But the people took some of the spoil, sheep and oxen, the choicest of the things devoted to destruction, to sacrifice to the Lord your God at Gilgal" (v. 21). Fifth, the prophet Samuel focuses once more on the livestock—which the Lord does not desire—and completely ignores the military aspect. Samuel apparently takes Saul at his word that he had "utterly destroyed" the Amalekites (Agag aside) and addresses what is the central issue—namely, listening to the people instead of God's command and preserving the animals: "Has the Lord as much delight in burnt offerings and sacrifices as in obeying the voice of the Lord? Behold, to obey is better than sacrifice, and to heed than the fat of rams" (v. 22). Finally, Saul's reply acknowledges that he has failed to be a leader but instead listened to the people about the animals: "I have indeed transgressed the command of the Lord and your words, because I feared the people and listened to their voice" (v. 24).

So all the Amalekite people, except for Agag, are said to be destroyed by Saul (vv. 8, 20). Moreover a few verses later (v. 33), the text records that Agag was executed. And the livestock that were spared were taken back to Gilgal as a sacrifice. Hence, taken literally, by the end of the chapter every Amalekite man, woman, child, and all Amalekite livestock would have been eradicated.

Nevertheless, we have reason for taking this text hyperbolically. The narrator proceeds to state quite emphatically that the Amalekites were *not*, in fact, entirely wiped out. For one thing, before Samuel hacked to death King Agag, he told him, "As your sword has made women childless, so shall your mother be childless among women" (v. 33). Apparently, Samuel himself assumed that Agag's mother was still alive; so not all the Amalekites were eradicated.

So could it be that with Agag killed, perhaps *now* every single Amalekite man, woman (save Agag's mother), child, *and animal* has been killed? Not so! In 1 Samuel 27:8–9, David invades a territory full of Amalekites: "Now David and his men went up and raided the Geshurites, the Girzites and the Amalekites. (From ancient times these peoples had lived in the land extending to Shur and Egypt.) Whenever David attacked an area, he did not leave a man or woman alive, but took sheep and cattle, donkeys and camels, and clothes. Then he returned to Achish." This text affirms not only that the Amalekites still existed, but the reference to Egypt and Shur states that they existed in the *very same area* where Saul "utterly destroyed" every single one of them (15:8, 20). What's more, David took sheep and cattle as plunder. Clearly, in terms of what the narrative says, the Amalekites were not all destroyed—nor were all the animals finally destroyed in Gilgal in chapter 15. Instead, many people and livestock from the region had survived Saul's attack.

This survival is reinforced by the fact that three chapters later we read that *a sizeable Amalekite army* attacked Ziklag! So even though Saul "utterly destroyed" the Amalekites (15:8, 20), the text makes clear that many Amalekites remained so that David would not only—once again!—fight against them so that "not a man of them escaped," but after this battle, *four hundred Amalekites* fled on camels (30:17 NASB).

Even beyond this, the Amalekites continue to remain, and we come across another Amalekite in 2 Samuel 1:8, a passage where one of them takes credit for killing Saul—presumably a tall task if Saul had "utterly destroyed *all* the people" of Amalek. And in 1 Chronicles 4:43, the nation of Amalek is still around during the reign of Hezekiah. And then in the book of Esther, we encounter a descendant of the Amalekite king, Agag—Haman "the Agagite" (8:3), also called "the son of Hammedatha the Agagite" (3:1)—who was determined to wipe out the Jewish people. Amalekites were around well after both Saul and David.

So while Saul's condemnation is compatible with both a literal and hyperbolic reading of the command, a literal reading contradicts the remaining narrative, whereas a hyperbolic reading coheres with it. If Saul engaged in "disabling raids" against Amalekite soldiers in their territory, "killing their local kings and such of the inhabitants that had not gotten clear,"[6] then it is unsurprising that a large number of Amalekites remain after the battle.

So we see in Morriston's argument a subtle incoherence. Morriston defends a literal interpretation because he wrongly thinks that a hyperbolic interpretation is inconsistent with other things affirmed by the text. So the grounds he mistakenly provides for rejecting hyperbole are also grounds for rejecting literalism.

Finally, not only does a hyperbolic interpretation cohere with the text better than a literal one; there is evidence within the section from which Morriston quotes that suggests it contains rhetorical exaggeration and hyperbolic syntagms like "utterly destroyed" or "left no man of them alive."

First, the way 1 Samuel 15 uses the language of how Saul "utterly destroyed [*haram*]" the Amalekites "with the sword" is the same syntagm that was repeatedly used as hyperbole in Joshua (8:24; 10:28; etc.) as well as 1 Chronicles 4:41. Compare the following passages:

So Saul defeated [*nakah*] the Amalekites, from Havilah as you go to Shur, which is east of Egypt. He captured Agag the king of the Amalekites alive, and utterly destroyed [*haram*] all the people with the edge of the sword. (1 Sam. 15:7–8 NASB)

[Joshua] captured it and its king and all its cities, and they struck [*nakah*] them with the edge of the sword, and utterly destroyed [*haram*] every person who was in it. (Josh. 10:39 NASB)

[They] attacked [*nakah*] their tents and the Menuites who were found there, and destroyed them utterly [*haram*] to this day. (1 Chron. 4:41 NASB)

Second, the language of the command is very similar to the hyperbolic syntagm in 2 Chronicles 36. Compare the following two passages:

Now go and strike [*nakah*] Amalek and utterly destroy [*haram*] all that he has, and do not spare him; but put to death both man and woman, child and infant, ox and sheep, camel and donkey. (1 Sam. 15:3 NASB)

Therefore He brought up against them the king of the Chaldeans who slew their young men with the sword in the house of their sanctuary, and had no compassion on young man or virgin, old man or infirm; He gave them all into his hand. (2 Chron. 36:17 NASB)

In light of such texts, it appears we have good reason for thinking that these similarities in language and context offer good grounds for seeing God's command to Saul to "utterly destroy" the Amalekites and his clearly carrying this out (1 Sam. 15:3, 7) as indicative of hyperbolic language.

Third, we noted (in chap. 8) that one feature of ancient war reports is the hyperbolic use of numbers, where the size of armies is exaggerated for rhetorical effect. If we take the number in 1 Samuel 15 literally, that Saul's army was said to be 210,000 men, this would have been astronomically large for this time in history. For perspective, consider this comparison: it is estimated that the Egyptian army during the time of Rameses II (thirteenth century BC) was 100,000 in size and that Assyria's army during the eighth century BC was the largest standing army the ancient Near East had witnessed up to that time—150,000 to 200,000 men.[7]

In a previous essay, we noted that another interpretation of these astronomical numbers (an interpretation of Cambridge's Colin Humphreys) is possible.[8] The point we make there and in chapter 8 is that the word '*eleph*—typically translated "thousand"—is more ambiguous and could be a smaller number; it can be translated as "unit," "troop," or "squad." While this interpretation is certainly *possible*, it appears we have a stronger reason for taking as hyperbolic the high numbers in biblical war texts such as 1 Samuel 15. The simple reason for this is the clear evidence of hyperbole in general ancient Near Eastern usage (e.g., "I will surely multiply your offspring as the stars of heaven and as the sand that is on the seashore" [Gen. 22:17 ESV]), and this is particularly so in military texts. As Daniel Fouts observes, "If numerical hyperbole was employed, and is especially prevalent in the largest numbers of Scripture, then the problems traditionally ascribed to the large numbers can be reconciled easily."[9]

Egyptologist James Hoffmeier notes how such hyperbole is the stock-in-trade of ancient war texts boasting of military success. For example, the Egyptian king Thutmose III has Amun-Re recounting victories gained through divine assistance: "The great ones from every foreign land are united in your grasp. . . . I fettered Nubian Bowmen for you by ten thousand thousands and northerners as a hundred thousand prisoners of war. . . . You trod on *all* foreign lands. . . . The heads of Asiatics are severed, none escape (death)." The text (the Poetic Stela) claims there were no survivors, yet the same text reports that thousands of prisoners of war were taken.[10] Again, Amenhotep II is commanded to "capture *all* lands without fail. . . . *All* foreign lands were bound under his soles."[11] Yet again, Egypt's Rameses II is said to have prevailed over 100,000 men—not to mention that under Pharaoh Merneptah (son of Rameses II), "*all* lands were united" and "*all* who roamed have been subdued."[12] Again, exaggeration makes the best sense of these immense numbers, as hyperbole was "a regular feature of Near Eastern military reporting."[13]

Another reason to take Saul's battle as hyperbolic is this: we are told that Saul struck the Amalekites from Havilah to Shur. Shur is on the edge of Egypt; Havilah is in Saudi Arabia. Old Testament scholar Ralph Klein suggests this too is ancient Near Eastern exaggeration: "it is impossible to imagine the battle actually traversed the enormous distance from Arabia almost to Egypt."[14]

We have noted in a previously published work that King Saul is primarily engaged in battle against the Amalekites *in a specific city*—not on a massive geographical scale.[15] The text focuses on Saul doing battle in a "city of Amalek" (1 Sam. 15:5). As David Firth argues, this was probably a fortified (perhaps semipermanent) military encampment.[16] This point about exaggeration is reinforced by the fact that later (in 27:8), David fights against the Amalekites in the same region of Shur up to the land of Egypt. Hoffmeier observes that we routinely find in ancient Near Eastern war texts "lofty assertions of universal conquest side by side with sober statements about taking individual cities."[17] That is *exactly* what we see in 1 Samuel 15: we have both localized fighting (v. 5: "the city of Amalek") as well as "universal conquest" (v. 7: Havilah to Shur). A close look at the text of verses 5–7 reveals that we have fighting on a lesser scale: "Saul came to the city of Amalek and set an ambush in the valley. Saul said to the Kenites, 'Go, depart, go down from among the Amalekites, so that I do not destroy you with them; for you showed kindness to all the sons of Israel when they came up from Egypt.' So the Kenites departed from among the Amalekites. So Saul defeated the Amalekites, from Havilah as you go to Shur, which is east of Egypt" (NASB). A literal reading of the massive geographical scope of the battle passage seems further precluded when we consider that the narrator is not clearly affirming that Saul literally killed all the Amalekites from Havilah to Shur—though he did strike or smite (*nakah*) them there (v. 7). A closer look at the text of 1 Samuel reveals that Saul is fighting against a smaller representation of the Amalekites—a group that had just earlier engaged in plundering the Israelites (14:48) and which provoked a military response from Saul.

So contrary to Morriston, we believe the evidence suggests a more plausible way of interpreting this text as hyperbolic. The account of Saul's fighting the Amalekites is built up with stock ancient Near Eastern literary devices that suggest exaggeration; these accounts are not affirming that Saul literally killed every single Amalekite at God's command—not even close.

Whether at a popular level or a scholarly one, Hoffmeier asserts, those who read this text as affirming divinely mandated genocide commit what historian David Hackett Fischer in his classic work *Historians' Fallacies* calls "the fallacy of misplaced literalism." This is "the misconstruction of a statement-in-evidence so that it carries a literal meaning when a symbolic or hyperbolic or figurative meaning was intended."[18]

Judges 1: Israel's Failure to Drive Out the Canaanites

A second line of evidence that Morriston cites for his rejection of a hyperbolic interpretation of the relevant passages is this: "After all, it was precisely the failure [of the Israelites] to destroy *all* the targets of the genocide that prevented one of the very things that God was supposed to be trying to do—namely, destroy the Canaanite religion. This left the Israelites in the exact situation that God was allegedly trying to change—namely, one in which they were continually tempted to intermarry with the surrounding people and to join them in the worship of their Gods. According to the biblical record, the Israelites repeatedly succumbed to this temptation."[19]

This assertion, however, is mistaken. Suppose, as we have argued, that this command was not a command to exterminate every single Canaanite or even the vast majority, but rather to drive them out, killing only those who remained and did not flee. Thus, if the Israelites followed this command, they would not be in a position to be tempted to continually intermingle with the surrounding people, as those people, having already fled, would not be there.

Interestingly, the biblical text itself brings clarity. The book of Judges attributes Israel's repeatedly succumbing to the temptations that Morriston mentions to their failure to "drive out the Canaanites." It is *not* that they failed to kill every one of them. The end of Judges 1 repeatedly emphasizes the failure to drive out the Canaanites:

Manasseh did not drive out the people of Beth Shan or Taanach or Dor or Ibleam or Megiddo and their surrounding settlements. (v. 27)

Nor did Ephraim drive out the Canaanites living in Gezer. (v. 29)

Neither did Zebulun drive out the Canaanites living in Kitron or Nahalol. (v. 30)

Nor did Asher drive out those living in Akko or Sidon or Ahlab or Akzib or Helbah or Aphek or Rehob. (v. 31)

Neither did Naphtali drive out those living in Beth Shemesh or Beth Anath. (v. 33)

The episode concludes with the angel of the Lord rebuking Israel:

> The angel of the LORD went up from Gilgal to Bokim and said, "I brought you up out of Egypt and led you into the land I swore to give to your ancestors. I said, 'I will never break my covenant with you, and you shall not make a covenant with the people of this land, but you shall break down their altars.' Yet you have disobeyed me. Why have you done this? And I have also said, 'I will not drive them out before you; they will become traps for you, and their gods will become snares to you.'" (Judg. 2:1–3)

Here the issue is failure to *drive out* the Canaanites, not failure to *physically exterminate* all of them. It is worth noting also that, while Judges criticizes generations after Joshua for failing to drive out the Canaanites, the continued existence of Canaanites in these regions cannot be attributed to Joshua's failure to obey God because (as we noted in chap. 8) the text is clear that Joshua *faithfully obeyed* God's (Moses's) commands on this matter (e.g., Josh. 11:12, 15, 20). Thus, the existence of Canaanites in the later chapters of Joshua and in Judges 1 would have to be compatible with faithfully carrying out God's commands. A *hyperbolic* understanding of the commands and their fulfillment makes sense of this; a *literal* reading does not.

The Case of Rahab

Another objection comes from Douglas Earl, who disputes the hyperbolic reading of the story of Rahab in Joshua 6—the kind of reading advocated by Nicholas Wolterstorff. We noted (in chap. 5) that in the narrative, Joshua encounters an angel who identifies himself as the commander of the Lord's army (5:13–15). When Joshua asks the angel if he is on Israel's side or the side of the Canaanites, the response is that the angel is not on either side. He is on the side of the Lord. After this, Rahab, a Canaanite woman who shows faith in God, is saved from destruction (6:17–25). But then Achan, an Israelite who disobeys, is destroyed (chap. 7).

The juxtaposing of these episodes and the similar language leads many commentators, such as Earl, to conclude that the author here is making an explicit point: that it is faithfulness to God's commands, and not one's ethnicity, that makes one a true Israelite. Moreover, it is disobedience, not ethnicity, that makes one subject to destruction. (We use "ethnicity" loosely here. After all, when it came to pottery, clothing, tableware, homes, language, and general appearance, the Canaanites and Israelites were indistinguishable.)[20]

How does this create a problem for Wolterstorff's hyperbolic reading? The objector suggests that, once one sees the point being made, the total destruction of every single Canaanite is essential to the story. If Israel did not kill absolutely every last man, woman, and child in Jericho (except for Rahab and her family), then Rahab's survival could have been explained in ways other than as a reward for her loyalty to God. The author, then, must be asserting literal extermination.

This conclusion, however, does not follow. First, consider the suggestion that unless the author asserts, literally, that everyone was killed, we cannot know Rahab was spared as a reward. This is dubious. Suppose you are given a reward of five thousand dollars for assisting the police with an investigation. The same day, another person wins five thousand dollars in the lottery. Does the fact that someone else got the same amount of money you received undermine the fact that you received a reward? Would it mean that those who saw you get the reward are suddenly unable to know you did because it could have been luck? Obviously not! Similarly, if the text tells us that Rahab was spared because of her fidelity to God, then we know that she was spared for that reason because the author has told us. And, we should add, she did so *at great risk* to her own life. At any rate, someone else also being spared (out of luck or any other reason) makes no difference.

Second, if the real point of the story is that it is *disobedience*, not *ethnicity* (or, more precisely, national identity), that makes one subject to destruction, then surely it is the *literalistic* reading that contradicts the point of the story, *not* the *hyperbolic* reading. Taken literally, Joshua 6–11 affirms that God commanded that everyone of a particular national identity be killed—namely, the Canaanites. And he commanded the "total destruction" of the Canaanites not just in Jericho, but in *the entire Promised Land*. But that shifts the focus to ethnicity—or more precisely, national identity—rather than disobedience, which goes against the Rahab-Achan contrast. So this command to kill every Canaanite would actually not be essential to the point of the story if the major emphasis is to contrast Rahab's obedience and Achan's disobedience; if it were essential, that would contradict the point of the story.

Judges 20–21

As we engage with critics in various forums, we encounter another objection—one that appeals to Judges 20–21. In this story, the allied tribes of Israel attack armies from the morally degraded tribe of the Benjamin. After several Israelite defeats, they eventually prevail, and a small number of Benjamite soldiers escape. After the battle, the allied forces proceeded to kill every last woman and child in the land of Benjamin. This shocking story occurs as one of many illustrations of Israel's moral degeneration: "In those days Israel had no king; everyone did as he saw fit" (Judg. 21:25; cf. 17:6; 18:1; 19:1).[21]

What is relevant for our purposes is that this account does *not* appear to be hyperbolic. After the massacre, the Israelites faced a problem: they wanted to show mercy on the tribe of Benjamin. However, only the few hundred soldiers who escaped are left; all their wives and children have been killed. The narrative consequently proceeds on the assumption that this is not hyperbole.

On the surface, it is difficult to see the objection. Interpreters like Nicholas Wolterstorff argue that the accounts of massacre in Joshua are hyperbolic. Indeed, we have emphasized how Judges 1–2 is the more "down-to-earth" account of what Joshua describes using ancient Near Eastern hyperbole. So if Judges 20–21 is not hyperbolic, this point is irrelevant. Since Wolterstorff is not talking about Judges, it is hard to see how this passage at the end of Judges calls his conclusion into question.

Some critics will offer a comeback, however. They point out that Judges 20–21 uses language similar to Joshua. Because the passage uses the same language as Joshua, and because the account in Judges is clearly not hyperbolic, the account in Joshua cannot be hyperbolic either.

There are two problems with this reply. First, the language in Judges 20:10—where the allied Israelite tribes kill every last woman and child in the land of Benjamin—does not use the language of *herem* ("utter destruction") that is used in Deuteronomy and Joshua. The command regarding the Canaanites in Deuteronomy 7:2 and 20:17 and its repeated fulfillment in Joshua 6–11 all use the technical term *haram* ("totally/utterly destroy"—or the noun *herem* ["something condemned/banned/devoted to destruction"]). The same is true of the command to Saul to "totally destroy" the Amalekites

(1 Sam. 15:3), followed by its recorded fulfillment (1 Sam. 15:7–8). This term is not used in Judges 20:10 ("Go and strike the inhabitants . . . with the edge of the sword").

The verb *haram* does occur later in Judges 21. There, in order to get wives for the Benjamites, the allied Israelite tribes attack Jabesh-gilead and "utterly destroy [the verb is *haram*] every man and every woman who has lain with a man" (v. 11 NASB). However, the problem here is that the book of Samuel (11:1) tells us that the city of Jabesh-gilead remained populated in the time of Saul, who would rescue the city's inhabitants from the invading forces of Ammon. Once again, we see in Judges 21 the language of "totally destroying" whole populations is followed by narrative that assumes the people in question remained alive in reasonable numbers.

Second, even if Judges 20–21 did use language similar to Joshua, this comeback fails to understand that the same language, even the same phrase, can have different senses, whether hyperbolic or literal, depending on the context. The very nature of hyperbole involves taking language that can be literal in certain contexts and using the same language in a nonliteral way. Consider an obvious example. Suppose your neighbor notices that his young son has thrown mud on his newly washed car. While he is looking at the mess, you hear him angrily mutter, "I am going to kill that kid!" In this context, a sensible and charitable interpretation would be to interpret this hyperbolically; you are not going to call the police because you fear your neighbor is going to literally kill his son—you understand that the son will only be punished. However, suppose that a Mafia boss, referring to a young store owner who has refused to pay protection money, states, "I am going to kill that kid!" In this instance, we would take the statement literally in spite of the fact that the same phrase is used nonliterally in other contexts. So the fact that a phrase is used literally in Judges 20–21 by itself does not provide grounds for thinking it is used that way in Joshua. What matters is the context in which it is uttered.

When one turns to context, it is clear that this argument is unsuccessful. The reason the objector contends that the account in Judges 20–21 is not hyperbolic is because the account is proceeded by a narrative which assumes, and only makes sense if, *the massacre actually happened*. This context, however, is the very *opposite* of what we find in Joshua. In Joshua, the language of wiping out all the inhabitants is included in narratives that assume the inhabitants were *not* wiped out and even existed in large numbers. This is an assumption that is carried over into the book of Judges. One can therefore read one account literally and another hyperbolically because they occur in different contexts.

Midian

A final appeal to the biblical text that we will address involves the apparent genocide of the Midianites in Numbers 31. After the Israelites "fought against Midian, as the LORD commanded Moses, and killed every man" (v. 7), Moses commanded them to "kill all the boys. And kill every woman who has slept with a man, but save for yourselves every girl who has never slept with a man" (vv. 17–18).[22] On the face of it, this text affirms that every Midianite was killed and only female virgins survived so they could be assimilated into the Israelite community. Critics argue that texts like this cannot plausibly be understood as being hyperbolic.

It's again hard to see an objection to the hyperbolic interpretation of Joshua here. For one thing, even if Numbers 31 wasn't hyperbolic, it wouldn't necessarily follow that the relevant passages in Joshua and Deuteronomy aren't hyperbolic. But more interestingly, the noted Jewish scholar Jacob Milgrom (d. 2010) makes the case that the Numbers 31 account does contain extensive hyperbole, and he notes several features of the text that suggest this.

First, Milgrom notes several cases of obvious rhetorical exaggeration.[23] The Israelite army is said to have killed "every [Midianite] male" in battle without a single Israelite fatality (Num. 31:7, 49).[24] Moreover, the spoil from the battle is said to be 32,000 maidens and 675,000 sheep and goats (vv. 32, 35)—these numbers are astronomically and absurdly large.[25] But in light of the ancient Near Eastern pattern of using hyperbolic numbers (as we have noted earlier in this chapter as well as in chap. 8), they are easily explicable.

Second, when we turn to the book of Judges, if we take that narrative literally, it states quite emphatically that the Midianites were not wiped out at all. In Judges 6 and 7, the Midianites invade Israel in numbers said to be "like swarms of locusts. It was impossible to count them or their camels" (6:5). Indeed, Israel was so overrun with Midianites that they fled to "mountain clefts, caves and strongholds" (v. 2). Unable to win in open battle, Gideon was forced to use deception to defeat them. This does not square with the Midianites having been literally "utterly destroyed." So it is not at all obvious that the battle recorded in Numbers is intended to be taken entirely literally.

Also, later in this book (chap. 17), we discuss a further point worth noting. We observe the distinction between *God's command* (to kill every male, Num. 31:7), which Israel did carry out *before the additional command from Moses* (to kill women and male children, vv. 17–18). This seems to be Moses's command solely—a command beyond what God had actually ordered and what had been carried out. As Old Testament scholar Robert Alter points out, "one should note that it is Moses's, not God's" command here.[26] But, some might ask, wasn't Moses justified in calling for the punishment of the Midianite seductresses? Perhaps three further responses could be given. First, God's command centered on the Midianite *men* being killed, since they had been complicit in this national Midianite plot hatched by Balaam; this was a corporate endeavor to incite Israelite treachery against Yahweh's covenant with them. And we are explicitly told that the Israelite men were killed. And this was certainly God's prerogative to bring such a judgment. Second, while Moses's command does highlight the women's guilt and judgment-worthiness, the text still indicates a distancing of the divine command (and its completion) from Moses's own command. Third, as John Goldingay notes, we are not told that Moses's command is actually carried out, and we well know that the Old Testament does not shrink from mentioning deaths by divine judgment: "so this raises the question of whether the slaughter actually happened."[27]

We further discuss Numbers 31, 1 Samuel 15, and related passages in chapter 17, but here we bring our preliminary explorations to a conclusion.

As we look at how critics often use these biblical texts, we are reminded of what Egyptologist Kenneth Kitchen says of various Old Testament scholars themselves. He maintains that even they have engaged in a "careless reading" of biblical war texts, particularly Joshua. This "has encouraged Old Testament scholars to read into the entire book *a whole myth of their own making*, to the effect that the book of Joshua presents a sweeping, total conquest *and occupation* of Canaan by Joshua, which can then be falsely pitted against the narratives in Judges. But this modern myth is merely a careless falsehood, based on the failure to recognize and understand ancient use of rhetorical summations. The 'alls' are qualified in the Hebrew narrative itself."[28]

Summary

- Some critics have not been impressed with the hyperbolic explanation. For example, God surely would not have been displeased if all the Amalekites had been wiped out by Saul (1 Sam. 15). Saul appeared to be rejected for not taking God's command literally ("do not spare").

- Actually, while the language in 1 Samuel 15 could be understood literally, a more coherent explanation is the hyperbolic one.

- As with the Canaanites, this passage relates to those who had not "gotten clear" (made their escape).

- The text states quite clearly that with the exception of King Agag, whom Saul spares, the command to destroy the Amalekite people (v. 3) *was carried out* (vv. 7–9): Saul *utterly destroyed all the people with the edge of the sword.* Saul notes this again in verse 20. We see the emphasis on taking the animals as spoil in verses 14, 15, 18, 19, 21, and 24. The killing of the Amalekites has dropped off the scene because Saul has carried this out (vv. 7–9).

- Then in 1 Samuel 27:8–9, David invades a territory full of Amalekites—the same massive territory from Arabia to Egypt where Saul had fought (exaggerated language again!). And four hundred of them escape (1 Sam. 30:17). Amalekites continue to show up in Scripture (2 Sam. 1:8; 1 Chron. 4:43; Esther 3:1; 8:3).

- If we take the number in 1 Samuel 15 literally (Saul's army of 210,000 men), this would have been astronomically large for this time in history (cf. the Egyptian army under Rameses II being 100,000 and Assyria's army being 150,000–200,000 men, the largest standing army up to that time in history).

- Again, a *hyperbolic* understanding of the commands and their fulfillment makes sense of these numbers; a *literal* reading does not.

- What of Judges 1, where Israel does not eliminate the entrenched Canaanites? Isn't this what God commanded? The text, however, often repeats that Israel *failed to drive out* the Canaanites from the land (which would keep their negative spiritual influence at a distance). The problem is not that Israel failed to exterminate every Canaanite. Note also that Joshua *had fulfilled* what God had commanded Moses.

- Some objecting to a hyperbolic reading claim that the story of Rahab emphasizes that she acts like a true Israelite and that the Israelite Achan acts like a Canaanite and is destroyed for his disobedience (Josh. 7). But if the narrative is to highlight Rahab's obedience and Achan's disobedience, then whether *all* the inhabitants of Jericho were killed is beside the point.

- Some raise the question of Judges 20–21, where the morally degraded tribe of Benjamin is nearly extinguished. Isn't this literal? Weren't they nearly "utterly destroyed"? We agree that the account doesn't appear to be hyperbolic, but it's hard to see the objection. The accounts in Joshua clearly *are* hyperbolic, and we have noted that Judges gives a more "down-to-earth" account of warfare.

- Another objection to the hyperbolic account is the apparent genocide of Midian (Num. 31). There are a number of indicators of hyperbole in the text itself (e.g., in Judges 6:5, we read that the "utterly destroyed" Midianites are too numerous to count). Also, note the difference between God's command and that of Moses. We read that the Israelites "fought against Midian, as the LORD commanded Moses, and killed every man" (Num. 31:7). However, Moses appears to go *beyond* God's command, adding his own command: "kill all the boys. And kill every woman who has slept with a man, but save for yourselves every girl who has never slept with a man" (vv. 17–18). And even though Moses highlights the adulterous Midianite women's culpability at Peor, just judgment has already fallen on the Midianite men (v. 7)—by God's command (v. 3)—who were complicit in Israel's act of national treachery. Finally, we have no indication that this act against the Midianite women and children was actually carried out.

10

Legal and Theological Objections concerning Genocide

I n this chapter, we want to look at further objections concerning the question of "genocide in the Bible"—namely, legal and theological objections.

Legal Objections: Genocide in International Law

We have argued that when the text says that Joshua "put the city and its king to the sword and totally destroyed everyone in it" (Josh. 10:28) or "put it to the sword . . . and everyone in it" (10:37) or "totally destroyed them, not sparing anyone that breathed" (11:11), the author is engaging in rhetorical hyperbole. He is not asserting that Joshua actually killed every man, woman, and child in Canaan. We have also argued that a careful reading of the texts suggests Israel's task was not aimed at exterminating every living Canaanite, but rather driving them out of the Promised Land. Only those who had not fled but remained would be killed. Consequently, it is inaccurate to describe the biblical text as depicting "genocide."

Critics might reply that, in arguing this way, we are operating under a faulty definition of genocide. They might claim our argument assumes that, in order for something to count as genocide, the goal has to be to kill off an entire people group. But if so, our assumption about genocide is incorrect. As genocide is defined in international law, even the killing of *part* of a people group and dispossessing the rest of them would count as genocide. So our argument fails.

To assess this kind of objection, it might be instructive to see how international law defines genocide. According to Article 2 of the International Convention on the Prevention and Punishment of the Crime of Genocide (ICPPCG), "genocide" means

any of the following acts committed with intent to destroy, in whole or in part, a national, ethnical, racial or religious group, as such:

(a) Killing members of the group;
(b) Causing serious bodily or mental harm to members of the group;
(c) Deliberately inflicting on the group conditions of life calculated to bring about its physical destruction in whole or in part;
(d) Imposing measures intended to prevent births within the group;
(e) Forcibly transferring children of the group to another group.[1]

Critics could point to a couple of features of this definition to establish their conclusion that driving the Canaanites out of the land by force and killing those who refuse to leave is genocide. First, they could say that according to (c), "deliberately inflicting on the group conditions of life calculated to bring about its physical destruction in whole or in part" would include "driving out" (expelling, relocating) people from their homeland.

Second, the critic could argue that the destruction of an ethnic or religious group does not have to be total to qualify as genocide. The above definition describes genocide as involving "intent to destroy, in whole *or in part*, a national, ethnical, racial or religious group." These facts, they argue, show very clearly that what's described in the Bible fits the legal definition of genocide.

In response we will address both of these points in turn. First, the critic is correct to acknowledge that forcible relocation could be involved in genocide, according to (c). However, this act *by itself* is insufficient to establish genocide. Central to legal definitions of genocide is the notion of *double* intention: (1) one must intentionally commit one of the acts (a)–(e) above, *and* (2) one must do so with a further intent to destroy a group in whole or in part as such. This is what we see in the proceedings of the International Criminal Tribunal for the former Yugoslavia (ICTY). In the case of *Prosecutor v. Goran Jelisic*, the accused was on trial for crimes against humanity and ethnic cleansing of the Bosnians. In the trial transcripts, we read this description:

Genocide is characterized by two legal ingredients according to the terms of Article 4 of the Statute:

- the material element of the offence, constituted by one or several acts enumerated in paragraph 2 of Article 4;
- the *mens rea* [literally, "state of mind," focusing on intent] of the offence, consisting of the special intent to destroy, in whole or in part, a national, ethnical, racial or religious group, as such.[2]

So driving a population off their land is insufficient to qualify as genocide. Rather it must be done with "special intent to destroy, in whole or in part." But what does the statute mean by "in part"? It seems that getting clear on this point is central to our discussion in this section.

Two things are noteworthy in understanding this term "in part." First, according to much of the case law surrounding the meaning of "in part," the destruction in question must be *physical destruction of the group*. In another case, *Jorgic v. Germany* (2007), the European Court of Human Rights stated that "a majority of scholars took the view that genocidal 'intent to destroy a group' under Article 220a of the Criminal Code had to be aimed at the *physical-biological destruction* of the protected group."[3]

It found a similar definition had been adopted based on case law. In *Prosecutor v. Krstic* (2001), for example, the Trial Chamber recognized that "customary international law limits the definition of genocide to those acts seeking the physical or biological destruction of all or part of the group."[4] This judgment was upheld by the Appeals Chamber in 2004: "The Genocide Convention, and customary international law in general, *prohibit only the physical or biological destruction of a human group*."[5] The Trial Chamber refused to broaden this definition and expressly recognized this definitional limit to genocide. Indeed, even prior to this (1996), the International Law Commission (ILC) recognized that genocide involved "destruction" only in the *material* sense—that is, "its physical or biological sense."[6] Similarly in *Prosecutor v. Kupreskic* (2000), the ICTY court stated that "in genocide, the persecutory intent is pushed to its uttermost limits through the pursuit of the *physical annihilation* of the group or of members of the group."[7]

Second, while the convention refers to "in whole or in part," most authorities require intent to physically destroy a substantial number of the group. In *Prosecutor v. Radislav Krstic* (2004), the ICTY stated: "It is well established that where a conviction for genocide relies on the intent to destroy a protected group 'in part,' the part must be a substantial part of that group. *The aim of the Genocide Convention is to prevent the intentional destruction of entire human groups, and the part targeted must be significant enough to have an impact on the group as a whole.*"[8]

Citing several previous cases, the ICTY affirmed that "the substantiality requirement both captures genocide's defining character as a crime of massive proportions and reflects the Convention's concern with the impact the destruction of the targeted part will have on the overall survival of the group."[9]

When we read passages like Joshua 6–11, Eric Seibert insists, we should "call a spade a spade: it is genocide."[10] He charges that we, in holding the position we do, "justify genocide."[11] But we would argue that, contrary to such criticisms, our position does not advocate genocide. And when we look more closely at international law's usage of "genocide," such accusations appear all the more misdirected. International law *does* assume that in order to count as genocide, the perpetrator's aim has to be killing off an entire people group. To count as genocide, the intent must be to physically destroy either the whole group or a significant proportion of that group; and if it is a significant group that is destroyed, it would be genocide if the destruction of the part is likely to have an adverse impact on the survival of the whole group.

What's more, we have noted that the Israelites' intent was not to annihilate, say, the Canaanite peoples but to put an end to their pernicious *criminal* influence—one that could affect Israel and seriously undermine its national mission and integrity. We noted in chapter 5 in this book that the activities of the Canaanites were not trivial; they would be prosecutable in virtually all Western countries and punished by the death penalty in certain jurisdictions.

What about the charge that *displacing* or *dispossessing* people is a genocidal act? Here again, international case law repeatedly repudiates that such acts are "genocide." Indeed, killing people for the purpose of driving them off a piece of land is not genocide. Consider, for example, the case of *Jorgic v. Germany*. The court stated, "Amongst scholars, the majority have taken the view that ethnic cleansing, in the way in which it was carried out by the Serb forces in Bosnia and Herzegovina in order to expel Muslims and Croats from their homes, did not constitute genocide."[12]

The case of *Prosecutor v. Kupreskic* provides another example. In this case, the court found that Croat soldiers had attacked a small village in central Bosnia, killing 116 inhabitants and destroying twenty-seven houses and several mosques. The court ruled that this persecution of Muslims was not genocide: "In the present case, according to the Prosecution—and this is a point on which the Trial Chamber agrees—the killing of Muslim civilians was primarily aimed at expelling the group from the village, not at destroying the Muslim group as such. This is therefore a case of persecution, not of genocide."[13] This is because "the primary purpose of the massacre was to expel the Muslims from the village, by killing many of them, by burning their houses and their livestock. The ultimate goal of these acts was to spread terror among the population so as to deter the members of that particular ethnic group from ever returning to their homes."[14]

This point is repeated in *Bosnia and Herzegovina v. Serbia and Montenegro* (2007):

The term "ethnic cleansing" has frequently been employed to refer to the events in Bosnia and Herzegovina which are the subject of this case. . . . General Assembly resolution 47/121 referred in its Preamble to "the abhorrent policy of 'ethnic cleansing', which is a form of genocide", as being carried on in Bosnia and Herzegovina. . . . It can only be a form of genocide within the meaning of the Convention, if it corresponds to or falls within one of the categories of acts prohibited by Article II of the Convention. Neither the intent, as a matter of policy, to render an area "ethnically homogeneous", nor the operations that may be carried out to implement such policy, can *as such* be designated as genocide: the intent that characterizes genocide is "to destroy, in whole or in part" a particular group, and deportation or displacement of the members of a group, even if effected by force, is not necessarily equivalent to destruction of that group, nor is such destruction an automatic consequence of the displacement. This is not to say that acts described as "ethnic cleansing" may never constitute genocide, if they are such as to be characterized as, for example, "deliberately inflicting on the group conditions of life calculated to bring about its physical destruction in whole or in part", contrary to Article II, paragraph (c), of the Convention, provided such action is carried out with the necessary specific intent (*dolus specialis* ["special intent"]), that is to say with a view to the destruction of the group, as distinct from its removal from the region.[15]

Particularly clear is the ICTY case of *Prosecution v. Milomir Stakic* (2003):

It does not suffice to deport a group or a part of a group. A clear distinction must be drawn between physical destruction and mere dissolution of a group. *The expulsion of a group or part of a group does not in itself suffice for genocide.* As Kreß has stated, "This is true even if the expulsion can be characterised as a tendency to the dissolution of the group, taking the form of its fragmentation or assimilation. This is because *the dissolution of the group is not to be equated with physical destruction*". In this context the Chamber recalls that a proposal by Syria in the Sixth Committee to include "imposing measures intended to oblige members of a group to abandon their homes in order to escape the threat of subsequent ill-treatment" as a separate sub-paragraph of Article II of the Convention against Genocide was rejected by twenty-nine votes to five, with eight abstentions.[16]

The *Stakic* case makes the point that the expelling of a group or part of a group from an area resulting in that group's assimilation, dissolution, or fragmentation so that the group no longer exists is not genocide. This is because dissolution is not the same as physical destruction.

This is further reinforced by the Appeals Chamber in the *Krstic* case, which took the view that "genocide is not forcible removal of a group from a specific place" but is intending their "physical disappearance from the earth."[17] For the term "genocide" to apply, one must intend the physical destruction of a group or of a substantive number of its members.

What we have examined runs contrary to the critics' charge of "genocide." If God's command was primarily to drive the Canaanites from the land and not to physically exterminate all or even the vast majority of the Canaanites, then the command was *not* obviously a genocidal one.

Of course, the fact that it is not genocide doesn't resolve all moral questions that arise from the text. Even if an act is not genocide, it could still be problematic on other grounds. We endeavor to address a number of these concerns throughout the book. What we do try to show here is that the claim "the Bible condones genocide" is false—and this is a significant point.

This point is significant because the accusation of "genocide"—whether coming from Old Testament scholars like Eric Seibert or New Atheists like Richard Dawkins—carries a heavy rhetorical punch, which often calls forth echoes of Rwanda or the Holocaust. The more modest claim that *at one particular point in history God made an exception to a general rule against killing noncombatants* (while still raising moral questions) does not carry that same rhetorical baggage. Certainly the general principle of noncombatant immunity is correct in most circumstances, but that it is nevertheless not absolute and can be overridden in specific circumstances is a position seriously proposed and defended in the contemporary literature on ethics. As we point out in chapters 15 and 16, by contrast, the claim that the Holocaust or Rwanda's genocide was justified by overriding circumstances is not likewise proposed and defended.

So it's not enough for opponents of biblical theism to draw rhetorical connections with these recent historical events. They need to deal with what the biblical authors of these texts actually say—not simply pick and choose certain verses containing phrases like "utterly destroy" while ignoring verses mentioning "dispossessing" or "they could not drive them out." These critics also need to consider what it is plausible to claim that God (assuming he is the primary author of Scripture) says by way of appropriating these war texts in the biblical canon, and critics need to offer arguments showing that God cannot give certain difficult—though not intrinsically evil—commands in order to accomplish his purposes.

Theological Objections: Clarifications and Avoiding Slippery Slopes

In this chapter, we have addressed some of the legal considerations of the charge of genocide. Another set of objections is broadly theological. As we speak to various audiences, we often encounter the charge that our acceptance of a hyperbolic interpretation of these Old Testament war texts is a threat to biblical authority.[18] We address this charge below.

Worries about Slippery Slopes

A common objection to understanding the literary phrasings (syntagms), such as "they left nothing alive that breathed" or "there were no survivors," as hyperbole is that this interpretation threatens the literal truth of everything else Christians believe. If one takes the commands to exterminate the Canaanites and Joshua nonliterally, then why not take the rest of the text nonliterally as well? Why not claim, for example, that the resurrection of Christ is nonliteral or hyperbolic?

The straightforward answer is that one should take the relevant passages in Joshua nonliterally because the evidence supports such a reading. There is compelling textual evidence for hyperbole both from within the text itself and also from parallels between Joshua and other ancient Near Eastern war texts.

To clarify, these parallels with war texts and textual considerations within the biblical text are not present across the board for other parts of the Bible. The resurrection accounts, for example, don't follow the literary type (genre) of ancient Near Eastern conquest accounts. Rather, these accounts are found in the four Gospels, which all follow the genre of ancient Greek biographies (*bioi*—"lives"). So the literary conventions governing their use will be different. Unlike the Joshua conquest accounts, the resurrection accounts are followed by other biblical books which assume that a bodily resurrection really happened. If we had biblical texts indicating that Jesus's body remained in the tomb, then we would have reason for interpreting the resurrection metaphorically. Perhaps one could say, "When I say Jesus is alive, all I mean is that Jesus 'lives' in my heart and gives meaning to my life—even though his body literally rotted in a tomb." But we don't have such texts.

In Joshua, on the other hand, the conquest accounts are followed up by passages that assume that the events as narrated did not *literally* happen—though we do not have to deny a fundamental historicity to these war texts, despite their hyperbole.

Perhaps it would be helpful to point out a much-abused phrase that some Christians readily use—"taking the Bible literally." If you treat a text metaphorically that other Christians take literally, they may charge you with being inconsistent by taking some parts of the Bible literally and others not. They might ask, "How much more straightforward can you get than 'utterly destroy' or 'there were no survivors'?" (We get this question *a lot*!)

There are at least a couple of problems with this approach. First, this "literal" approach will not be consistent. Scripture contains many literary genres—historical narrative, poetry, prophecy, epistle/letter, apocalypse, Gospel, parable, proverb, and so on. We don't interpret each genre the same way, and there will be varying proportions of literal and figurative language within each. For example, the biblical authors don't literally believe that the mountains will sing and the trees will clap their hands (Isa. 55:12). When Jesus says he is a "door" (John 10:9) or "bread"/"manna" from heaven (6:31–35), or that Herod is a "fox" (Luke 13:32), he is not being "literal." And when we come to the book of Revelation, we typically have to assume that much of the language is most likely figurative unless we have good reason for taking it literally—the very opposite of how we approach historical narrative.[19] A good rule of thumb is that we should *always treat the Bible literarily* (according to the author's intended literary genre), *but not always treat it literally* (which would lead to absurdities).

Second, this kind of argument relies on a peculiar assumption: if one grants that one part of a text is nonliteral, then one cannot take any other part of the text as literal—or vice versa—without being arbitrary. This assumption is false. For instance, consider Exodus 14 and 15, where we have both the historical narrative of Israel's passage through the Red Sea (chap. 14) followed by a song/poetry based on this historical event (chap. 15). Even though the poem refers to God's "right hand" and "nostrils" (vv. 6, 8, 12), it is based on the historical event recounted in chapter 14.[20]

Or consider a recent example. In my (Matt's) debate with Raymond Bradley at Auckland University in 2010, Bradley gave this opening statement:

> I come not to praise God but to bury him along with the dead gods of now forgotten religions. Not to praise him as the source of all that's good in the world, and hence the ultimate guide to human morals. . . . I will assume the role of prosecutor in providing grounds for agreeing with God's self-indictment. And having conducted God's trial in accord with the principles of morality and logic, I will hope to see him put, first, into a straightjacket, and then forever in his grave, no longer to command the belief of men.[21]

Now Bradley obviously does not literally mean that he will bury God, as though God were a physical person whom he would attempt to cover with dirt. Nor is he literally putting God on trial. Nor does he mean God exists and can be put in a straightjacket made of logic. Bradley, of course, is speaking metaphorically. Does this fact mean that we cannot take *anything* Bradley says literally, that we must take his whole argument as a figure of speech?

As to the texts in Joshua, we have argued there is compelling *textual* evidence both from within the text itself and also from comparisons between Joshua and other ancient Near Eastern texts suggesting that such phrases as "utterly destroy" and "leave alive nothing that breathes" are hyperbolic. What we are advocating is taking a *closer* look at these texts rather than *glossing over* them! These parallels and textual considerations are not present with the resurrection accounts. For example, we don't have a couple of Gospels saying that the tomb was empty and other Gospels claiming that Jesus's body remained in it. Jesus's resurrection and the empty tomb are taken for granted. But with Joshua, we have texts stating that the Canaanites were "utterly destroyed" alongside texts indicating that many Canaanites remained "to this day."

Again, we must examine texts and their respective genres to discern whether hyperbole exists within a given passage. But we should not make the mistake of inferring that because *some* biblical texts are hyperbolic, it follows therefore that *all* are.

The Worry of Miscommunication

A further objection is that God, by allowing his Word to be mediated through the literary conventions of ancient Near Eastern military texts, should have foreseen that future generations would misinterpret it. Now, it's correct that church history has seen its share of biblical *mis*interpretation. But it's still unclear why this means the text should always be taken literally. After all, it seems that *any* language through which God mediates his Word, whether literal or figurative, will carry this possibility. A message mediated through the more literalistic, less-hyperbolic conventions of English, history, or moral philosophy in the twenty-first century could readily be misunderstood by numerous people in non-Western cultures, to whom our literary conventions are quite alien. Just think about attempting to accommodate the secularist by using the deist Thomas Jefferson's "Bible"—a cut-and-paste version of the Gospels, in which all references to Jesus's miracles, unique identity claims, and bodily resurrection are removed. This would distort the message of Scripture rather than clarify it.

The worry about miscommunication seems to be more a problem with divine verbal *revelation* in general than with any particular *interpretation* of that revelation. As philosopher Peter van Inwagen notes,

The Bible has not been translated into more languages than any other book *only* because missionary societies believe it to be the inspired word of God; another important part of the explanation is that missionaries know from experience that the Bible is one of their most effective tools. They know that those to whom they preach "take to it" with very little prompting or preparation. They know it captures their attention. They know people of most cultures will listen to the words of the cloud of witnesses who speak to them across the millennia from its pages. And quite possibly—who is in a position to deny this?—a version of, or replacement for, the Bible that a secular reader of our culture would find more appealing (or less appalling) than the actual Bible would have very little meaning for the peoples of most times and most cultures.[22]

Resorting to False Analogies

In the various chapters leading up to this one, we have been looking at the question of whether God commands us to kill innocent human beings—particularly whether the descriptions of the biblical text made by critics accurately reflect what the author(s) intended to say.

Perhaps we can bring some of the loose strands together at this point by noting Wes Morriston's criticism of the view that Scripture is truthful in what it (actually!) affirms. Let's examine an analogy suggested by Morriston that would, he thinks, undermine confidence in biblical authority, using the charge that God commanded genocide:

> If the President of the United States were to announce that God had told him to use the vast military power at his disposal to obliterate, say, the nation of Iran, "saving alive nothing that breathes," people would assume that he was mad and he would speedily be dismissed from office. No one—well, almost no one—would take seriously the idea that God had instructed him to do this terrible thing.[23]

The discussion of what we have written thus far reveals significant disanalogies between the biblical narrative and Morriston's example. Let's review some of them.

First, Morriston's example involves the United States; the biblical text refers to Israel. While both are nations, the similarities end there. Nationalistic fervor aside, the United States is not God's chosen people; they are not in a special covenant with God to be a light to the nations and the channel through which all nations will be blessed and restored.

Second, while the United States is the most powerful economic and military nation in the world today, the ancient Israelites were refugees fleeing oppression in Egypt. The citizens of the United States are not landless refugees needing a place to live.

Third, Iran is not part of the United States. By invading Iran, the United States would be invading a foreign country. By contrast, Canaan was land that belonged to Israel. Indeed, this was the land of Israel's roots beginning with Abraham, when God had covenanted to give him this land. Abraham and the other patriarchs had title to land within Canaan (not to mention that, as noted in the last chapter, the Canaanites were culturally and ethnically indistinguishable from the Israelites).[24] By contrast, Iran is not and never has been land to which the United States has legitimate title.

Fourth, whatever one thinks of the regime in Iran, the Iranian population has not been busy engaging in practices such as incest, adultery, bestiality, ritualized sex, and human sacrifice as part of the normal religious repertoire of their culture.[25] Such practices are not entrenched in Iranian culture, and even if they were, Iran has not been engaging in these practices for four hundred years on US soil without repentance.

Fifth, it is not the case that the population of the United States risks being assimilated into Iranian culture such that, if they coexisted, Americans would be drawn into all these practices.

And finally, in Morriston's example, the president is divinely ordered to use the "vast military power at his disposal to obliterate . . . the nation of Iran." The vast military power of the United States involves nuclear weapons, a massive air force, navy, and military. In this context the command is clearly literal. In the Bible, however, the reference to annihilation is hyperbolic. The United States is not trying to drive the population out, killing only those who refuse to leave. Nor is the attack happening after a significant number of people, warned about an impending attack, have fled. Nor is it referring to "disabling raids" described in maximal hyperbolic terms.

What would we have to do to adjust Morriston's portrayal to make it a more accurate analogy? Imagine Iran has assumed possession of land that belongs to the United States. They occupy this land and refuse to leave. They are heavily armed, and a certain number will resist eviction with force. Imagine Iran is not comprised of Shi'ite Muslims but rather of members of a religious sect whose rituals involve criminal activities such as incest, bestiality, and burning children alive as sacrifices. For centuries, they have been squatters on US territory, engaging in these activities without repentance and having a pernicious influence on those around them.

Suppose further that all the citizens of the United States have lost their land and are refugees fleeing persecution and in need of land. The number of remaining Americans is so small that if they coexist in the land with the Iranians, the Americans will be assimilated. America's identity, ideals, and ethos will disappear, and the entire US citizenry will become part of the criminal cult.

Imagine further that in such a setting, the president announces his belief that it is God's will for him to forcibly drive Iran from their land. A generation ago, an ultimatum had been given to the Iranians that if any of them remained behind, they would be killed. Large numbers leave, but other refuse to heed the warning. The president regretfully announces that, as a last resort, Americans must go in and kill those who did not heed the warning and flee. The president stresses that these are highly unusual circumstances and certainly not the norm. He tells his people that he would not take such action under normal conditions. But he believes that for this specific situation, on the basis of God's assurance, that greater evils will be averted by this course of action than by any alternative strategy. So in this specific case the normal rules are overridden.

We acknowledge that this counteranalogy to Morriston's does not eliminate all moral questions. However, we are attempting to portray a situation that resembles far more closely the biblical text. This is a picture that is markedly different from the one painted by critics who typically portray a flawed scenario in which God commands the US president to use nuclear weapons against a peaceful foreign country for little or no reason at all.

Summary

- Some raise legal objections to the biblical text and say that "not sparing anyone that breathed" would be considered "genocide" in today's international human rights courts. Even if we say that we are only talking about killing *part* of a people group and dispossessing the rest, the critic will say that our argument fails; our position still doesn't square with international law.

- Actually, as we look at specific international laws and rulings from human rights courts, our interpretation of these biblical texts simply does *not* qualify as "genocide." Rulings consistently show that there must be *intent* "to destroy, in whole or in part, a national, ethnical, racial or religious group"; this intent along with the following conditions—killing, causing serious bodily or mental harm, inflicting conditions that would lead to a group's physical destruction, and so on— would qualify as "genocide."

- However, we have noted that the intent is not to destroy, say, the Canaanite peoples but to put an end to their pernicious *criminal* influence—activities that are not trivial but would be prosecutable in virtually all Western countries.

- Even the displacement of persons cannot be defined as "genocide" in international law courts; this charge has been repeatedly rejected in multiple rulings. The intent (*mens rea*) must be to destroy another people *physically*. The mere dissolution of a group does not, by itself, constitute genocide.

- One ruling affirms the Genocide Convention's goal: "The aim of the Genocide Convention is to prevent the intentional destruction of entire human groups, and the part targeted must be significant enough to have an impact on the group as a whole." Another ruling (on events in the former Yugoslavia) stated that to count as genocide, the intention must be a people's "physical disappearance from the earth."

- While the charge of "genocide" carries a certain rhetorical punch, it is a false charge. It's not enough for opponents of biblical theism to draw rhetorical connections with recent historical events. Picking out verses that say "utterly destroy" while ignoring passages commanding Israel to "drive out" will not do.

- As to *theological* objections to our position, some might raise the slippery slope argument—if these seemingly clear texts to "utterly destroy" are called hyperbole, why not say the same about the resurrection of Jesus? In reply, we are dealing with a different type of literature in Joshua than in the Gospels, and we don't have conflicting resurrection narratives where one says Christ's body is no longer in the tomb while another says his body is still in the tomb. We approach Revelation as a book that is highly symbolic, no matter how people may attempt to literalize the "beast," the "dragon," the "144,000," and "1,000 years."

- A good rule of thumb is that we should *always treat the Bible literarily* (according to the author's intended literary genre), but we should *not always treat it literally* (which would lead to absurdities).

- Some might claim that if these war texts are hyperbolic, then interpreters are liable to *miscommunication*. But this still doesn't show that the text ought always to be taken literally. The problem is not restricted to Scripture alone; it applies to any work of literature.

- We run the risk of distorting the meaning of Scripture by trying to accommodate the secularist with a more "appealing" version of the biblical text (like the "Jefferson Bible," in which all references to Jesus's miracles or unique identity claims are removed). But doing so would leave us with a text that would have very little meaning for the peoples of most times and most cultures.

- Another attempt to challenge the biblical account is the use of *false analogies*—such as imagining a US president's announcement that God told him to obliterate the nation of Iran. Such analogies are problematic at many different points (president vs. proven prophet, nontheocratic United States vs. theocratic Israel, Iranians not engaged in morally-reprehensible activities vs. the Canaanites' practices, etc.).

PART 3

Is It Always Wrong to Kill Innocent People?

11

Divine Command Theory

PRELIMINARY CONSIDERATIONS

Reviewing Where We've Been

Before launching into the next several chapters, we want to do a bit of reviewing. In part 1, we explored a representative version of the argument that we discuss throughout much of this book. This was the claim that a "biblical theist"—a person who accepts both that God exists and that the Bible is his authoritative Word—is rationally committed to the following four inconsistent propositions, which we have tweaked and clarified along the way.

1 Any act that God commands us to perform is morally permissible.
2′ God is the author of the Bible.
3 It is morally impermissible for anyone to commit acts that violate the Crucial Moral Principle: "It is morally wrong to deliberately and mercilessly slaughter men, women, and children who are innocent of any serious wrongdoing."
4‴ The divine author of the Bible uses the text to perform the speech act of commanding us to perform acts that violate the Crucial Moral Principle.

Bradley points out that statements 1–4‴ are inconsistent. The biblical theist, however, is committed to 1 and 2′ and so must reject either 3 or 4‴. In part 2, we found reason to call into question the claim that a biblical theist is committed to 4′′′.

In particular, we argued that those accepting biblical authority are not at all required to believe that God commanded the extermination of every single man, woman, and child in Canaan ("genocide"); the biblical narrative is far more nuanced. Rather, the picture is predominantly one of God commanding the Israelites to drive out people who were occupying land the Israelites had title to. The Canaanites had been using that land for centuries, engaging in serious criminal practices without repentance. These practices had become so widespread and pervasive that Israel could not use the land for the purposes for which it was given them without themselves being corrupted by those practices and being led into imitating them.

Furthermore, there is evidence within the text itself that exceptions could readily be made and that Canaanites who rejected these evil practices were spared. Moreover, many of the accounts of killing are highly hyperbolic and are not to be taken as literally affirming the extermination of every single man, woman, and child. Also, we pointed out that this hyperbolic command was an occasional one—that is, a command for a specific situation and not a general requirement for all people at all times. According to Deuteronomy 20, all wars after Israel settled in the Promised Land were to be governed by the principle of noncombatant immunity.[1]

It is important to note that in addressing this question, we have been asking only what the author(s) of the text can plausibly be said to have affirmed. Specifically, we have asked what a person who accepts these texts as the authoritative Word of God is committed to and can defensibly claim as the text's affirmations or commands. In part 2, we did not attempt a moral evaluation of what these texts say.

Making Moral Assessments: What If Some Innocent Persons Were Killed?

At this point, however, moral evaluation clearly comes into play. No doubt the critic will respond that, even given our nuanced response, an important question still remains. In granting the general wickedness of the Canaanites and the presence of extensive hyperbole, it seems implausible that in such battles no innocent people were killed—or that every single innocent person escaped destruction. Hence, even if God does not command *us* with these texts to kill innocent people, and even if the texts don't envisage genocide, they still seem to suggest that a loving and just God did command killing the innocent on a particular occasion. This would mean that God on at least one occasion endorsed violations of the principle of noncombatant immunity.

Even those who grant the hyperbolic interpretation of these passages seem to concede this. Consider again Kenneth Kitchen's summary:

> The conflict with Canaanite city-state rulers in the south part of Canaan is worth close observation. After the battle for Gibeon, we see the Hebrews advance upon six towns in order, attacking and capturing them, killing their local kings and such of the inhabitants as had not gotten clear, and *moving on, not holding on to these places*. Twice over (10:15, 43), it is clearly stated that their strike force *returned to base camp at Gilgal*. So there was no sweeping takeover and occupation of this region at this point. And *no* total destruction of the towns attacked.[2]

He goes on to add:

> What happened in the south was repeated up north. Hazor was both leader and famed center for the north Canaanite kinglets. Thus, as in the south, the Hebrew force defeated the opposition; they captured their towns, killed rulers and less mobile inhabitants, and symbolically burned Hazor, and Hazor only, to emphasize its end of its local supremacy. Again Israel did *not* attempt to immediately hold on to Galilee; they remained *based at Gilgal* (cf. 14:6). These campaigns were essentially *disabling raids*; they were not territorial conquests with instant Hebrew occupation. The text is very clear about this.[3]

Kitchen notes that when the hyperbolic rhetoric is taken into account, the text states Israel engaged in disabling raids in which they killed the less mobile inhabitants—those who had not cleared out. William Lane Craig similarly concedes that "it was first and foremost a command to drive the tribes out of the land and to occupy it. Only those who remained behind were to be utterly exterminated."[4] So even if we accept that God did not command the *extermination* of all the Canaanites, and even if we grant the type of warfare involved, then it still seems to involve the killing of the innocent in the sense of killing noncombatants. Even if the phrases "they completely destroyed everyone in it" and "left no survivors" are obvious hyperbole, where does that leave us? How many women and children is it acceptable to slaughter before it becomes morally problematic? Raymond Bradley rejoins, "Does this make God any less guilty? What sort of perverted morality would lead one to conclude: 'Not all of them? Oh! I suppose that's OK then'?"[5]

This therefore brings us to our next question: Can the biblical theist reject 3? Proposition 3 states: "It is morally impermissible for anyone to commit acts that violate the Crucial Moral Principle"—namely, that "it is morally wrong to deliberately and mercilessly slaughter men, women, and children who are innocent of any serious wrongdoing." Bradley suggests a biblical theist cannot reject 3. "To do so would be to ally oneself with moral monsters like Genghis Khan, Hitler, Stalin, and Pol Pot. It would be to abandon all pretense to a belief in objective moral values. The denial of 3, then, would be tantamount to an embrace of moral nihilism. And no theist who believes in the Ten Commandments or the Sermon on the Mount could assent to that."[6]

Theologian Randal Rauser makes similar claims. Rauser states that biblical theists who reject 3 display "cognitive dissonance given their unqualified revulsion to the bludgeoning of Tutsi babies."[7] He asks, "Are we to believe an act of baby bludgeoning is suddenly defensible if we replace 'Hutu bludgeoner' with 'Israelite bludgeoner,' 'Tutsi baby' with 'Canaanite baby,' and 'the year 1994' with '1450 BC'?"[8] As we saw earlier, a similar line of thought is expressed by Richard Dawkins when he states that Joshua's destruction of Jericho is "morally indistinguishable from Hitler's invasion of Poland, or Saddam Hussein's massacres of the Kurds and the Marsh Arabs."[9]

Bradley claims that denying 3 has two problematic implications. First, denying 3 entails nihilism—that is, that no action is morally wrong. Second, denying 3 entails that the atrocities of Genghis Khan, Hitler, Stalin, and Pol Pot (Rauser adds the Hutus in Rwanda) were not morally wrong. Both stances are incompatible with the moral teachings of Scripture and hence with what a biblical theist is committed to.

William Lane Craig's Argument

Recently, William Lane Craig has provided a straightforward way that a biblical theist can deny the Crucial Moral Principle without embracing nihilism (the view that denies the meaningfulness of objective morality). Bradley's argument relies on the claim that the Crucial Moral Principle is a "universal principle" in the sense of "being exceptionless—of holding, that is, for all persons, places, and times." However, Craig argues that, technically, the Crucial Moral Principle is not an exceptionless principle. Reflecting on God's command to Abraham to sacrifice Isaac, Craig argues that in this highly unusual case, God, for the sake of some greater good, exempted Abraham from a moral principle that otherwise would be binding on him by commanding him to kill his son.[10] Craig suggests that the "same considerations are relevant for the case of the destruction of the Canaanites at God's command."[11]

Examining Three Claims

Craig's support for this conclusion consists of three premises.[12]

a "Our moral duties are constituted by the commands of a loving and just God."[13] (Craig here proposes a divine command theory of ethics whose thesis is analogous to the way water is constituted by H_2O; just as one can know what water is without knowing it is H_2O, so one can know one's moral duties without knowing they are divine commands.)

b A loving and just God, in normal circumstances, prohibits killing the innocent.

c In very unusual circumstances in the past, God commanded people to kill the innocent for the sake of some greater good.

These three claims entail that 3—it is morally impermissible to violate the Crucial Moral Principle—is false. Now a and b entail that killing the innocent is *normally* wrong. However, a and c entail that killing the innocent in those *highly unusual situations* is morally permissible, where a loving and just God had morally sufficient reasons and valuable ends in mind when commanding killing in these instances. Hence, strictly speaking, the Crucial Moral Principle does not hold for *all* persons, places, and times.

Is Craig's statement radical? Or novel? No, not at all. Another Christian philosopher, Philip Quinn, has noted the long tradition of interpretation in which God can, on rare occasions, grant exemptions to the moral rule against killing the innocent.[14] Stephen Grabill makes a similar observation:[15] Augustine, Bernard of Clairvaux, Duns Scotus, Gabriel Biel, William of Ockham, John Calvin, Francis Turretin, Peirre d'Ailly, and Paul Althaus all held that God could grant dispensations from the divine law; God could on specific occasions for the sake of a greater good exempt an individual from the obligation of the law. The history of this idea is rich and interesting.

What is important for our purposes, however, is that Craig's argument suggests a way biblical theists can reject 3—that violating the Crucial Moral Principle is never morally permissible—without committing themselves to either of the problematic implications that Bradley points to. Craig's position does not entail that no action is morally wrong (i.e., nihilism). Both a and b entail that, with the exception of a few highly unusual cases, killing of the innocent is wrong. Craig's position also does not commit a biblical theist to endorsing the atrocities of Genghis Khan, Hitler, Stalin, and Pol Pot or the genocide of the Tutsis in Rwanda. This would follow only if the biblical theist believes that Hitler, Stalin, and Genghis Khan or the Hutus were commanded by God to do what they did. However, nothing about Craig's position commits a biblical theist to this claim. Craig maintains that cases where God commands such killings are highly unusual past occurrences. He believes they occurred only because there is compelling scriptural evidence that they did. There is no comparable evidence that Hitler or Stalin received such a command, and in the absence of such evidence, "we should be highly skeptical of someone who says, 'God has commanded me to kill so-and-so!'"[16] In fact, a biblical Christian may have theological reasons for thinking that such commands would not occur outside of the extremely unusual events of salvation history recorded in Scripture.[17] Therefore, adopting this view, one could even accept that killing the innocent is, for practical purposes, absolutely wrong.[18]

The success of Craig's position depends on whether a biblical theist can rationally accept a, b, and c. The claim that a biblical Christian can accept b seems uncontroversial. The biblical theist already accepts that a loving and just God exists, and it is obvious that such a God would, in normal circumstances, prohibit killing the innocent. The question, then, is whether a biblical theist can accept a and c.

In chapters 12 through 14, we defend both a and b; there we will defend a divine command theory of ethics—"the thesis that our moral duties are constituted by the commands of a loving and just God."[19] There we will give some general definitions followed by false definitions and misrepresentations of divine command theory. Then in chapters 15 through 17, we will defend the thesis that in very unusual circumstances, God commanded people to kill the innocent for the sake of some greater good. In chapters 18 and 19, we will look at a final problem raised by this position—the concern that any fanatic today can get away with committing atrocities simply by saying God commanded to do it.

Summary

- Raymond Bradley has charged that the "biblical theist" must believe that what God, the author of Scripture, commands is morally permissible and that God commands us to violate the Crucial Moral Principle. So the believer must hold to a contradiction.

- We have argued that the believer is not required to believe God commanded literal extermination of the Canaanites but that they were to be driven out. The text speaks hyperbolically; it is an occasional (not universal) command—and thus not for *us* to carry out—and it presupposes that the Canaanites could have responded favorably to God, or at least fled without needing to fight against Israel. So, in principle, *every* Canaanite could have been spared.

- But what if some innocent people were killed? Has God commanded that on at least one occasion, the principle of noncombatant immunity be violated? Is that moral principle *exceptionless*? Is it possible that for the sake of some greater good, God commands the killing of the innocent? This brings us to the topic of divine commands.

• Our moral duties are constituted by the commands of a loving and just God (just like water is constituted by H_2O). Normally, God prohibits killing the innocent, but God may override this for a greater good. However, *this is not a radical or novel notion* either in theology or ethical theory. Nor does it commit us to overturning the Crucial Moral Principle as a general prohibition.

12

The Divine Command Theory of Obligation: What It Is—and Is Not

We saw earlier that William Lane Craig's purported solution to William Bradley's objection involved an appeal to a divine command theory of ethics. This view affirms that "moral rightness and wrongness consist in agreement and disagreement, respectively, with the will or commands of a loving God."[1] To many, this statement alone is enough to call into question the soundness of this response. Within contemporary secular discussions of ethics, a divine command theory is often proposed as a text-book case of how *not* to think about ethics. A generation ago the philosopher Peter Geach wrote, "In modern ethical treatises we find hardly any mention of God; and the idea that if there really is a God, His commandments might be morally relevant is wont to be dismissed by a short and simple argument that is generally regarded as irrefutable."[2] Geach's comments are no doubt an accurate description of how divine command theories are often viewed in contemporary secular ethics. A perusal of many ethics textbooks bears out Geach's suggestion that many thinkers simply reject out of hand any idea of divine command theory. And they usually do so by appealing to the same simple arguments to which Geach refers.[3]

However, in a recent critique of divine command theories, Mark Murphy notes that these dismissals are somewhat dated.[4] Within the field of philosophy of religion, such theories have undergone an unexpected revival. The work of people like Philip Quinn[5] and Robert Adams[6] has provided rigorous formulations and defenses of a divine command theory that have addressed the standard criticisms Geach refers to. Since their pioneering work, similar defenses have been made of divine command theories by a significant number of contemporary theists. Those who have defended these theories (or close versions) include John Hare,[7] William Alston,[8] William Lane Craig,[9] C. Stephen Evans,[10] Edward Wierenga,[11] Matthew Carey Jordan,[12] Janine Marie Idziak,[13] William Wainwright,[14] William Mann,[15] Thomas Carson,[16] Alvin Plantinga,[17] and David Baggett and Jerry Walls.[18]

In a book of this size, we can't review all the literature. In this and the next chapter, we'll clarify what divine command theory is (particularly the version articulated by Craig) before looking at objections to it based on Plato's Euthyphro argument (chaps. 13 and 14) and various other attempts to challenge it (chaps. 15 through 17). We will conclude that Craig's appeal to this theory is defensible.

What Is a Divine Command Theory?

Craig makes the argument that if theism is true, then we can plausibly explain the nature of moral obligations or duties by identifying them with God's commands; this is analogous to the way "we explain the nature of water by identifying it with H_2O or explain the nature of heat by identifying it with molecular motion."[19]

Craig appears to use the word "God" here as a title or description.[20] He makes clear that he is using the definition of God made famous by the eleventh-century theologian Anselm of Canterbury. "God" is the title given to any personal being who is "the greatest conceivable being" (or "greatest possible being"), who is "worthy of worship"—just as the title "Caesar" designated "whoever is emperor of Rome." On this understanding, the word "God" functions more like a title than a proper noun. Furthermore, if this being is worthy of worship or maximally great, then it must be "morally perfect." That is, this being must have certain character traits essentially or necessarily—being loving, generous, kind, faithful, and so on.[21] In Craig's debate with atheist philosopher Stephen Law, he affirmed:

> God, by definition, is a being which is necessarily good. Peter Millican, Professor of Philosophy at Oxford University, says, "what makes the Supreme Being worthy of worship is not simply his power but rather his moral excellence. . . . For the Supreme Being to be an *appropriate* object of religious attitudes, therefore, He must above all be morally good." So you cannot have, literally speaking, an evil

God because he would not be worthy of worship. What you *could* have would be an evil Creator of the universe who is not God.[22]

Similarly in his debate with Sam Harris, Craig stated:

> God is a being worthy of worship. Any being that is not worthy of worship is not God. And therefore God must be perfectly good and essentially good. More than that, as Anselm saw, God is the greatest conceivable being, and therefore he is the very paradigm of goodness itself. He is the greatest good. So once you understand the concept of God, you can see that asking, "Well, why is God good?" is sort of like asking, "Why are all bachelors unmarried?" It's the very concept of the greatest conceivable being, of being worthy of worship that entails the essential goodness of God.[23]

So as Craig has defined his terms, then, it is impossible for God not to be essentially good, in the same way it is impossible for Caesar not to be the emperor of Rome. A person might claim there is another person who currently holds this title, and one might dispute as to who at a particular point in time in fact did—saying that Nero is Caesar as opposed to Claudius, let's say. But one cannot claim that someone is Caesar but is not the emperor of Rome. Similarly, as Craig has defined his terms, it is impossible for any being to be God and not be essentially good. One can deny that any existent being is God, and one can deny certain candidates such as Yahweh or Allah are God. But if a being is God, then he is good. This point is an important one. We will argue that *some important celebrated objections to Craig's divine command theory fail precisely because they do not note this point.*[24]

In emphasizing God as *loving* and *just* as well as the relationship between *God's commands* and *moral obligations*, we could call Craig's view a version of the so-called modified divine command theory.[25] This view has been defended most ably by Christian philosopher Robert Adams.[26] Adams asserts that "ethical wrongness *is* (i.e., is identical with) the property of being contrary to the commands of a loving God,"[27] and the similarities to Craig's version of the divine command theory are fairly clear; indeed, it can be rightly said that Craig is elaborating on and popularizing Adams's argument.[28]

Two Important Aspects of Divine Command Theory

Craig specifies two important aspects of the divine command theory as he presents it.[29] First, this understanding of the divine command theory deals with the *right* (*moral obligations or duties*) and not the broader category of the *good* (*value*)—this category includes, for example, the topic of beauty (aesthetics), virtue, and even rationality. On the other hand, the *right* is much more specific; it has the quality of "being morally permitted, being morally forbidden or prohibited, and being morally obligatory or required."[30] This is different from the nature of goodness in general. For example, it is a *good* thing for you to donate a kidney to a stranger in need of one, but it is not a *duty* that you donate your kidney to a stranger. What may be a good thing to do is not identical to what is morally obligatory.[31] Goodness is much broader than the concept of duty (the *right*).

Here many critics of this version of the divine command theory get matters terribly confused. They assume that divine commands "define" goodness—a point that becomes clear when they use the Euthyphro argument, which we discuss later on. No, the divine command theory is not a theory about the nature of goodness in general, which deals with value and what is praiseworthy or commendable. Acts that are obligatory (*duties*) are things we are *required* to do. Not doing so without adequate justification renders us blameworthy, and others can justifiably censure us, rebuke us, and even punish us. Failure to comply makes one guilty and in need of forgiveness.

Second, Craig notes that the claim that moral obligations are *identical* with God's commands needs to be distinguished from two other, different claims. These are (1) *the claim that the word "wrong" means "prohibited by God"* and (2) *the claim that one cannot know or recognize one's moral obligations unless one believes in God*. Craig states:

> To give an illustration, think of light. Light is a certain visible range of the electromagnetic spectrum. But obviously, that isn't the meaning of the word "light". People knew how to use the word "light" long before they discovered its physical nature. And, I might also add, they certainly knew the difference between light and darkness long before they understood the physics of light. Now, in exactly the same way, we can know the meaning of moral terms like "good" and "evil", "right" and "wrong", and know the difference between good and evil, without being aware that the good is grounded in God ontologically [i.e., in reality].[32]

Craig here is taking for granted certain developments in contemporary philosophy of language spearheaded by certain key thinkers.[33] They have helpfully distinguished between the idea that *two words have a synonymous meaning* and the idea that *the things to which those words refer are identical*. One of the most famous examples is the relationship between water and H_2O. Water *is* H_2O—this is a claim of *identity*. The liquid on earth that we call water is dihydrogen monoxide (or H_2O). However, the claim that "water is H_2O" is *not* true in virtue of the meaning of the words (what philosophers call an *analytic* truth). Rather, we discover this through empirical investigation. Moreover, a competent speaker of English could refer to "water" without needing to know anything about the atomic structure H_2O. Similar examples are available: "the morning star is the evening star" (i.e., Venus), "Mark Twain is Samuel Langhorne Clemens," or "Superman is Clark Kent."

Despite the careful articulations of divine command theories that have taken place in the last forty years, critics of divine command theories fail to explore or grasp these distinctions. This will become quite clear in our examination of two such critics below.

Two Kinds of Mistakes Critics Make

Objection Based on Mistaken Meaning (Semantics)

We saw that *right* and *good* (or *duty* and *value*) are not identical terms and that the "modified divine command theory" assumes this distinction. Yet a surprising number of contemporary philosophers mistakenly label divine command theories as theories about the "meaning of the word good."[34] With this flawed starting point, they then attempt to dismantle divine command theories by offering arguments to show that the words "good" and "commanded by God" do not have a synonymous meaning. Harry Gensler is an example:

> Imagine an atheist who says the following: "kindness is good, but there is no God." *If "x is good" meant "God desires x"*, then this claim would be self-contradictory (since it would mean "God desires kindness, but there is no God"). But it isn't self-contradictory. So "x is good" doesn't mean "God desires x."[35]

Gensler is probably correct when he says that the word "good" does not mean "desired by God" just as the word "water" probably does not mean "H_2O." An ancient Greek who accepted an Aristotelian account of reality as opposed to an atomic one could without self-contradiction claim, "The Aegean Sea is water and atoms don't exist." But this doesn't tell us that water is not H_2O, nor does Gensler's point show that moral obligations aren't divine commands. The claim that two words aren't synonymous in their meaning is quite compatible with the thesis that those words both refer to the same thing. The examples of H_2O and water, and molecular motion and heat, illustrate this.

Objection Based on Moral Knowledge (Epistemic)

Similarly, many critics of divine command theory continue to argue that because people can *know* the truth of moral claims independently and prior to any belief they have about *God or divine commands*, a divine command theory is false. Critics making this blunder include Patrick Nowell-Smith,[36] James Cornman and Keith Lehrer,[37] Louise Antony,[38] and Walter Sinnott-Armstrong.[39]

It is, of course, true that many people believe in the existence of right and wrong without believing in any divine revelation or even in God. It is also true that many people form moral beliefs independently of and prior to beliefs they form about God. Atheists and agnostics can know their moral duties without belief in God. But that doesn't show that moral obligations are not identical with God's commands. For centuries people recognized, swam in, sailed on, and drank water before they knew anything about modern chemistry. That fact doesn't prove that water is not H_2O.

In a somewhat similar vein, the atheist Paul Kurtz makes an argument from "exemplary lives."[40] He adds, "If God is essential, then how can it be that millions of people who do not believe in God, nevertheless behave morally? On [Craig's] view, they should not. And so, [Craig's] God is not essential to the moral life."[41]

The problem with such an argument is that Craig's view doesn't entail that people who don't believe in God cannot behave morally or have moral knowledge. Craig writes, "It would, indeed, be arrogant and ignorant to claim that people cannot be good without belief in God. But that was not the question."[42] He writes elsewhere: "My concern here is with moral ontology [i.e., the actual grounding of moral obligation] not moral epistemology [i.e., having moral beliefs/knowledge]."[43] In fact, Kurtz gives his response (above) to Craig in a debate, even though Craig's opening statement began with this very point: "Let me say just at the outset, as clearly as I can, that I agree that a person can be moral without having a belief in God, but that is not the topic under debate. We are not talking about goodness without *belief in God*, but rather goodness without *God*."[44] So it is odd that Kurtz would make this argument.[45]

Atheist Jerry Coyne makes a similar mistake when he argues that secular European countries like Sweden and Denmark "are full of well-behaved and well-meaning citizens, not criminals and sociopaths running amok."[46] Kurtz's and Coyne's observations about the character of some atheists may well be true, but all they show is that people can recognize moral obligations and live in accordance with them without believing in God. That no more shows that moral obligations can exist without God or that moral obligations are not divine commands than the fact that for centuries people could recognize water and swim in it without knowing anything about how modern chemistry shows that water is H_2O.

Note well: *a divine command theory is not the claim that morality is based on knowledge of, or belief in, commands revealed in a sacred text such as the*

Bible, Torah, or Qur'an. While most divine command theorists accept that God has revealed his commands through a sacred text, this is due to other theological commitments they have, independent of belief in a divine command theory. A divine command theorist could argue that, in principle, the rightness or wrongness of an action is identical to and constituted by God's commands and prohibitions but that we *know* what is right and wrong through our conscience and not from any purported written revelation like the Bible. In fact, the divine command theorist Philip Quinn has suggested this scenario.[47]

Moreover, even some of those divine command theorists who accept the authority of a sacred text through which God issues commands have emphasized that God can and does make known basic moral duties and prohibitions by other means and that those who don't believe in God can know what God's commands are by those methods. For example, the philosophers George Berkeley and William Paley—both Christians—assumed that the criterion for right and wrong is the will of God and that God desires the happiness of his creatures. Knowing that God desires the happiness of his creatures, we can discern what actions are right or wrong by examining which general rules, when followed, tend to promote the happiness of his creatures.[48] Given this approach, one can know right and wrong at least *partially* as a result of following this method.

Interestingly, this is comparable to what secular utilitarians do: they follow what could be called the "greatest happiness principle" that seeks the greatest happiness for the greatest number. However, we should note that these utilitarians would differ about the definition of happiness. For example, utilitarians like Jeremy Bentham have emphasized what enhances short-term physical pleasure and minimizes physical pain while others have emphasized the deeper and more satisfying—though long-term—pursuit of cultural and intellectual happiness. And certain secular utilitarians like Peter Singer have denied any intrinsic worth to individual human beings since the "greatest number" takes priority over the individual, who is often seen as a means to the end of benefiting society. At any rate, the point we are making here is that some theists who endorse a divine command theory have emphasized that God is attempting to maximize creaturely well-being, and they have advocated a method much like utilitarians have used to make moral judgments rather than appealing to the Bible.

In a similar way, what ethicists call a "moral sense theorist" or "intuitionist" could argue that God has so constituted people that they immediately perceive certain actions to be either prohibited or permissible—that torturing babies for fun is wrong or that one ought to be kind rather than selfish.[49] The Scriptures themselves suggest this kind of intuitive awareness—that those without the Scriptures can know that it is wrong to break treaties, deliver vulnerable refugees into the hands of their enemies, and rip open pregnant women (Amos 1–2); that humans can recognize moral duties that should not be violated (Rom. 1:28–32); and so on.

So the divine command theory Craig proposes simply claims that moral obligations, moral prohibitions, and moral permissions are identical with that which has been commanded, forbidden, and permitted by God. Questions about how we know these moral matters (moral epistemology), whether a purported sacred text is divinely authoritative, or how we use moral language are logically distinct questions. Divine command theorists may or may not have answers to these questions, but that is beside the point and is distinct from the general thrust of divine command theory.

An Attempted Revision of Objections to Divine Command Theory

More sophisticated critics have acknowledged the error in these critiques of divine command theory, and they have attempted to offer updated responses without the kinds of mistakes we've mentioned. The atheist philosopher Wesley Morriston is one such example. He grants that Craig "is not concerned with the foundation of moral knowledge. He acknowledges that theists and atheists often make similar moral judgments on similar epistemic grounds. But only theists, he says, can give an adequate account of the ontological ground or foundation of morality."[50] However, despite this, there is still an "obvious problem" for those holding to a divine command view of ethics, says Morriston—namely, the existence of people who don't believe that there is a God. Why is this a problem? Morriston answers:

> The reason is that commands are speech acts in which a person tells others what to do. In order successfully to issue a command, one must *deliver* it to its intended recipients. This brings us right back to the problem of the reasonable nonbeliever. On the face of it, God has not succeeded in speaking to *her*. And since she is a *reasonable* non-believer, God has not even succeeded in putting her in a position in which she *should* have "heard" a divine command. How, then, can *she* be subject to God's commands? How can *her* moral obligations be understood by reference to what God has commanded *her* to do?[51]

Let us grant that divine commands are speech acts in which God tells another what to do.[52] The problem appears to be that, if a person does not believe in God and that person's nonbelief is reasonable, then that person cannot have "heard" God issue a command.[53] But God cannot command people to do something unless they recognize that they have heard the command and that it is God doing the commanding.

This, however, seems implausible. Surely it is perfectly possible to hear a command or discern a speech act, such as a promise or assertion, without knowing who the author of the speech act was. Consider the New Testament book of Hebrews. Some have speculated about who the author was (e.g., Barnabas, Apollos), but the book was written anonymously; and many scholars contend we just do not know who the author was. (The church father Origen put it best: "But who wrote the epistle, in truth God knows.")[54] Does it follow that one cannot read or interpret the speech acts made by the human author in that text? Suppose you receive an anonymous death threat in the mail, ominously stating, "I am going to kill you. Watch out!" Does it follow that you haven't been truly threatened since you don't know who wrote it? Or suppose you are hiking in the woods and you hear someone crying out for help. But you have no idea who it is. Does it follow that you should show no concern since you don't know who is calling out and so don't *really* "hear" anyone? Of course not!

Now Morriston does show some awareness of the problem; he points out that even if a "reasonable non-believer" can be aware that a particular action is prohibited or permitted, his lack of belief in God will prevent him being "subject" to the command.

> Even if he is aware of a "sign" that he somehow manages to interpret as a "command" not to steal, how can he be subject to that command if he doesn't know who issued it, or that it was issued by a competent authority?
>
> To appreciate the force of this question, imagine that you have received a note saying, "Let me borrow your car. Leave it unlocked with the key in the ignition, and I will pick it up soon." If you know that the note is from your spouse, or that it is from a friend to whom you owe a favor, you may perhaps have an obligation to obey this instruction. But if the note is unsigned, the handwriting is unfamiliar, and you have no idea who the author might be, then it's as clear as day that you have no such obligation. In the same way, it seems that even if our reasonable non-believer gets so far as to interpret one of Adams' "signs" as conveying the message, "Do not steal," he will be under no obligation to comply with this instruction unless and until he discovers the divine source of the message.[55]

Here, Morriston joins together two issues that should be kept separate: (1) whether the person recognizes the command as issued by a "competent authority" and (2) whether the person recognizes "the divine source" of the command. To be subject to the command in the way Morriston suggests, only the *first*, not the second, is necessary.

To see this, consider a slight variation of Morriston's analogy. In the 1990s, the New Zealand police force merged with the Ministry of Transport. Prior to this time, these two were separate organizations. The former dealt with criminal offenses and the latter driving offenses. After the merger, both fell under the jurisdiction of the police.

With this background in mind, consider the following hypothetical situation. Prior to the 1990s, a Canadian tourist visits New Zealand. She is driving down State Highway One. Looking in her rearview mirror, she sees a black and white car with red flashing lights driving behind her and hears a voice over the loudspeaker booming, "Pull over." Unaware of the subtleties of New Zealand's system, she mistakenly believes that the order comes from the police, when in reality it is from the Ministry of Transport.[56] Does it follow that she isn't "subject" to the command or has not "heard" the command? The answer is clearly negative, regardless of whether it is the police or the Ministry of Transport. The Canadian tourist recognizes that someone in authority has ordered her to pull over. The fact that she cannot identify who issued the order, or which particular authority it is, is irrelevant.[57]

One could make a similar point about federal and state law. A person who was aware that a particular law existed but was unsure whether the law was passed by the federal or state authorities would still have legitimately received a command. Whether the law originates from the state or federal government is irrelevant; the law is legally obligatory. And it is legally obligatory independent of whether a person recognizes it to be so or not. In both cases a legitimate authority has passed the law, and hence all people (in the jurisdiction) are subject to it.

Examples like this show that this argument of Morriston's is mistaken. To be "subject" to the command in the sense mentioned, one does not need to recognize that the command has divine origin. One simply has to recognize an action as prohibited and the prohibition as being authoritative and having a claim on one's own behavior. We would contend that reasonable nonbelievers plausibly do experience obligations as authoritative demands or prescriptions on their conduct. The idea that moral properties are both prescriptive (obligatory) and have authority over our conduct seems to be part of our commonsense, intuitive, pretheoretical moral experience.

Summary

• Moral *rightness* and *wrongness*—*duties* and *prohibitions*—consist in agreement and disagreement, respectively, with divine commands.

- Many philosophers and other scholars dismiss divine command theories, but these criticisms are often naïve and virtually all outdated. Excellent philosophical work has been done to defend the coherence of divine command theory (e.g., Philip Quinn, Robert Adams).

- Our moral duties are constituted by the commands of a loving and just God (just like water is constituted by H_2O or the nature of heat is constituted by molecular motion).

- *God* is a title (as "Caesar" is the title for "the emperor of Rome")—a description of the greatest conceivable being, a being that is worthy of worship. So if some evil being is responsible for creating the world, this being cannot be called God. An evil being is not worthy of worship. Goodness is essential to God. If a being is God, then he is good—just as a bachelor is an unmarried male.

- We must emphasize God's character as *loving* and *just*, which must be assumed to make sense of God's commands (and our moral obligations).

- The divine command theory deals with the *right* (*moral obligations or duties*) and not the broader category of the *good* (*value*)—this category includes duties but also beauty (aesthetics), virtue, and even rationality. On the other hand, the *right* is much more specific. Donating a kidney to a stranger is *good*, but it is not a *duty* ("*right*").

- God's *commands* are our *duties*, and this is true even if people don't *know* that these are commanded by God. This is like knowing what water is without necessarily knowing that it is H_2O. People can know their duty

without knowing that this duty is grounded in God.

- Some critics of divine command theory wrongly assume that "good" equals "commanded by God" (this often comes up in the Euthyphro argument).

- Critics also assert that they *know* moral truths independently of any belief they have about God or divine commands. We can agree that atheists can *know* moral truths, but there is a difference between *knowing* and *being*—between goodness without *belief* in God (which is not at issue) and goodness without the *existence* of God.

- A divine command theory does not make the claim that morality is based on knowledge of, or belief in, commands revealed in a sacred text such as the Bible, Torah, or Qur'an. For example, some divine command theorists believe that we can discern what actions are right and wrong by examining general rules and seeing what promotes the happiness of creatures. This is in line with a God who commands and desires the happiness of his creatures. One can follow such a method—or even basic moral intuitions (Amos 1–2; Rom. 1:28–32)—without using sacred texts and get a clear understanding of basic human duties and thus divine commands.

- Some claim that for us to be bound to God's commands, we would have to "hear" God first to know to obey. But we can know something is authoritative without knowing its precise origin (e.g., the author of the book of Hebrews is unknown to us, but Christians take the commands in this book seriously). And we take the law of the land seriously, even though we may not know the origination of these laws (local, state, or federal).

13

Arbitrary Divine Commands?

THE EUTHYPHRO DILEMMA

As we have seen, key objections to divine command theory actually attack a straw man (the semantic and epistemological), and Morriston's attempt to salvage the epistemological objection fails. Though prevalent in the literature, these objections are not normally those considered decisive. The reason critics typically see a divine command theory as coming to ruin is due to a more substantive family of objections clustered around an argument known as the Euthyphro dilemma.[1]

So what is this dilemma? In Plato's *Euthyphro* dialogue, Socrates is conversing with Euthyphro, who is on his way to prosecute his elderly father for murdering one of the household servants. Socrates wonders whether such legal action is fitting for a son; instead, it seems an "unholy" breach of loyalty. Eventually the topic of discussion comes around to defining what "piety" or "holiness" actually is. Then Socrates poses the most famous question of the entire dialogue: "Is what is holy holy because the gods approve it, or do they approve it because it is holy?"[2] Initially, Euthyphro claims it is what the gods approve or find pleasing that determines piety or holiness. Socrates, however, shows this to be an arbitrary criterion—the will of the gods determines what is good, and they could just as easily will the opposite. Euthyphro comes to see that the gods are pleased with holiness or justice because these qualities are virtuous in themselves.[3]

Most contemporary discussions of the Euthyphro dilemma don't focus on Plato's original argument, which was applied to polytheistic religions and which exposed the contradictions bound up with such a view. Rather, they involve an adaptation of the argument for a monotheistic context, and they are rhetorically cast as a dilemma: "Are actions wrong because God prohibits them, or does God prohibit them because they are wrong?" Many a questioner assumes that *no matter which* option is taken, the result will be theological trouble.

Philosopher James Rachels gives a useful summary of the landscape. "Suppose God commands us to do what is right. Then *either* (a) the right actions are right because he commands them *or* (b) he commands them because they are right."[4] Rachels goes on to note that either option yields problems for the believer in divine commands:

> If we take option (a), then God's commands are, from a moral point of view, arbitrary; moreover, the doctrine of the goodness of God is rendered meaningless. . . . If we take option (b), then we have admitted there is a standard of right and wrong that is independent of God's will.[5]

Rachels concludes: "Therefore, we must *either* regard God's commands as arbitrary, and give up the doctrine of the goodness of God, *or* admit there is a standard of right and wrong that is independent of God's will and give up the theological definitions of right and wrong."[6]

Obviously, a divine command theorist can't accept the second option (b). To take that option—that God commands actions *because* they are right—entails that rightness and wrongness exist independently of and prior to God's commands. For his position to be defensible, the argument proceeds, the believer in divine commands must adopt a version of option (a). But that option, too, is said to be problematic.

Rachels offers two fairly standard criticisms of divine command theory. The first is that a divine command theory makes God's commands *arbitrary*. It's like an episode of the television series *M*A*S*H* in which chaplain Father Mulcahy is shocked to read a misprint in the Bibles he's received for the troops. Exodus 20:14 reads: "Thou *shalt* commit adultery." A critic like Rachels would ask something approximating this: Why can't God command the opposite of what he does if morality is the creation of God's will? So why can't God command murder and adultery just as he prohibits them? This we'll call *the arbitrariness objection*.

The second objection Rachels highlights is that divine command theory renders *empty* or *meaningless* the doctrine that God is good. That is, if what is good is what God commands, then when we say an action is good, we are saying, "That action is what God commands." And what sense does it make to say, "God is good," which means nothing more than, "God is what God commands"? This we label *the emptiness objection.* It is these two objections that will occupy us for this and the next chapters.

The Arbitrariness Objection

As with the Father Mulcahy example above, Rachels argues that the divine command theory leads to all manner of troubles "because it represents God's commands arbitrary. It means God could have given us different commands just as easily. He could have commanded us to be liars and then lying, and not truthfulness, would be right."[7]

Now we can distinguish two versions of this objection. One is that a divine command theory implies that *God's commands are arbitrary*—that God can have no reasons of any sort for commanding as he does and that his decisions are purely whimsical and capricious. The other version is that a divine command theory implies that *the content of morality is itself arbitrary.*[8] We will examine both versions of the objection below—with an excursus in between addressing a related objection raised by the atheist philosopher J. L. Mackie.

"Arbitrary Because God Has No Reasons" Objection

Philosopher Russ Shafer-Landau argues that a divine command theory makes God's commands arbitrary. The reasoning is this: *God can have no reasons for issuing the commands he does.* Shafer-Landau offers the following dilemma to show how this is so: "Either there are, or there are not, excellent reasons that support God's prohibitions on (say) torture and rape. If there are no such reasons, then God's choice is arbitrary"—that is, "insufficiently well-supported by reason and argument."[9] On the other hand, if God issues "commands *based on* excellent reasons . . . then it is those excellent reasons, and not the fact of God's having commanded various actions, that make those actions right. The excellent reasons that support the requirements of charity and kindness are what make it right to be charitable and kind."[10]

This argument is flawed as Shafer-Landau gets a bit slippery with his terminology. He says that if God has excellent reasons for his commands, then those reasons—and not the command—*make* the commanded action right. But in this context, the word "make" can be used in two very different senses—the *constitutive* explanation and the *motivational* explanation:[11]

- *Constitutive* explanation: This kind of explanation explains or lays out the factors that *make up* or *constitute* a thing. What *makes* a cup of clear liquid a cup of water is the fact that the liquid is H_2O.
- *Motivational* explanation: This kind of explanation attempts to tell us *why* an agent acted the way they did by giving us the *reasons* and or *motivations* the agent acted upon. A parent's love for his child *makes* him persevere over the long haul of parenting. This is a different explanation from laying out the factors that constitute a thing or make it up.

Now let's go back to Shafer-Landau's central affirmation: If God's commands are based on reasons, then it is *those reasons*—not God's commands—that *make* the commanded actions right. So if Shafer-Landau is using the word *makes* to refer to a *motivational* explanation, then his affirmation is quite correct. If God has *reasons* for commanding as he does, then those reasons do *motivate* God's decision to command what he does.

The problem here is that, given this *motivational* use of the word *makes*, Shafer-Landau isn't saying anything that divine command theorists would disagree with. When a divine command theorist claims that God's commands *make* an action wrong, they're claiming that God's commands provide a *motivational* explanation for why actions are wrong. Obviously, God's *reasons* for commanding something are not that he has commanded it!

As we have noted earlier, divine command theorists offer a *constitutive* explanation of moral obligation. The claim of Craig, Adams, Alston, and others is that moral obligations are identical with or constituted by God's commands, in the way water is identical with or constituted by H_2O. So for Shafer-Landau's argument to have any bite to it, he can't simply affirm what divine command theorists affirm. So what happens when he uses the word *makes* to refer to a *constitutive* explanation, not a *motivational* one? Let's make the adjustment to see: If God's commands are based on reasons, then it is those reasons and not God's commands that are identical with moral rightness. Once this is realized, however, Shafer-Landau's argument is clearly false.

Suppose we note that a judge has excellent reasons for issuing a verdict in a case. Shafer-Landau's reasoning would entail that those reasons *are* the verdict. Or if a university has good reasons for conferring a degree on a doctoral candidate, then those reasons are *identical to* the conferral of a degree. Or suppose John has good reasons for being a bachelor; then those reasons would be identical with being a bachelor. Such conclusions or inferences are, of course, seriously flawed.[12]

Elsewhere in the same essay, Shafer-Landau offers a different argument to show that divine command theory makes morality arbitrary. Suppose we grant that God has an excellent reason for commanding us not to rape. Wouldn't the reason be that rape truly is morally wrong? And if the reason is something *other* than the recognition that rape is morally wrong, then this would appear to be the wrong kind of motivating reason for issuing the command.[13] Shafer-Landau states,

> Absent divine disapproval, nothing is immoral. And yet if we want to see God's moral proclamations as backed by excellent reasons (rather than as arbitrary choices), we are compelled to think that it is the immoral nature of certain actions that provide God with the best possible reasons for their prohibition.[14]

This, however, seems mistaken. God could prohibit rape for reasons other than the fact that rape is morally wrong, and the prohibition could still be backed by the right kind of nonarbitrary reasons. Consider a case of a violent rape, and remove the command of God from the equation. Without the command of God, this action would not have the property of being wrong. However, it could still have other nonarbitrary characteristics: being an action that causes severe harm, being an action that violates someone's autonomy, being an action that expresses domination and contempt for the person in question, being an action that is unloving, being an action that is contrary to the flourishing of the victim, being an action that—if allowed—would not promote the general well-being of society, and so on. Of course, God could prohibit rape because it has these characteristics, and his doing so would seem to be the right kind of motivating reason for issuing the command in question.

Note also that divine command theory proposed by Craig, Quinn, Adams, and others is a theory of moral *obligation* (*wrong* and *right*) and not a broader theory of *value* (or *goodness*) in general. Keep in mind our distinction between *duty* (the *right*) and *value* (the *good*). We noted that goodness cannot be reduced to moral obligation; we observed that there are many *good* things (like donating a kidney to a stranger) but that something being good does not *obligate* us to carry it out.

So if we could theoretically or logically remove God's *command* (and thus *duty*) from the equation, an action like rape would not be *wrong*, but this act would still have *bad-making qualities*, and the *badness* (as distinct from *wrongness*) of the action could also be part of the motivating reasons for prohibiting it—such as not enhancing human flourishing. To illustrate, consider the *goodness* of being healthy rather than sick due to deteriorating kidneys—a *bad* state of affairs. There are *good* acts that would enhance human flourishing—such as donating a kidney to a stranger—but the fact that such acts are good does not *obligate* us to do all of them.

Perhaps the perceived problem here is that the existence of such goodness-enhancing reasons makes a divine command theory appear explanatorily unnecessary. If an action's causing severe harm is sufficient reason for God to prohibit it, why will it not also be true that the action's causing severe harm provides us with sufficient reason not to do it (quite apart from any command that God might issue)? And hence God's commands are not needed to explain the nature of moral obligation.

As we've already suggested, this perception is mistaken for at least two reasons. First, *it relies on fallacious reasoning*. Even if certain characteristics of an action provide *God* with a sufficient reason for prohibiting that action, it doesn't follow that (apart from God's issuing a command) *we* have sufficient reason to refrain from it. God, being omniscient, is aware of numerous facts and reasons which humans are not. Hence, while these facts can give *God* reason to prohibit a given action, they don't provide *us* with a reason to not do that action *because we do not know about them and cannot know*. But not only is God all-knowing. He is also impartial, loving, just, and so on. So he will have a *different* motivational state than that of human beings.

But second, even if one grants this kind of reasoning, it's not clearly a problem for the divine command theorist. Suppose the matter of severe harm provides us with sufficient reason to *refrain* from rape (apart from any consideration of God's issuing a command). Or we may have sufficient reasons to *perform* some action, but these still may not *obligate* us to carry out that action apart from God's command. That only follows if one equates obligations with what we have a sufficient reason to do. But these aren't the same thing. Stephen Evans observes:

> People frequently have reasons to perform actions, even powerful and decisive reasons, which they have no moral obligation to do. Suppose I am offered $5,000 to give a lecture this afternoon. The lecture is one I have given before and will require little work for me. I have the time to give the lecture and no pressing responsibilities that would conflict. In this situation I have very powerful reasons indeed to accept the invitation, but it does not follow I am morally obligated to do so.[15]

Evans observes that if a person spent the afternoon reading a novel instead of giving the lecture, she might be judged unwise or frivolous, but not immoral.

Adams makes the same point. Imagine a situation in which abundant reasons support you not walking on the lawn. However, those reasons give you no grounds for caring much or feeling guilty about doing so. Suppose also that it would be irrational in this situation for other people to make you feel that you have to stay off the lawn or to blame and reproach you for walking on it. Adams plausibly suggests that in such a case, while it might be best that you don't walk on the lawn, there is no *obligation* to stay off it. The fundamental point is this: *moral obligation is not identical with what one has good reasons to do.*[16] Obligations involve a certain type of reason to act: one that involves a demand with which we must comply, one by which others can rationally blame us and reproach us for failing to do so, one for which we can rightly be held accountable and feel guilty for violating, and one that is rational to inculcate into others.

Divine command theorists like Adams, Evans, and Craig argue plausibly, we believe, that these features of moral obligation are best explained by identifying obligations with demands made by a *personal being* rather than in terms of *facts* or *reasons* abstracted from particular contexts.

Excursus: God's Commands and Prior Reasons

Before we look at the second "arbitrariness objection," perhaps here is the place to address a matter related to the first arbitrariness objection, which dealt with God having no reasons for issuing his commands. The late Oxford philosopher J. L. Mackie has presented a different, though related, argument against divine command theory—what can be called an appeal to "prior reasons." Here is his argument:

> The commands of a legitimate human ruler do not *create* obligations: if such a ruler tells you to do X, this makes it obligatory for you to do X only if it is *already* obligatory for you to do whatever the ruler tells you (within the sphere in which X lies). The same applies to God. He can make it obligatory for us to do Y by so commanding only because there is first a general obligation for us to obey him. His commands, therefore, cannot be the source of moral obligation in general. . . .[17]

Mackie's objection here simply restates an objection to early modern divine command theories proposed by the seventeenth-century English philosopher Ralph Cudworth.[18] Despite its initial appeal, this argument fails for at least two reasons.[19]

First, the argument *generalizes.*[20] That is, the argument would apply to every account of moral obligations within any given ethical theory, secular or theological. Let's look at two examples to show this. One influential account of what moral obligations are is the social contract theory. According to a social contract view, moral obligations are those requirements that rational, impartial persons in a society would agree to. But Cudworth (and Mackie) could argue that one is morally obligated to such a contract only if there is *already* an obligation to follow such hypothetical agreements. So the hypothetical agreement can't itself be the source of moral obligation.

Or again, suppose someone advocates a *naturalist* theory of moral obligation, where our moral duties are identified with certain natural properties such as human flourishing. An analogue of Mackie's argument is applicable: A natural fact can make it obligatory for you to do some action only if there is already an obligation to do any action which has that property. Natural properties, therefore, cannot be the source of moral obligation.

We believe the same thing can be said about every major account of moral obligations defended today. If Cudworth's argument is successful, then it could show that not all obligations can be explained by God's commands—and also that not all moral obligations can be explained by other sources (self-interest, social contracts, what promotes the greatest good for the greatest number, and so on).[21]

What has gone wrong with the argument? It plays on an ambiguity between two claims—what is called "the fallacy of equivocation." Note the ambiguity between the following two claims:[22]

1 If God commands X, then we have an obligation to do X.
2 There is an obligation to do what God commands.

Only the second of these claims, 2, affirms the actual existence of an obligation to obey God. The first claim, 1, does not. Rather, 1 makes a conditional claim: it claims that *if* God commands a specific action, *then* we have an obligation to do that action. Claim 1 doesn't affirm the existence of an obligation; in fact, its truth is compatible with there being no obligations at all. All it asserts is that there *would* be an obligation if God commanded something. A person can correctly assert, "If Matthew were shot dead while writing this book, then he would not have finished this book." That does not mean that Matthew was shot dead or that the book was not completed.

So when Mackie states that "[God] can make it obligatory for us to do Y by so commanding only because there is first a general obligation for us to obey him," he assumes that God's commands cannot generate a moral obligation unless 2 is true—that there is an obligation to obey what God commands. But this is clearly false. All that is needed is for 1 to be true—that if God commands X, we have an obligation to do X. Given that 1 does not assert there exists any obligation to obey God, Mackie's central premise is false. Mark Schroeder notes that on the surface the conditional claim "If God commands X, then we have an obligation to do X" is what is needed to "explain the difference between me and God: that His commands, but not mine, generate obligations." He points out that God has a particular status—namely, that "His commands lead to obligations. I lack that status." It is this distinction—not some prior obligation we have to God—that the divine command theorist rightly emphasizes. One does not need to hold that we have a prior obligation to God.[23]

Consequently, the divine command theorist need not hold that there is a prior obligation to obey God. All he needs to hold is that God jointly possesses various characteristics or traits such that his act of commanding is sufficient to constitute moral obligations. And this is precisely what divine command theorists argue. In light of a similar objection, Robert Adams makes this same point in response to Stephen Sullivan:

> Creation, benefaction, and covenant, on my view, are among the factors that make God a good candidate for the role of a constitutive standard of right and wrong. Why should we not say that what contributes to making God a good candidate for that role contributes something to our obligation to obey God? Sullivan's insistence that we are motivated to obey God "by the belief that they *owe* obedience *because* God is related to them" in relevant ways suggests that perhaps he sees nothing as "contributing to an obligation" unless it is by a *prior* and *independent* moral principle. This seems to rule out *a priori* that creation, benefaction, and covenant contribute to God's will being a constitutive rather than a derivative moral standard. Can I fairly complain at this point that the question is being begged against me?[24]

"Divine Command Theory Makes the Content of Morality Arbitrary" Objection

The first arbitrariness objection dealt with God's not having reasons for issuing his commands. We concluded that the commands from an all-good, infinitely just, worship-worthy personal being are not arbitrary; abstracted facts or reasons themselves are not sufficient to ground duties. That said, many critics maintain these commands are arbitrary in another important sense. If a divine command theory is true, the critic argues, then God could have given us different commands just as easily. For example, God could have commanded *atrocious* acts; so if he had, those acts would be morally obligatory. This objection was pressed forcefully by the atheist philosopher Michael Tooley in a 1994 debate with William Lane Craig. Tooley stated that a divine command theory "is quite a hopeless theory because of its implications. One of its implications, for example, is that if God had commanded mankind to torture one another as much as possible, then it would follow that that action was obligatory. Perhaps Dr. Craig would be happy with that consequence. But many people, including many religious thinkers, are very unhappy with that consequence, and so have rejected the divine command theory of morality."[25] Robert K. Garcia and Nathan L. King articulate the concern that critics of the divine command theory routinely raise: "DCT [divine command theory] implies that it is *possible* for any kind of action, such as rape, to not be wrong. But it seems intuitively impossible for rape not to be wrong. So, DCT is at odds with our commonsense intuitions about rape."[26]

A similar line of argument has been made by atheist philosopher David Brink: "We might also notice a counterintuitive implication of voluntarism [divine command theory]. Voluntarism implies that all moral truths are contingent on what God happens to approve. . . . Thus, for example, had God not condemned genocide and rape, these things would not have been wrong, or, if God were to come to approve these things, they would become morally acceptable. But these are awkward commitments, inasmuch as this sort of conduct seems necessarily wrong."[27] If we single out the example of rape, this line of argument can be constructed as follows:

1 If divine command theory is true, then if God commanded us to rape, we would be required to rape.
2 God could command us to rape.
3 It is absurd that we could be required to rape.

Therefore:

4 Divine command theory is absurd.

The key claim here is 2—that God could command us to rape; however, that is seriously questionable. Divine command theorists don't maintain the view that moral obligations are identified with the commands of just *anyone*. They explicitly identify them with the commands of *God*—a personal being understood to be the all-good, all-powerful, all-knowing, loving, just, immaterial, worship-worthy Creator of the universe. So claim 2—that God could command us to rape—holds only if it is *possible* for the Greatest Conceivable Being, who is necessarily good, to command rape. What's more, Scripture itself makes clear how misguided such Tooley-like criticisms are. Because of his intrinsically good nature, God just could not command certain things: "[They] have built the high places of Baal to burn their sons in the fire as burnt offerings to Baal, a thing which I never commanded or spoke of, nor did it ever enter My mind" (Jer. 19:5 NASB). Furthermore, God cannot break his promise (Ps. 110:4; Heb. 7:21) or lie (Rom. 3:4; Titus 1:2;

Heb. 6:18). Nor would God command us to hate him rather than love him or to torture babies for fun.

The very reason people like Tooley and Brink cite examples of rape is because they view it as a paradigm of an action that no virtuous person could ever knowingly entertain.

However, suppose for the sake of argument that it is possible for a just, loving, and omniscient being to command rape. Because God is loving, just, and omniscient, it would follow that rape could only be commanded in situations where a just and loving person, aware of all the relevant facts, could endorse it. And under these circumstances it is hard to see how 2—that God could command us to rape—could be maintained. Thus, it is hard to see how both 3 and 2 can be true—that is, it is absurd that we be required to rape *and* that an all-good, all-knowing God could command rape; hence, this argument contains at least one false claim.

This response to the arbitrariness objection is known as the *essential goodness response*—that is, an essentially good God could not command what is intrinsically evil—to hate him, to worship Satan, to rape. Are there *difficult* divine commands in Scripture? Yes, but not impossible or intrinsically evil ones ("nor did it ever enter My mind"). We believe this fact is decisive against the objection that a divine command theory makes the contents of God's commands arbitrary. So instead of saying, "God couldn't command the killing of the Canaanites because he is necessarily good," we could turn this around: "Because God is necessarily good, he would have a very good reason for commanding the killing of the Canaanites in utterly unique circumstances."

Recently, several critics of divine command theories have offered several rejoinders to the essential goodness response. In the next chapter, we will argue that they all fail—in addition to various other Euthyphro-related objections from arbitrariness and emptiness.

Summary

- Plato's Euthyphro dialogue raises the question: "Is what is holy holy because the gods approve it, or do they approve it because it is holy?" Or, "Are actions wrong because God prohibits them, or does God prohibit them because they are wrong?" This leads to the charge that God's commands are either *arbitrary* (God could command the exact opposite of what he does) or *empty* (another standard of goodness is assumed that is independent of God and therefore "right" and "wrong" don't depend on God; to say an action is "good" is just to say "it is commanded by God").

- Are God's commands merely arbitrary?

- Russ Shafer-Landau incorrectly says that if God's commands are based on *reasons*, then those reasons *make* an action right—not God's commands. But we have to ask: How is the word *make* to be understood? There are two different senses to consider: the *constitutive* explanation ("water is made up of/ is H$_2$O") and the *motivational* explanation (the *reasons why* agents act the way they do). We don't disagree that God has *reasons* for commanding what he does. But this position is like saying a judge's reasons for a verdict are the verdict itself. God's *reasons* for commanding are not the *command* itself.

• *Goodness* can't be reduced to *duty*—an unfortunate assumption made by critics who use the Euthyphro argument. There are many *good* things (like donating a kidney to a stranger), but that good thing does not *obligate* us to carry it out.

• Furthermore, an omniscient *God* will have reasons for commanding or prohibiting— reasons that we ourselves may not or even cannot know. So God's motivational state will be different from our own, which is why we need commands even if we don't know all the reasons behind them.

• Also, we may commend the pursuit of *good* states of affairs (like good health), but this good in itself does not constitute a *duty* to, say, donate a kidney to a stranger. Having sufficient reason to donate a kidney (it would improve a person's health, say) does not constitute a duty to do so. *Moral obligation is not identical with what one has good reasons to do.*

• Furthermore, these duties originate from a personal being rather than mere facts or reasons abstracted from particular contexts.

• Atheist J. L. Mackie's argument against divine command theory is that God can make it obligatory to do some specific action only if there *already* exists a general obligation to obey him. But while God through creation, kindness, and covenant is rightly positioned to wisely command us, we can bypass Mackie's objection. That is, we can still have moral obligations without needing to affirm that there already exists a general obligation to obey God. All we need to affirm is that if God commands something, we have a duty to do it—that is, God's commands generate obligations.

• The charge that God's commanding intrinsically evil or atrocious acts would thereby make those acts obligatory is fallacious. Divine commands come from an intrinsically good God. So it's absurd for the greatest conceivable being to command rape. This is like saying that square circles or married bachelors exist. God cannot command what is intrinsically evil.

• Scripture itself tells us there are things that God simply will not do because they violate his good nature (Jer. 19:5; Ps. 110:4; Rom. 3:4; Titus 1:2; Heb. 6:18; 7:21).

• Instead of saying, "A good God would never command the killing of the Canaanites," we can say, "If God is all-good, he would have overridingly good reasons for commanding this."

14

Other Euthyphro-Related Objections

I n this chapter, we continue the Euthyphro-based objections that use the *arbitrariness* argument; then we move to the *emptiness* objection.

More Arbitrariness Objections

In the last chapter, we left off with the essential goodness response, which we continue here. Let's look now at a few more objections to the essential goodness response.

The Objection from Omnipotence

Let's go back to Wes Morriston at this point. He offers a comeback to the essential goodness response by appealing to God's omnipotence—the doctrine that God is all-powerful: "Few divine-command theorists would want to give up the claim that God is omnipotent, but I believe that quite a strong case can be made for saying that omnipotence entails the ability to command X, in which case premise [2] [i.e., that God could command us to rape] must be true."[1]

The initial problem is that while divine command theorists do typically accept that God is *omnipotent*, they also accept that God is essentially *good*. That is, God has certain character traits such as being loving, impartial, just, and so on—and he has these traits essentially. That is, God could not be God without them. Hence while divine command theorists accept that God is omnipotent, they also accept that it is impossible for God to act in a manner that is capricious, malicious, unjust, and so on. So, Morriston's argument goes, if omnipotence is understood so as to entail the possibility of God issuing such an intrinsically evil command, then it is impossible for God to be both omnipotent and essentially good. He is either one or the other.

The technicalities of defining omnipotence are beyond the scope of this book. Here we will simply note a couple of options that eliminate Morriston's objection. One option is to deny that the two are incompatible, which is what various philosophers have shown—even on the atheistic side.[2] Omnipotence involves the *power* to do what is logically possible. While it is not logically possible for God to issue malicious commands, this is not because he lacks the power to do so but because in no possible situation does he *choose* to issue such commands.

Others have offered rigorous accounts of omnipotence in terms of God bringing about logically possible states of affairs. Such power isn't simply the ability to do anything at all. For example, God can't make himself cease to exist, create square circles, or change past events from already having occurred. These are acts that are incoherent and nonsensical. No power, however great, can produce something self-contradictory. Also on this account, God's power is *bound up with his goodness*. Not *every* ability to do something should be considered worthy of divine power—including commanding something intrinsically evil. There is no possible state of affairs in which God commands something abhorrent. His failure to do so does not contradict his omnipotence.[3] If either of these accounts of omnipotence is correct, then the problem Morriston cites does not even arise. Omnipotence does not entail that God can issue malicious commands.

For the sake of argument, though, let's revisit the idea that omnipotence and essential moral goodness are incompatible. In this case, God will either not be essentially good, or he will not be omnipotent. Does this actually create a problem for the divine command theorist? Not necessarily. Now, it *will* create a problem if the divine command theorist responds to this dilemma by *denying* that God is essentially good and *embracing* full omnipotence. So if divine command theorists take this route, then it will be possible for God to command evil, and they would be forced to embrace both claims 2 and 3—that God could command us to rape and that it is absurd that we could be required to rape. But nothing in Morriston's argument requires that divine command theorists must resort to such measures in an effort to address this so-called dilemma.

An alternative is for the divine command theorist to *qualify* what is meant by *omnipotence*. The divine command theorist could replace the claim that

God is omnipotent with something weaker—the claim that "God has as much power as is compatible with essential goodness."[4] Morriston acknowledges that even given this weaker claim, God would be

> very powerful indeed—powerful enough to create the world, powerful enough to perform all sorts of (good) miracles. Powerful enough to ensure that evil will eventually be defeated, that world history will have a wonderfully good outcome, that virtue will not go unrewarded, and that innocent suffering will not go uncompensated. Such a being would have enough power to satisfy our deepest longings for love and peace and justice. In sum, it would have enough power not to detract in any way from God's greatness or make Him unworthy of unconditional worship and devotion.[5]

So even if God's omnipotence were somehow incompatible with essential goodness, the divine command theorist could escape Morriston's objection simply by qualifying omnipotence. So even after raising the omnipotence objection by stating that "few divine-command theorists would want to give up the claim that God is omnipotent," Morrison goes on to frankly admit this is a defensible option: "Even if the weaker claim about God's power is accepted, one might still consistently say that He has the best possible combination of attributes. So perhaps this particular implication is not a deal-breaker."[6] Morriston's appeal to omnipotence, therefore, does not pose a problem for a divine command theory; in fact, we can thank Morriston for even offering the biblical theist one possible way out of the alleged dilemma!

Either omnipotence is compatible with essential goodness or it is not. If it is, no problem arises. If it is not, then the divine command theorist can simply respond by rejecting omnipotence as Morriston defines it yet maintain that God still has unfathomable power—power sufficient to be considered both worthy of worship and the greatest conceivable being. To create a problem, Morriston would need to argue that the only defensible solution to his proposed dilemma is to deny essential goodness. He has not done this, and in fact he affirms the contrary.

"Even if a Good God Could Command Rape . . .": Impossible Counterfactuals

In this section, we use the word *counterfactual*. Though we don't use this word in everyday conversation, we readily recognize it. For example, "*If I were you*, I would not venture out in such terrible weather." Or, "If Abraham Lincoln's bodyguard, John Frederick Parker, *hadn't left* his post at Ford's Theater on April 14, 1865, then Lincoln probably wouldn't have been assassinated that evening." These are *conditional statements using the subjunctive mood.* The language of the subjunctive mood—*if I were* or *if he had*—are conditionals that are *contrary to fact.* "If I were you" assumes that I am *not* you. Not only are counterfactuals conditionals that are contrary to fact, they may also be conditionals that *could be realized if the condition were met*: "If you were to go to the game, we would have a good time together." Also, the *if*-clause is the *antecedent* ("if I were you") which is followed by the *consequent* ("then I would go to Oxford University"). Modal logic studies the truth status of such conditional statements or statements such as "it is necessary that" or "it is possible that" (that is, *modes* or *modalities* in which a statement may be true). With this in mind, let's look at counterfactuals regarding God's commands raised by critics such as Walter Sinnott-Armstrong and Louise Antony.

Walter Sinnott-Armstrong has recently suggested a further reply to this response to the charge of arbitrariness in divine commands. He affirms: "Assuming God is good, *of course* he would command us not to rape."[7] He suggests this corrective: "Moreover, *even if God in fact never would or could* command us to rape, the divine command theory still implies the counterfactual that, if God did command us to rape, then we would have a moral obligation to rape. That is absurd."[8]

Unfortunately, Sinnott-Armstrong gives no argument for the claim that the counterfactual is absurd. He simply asserts it as obvious. The problem is that it is not obvious. If there is no logically possible world where God issues such a command (to rape), then the counterfactual has a logically impossible antecedent (e.g., "If God were to command rape . . ."). According to the standard view of modal logic, a conditional statement with a logically impossible antecedent (again, the antecedent is the *if*-clause) is *true.* So Sinnott-Armstrong's suggestion that the consequent (e.g., "*then* we would have a moral obligation to rape") is obviously false is far from obvious. In his later work, *Morality without God*, Sinnott-Armstrong states that the falsehood of the counterfactual—that *if God did command us to rape, then we would have a moral obligation to rape*—"seems plausible to most people, regardless of technical details about counterfactuals with impossible antecedents."[9] Antony makes a similar point by admitting that she is going *against* the standard modal logic; she sides with her "intuitions" and does not "treat all counterfactuals with impossible antecedents as true."[10]

One problem with Sinnott-Armstrong's and Antony's critiques is that they appear to rule out not just a divine command theory but every other notable ethical theory on offer today.[11] Consider *utilitarianism*—the position that wrongness is whatever fails to maximize utility or usefulness. Even if rape never would or could maximize utility or usefulness for society, utilitarianism still implies the counterfactual that if rape were to maximize utility, then it would be obligatory. The case is true with *Kantianism*—the view that moral duties are categorical (absolute) requirements of reason: even if rape never would or could be categorically required by reason, Kantianism implies the counterfactual that if rape were categorically required by reason, then it would be obligatory. The same is true with *virtue ethics*. Even if a perfectly virtuous person never would or could commit rape, on Sinnott-Armstrong's and Antony's reasoning, virtue theories imply the counterfactual: that if a virtuous person were to rape, then rape would be permissible. We could add other examples.

The point is this: if Sinnott-Armstrong and Antony are correct, then *they would render every leading ethical theory arbitrary—not simply a divine command theory*. So if it is absurd that rape could be permissible even if a perfectly rational, loving, just, and omniscient being commands it, then it must be absurd that rape could be obligatory if it's required by reason, compatible with virtue, or maximizes happiness. So unless one wants to declare all substantive ethical theories to be arbitrary, the claim that these counterfactuals are obviously absurd needs to be reconsidered.[12]

"Imagine God Is Cruel and Capricious": Erik Wielenberg's Variation on a Theme

Atheist philosopher Erik Wielenberg has offered this variation of the "arbitrariness argument" against the divine command theory: "Implicit in the proposal is the notion that God has the *power* to make any logically consistent ethical claim true; it is only His character that prevents Him from being able to exercise this power. This implies that if, *per impossible* [though impossible], God were not loving, He could make it the case that it is obligatory for someone to inflict a gratuitous pummelling on another human being."[13] On the one hand, Sinnott-Armstrong and Antony ask us to imagine a logically impossible world where an essentially loving and just God commands rape. Wielenberg, on the other hand, asks us to imagine a situation in which God does not have those character traits but instead is cruel and capricious and commands humans to unnecessarily assault one another.

Wielenberg draws two opposing conclusions about this admittedly impossible hypothetical: (1) a divine command theory entails that gratuitous assault would be morally obligatory in this situation, on the one hand, and (2) it is false that in this situation, gratuitous assault is obligatory, on the other.

An immediate problem with this objection is that as the terms have been defined in the discussion, conclusion 2 is false. It is not at all obvious that *in the hypothetical situation envisaged*, gratuitous assault would not be morally required.

To see this we need to remember a terminological point we made in chapter 12. We were citing William Lane Craig who referred to the title "God" as a description of "the greatest conceivable being" who is "an appropriate object of worship." However, if "God" is a title, like the word "Caesar," then the word "God" refers to whichever being possesses the title or status of being worthy of worship. This means that the situation Wielenberg envisages is one where the character traits of some being that is hateful and cruel are possessed by the being that is maximally excellent and worthy of worship.

Wielenberg's argument is problematic. He presents an utterly impossible world where hatred and cruelty can be features of a maximally excellent being; the result is that we cannot say with confidence that gratuitous assault is wrong. Presumably, in such an impossible world, Wielenberg thinks that endorsing beating people up for no reason is compatible with excellence and worship-worthiness. But if beating people up for no reason is an excellent, worship-worthy thing to do, it would not be wrong. The reason we believe such an action *is* wrong is because we believe a maximally great being could never endorse such actions.

Wielenberg could respond that, while Craig is using the term "God" as a *title*—that is, a description—he, in making this objection, is doing something else. If "God" is only a *proper name* that refers to a particular deity who happens to have the title of being worship-worthy, then Wielenberg's world is an impossible world. A hateful and cruel being has no claim to the title "greatest conceivable being" or "maximally excellent being." So in the impossible situation envisaged, supporting assault is not compatible with being worthy of worship or excellence.

So our reply might enable Wielenberg to escape our objection to 2, which claims that it is false that in this situation, gratuitous assault is obligatory. The problem is that if the term "God" is understood in the way this rejoinder suggests (i.e., as a proper noun as opposed to a title), then 1 is false; in other words, *it is false that a divine command theory entails that unnecessarily assaulting others would be morally obligatory*. But as we have seen, Craig's divine command theory is that moral obligations are identified with the commands of God, where God is defined as the greatest conceivable being, a being worthy of worship. And when Craig states that our moral obligations are identified with the commands of God (he is using the word God as a *title*), they are identified with the commands of whoever is worthy of worship or the greatest conceivable being. So if, in these impossible situations proposed by Wielenberg, a personal being does not hold this title of maximally great being, then the divine command theory does not identify that personal being's commands with our obligations.

The Psychopathy Objection

"New atheist" Sam Harris suggests a different kind of reply. He claims that with divine command theory, "we are being offered a psychopathic and psychotic moral attitude."[14] He continues:

> It is psychopathic because this is a total detachment from the well-being of human beings. This so easily rationalizes the slaughter of children. Ok, just think about the Muslims at this moment who are blowing themselves up, convinced that they are agents of God's will. There is absolutely nothing that Dr. Craig can say against their behavior, in moral terms, apart from his own faith-based claim that they're praying to the wrong God. If they had the right God, what they were doing would be good, on Divine Command theory.[15]

Here Harris suggests three things. First, like Sinnott-Armstrong and Antony, he notes that a divine command theory entails the following conditional: *If God commands you to blow up a bus full of children, then you are required to blow up a bus full of children.* Second, he suggests accepting the truth of this conditional requires a psychopathic perspective. What is it that characterizes a psychopath? Perhaps something like a shocking degree of callousness and a lack of empathy for others. Third, accepting the truth of this conditional "so easily rationalizes the slaughter of children." Let's examine each of these points in turn.

First is Harris's contention that the divine command theory entails this conditional: *If God commands you to blow up a bus full of children, then you are required to blow up a bus full of children.* This conditional is indeed an implication of divine command theories. Undoubtedly that sounds shocking at first, but note two important points which Harris skims over.

1. *This is a conditional or hypothetical statement.* It states that *if* God commanded blowing up buses, then blowing up buses would be morally obligatory. Nothing about this conditional entails that God actually ever does, or even could, command such a thing, nor does it entail that one is ever rationally justified in believing that he does. It simply states that *if* this situation occurred, then the action would be permissible.

It is a well-known point in logic that a person can affirm that one thing would be true if a certain situation occurred without being committed to claiming it ever occurs. It would be true, for example, that *if* we had never been born, then we would not be writing this book right now. That does not mean we believe we were never born. That would be a gross misconception.

2. *The divine command theory entails that blowing up buses is morally obligatory only if God commands doing so.* As we have already noted, the context in which the divine command theory has been discussed presents God as the omniscient, omnipotent, morally perfect personal being who created and sustains the universe. To say God is morally perfect is to say he possesses certain character traits such as being loving, just, impartial, and so on. And God is necessarily morally perfect, which means he possesses these traits in all possible worlds.

So what a divine command theory entails is that blowing up a bus full of children is right only under hypothetical conditions (which may well be impossible), where a personal being who is fully informed, rational, loving, just, and impartial would knowingly endorse the action. It is under those circumstances and *only* under those circumstances that a divine command theory entails such acts would be permissible.

Notice also the hypothetical is one where God *actually* issues the command; the action is *actually* endorsed by a fully informed, rational, loving, just, and impartial personal being. *It is not a hypothetical situation where someone claims falsely or mistakenly that God did so.*

Having clarified the relevant conditional, we can now turn to Harris's second claim. Harris contends that accepting this conditional requires a psychopathic outlook—a startling degree of callousness and lack of empathy for others. But this is clearly false. What is being envisaged is not that it is permissible to blow up buses *per se*, but rather blowing up buses under certain hypothetical situations—namely, where it is *not* unloving, *not* unjust, *not* based on false information, and *not* irrational. The circumstances are such where an impartial, compassionate being—after a fully rational consideration of the facts—would knowingly endorse killing. These kinds of conditions are quite different than the scenario Harris raises. By definition, these are cases where impartial, empathic concern demands such action.

Consequently, Harris's second claim is incoherent. It affirms that only the person who lacked empathy and was morally calloused could accept killing in circumstances where a fully loving, impartial being (i.e., one who was empathetic) has in fact endorsed it. Far from being a sound argument, this is a contradiction.

Finally, let's look at Harris's third claim, that accepting this conditional "so easily rationalizes the slaughter of children." Why does Harris think this? Because Islamic terrorists "are blowing themselves up, convinced that they are agents of God's will" and a divine command theory can say nothing "against their behavior, in moral terms, apart from . . . [the] faith-based claim that they're praying to the wrong God."[16]

Harris's reasoning here is unsound. A divine command theory insists that an action is obligatory only if God *actually* commands that action. It does not contend that an action is obligatory if someone *claims* or *believes* that God commands it. Obviously, simply believing something is the case does not mean that it is true. Harris as an atheist surely recognizes this; after all, many people believe and are convinced God exists, yet Harris thinks they are mistaken.

Hence, the mere fact that a group of Islamic terrorists believe God has commanded them to "blow themselves up" does not commit the divine command theorist to supporting terrorism. All a divine command theorist needs to say in response to Islamic terrorists is that God did not command them to engage in terrorism. This is not the same as claiming "they are praying to the wrong God." It's theoretically possible that an evildoer is acting or praying in the name of "the right God" but is also violating his commands, as Jesus himself pointed out: "An hour is coming for everyone who kills you to think that he is offering service to God. These things they will do because they have not known the Father or Me" (John 16:2–3 NASB; cf. Matt. 7:22–23).

Praying to God does not mean one is obeying him. Faithful, biblically informed believers with earnest prayer lives will candidly admit that they fail to obey God perfectly. Moreover, if a divine command theory is correct, then every person—theist, agnostic, or atheist—who refrains from murder, rape, or theft is obeying God's commands. Harris here seems to presuppose a caricature of a divine command theory whereby it affirms that an action is right only if it is done by someone who prays to "the right God." No divine command theorist we know of—and certainly not William Lane Craig—has made such a claim.

Suppose then that a divine command theorist—say, from the Christian community—responds to Islamic terrorism by affirming that God did not command any terrorists to blow themselves up. What is the problem? Harris seems to suggest this denial is a "faith-based claim"—that only those within a particular faith-community can make this assertion and that it cannot be known or accessed apart from "faith." This, however, is extremely implausible. Is Harris really suggesting that a person—independent of that particular "faith commitment"—cannot know that a loving and just God doesn't command people to engage in terrorism apart from faith? Harris *himself* presumably thinks that a good, just God—if he existed—did not command Islamic terrorists to blow themselves up. Has Harris based his conclusion on faith?

This point was made by Craig in his debate with Harris on this subject:

HARRIS: This is the kind of morality that you get out of divine command theory that, again, offers no retort to the jihadist other than, "Sorry, buster, you happen to have the wrong god."

CRAIG: But that's exactly your retort, Sam, that God has not issued such a command, and therefore, you're not morally obligated to do it.

HARRIS: No, if God did, he would be evil. So I can't get behind that God; if God is issuing that command, he's an evil bastard.[17]

This exchange is insightful as it shows the special pleading or question-begging by Harris and—as we've seen in this and the previous chapters—other thinkers like Antony and Sinnott-Armstrong, who take a similar position. Harris objects that the only retort a divine command theorist can make to a jihadist is "you happen to have the wrong god." Yet his own response to the jihadist is "the God you're following is an evil bastard." By this we assume Harris means that the conception of God the jihadist holds is one that is atrocious; a being fitting that description would be unworthy of worship. But isn't this just another way of saying the jihadist is following the wrong God?

Contrary to Harris's protestations, the answer he gives the jihadist is actually the same as the one Craig suggests: *God has not issued such a command.* The only reason it appears to be a different answer is terminological. As we pointed out earlier in the chapter, Craig in this debate is using the term "God" as a title given to any personal being who is "the greatest conceivable being" and who is "worthy of worship." Hence, when Craig says that God has not issued such a command, what he means is that the command was not issued by a person worthy of worship; it was not issued by a person who was maximally great. Consequently, to point out that any being who issued a particular command is an "evil bastard" is, given Craig's terminology, to affirm that it was not commanded by God. There is therefore no substantive difference between the reply Craig offers the jihadist and that offered by Harris.

This raises an obvious problem for Harris. If the claim that God did not issue the command is merely a "faith-based claim," then Harris's own response must be a faith-based claim, as it is the *identical* reply. Harris seems to think that the divine command theorist's response is inadequate, yet his own reply is no different!

Harris's comments show the divine command theorist can offer an adequate answer to jihadists without reverting to mere (apparently insulated and empirically unsupportable) "faith" claims. Harris's comments show that when a person asserts that God has commanded some atrocity, one can use normal moral reasoning to show that it is unlikely that God (understood as a personal being worthy of worship) commanded the action in question. Because we have some grasp of what justice and love are, we can tell that certain actions are likely to be commanded by a just and loving person—and that certain actions are not. Harris's repeated verbal attack against jihadism and the Taliban involves just that assumption: these terrorist groups who claim to be following God are false because only "an evil bastard" would command the sorts of things those groups claim God commands. Hence, those actions were not commanded by a just and loving God who is worthy of worship. This attitude is no more psychopathic when expressed by Craig than it is when expressed by Harris.

Another odd feature of Harris's criticisms is worth mentioning here. In the dialogue we cited above, Harris offers the objection that if jihadists had the right God, then what jihadists do would be good according to divine command theory. What exactly is the problem here? It is true that *if* the theology of Osama bin Laden is true, then 9/11 was justified. Similarly, *if* what Hitler believed was true, then exterminating Jews is permissible. *If* what Marxists claim is true, then the dictatorship of the proletariat (the laboring class) is just. This is simply the uncontroversial point that *false ideologies often have false implications.* It is unclear to us why Harris would want to deny this. Much of his argumentation involves claiming that certain religious beliefs are such that if true, they have false or absurd implications. In fact, as we noted above, Harris states that he would reply to the jihadist: "If God is issuing that command, he's an evil bastard." This suggests his belief that *if jihadism is true, then evil things follow.*

In our review of the *arbitrariness* objection to divine command theory in the Euthyphro argument, we looked at a sampling of the philosophical criticisms on offer. Yet these attempts to undermine the divine command theory from Morriston, Sinnott-Armstrong, Wielenberg, Antony, and Harris are unsuccessful and often confused. We move now to the *emptiness* objection.

The Emptiness Objection

As we say in the last chapter, James Rachels's second objection to a divine command theory is that "the doctrine of the goodness of God is rendered meaningless."[18] Here we look at two possible renderings of this objection.

"Can God Be Good If He Has No Moral Obligations?"

Christian philosopher Peter van Inwagen has recently developed this objection in some detail: one implication of a divine command theory of ethics is that God does not have obligations and hence, strictly speaking, nothing he does can be right or wrong.[19] Craig himself observes that God is not "bound by moral duties since he does not issue commands to himself."[20]

What are the implications of a God not having moral duties? Here van Inwagen draws the following conclusion from the idea that God has no duties: "Presumably, there is no such property or attribute as 'moral perfection.' . . . If there is no such attribute as moral perfection, the *aliquid quo nihil maius cogitari possit* [that than which nothing greater can be conceived—that is, God] will not be morally perfect—and not because it will be morally imperfect, but because there will not be any such thing for it to be."[21] So van Inwagen appears to think that a person can be morally perfect, in the sense he defines these terms, only if there is an objective moral standard that applies to that person and that person perfectly conforms to this standard. God can be morally perfect only if God has duties and acts in accord with them.

Now there is a grain of truth to the suggestion that *if* God has no duties, then he cannot be said to be good in any meaningful sense. If we are going to understand God's goodness in terms of God having duties that he consistently fulfills, then a divine command theory cannot account for God's goodness. However, why must the statement *God is good* be explained in terms of God having duties? We do not see why it should.

Many theologians and philosophers have suggested an alternative;[22] God's goodness should be understood in terms of God having certain character traits. To claim God is good is to claim that he is truthful, benevolent, loving, gracious, merciful; it is to hold that he is opposed to certain actions such as murdering, raping, torturing people for fun, and so on. Now even if God does not have duties, it does not follow that he cannot have character traits such as these. It is true that God is not under any obligation to love others or to tell the truth or what have you, but that does not mean he *cannot* love others or tell the truth. God does not have to have a duty to do something in order to do it.[23] That is, God by his very nature acts lovingly, justly, and truthfully. He does not consult some prior moral standards or obligations to which he is duty-bound. He simply acts, and it is good.

Interestingly, van Inwagen recognizes this point:

> But no doubt anyone who felt compelled to remove "moral perfection" from the list of properties a "something" must have if it is to be a something than which a greater cannot be conceived (having been convinced by some argument or other that there was no objective moral standard) would want to "replace" it with some attribute whose existence did not presuppose an objective moral standard: "benevolent in the highest possible degree," perhaps, or "exhibiting perfect love toward all creatures."[24]

God is not "morally perfect" in the sense that van Inwagen defines this term—namely, God *conforming to duties*. But this doesn't preclude attributing *goodness* to God in the sense that he has certain excellent character traits. We are wise to keep in mind the distinction we made earlier between the *good* and the *right*. The *good* refers to the broader category of *value*, which includes a range of areas such as beauty, virtuous character, and even rationality. The *right*, by contrast, pertains to *duty and prohibition*—a more narrow subcategory of the *good*.

So in the absence of any solid argument as to why God's goodness must be construed in terms of divine duties, it is hard to see any substantive objection here.

"God Does Not Have to Be Good"

Another version of the emptiness objection comes from Sam Harris. He counters that the absence of duties compromises the claim that God is essentially good. "According to Dr. Craig's Divine Command theory, God is not bound by moral duties; God doesn't have to be good."[25] Whether this inference is sound depends on what Harris means by "doesn't have to be good." There are at least two possible things he could mean by this.

Sometimes when we say someone does or does not "have to" do something, we mean they are not morally obligated to do it. When we tell our children that they "have to" tell the truth, for example, we are saying they have a duty to tell the truth. In other contexts, however, when we say that someone does or does not "have to" do something, we mean it is "possible" for them to do it. For example, if I say a triangle does not have to be red, but it does have to have three sides, I am using the phrase "have to" to refer to what is logically possible.

So if Harris's statement "God doesn't have to be good" means "God is not under an obligation to be good," then technically his inference is sound. If God is not bound by duties, then he obviously does not have an obligation to be good. This, however, does not entail that it is logically possible for God to lack goodness. As we noted, God by his very nature does what is good, not because he has moral duties imposed upon him.

If, on the other hand, Harris's claim that "God doesn't have to be good" carries the implication that it is possible for God to do evil, then it is a flat-out straw man—a caricature of a divine command theory position. Craig's position is that our moral obligations are constituted by God's commands. He explained what he meant by the term "God" earlier in the debate:

As St. Anselm saw, God is by definition the greatest conceivable being and therefore the highest Good. Indeed, He is not merely perfectly good, He is the locus and paradigm of moral value. God's own holy and loving nature provides the absolute standard against which all actions are measured. He is by nature loving, generous, faithful, kind, and so forth. Thus if God exists, objective moral values exist, wholly independent of human beings.[26]

As Craig has defined his terms, it is impossible for God not to be good. Harris's argument here simply ignores what Craig has explicitly stated he meant when he said he was using the term "God."

Conclusion

We conclude, therefore, that the standard objections to a divine command theory fail. Semantic and epistemological objections attack a caricature, and the Euthyphro dilemma equally fails to refute a divine command theory. Though we have given a fair representation of the critics' arguments here, we contend that the other objections raised in the literature fare no better.[27] It is therefore defensible to claim that right and wrong consist in agreement with and disagreement with, respectively, God's commands.

Summary

• If God is all-powerful (omnipotent), then wouldn't God be able to command what is evil? This ignores the fact that God is intrinsically good. We simply don't need to accept the choice between God's goodness and power—a false disjunct (either/or).

• There are a couple of alternative responses. (1) Perhaps one could say that omnipotence means that God has the power to command evil, but (because of his goodness and good purposes) he never chooses to exercise that power. (2) Power isn't the ability to do anything at all. It has to do with bringing about logically possible states of affairs—not nonsensical, self-contradictory ones. God can't make himself cease to exist, create square circles, or change past events from already having occurred. However, the idea that an intrinsically good being, who is essentially loving and just, would issue intrinsically evil commands is a nonsensical, self-contradictory state of affairs. (3) One can slightly revise "omnipotence" to "extremely

powerful" such that God can only command what is in keeping with his power. But we still have no good reason to think that omnipotence and perfect goodness cannot be compatible. This is a false dilemma.

• Counterfactual statements like, "If I were you, I would go to Oxford University," are in the subjunctive mood; they are contrary to factual statements or are statements that could be realized if certain conditions were met.

• Some philosophers claim that if God *did* command us to rape, then we would have a moral obligation to rape. Again, the problem is that this is logically impossible for an intrinsically good, maximally great being to command. And such a view would render arbitrary *any ethical theory* on offer today (e.g., if a virtuous person were to rape, then rape would be permissible; if rape were to maximize usefulness, then it would be obligatory; if rape were categorically required by reason, then it would be obligatory). Such claims are just absurd.

• Another objection (from Erik Wielenberg) asks us to imagine a world in which God is not essentially loving and just but instead is a capricious deity that commands us to commit assault. But again, why accept such a scenario? We are no longer talking about the greatest conceivable being.

• So if in these impossible situations a personal being does not hold this title of maximally great being, then the divine command theory does not identify that personal being's commands with our obligations.

• Sam Harris's psychopathy objection gives this conditional scenario: If God commands you to blow up a bus full of children, then you are required to blow up a bus full of children. It would be a sick person who commands this, says Harris. There are problems here. (1) Nothing is said about whether this entails that God ever does or could command this—just a "what if" question and nothing more ("if we hadn't been born, we wouldn't be writing this book"). (2) This scenario ignores the very definition of God as the greatest conceivable being, which renders the argument self-contradictory: it affirms that only the person who lacked empathy and was morally calloused could accept killing in circumstances where a fully loving impartial being (i.e., one who was empathetic) has in fact endorsed it. (3) The mere fact that a group of Islamic terrorists believe God has commanded them to "blow themselves up"

does not commit the divine command theorist to supporting terrorism.

• A divine command theory insists that an action is obligatory only if God *actually* commands that action; it does not contend that an action is obligatory if someone *claims* or *believes* that God commands it.

• Harris responds that the denial that God could command this terrorist act is a "faith-based claim." But surely the traditionally religious person (or the atheist independent of philosophical or religious commitments) can say that a loving and just God doesn't command people to engage in terrorism. *Both Harris and the biblical theist can agree: God has not issued such a command and if jihadism is true, then evil things follow.*

• An "emptiness" objection states that God can't be good if he has no moral obligations. But surely we can understand God's goodness even if he has no duties. God's goodness should be understood in terms of his character traits; God by his very nature acts lovingly, justly, and truthfully. He does not consult some prior moral obligations or standards to which he is duty-bound. He simply acts, and it is good.

• Another "emptiness" response is that God does not have to be good; if this means God has no duties (to follow his own commands), this is no problem. God naturally does what is good since God is the greatest conceivable being. But if this means God can do good or evil, this is a caricature of the divine command theory.

15

Can One Coherently Claim
That God Commanded
the Killing of Innocents?

I n this book, we have engaged with some of the work of William Lane Craig, and we have emphasized how his argument depends on two affirmations. The first is a divine command theory of ethics, which we have defended in previous chapters. However, many philosophers embrace a divine command theory without accepting that God commanded the killing of Canaanite noncombatants. The real question about Craig's argument involves a second claim—*that in very unusual circumstances in the past, God commanded people to kill the innocent for the sake of some greater good*. In this and the next two chapters, we defend this second claim against two important objections. First, in this chapter we reply to the claim that it is incoherent to attribute such commands to a loving and just God. Second, in the next two chapters we respond to the claim that even if it is coherent, one cannot rationally claim God has ever issued such a command.

Can One Coherently Claim That God Commanded the Killing of Innocents?

Several writers have suggested the claim that a loving and just God could command the killing of the innocent is simply incoherent. Biblical scholar and theologian C. S. Cowles writes: "If the indiscriminate slaughter of human beings for any reason can be called a 'good' and 'righteous' act. . . then all moral and ethical absolutes are destroyed, all distinctions between good and evil are rendered meaningless, and all claims about God's love and compassion become cruel deceptions. It represents the ultimate corruption of human language and makes meaningful theological discourse virtually impossible."[1]

Old Testament scholar Eric Seibert (see chap. 3) makes a similar claim: "If God's standard of justice is so fundamentally different from ours that physical abuse and the slaughter of babies can be considered just, then it no longer seems possible to have meaningful conversation about what constitutes justice."[2] In the same vein, atheist philosopher Raymond Bradley asserts: "For holy is as holy does. That is to say, if anyone at all is properly to be described as morally perfect, then their acts of commission, of command, and of permission, must also be morally perfect. To say that God is holy despite the evil nature of what he does would be to play with words: it would be to deprive the word 'holy' of its ordinary meaning and make it a synonym for 'evil'."[3] These comments offer a number of rapid-fire assertions and inferences, and in some cases these comments obviously do not follow. Consider Cowles's statement, for instance. It is simply false to claim that if a person denies there is an absolute prohibition on killing noncombatants, it follows that there are *no* moral absolutes or that all moral and theological language has lost its meaning.

Let's unpack this type of assertion so that we might get clear on what the argument actually is and what inferences can and cannot be properly drawn here.

Calling Right Wrong and Wrong Right? Robert Adams's Version of the Coherence Objection

More careful and plausible versions of this argument have been developed by Robert Adams. Adams's starting point is "the arbitrariness objection" to divine command ethics, which we discussed in chapters 13 and 14. There we say that to escape the objection that a divine command theory makes morality arbitrary, the divine command theorist must appeal to the fact that God is essentially good: he possesses certain virtues such as being loving, just, truthful, benevolent, gracious, merciful, and so on. God's possession of these traits means that it is not possible for him to command just anything, such as rape or the torture of children.

Adams has argued this means there are limits to the commands one can coherently attribute to God.[4] We have some grasp of what goodness is and what kinds of things a good person does not command. It follows that God cannot coherently be called good if what he commands is contrary to "our *existing* moral beliefs."[5] To do so, as Raymond Bradley contends, would be "playing word games which are intellectually dishonest."[6] But, the argument goes, one of our existing moral beliefs is the Crucial Moral Principle—that it is wrong to kill innocent human beings. So we cannot coherently attribute this command to a loving and just God.

A Reply to the Coherence Objection

Adams's argument is too quick. Critics of Adams have pointed out that his conclusion is more qualified than it appears. While he states that "our *existing* moral beliefs" are a constraint on our beliefs about God's commands, he goes on to state that God cannot issue "a set of commands that is *too much* at variance with the ethical outlook we bring to our theological thinking."[7] The phrase "too much" suggests that one can accept a set of commands that is *somewhat* at odds with the outlook we bring to our ethical thinking.

Elsewhere Adams makes the same point. He suggests that one cannot identify moral obligations with God's commands if what God commands is contrary to "an important central group" of what we consider to be right and wrong. He grants that it would be "unreasonable" to expect God's commands to "agree perfectly with pre-theoretical opinion." He states that an ethical theory—like a divine command theory—may "give guidance in revising one's particular ethical opinions. But there is a limit to how far those opinions may be revised without changing the subject."[8]

Elsewhere, Adams makes two points that suggest this qualification is necessary. First, while we do have some grasp of what is good and some idea of what is right and wrong, it is clear that *our moral judgments can be fallible.*[9] While God does not command wrongdoing, it is likely that a perfectly good, omniscient being would command something contrary to what *we think* is wrong. To say otherwise dogmatically assumes we are such good judges of morality that God could never disagree with us.

Second, *our moral concepts are subject to revision.* We change our opinions about the goodness and rightness of certain things—that is, we *do* adjust "our *existing* moral beliefs." (And contrary to Bradley, this is not "intellectually dishonest" or calling what is holy "evil.") If this were not the case, one could *never* honestly or rationally change one's mind on an ethical issue. Indeed, Adams accepts "the possibility of a conversion in which one's whole ethical outlook is revolutionized, and reorganized around a new center."[10] But he recognizes that "we can hardly hold open the possibility of anything too closely approaching a revolution in which, so to speak, good and evil would trade places."[11]

These points, however, limit Adams's conclusion. What his argument in fact shows is not that "our existing moral beliefs are bound in practice, and I think ought in principle, to be a constraint on our beliefs about what God commands,"[12] but rather that *certain types* of our existing beliefs do this. What he has in mind are those ethical beliefs that are so central to our concept of goodness that rejecting them would create a more revolution of sorts in which good and evil would switch places.[13] Those moral convictions or beliefs are such that rejecting them would be such a moral revision as to utterly change the subject. As Christian philosophers David Baggett and Jerry Walls observe, these would be such fundamental, deeply imbedded, nonnegotiable convictions "that they are truly nonnegotiable, and unable to be relinquished—not just psychologically, but rationally, at least without perverting morality itself."[14]

Philosopher James Rissler gives two examples of cases where a purported divine command violates a nonnegotiable belief.[15] The first is where God issues a command to *reverse* one's conception of right and wrong or issues a set of commands that negates a large number of moral imperatives that one currently accepts. Second, he suggests that a command might contradict a moral belief "sufficiently integral to one's conception of morality"[16] that abandoning that belief would force such a radical revision as to destroy one's concept of goodness altogether. Imagine a command to kill everyone around you purely for entertainment, or a command that said harming, hurting, and inflicting suffering on people for no reason at all is permissible. Or consider a command to hate God and despise all other human beings. Similarly, one cannot accept a system of divine commands where every duty we believe in is declared false. Nor can we accept a system that suggests that the vast majority of our moral beliefs are mistaken. This would come too close to the problematic revolution of which Adams speaks.

The key question, then, is not whether the Crucial Moral Principle is one of our existing moral beliefs, but whether it is a nonnegotiable belief. On closer investigation, it becomes apparent that the Crucial Moral Principle—the wrongness of killing innocent people—is *not a nonnegotiable belief*. Many ethicists contend that while the claim "it is wrong to kill innocent people" is correct as a general rule, it can be overridden in rare circumstances of "supreme emergency"[17]—for example, when the alternative to killing noncombatants in war is to tolerate significantly greater evils, and the consequences of refraining from killing are significantly bad. Whatever one thinks of this position, it cannot be dismissed as conceptually incoherent. If a proponent of an absolutist position on killing noncombatants examined the arguments and concluded that, in rare circumstances of supreme emergency, killing noncombatants was not wrong, then it is implausible to suggest that their concept of goodness was so radically at odds with prior beliefs that "good and evil would trade places," or that their position consisted of mere word games. This position may be false, but it is not obviously incoherent. Hence, taken as a universal, the Crucial Moral Principle about the wrongness of killing innocent people is not a nonnegotiable principle.

Of course, it is plausible that the Crucial Moral Principle is a nonnegotiable belief when it is not taken as universal. The claim that in *normal* circumstances it is wrong to kill the innocent *is* central to our understanding of morality. Craig's position accepts the Crucial Moral Principle as a generally valid principle. He states that only in highly extraordinary, unusual cases in the past has God commanded such killing.

Once this is realized, it is evident the arguments of Cowles, Seibert, and Bradley cited at the beginning of this chapter fail. These arguments assume that the claim that it is always wrong to kill the innocent is a nonnegotiable belief. But this is false. Note that this point also serves as a response to the objection to a hyperbolic interpretation we noted earlier from Bradley: "Hence his second ploy, that of claiming that God didn't really mean what he said; he was indulging in a bit of hyperbole. 'Kill all' just meant, 'Kill most.' Does this make God any less guilty? What sort of perverted morality would lead one to conclude: 'Not all of them? Oh! I suppose that's OK then'?"[18] This argument, however, misses what we believe to be of central significance in the command to kill the Canaanites—namely, that this was a *rare exception*. If we were arguing that killing large numbers of people was permissible providing only some were killed, and that killing some but not all makes one innocent, then Bradley's response here would be correct. The moral status of homicide is not determined by how many homicides one engages in, and simply killing fewer people or doing it only once does not give anyone a free moral pass.

However, that is not what we (or anyone we know of, for that matter) have argued. The question is whether one can coherently attribute such a command to God. Craig's point is that one cannot coherently attribute to God a command that suggests it is permissible to kill or harm in general. That would violate a nonnegotiable moral belief. However, the claim that God on rare or highly unusual occasions allows exceptions to a general rule against killing for the sake of some greater good does not violate a nonnegotiable moral belief. Hence one can coherently attribute it to God. So to refute *this* argument, Bradley would need to offer an argument that it is impossible that a perfectly good being would ever allow rare exceptions to the rule against killing for the sake of some greater good—and he has not done so—or that such a belief is a nonnegotiable moral claim.

Randal Rauser offers an argument in favor of an absolute prohibition against killing the innocent, which could be used to contest what we have argued. He writes, "Given the staggering implications of slaughtering an entire society, at the very least one should demand clear and compelling criteria for when a slaughter is required."[19] Rauser here assumes that the command to kill the Canaanites is a command to physically slaughter an entire society. We have already argued against this assumption.

However, this does bring us to consider an important argument raised by C. A. J. Coady against alleged exceptions to an absolute prohibition on killing noncombatants.[20] Commenting on Michael Walzer's argument that the prohibition on killing noncombatants can be overridden in extremely rare cases of extreme emergency,[21] Coady notes that the criteria for extreme emergency is "conceptually opaque"; furthermore, it requires calculations that are difficult to accurately weigh in situations where people are prone to rationalize their behavior. Walzer's own historical examples suggest such exceptions are more often abused, or rationalized, than correctly applied. For this reason, adopting an absolute rule against killing the innocent actually will have better results morally than allowing an exception. General acceptance and conformity with an absolute rule will bring about more good than the acceptance of a rule allowing supreme emergency exceptions.

Stephen Nathanson and Alan Donagan make similar criticisms.[22] Nathanson, arguing from a utilitarian perspective, suggests that widespread adoption and conformity to an absolute prohibition on noncombatant immunity will result in better overall consequences than adopting and conforming to a rule that allows rare exceptions in emergency cases. This is because concrete cases where greater goods result from killing the innocent are so rare and the criteria are so opaque and difficult to apply. And what's more, humans have the pervasive tendency to rationalize and be tempted to apply such an exception when it is not legitimate. Donagan argues that when we allow for an "escape clause" to traditional morality, nearly everyone's moral judgment will be clouded in the heat or tension of the moment, and "it is probable that much of what is done on the ground of such escape clauses will be mistaken."[23]

We have considerable sympathy with this argument. However, two things are important to say in response. First, while our argument above refers to Walzer's concept of supreme emergency, it does not depend on Walzer's position being correct. Our position is that, whatever one thinks of Walzer's position, it cannot be dismissed as conceptually incoherent. Some who adopted it would not have a concept of goodness that was so radically at odds with prior beliefs that "good and evil would trade places." Nothing in this argument contests *this* point.

Second, note that it is based on the fact that humans are limited in knowledge and moral judgment. What the argument shows is that for humans—who are prone to bias, factual error, and moral temptation—adopting and following an absolute rule is preferable to one with exceptions. Humans should not attempt to work out when greater goods will be preserved by killing and when they will not be. Humans and human authorities should not presume to make exceptions along these lines. In the matter under discussion, however, the claim is not that human beings are going to make the calculations in question. The question is whether *God*— who is not prone to bias or temptation and is omniscient—could ever make exceptions.[24]

Granted that the command to kill innocent human beings is understood as a *rare exception* to the normal rule against doing so, it seems perfectly coherent to attribute an occasional command to a good and just God who has some greater good or purpose in mind and is not erroneous in his judgment.

Summary

• Various philosophers accept a divine command theory without accepting that God commanded the killing of Canaanite noncombatants. The challenge to address now is the objection that, *in very unusual circumstances in the past, God commanded people to kill the innocent for the sake of some greater good.* Various biblical scholars and philosophers reject this idea.

• We have seen that God's goodness and justice prevent him from commanding just anything, such as rape or the torture of children.

• Does violating the Crucial Moral Principle overturn our basic moral understanding, as Robert Adams suggests?

• We should keep two facts in mind: (1) *our moral judgments can be fallible* (we should never take the arrogant position that God would never disagree with our moral judgments); (2) *our moral concepts are subject to revision* (we find ourselves changing positions on moral matters as we grow in experience and gain a better understanding of the relevant considerations in making moral judgments).

• The point is not that our *existing* moral beliefs must serve as a constraint on our beliefs about what God commands, but rather that *certain types* of our existing beliefs do this. We can affirm that God would not command something that would overturn our moral understanding such that good and evil switch places and we would get rid of fundamental, nonnegotiable beliefs.

• Our question has to do with whether the Crucial Moral Principle (the wrongness of killing innocent people) is a nonnegotiable belief. We argue that in rare cases of supreme emergency, this principle can be overridden.

• We argue that under normal circumstances, we should not take innocent human life. But the killing of the Canaanites was just such a *rare exception*. To refute this argument, critics like Raymond Bradley and others would need to offer an argument that it is impossible that a perfectly good being would ever allow such rare exceptions to the rule against killing for the sake of some greater good.

• Theologian Randal Rauser calls for clear and compelling criteria for when slaughter is required. Others argue that it's better not to allow exceptions (given the power of human rationalization, especially in the heat of the moment when moral judgment is often clouded).

• We should keep two points in mind: (1) the concept of "supreme emergency" can't be dismissed as conceptually incoherent; (2) the fact that humans can make mistaken judgments is not at issue, but whether we should trust in the judgment of a good, unbiased, omniscient being to ever make exceptions for a greater good.

16

Can One Rationally Believe God Commands a Violation of Innocent Human Beings?

I n the previous chapter, we argued that a person can coherently attribute to God a command to kill innocent human beings. Provided the command to kill innocent human beings is understood as a rare exception to the normal prohibition against taking innocent human life, which God issues for the sake of some greater good, then attributing this command to God does not violate a nonnegotiable moral belief. While the claim that it is *normally* or *generally* wrong to kill the innocent is a nonnegotiable moral belief, the claim that it is *absolutely* or *always* wrong under *any* circumstances is not.

In this chapter, we want to do two things. First, we'll look at Immanuel Kant's (1724–1804) objections to difficult divine commands based on historical revelation claims that seem to go against unquestionable, universally known moral certitudes. Then we'll look at more recent objections along these lines.

Universally Known Truths versus Doubtful Theological Assertions? Immanuel Kant's Objections

Here we encounter an objection to the theoretical possibility of a divinely commanded exception to the Crucial Moral Principle. Even if one can coherently believe that God commanded a violation of the Crucial Moral Principle, questions can be raised as to whether it is ever rational to believe this. The classic motivation for this objection comes from the notable philosopher Immanuel Kant, who raises the question of God's command to Abraham to sacrifice Isaac: "Abraham should have replied to this supposedly divine voice: 'That I ought not kill my good son is quite certain. But that you, this apparition, are God—of that I am not certain, and never can be, not even if this voice rings down to me from (visible) heaven.'"[1] Kant makes a similar argument in his work "The Conflict of the Faculties":

> That to take a human being's life because of his religious faith is wrong is certain, unless (to allow the most extreme possibility) a divine will, made known to the inquisitor in some extraordinary way, has decreed otherwise. But that God has ever manifested this awful will is a matter of historical documentation and never apodictically [i.e., indisputably or necessarily] certain. After all, the revelation reached the inquisitor only through the intermediary of human beings and their interpretation, and even if it were to appear to him to have come from God himself (like the command issued to Abraham to slaughter his own son like a sheep), yet it is at least possible that on this point error has prevailed.[2]

Kant's argument is addressed to the issue of whether it is wrong to kill people merely for their religious belief. His *conclusion* in this context is undoubtedly correct. However, the argument has applications in other contexts, and the argument itself is subject to several difficulties.

Kant accepts the possibility that killing an innocent person would be justified if "a divine will . . . has decreed" it. However, he maintains that no one is ever rationally justified in believing God has done this. His argument involves two steps. First, he suggests as plausible the following rule of thumb: *whenever two conflicting claims differ in epistemic (or knowability) status, the claim with the lower status is to be rejected.*[3] Second, he contends that *moral claims such as "it is always wrong to kill innocent people" are certain.* And claims that God commands or forbids a certain action are not certain and never can be. The claim to divine revelation in history is less sure than universal moral principles that are accessible to all human beings. The conclusion is that even if it is coherent to claim that God has commanded a violation of the Crucial Moral Principle, one can never rationally accept that such a claim is true.

Philip Quinn points out two problems with Kant's argument. While Quinn doesn't disagree with the first principle suggested by Kant, Quinn observes that "Kant has an extremely optimistic view of our ability to attain epistemic certainty [i.e., confident knowledge] about principles of moral wrongness."[4]

He thinks we can be *certain* of moral claims *across the board*.[5] This, however, is doubtful. True, there are some moral claims of which we can be very confident. We are certain, for example, that it is wrong to inflict as much pain as we can on another merely for our own entertainment. We are quite certain that killing, assault, theft, and lying are wrong *in general* or *all things being equal*. Philosophers use the term *prima facie* ("at first appearance"). That is, killing, assault, theft, and lying are generally wrong *but not absolutely so*. Such actions can only be justified if some overriding moral reason applies. A classic case is that of lying to Nazis about hiding Jews in your basement; it is precisely because Nazis are intent on taking innocent human life that they are deprived of any right to know the truth of the whereabouts of those Jews—a point we see played out in Scripture as well (cf. Exod. 1:15–21; 1 Sam. 16:1–2; Heb. 11:31; James 2:25).[6] However, many moral claims are far from certain at all. Similarly, consider moral debates about capital punishment, end-of-life issues, warfare, or church-state relations. While there are defensible and justified answers to these questions, we doubt that we can claim *certainty* about these answers.

Second, Kant claims that we can *never* be certain that God has commanded a particular action. Even if this is true, Quinn notes, "It would thus seem to be well within God's power to communicate to us a sign that confers on the claim that God commands some intolerant behavior, for example, issuing threats to heretics, a fairly high epistemic [i.e., knowable] status."[7] So there appears no reason for thinking that claims about God's commands cannot have a higher knowability status than moral claims about the wrongness of specific actions. Some moral claims we hold to are less than certain, and God could in principle communicate a command with higher knowability status to human beings.

In fact, the assertion that *moral* claims have a higher knowability status than *theological* claims is highly doubtful. Indeed, many skeptical worries raised about belief in God's commands apply with equal force to moral beliefs.[8] Consider the problems bound up with moral beliefs: Are the moral issues generally understood (public intelligibility)? Do people in society have ready access to the details and nuances of these issues (public accessibility)? Are the moral claims supportable through repeated confirmation (replicability)? Do the moral claims take into account human error (fallibilism)? Are they open to critique (external criticism)? Do other groups with no axe to grind make similar assessments (independent confirmability)? What evidence exists that these moral beliefs are solidly grounded (proof of reliability)?[9] The same kinds of challenges leveled against *theological* beliefs all apply to *moral* beliefs. Moreover, many of the very same arguments used to motivate skepticism about theological claims motivate skepticism about moral claims. It is simply not true, then, that moral beliefs always have a higher knowability status than beliefs about God's commands. And let us not forget that Kant's own moral understanding was largely shaped by the influence of the biblical revelation in Western culture.[10]

At this point the objector could offer this comeback: True, not all moral claims have a high knowability status, but surely the claim that it is morally wrong to deliberately kill the innocent is one that does. But this response is inadequate. We agree with the claim that *in normal circumstances*, it is wrong to kill innocent people; this strikes us as quite certain. However, the claim that *it is never permissible under any circumstances* is extremely controversial in contemporary ethical theory.[11] That there are rare exceptions to rules against killing when there is some greater good or even moral conflict involved is a widely accepted conclusion in a broad range of schools of contemporary ethics.[12] *It is at best controversial that a principle rejected by almost all of the major ethical theories on offer today is more plausible than belief that God, on rare occasions, commanded violations of the Crucial Moral Principle.* Surely some argument is needed before the biblical theist is required to accept this controversial claim.

More Recent Objections to Difficult Divine Commands

Theologian Randal Rauser has recently presented a kind of Kantian argument concerning Canaanite texts. He doubts that "a literal reading of these ancient narratives" (that is, "belief that Yahweh commanded the killing of babies in scripture") is "really stronger" than belief that it is never permissible to kill the innocent.[13] In the remainder of this chapter, we will look at four defenses of this conclusion.

Bludgeoned Babies

Rauser's first argument is that "every rational, properly functioning person cannot help but know: *it is always wrong to bludgeon babies.*"[14] To support this claim, Rauser cites several cases, including the 1994 Rwandan genocide "when Hutus slaughtered approximately four thousand Tutsi and moderate Hutu children."[15] Rauser asks, "My question is simple: When we hear these accounts is our moral condemnation in any sense qualified? Do we withhold judgment pending further information about context, location, and other extenuating circumstances? . . . On the contrary, I would submit that any properly functioning, moral, and intellectually honest human being will condemn these events without qualification."[16] While we share Rauser's unqualified condemnation of the Rwandan genocide, this argument simply does not follow. Rauser suggests that any intellectually honest, moral person would condemn the events he describes *without qualification*. By this he means they condemn it immediately without withholding judgment pending further information. The conclusion he draws, however, is that killing infants is *always* wrong. That is, it is absolutely wrong without any exception.

This conclusion, however, doesn't follow. It's possible for a person to condemn a particular *example* of an action "without qualification" yet deny that this *general* action is always wrong. It is common in moral philosophy to hold that under normal circumstances, or in general, the killing of innocent human beings is wrong. That is, there is a strong moral presumption against killing with the default position being that killing innocent people is wrong. Yet it is also possible to hold the view that under certain conditions, this presumption can be overridden when compelling reasons in favor of killing are forthcoming. If killing is presumptively wrong, then when we reflect on a case of killing an infant, we will condemn it without qualification. Because the default presumption is that any act of killing is wrong, we will condemn it immediately without withholding judgment pending further information. This, however, doesn't warrant the claim that killing is always wrong.

This is important because the position defended by Craig that we have spelled out takes for granted that killing the innocent is presumptively wrong. And God himself issues a general command to all people to not kill the innocent. The *default* position for everyone is that one should not kill the innocent. No further "information about context" is needed. However, if God later withdraws this command for a specific individual on a specific occasion, then the default presumption no longer applies. Hence, Rauser's observation that any properly functioning individual will condemn the actions he mentions without qualification is compatible with and does not refute Craig's or our position.

Rauser continues: "My unqualified condemnation of those who bludgeoned babies to death in Rwanda is rooted in the belief that you ought never to bludgeon babies." He states that this belief "is not only a basic belief; it is as indubitable as any belief I have (and more indubitable than most)."[17] Here he claims, quite plausibly, that our commonly held belief that it is wrong to kill infants is a basic belief. It is one we know "immediately" without being based on some inference or argument. He goes on, however, to make two further very strong claims. First, killing infants is not just generally or presumptively wrong, but it's always wrong; so there can never be any circumstance or situation where killing them is permissible. Second, the claim that there can *never* be any circumstance where killing infants is an indubitable one is a claim that cannot be sensibly called into question.

These strong claims are themselves doubtful. To see why, consider the following example. Four civilian airliners have been hijacked by terrorists. The terrorists are using these planes as weapons against a civilian population. Two planes have been flown into tall skyscrapers, destroying both buildings and killing thousands of innocent men, women, and children. A third has been crashed into a university stadium during a sporting event, again killing thousands of people. The final plane is still in the air and in transit to a fourth civilian target. F-16s have intercepted the plane and ordered it to deviate from its course. The terrorists who have commandeered the plane refuse to comply. Is it justifiable for the president of the United States to order the plane to be shot down?

Most people will intuitively respond to this case with an affirmative answer, and they will do so despite knowing that shooting down a civilian airliner undoubtedly involves killing innocent men, women, and children who are on the plane. Moreover, even if a person is disinclined to endorse shooting down the plane, it is implausible to suggest that the case does not lead some properly functioning, intellectually honest, morally upright people to doubt at least that it is always wrong to kill innocent people. Similarly, several studies found that more than 80 percent of people from a variety of cultures, ethnicities and nationalities and from both genders stated that you should throw a switch that would divert a trolley that will otherwise kill five innocent people, even if diverting it means you will kill an innocent bystander.[18]

We suggest reflection on cases like this and many others will lead to the conclusion that properly functioning individuals do not have an *indubitable* belief that it is *always* wrong to kill infants. Rather, we know intuitively that it is generally or presumptively wrong to do so. In most everyday cases, infanticide is a terrible crime; however, there are cases where it is at least plausible that this presumption can be overridden.

Calley's Corruption

Rauser's second argument is that even if killing noncombatants is on a given occasion morally permissible, then commanding someone to do this would still be a moral atrocity given its psychological and moral impact on the person carrying out the command. To substantiate this, Rauser cites numerous cases where the experience of combat has "deeply scarred the psyche" of soldiers. "War is the mother lode of traumatic experiences, and the chief source of the concept of PTSD [post-traumatic stress disorder]."[19] In addition to these negative psychological effects, Rauser mentions cases where participation in combat has corrupted individual soldiers so that they become desensitized to and willing to engage in morally heinous acts. Rauser cites cases such as the My Lai massacre during the Vietnam War in 1968, during which Lieutenant William Calley murdered twenty-two villagers (though several hundred other villagers were also murdered), and Private Jesse Spielman's rape and murder of a fourteen-year-old girl while he was serving in Iraq.

Again, while we join Rauser in his condemnation of Calley and Spielman, this argument is mistaken. Rauser's argument presupposes the premise: *if an action has a tendency or propensity to corrupt the individuals who commit it, then it is wrong to command someone to do it.* In fact, Rauser suggests something stronger—namely, that commanding someone to engage in such action is itself a moral atrocity. Rauser follows Marilyn McCord Adams who defines "moral atrocity" in this way: "evils the participation in which . . . constitutes prima facie reason to doubt whether the participant's life could (given their inclusion in it) be a great good to him/her on the whole."[20]

This, however, is false. Rauser himself advocates that just wars are possible, and he accepts that a government can, when necessary, use military force to defend those living within its borders from aggressive attacks by foreign armies.[21] Yet, as he notes, the corrupting tendencies he refers to are associated with military combat *per se.* In making his case that the killing of noncombatants is corrupting, Rauser appeals to studies which show that participation in combat *in general* is corrupting, even combat where only combatants are targeted. Consequently, if Rauser's central premise were true, it would be wrong for a government to order soldiers to engage in combat at all, even defensive wars against foreign invasion.

Perhaps some would respond by rejecting Rauser's claim that defensive wars can ever be legitimate (we address the just war issue in chap. 23). However, other counterexamples are available. A. A. Howsepian notes that only 15 percent of cases of PTSD occur as a result of combat. Similar psychological effects can result from having to identify charred human remains, and even therapists who treat PTSD can suffer from "vicarious traumatization" by virtue of being exposed to their patients' (often horrific) narrative accounts of traumatization.[22] If Rauser's argument is sound, one would have to conclude that requiring someone to identify charred remains or provide therapy to a PTSD sufferer is a moral atrocity. This is surely implausible.

Nor is it difficult to see how a loving and just person who is aware of post-traumatic stress and the corrupting influence of combat could still nevertheless command people to engage in combat.[23] If the alternative is between a country being invaded and annexed and millions killed, and soldiers risking being corrupted by combat, then a loving and just person could endorse engaging in combat. Here again the question is not whether there are good reasons that provide a strong presumption against killing. It is whether there can be circumstances where the goods and evils at stake are sufficient to override this presumption. The fact that Rauser accepts that combat can be justified in some circumstances, despite it having the effects he cites, shows he accepts that these reasons can be overridden.

Rationalizing Genocide

Rauser's third line of argument appeals to the "ubiquitous human tendency to rationalize illegitimate violations of the principle of universality (also known as the categorical imperative or the golden rule)." Using Noam Chomsky's definition, Rauser cites the principle of universality in this way: "we must apply to ourselves the same standards we do to others, if not more stringent ones."[24] Rauser suggests that while exceptions to this principle are common, they "typically come with a purported rationale" and "for every legitimate rationale there are a hundred spurious rationalizations."[25] He proposes two criteria for distinguishing legitimate rationales from spurious rationalizations and then argues that the biblical command to "destroy" the Canaanites is a violation of the principle of universality and fails to meet these criteria. We will make two lines of response.

First, the command to destroy the Canaanites does *not* violate the principle of universality. Craig's position is that it is permissible to kill innocent people if a loving and just God commands it. If God were to command us to kill innocent people, we would be morally permitted to kill innocent people. Similarly, if God were to command other people to kill us, then it would be permitted for those other people to kill us. There is nothing about this principle that suggests it applies only to us and not to others.

Second, Rauser's proposed criteria are problematic. His first is the "criterion of extraordinary exceptions" which proposes "that our skepticism of an alleged rationale should increase in direct proportion to the radicalness of the exception being proposed. A stranger in your backyard could provide a good rationale for invading your property uninvited (for example, the need to check your gas meter). But you would require a much better rationale from a stranger caught rummaging through your underwear drawer."[26] True enough, a stranger may step into your backyard for various reasons—a kid looking for an overthrown baseball or a lawn service worker who has the wrong house; the level of skepticism about the rationale for their presence in your backyard is *low*. And it's also true that it would be quite extraordinary for a stranger to look into your underwear drawer because of the multiple levels of inappropriateness (inside your house, inside your bedroom, inside your underwear drawer); thus the level of your skepticism about the person's rationale is quite *high*.

Even so, this reinforces our very point about *prima facie* or *general* prohibitions as opposed to justifiable actions in cases of *supreme emergency* or *unusual circumstances*. The general plausibility of such a criterion does not rule out exceptions. To expand on Rauser's analogy, we could imagine a female clothing designer who meets with a female owner of an exclusive clothing retailer at the latter's home. As they converse, the designer suggests to the owner: "Let me look at your underwear drawer to show you something I have in mind." (As the apostle Paul said, we "speak as if insane" [2 Cor. 11:23]!) Here we would have a stranger rummaging around another's underwear drawer—an exceptional scenario but with a justifiable rationale. Likewise, we have argued that in unusual cases, an all-good and all-knowing God would have a reason for issuing a difficult command.

Furthermore, Rauser's point about a better or worse rationale is itself inapplicable here. He incorrectly asserts: "A stranger in your backyard could provide a good rationale for invading your property uninvited (for example, the need to check your gas meter)" as opposed to a stranger rummaging through your underwear drawer. A brief comment is in order. We have no reason to be skeptical of the fashion designer's rationale for looking through an underwear drawer. But if the "stranger in your backyard" were dressed as a cat burglar with a large bag and crowbar in hand, you would be skeptical of his claim to be a service worker. Whether we are skeptical or not depends on particular contextual features, not mere abstract criteria. Rauser's example only has plausibility because we tend to fill in details that aren't there. We assume the stranger in the backyard in his example is not dressed like a cat burglar, and we assume the person rummaging through our drawers is not a fashion designer having a friendly conversation with the owner of a clothing retailer. Once we move beyond abstractions and realize these details are not specified and we consider the cases in the absence of any such assumptions, it turns out that we are not inherently more skeptical of one over the other. We would be more skeptical in certain contexts and not skeptical in others, but this often depends on the details and facts of the case.

Rauser's second criterion for distinguishing legitimate rationales from spurious rationalizations is equally erroneous. He proposes the "criterion of common origin" which "demands suspicion if an alleged rationale conforms to a well-established pattern of rationalization." Rauser suggests that there are three elements typical to "narratives used to justify genocide." They are: (1) "*divide*: First you distinguish between an in-group and an out-group while attributing a superior authority or ontological status to the former." Rauser elaborates: "often the in-group's status is attributed to ontological superiority, but the division may also be rooted in what Ben Kiernan calls . . . 'historical anteriority,' that is, the view that the out-group has somehow abdicated their status or rights." Then, (2) "*demonize*: next you accuse the out-group of promoting an injustice, inequality or threat over against the in-group." Finally, (3) "*destroy*: . . . you implore the in-group to redress the injustice, often with a divine or transcendent imprimatur [i.e., stamp of approval]."[27]

The problem is that while these three elements are common, not just too common, narratives justifying illicit killing, they are present in many paradigmatic cases of *justified* uses of force as well. Consider a paradigm of justified killing: A group of police officers shoot dead a group of assailants who have broken into a woman's house and are attempting to murder her. In this case elements 1, 2, and 3 are present.

1　A person defending the police shooting will note both that the police act as agents of the government and hence have a justified authority over the assailants. The defender of such police action will also typically contend that the assailants, by attacking the woman, have forfeited their right to not be killed.[28]

2　Part of the justification for the shooting will involve the fact that the assailants were violating the woman's rights and hence by definition perpetuating injustice.

3　Justification for killing in this situation assumes the police officers' official and stated duty to not stand by and watch the woman's rights be violated but to use lethal force to prevent the murder. Often, in fact, the authority of the state to use force, or the right to kill in defense of others, will appeal to a transcendent source of authority or justification. Such things include the law of nature (or "natural law"), God-given natural rights, or the state's God-given authority to "bear the sword" (Rom. 13:4). Indeed, these have been historical and traditional defenses of the right to kill in defense of another by prominent legal experts like William Blackstone and political philosopher John Locke.[29]

If we adopt Rauser's criteria, then even paradigmatic cases of justifiable killing will have to be dismissed as "spurious rationalizations" sharing common features with the narrative used by the Nazis to justify genocide.

Pragmatic Argument

Rauser proposes a prudential or pragmatic reason for rejecting the claim that God would ever command killing the innocent. This one is based on the practical consequences of doing so. Rauser contends that believing God commanded the killing of the Canaanites has "contributed to a long history of moral atrocities."[30]

Rauser cites two examples. First, he refers to John Howard Yoder's claim that "for centuries at least from the time of Augustine to the age of Enlightenment, mainstream Christians took it for granted that the ancient Hebrew model does count as justification for empire and genocide."[31] Second, he refers to Jeremy Cott who "summarises the historic link between brutalising violence in Canaan" and activities such as the Crusades and Charlemagne's massacre of the Saxons.[32]

Rauser is not alone in this. Like him, several writers in particular single out the Crusades as an example of the biblical conquest narratives being used to justify widespread atrocities. Atheist philosopher Evan Fales states that "time and again" Christians appealed to the conquest narratives to motivate Crusades against heretics and infidels.[33] Susan Niditch similarly suggests these texts were used by Europeans to join crusading wars against Saracens (a term used for Muslims during the Middle Ages).[34] The Crusades appear to be the standard historical example.

There are two problems with this argument. First, Rauser's historical claims are dubious. Although we examine some of Yoder's inaccurate historical argument in chapter 23, let's briefly examine Yoder's first claim: from "Augustine to the age of Enlightenment, mainstream Christians" appealed to these texts as models to justify "empire and genocide." Daniel Heimbach notes that Augustine, in fact, *rejected* the claim that the Scriptures justified empire-building.[35] Augustine's perspective runs utterly contrary to towering philosophers such as Aristotle and Cicero, who had earlier argued in favor of attacking and conquering weaker or inferior nations—nations that nature had destined to be ruled. Augustine fully repudiated this claim: "But perhaps it is displeasing to good men to fight with most wicked unrighteousness, and provoke with voluntary war neighbors who are peaceable and do no wrong, in order to enlarge a kingdom? If they feel thus, I entirely approve and praise them."[36] Augustine's position was that a war was justified only if another nation had engaged in aggressive attack on one's citizens. Here is a passage by Augustine favorably cited by Thomas Aquinas: "A just war is wont to be described as one that avenges wrongs, when a nation or state has to be punished, for refusing to make amends for the wrongs inflicted by its subjects, or to restore what it has seized unjustly."[37] No, Augustine's view was *not* rejected by mainstream Christians. Furthermore, in the standard twelfth-century medieval textbook on canon law and jurisprudence—Gratian's *Decretum*—Augustine is cited alongside Isidore of Seville (AD ca. 560–636) defining a just war as "one waged by an edict either to recover lost goods (*res*) or to repel an enemy attack."[38]

Neither is genocide standardly justified by mainstream Christians through this period. In canon law, various classes of noncombatants were declared immune from attack. These prohibitions drew on traditions dating back to the Peace of God (*Pax Dei*) movement in the tenth century that increasingly sought to use legal means to reduce violence. The Peace of God movement sought to protect church property, priests, women, pilgrims, merchants, and other noncombatants from violence. This would extend to the twelfth century.

In the thirteenth century, Aquinas contended that it was always unlawful for a human being to kill an innocent person. One could kill a person who was sinning and whose sin was a danger to the common good of society, but the innocent one could not kill.[39] Francisco Vitoria applied Aquinas's reasoning in his fifteenth-century tract on the ethics of war: "Let my first proposition be: The deliberate slaughter of the innocent is never lawful in itself. This is proved, firstly, by *Exodus*, ch. 23: 'The innocent and righteous slay thou not.' Secondly, the basis of a just war is a wrong done, as has been shown above. But wrong is not done by an innocent person. Therefore war may not be employed against him."[40] He continues:

> It follows that even in war with the Turks it is not allowable to kill children. This is clear, because they are innocent. Aye, and the same holds with regard to the women of unbelievers. This is clear, because so far as the war is concerned, they are presumed innocent. . . . This same pronouncement must be made among Christians with regard to harmless agricultural folk, and also with regard to the rest of the peaceable civilian population, for all these are presumed innocent until the contrary is shown.[41]

The mainstream Christian just war theory, therefore, did not endorse genocidal wars of conquest as normative.

A second problem has to do with the widespread but incorrect assumption of the Old Testament war texts' influence on the Crusades. In chapter 22, we go into detail on this point; there we explore other widely accepted myths related to the Crusades. We point out that Old Testament scholar Douglas Earl's survey of several representative medieval texts, written when crusading ideology was dominant in Europe, shows that accounts of Joshua's warring in Canaan received, at most, a wisp of a mention in these documents and played little or no role in justifying the Crusades.[42] Instead, the biblical texts cited to justify participation in the Crusades were predominantly the teachings of *Jesus* in the New Testament—references to love, humility, self-sacrifice for the good of one's neighbor, and so on. The Crusades were understood as an act of humble, loving service in which people risked their lives to liberate Eastern Christians from the threat of Muslim invasion of Christianized lands as well as Muslim attacks and actions of humiliation against Christian pilgrims to the Holy Land.

This brings us to the second problem with Rauser's argument: It assumes as an implicit argument that *if a belief has "contributed to a long line of historical atrocities,"*[43] *then we should reject that belief.* While this claim is not made explicitly by Rauser (although Eric Seibert repeatedly makes this point in his works),[44] something like it is necessary in Rauser's argument—namely, that if believing God commanded the killing of the Canaanites has "contributed to a long line of historical atrocities," this is to be grounds for rejecting that belief.

This implicit premise is false. Earl's study, in fact, provides some obvious counterexamples. His study shows that believers who had read the Gospels about loving one another, engaging in selfless service, and defending the weak and oppressed, for example, were influenced by them, thus contributing to a long history of "moral atrocities." These are the same kinds of atrocities to which Rauser appeals to make his case. Does it then follow that we should reject the claim that we should love one another and self-sacrificially care and serve? Do we have a strong prudential or pragmatic argument that God would never command love and humility?

Various other counterexamples can be provided. The belief that the atom could be split is one that has been used to kill thousands of people, yet that belief is true and was an important scientific discovery.[45] The belief that theft is wrong has in the past led to the lynching of thieves. Does this show that theft is not really wrong, and we should not oppose it? Take Rauser's reference to the Inquisition-like strategy of *divide, demonize,* and *destroy.* Terrence Cuneo and Christopher Eberle point out that typically the suppression of heretics was defended by an appeal to various *secular* reasons.

> When such rights have been violated, the justifications offered, even by religious believers, appeal to alleged requirements for social order, such as the need for uniformity of belief on basic normative issues. One theological apologist for religious repression, for example, writes this: "The king punishes heretics as enemies, as extremely wicked rebels, who endanger the peace of the kingdom, which cannot be maintained without the unity of the faith. That is why they are burnt in Spain."[46]

Aquinas similarly appealed to the belief that counterfeiting money was wrong as a central premise for his defense of Inquisitional practice.[47] Does it follow then that we should reject publicly available moral claims against counterfeiting as wrong? Should we reject public reasons offered that civil peace should be promoted and rebellion against civil governments that threatens this peace suppressed? (Along these lines, in chap. 20 we respond to the common but mistaken modern notion that "religion"—and more specifically monotheistic belief—promotes violence and intolerance.)

Other examples illustrate the absurdity of this claim. The "Reign of Terror" (1793–94) during the French Revolution was justified by appeals to liberty, equality, fraternity, and the rights of humankind; one victim of the guillotine famously remarked, "Oh, Liberty, what crimes are committed in your name!" In the twentieth century, tens of millions have been slaughtered by appeals to the greater good of society or the liberation of the oppressed classes, and it is well known that people have defended wars on the basis of "social justice," "change," and "peace."[48] Should we therefore avoid liberty, equality, peace, opposing oppression, seeking justice, or altering an oppressive, unjust status quo? Rauser's appeal to a prudential argument, therefore, fails.

Conclusion

We can conclude then that one can coherently and defensibly attribute to God commands to kill innocent human beings under certain conditions. In the previous chapter, we maintained that one can coherently attribute to God commands that appear immoral, provided that these commands do not violate a nonnegotiable moral belief. We argued that as long as the command to kill innocent human beings is understood as a rare exception to the normal rule against homicide which God issues for some greater good or purpose, it is perfectly coherent to attribute that command to God.

In this chapter, we have argued that one can rationally attribute to God a command that under ordinary circumstances would be immoral to carry out when the grounds we have for thinking that God issued such a command are stronger than those we have for thinking the command is immoral. We rejected the arguments of Kant and Rauser who attempt to show that the belief that it is always wrong to kill the innocent is always more plausible than the belief that God could, on occasion, issue such a command.

Summary

• Provided the command to kill innocent human beings is understood as a rare exception to the normal prohibition against taking innocent human life that God issues for the sake of some greater good, then attributing this command to God does not violate a nonnegotiable moral belief.

- While the claim that it is *normally* or *generally* wrong to kill the innocent is a nonnegotiable moral belief, the claim that it is *absolutely* or *always* wrong under *any* circumstances is not.

- Immanuel Kant objected to the idea that there could ever be a violation of the Crucial Moral Principle, and he argued that it is more rational to hold this view than to believe that God could command something contrary to it (e.g., God's command for Abraham to sacrifice Isaac).

- Kant held that (1) *whenever two conflicting claims differ in epistemic (or knowability) status, the claim with the lower status is to be rejected*; and (2) *moral claims such as "it is wrong to kill innocent people" are certain*. The claim to divine revelation, however, is less sure than universal moral principles, Kant argued.

- However, Kant is overly optimistic about achieving confident knowledge about principles of wrongness. He thinks we can be fully certain across the board when it comes to moral judgments.

- Kant's conclusion is doubtful because moral clarity comes in degrees: (1) We can be *certain* that acts like torturing babies for fun are wrong. (2) We can agree that assault, theft, killing, and lying are wrong *in general* (*prima facie*, or "at first appearance"), but deceiving Nazis about hiding Jews in your basement would be a morally permissible exception. (3) Various moral claims are *not as certain*—issues such as capital punishment, end-of-life issues, just warfare, or church-state relations. We just don't have the kind of certainty about these matters that Kant claims we can have.

- Kant is incorrect that we can never be certain that God commanded a particular action. Given that a number of ethical questions are debatable, why couldn't God grant a higher knowability status to some particular command than to certain moral principles?

- It's highly doubtful and disputable that moral claims have a higher knowability status than theological beliefs.

- Also, Kant's own moral understanding was largely shaped by the influence of biblical revelation in Western culture.

- Most ethical schools recognize that there are certain rare exceptions to general moral rules including not killing innocent human beings.

- More recent objections take a similar approach to Kant. Consider the statement that bludgeoning babies is always wrong—as in the 1994 Rwandan genocide. While we would also condemn this act and agree that killing innocent people is wrong, we would not say this is true *without qualification*. If planes are hijacked by terrorists, and their goal is to fly these planes into buildings or where many people are gathered, the president would be warranted in having these planes shot out of the sky, even though this means that innocent people, including infants, would be killed. This is not an implausible, outrageous idea.

- Wide-ranging studies show that more than 80 percent of people affirm that one should throw a switch to divert a trolley that will otherwise kill five innocent people, though throwing the switch will kill an innocent bystander. So while infanticide is a crime in most cases, there are cases where it is at least plausible that this presumption could be overridden.

- What about the psychological and moral impact of Israelites being commanded to kill (cf. the My Lai massacre)? If just wars are possible (as we believe), then the use of military force is necessary to protect against aggressors. Most cases of PTSD (post-traumatic stress disorder) in the military do not occur as a result of combat (only 15 percent do); most of them result from having to identify charred human remains. But doing so is appropriate and even demanded. The order to identify charred remains is not immoral, despite the trauma it may bring with it. And surely it would not be immoral to encourage therapists to counsel PTSD patients, despite the therapists' ensuing exposure to accounts of traumatization, however emotionally taxing this is.

• What about the argument that when exceptions to killing are allowed, people can easily rationalize killing? Doesn't this create an us-versus-them perspective ("we are innocent; they are guilty")? True, but that is not the central issue here. We have seen that killing innocent people may be permissible in rare cases—all the more clearly if a good God commands this for a greater good. Furthermore, we could affirm that if God commanded that *we* be killed by others, this command would be morally justified.

• What about those who not only *divide* (us-versus-them) but *demonize* (accuse the out-group) and *destroy* (appealing to some divine or transcendent source of approval)? The problem is that *each* of these steps typically occurs in the state's response to criminal activity, including legal experts appealing to transcendent "natural law" (e.g., Blackstone and Locke).

• There is the claim that the belief that God actually commanded the killing of the Canaanites has resulted in atrocities throughout history (e.g., the Crusades), and so we should doubt that God actually commanded this. However, this school of argument (e.g., John Howard Yoder) is often historically inaccurate and misguided. Indeed, even Christians during the Middle Ages were defending just-war principles—not principles based on Old Testament warfare.

• Furthermore, the key biblical texts that inspired crusading were from the *Gospels*, not Joshua (see chap. 22). But should we therefore reject the Gospels and the words of Jesus himself? It doesn't follow that if a belief has contributed to a long line of historical atrocities, then we should reject that belief.

17

Is It Rational to Believe God Commanded the Killing of Innocents?

Our discussion so far has led us to conclude that the biblical text does *not* present God as commanding genocide. It does, however, suggest that on rare occasions, God, for the sake of some greater good, exempted Israel from the moral principle that otherwise would be binding on them—the principle that it is wrong to kill innocent human beings. That is, the Crucial Moral Principle is not absolute. We have argued that, contrary to what various critics contend, the grounds for this assertion are coherent and thus this claim is rationally believable *when the grounds for thinking God issued such a command are stronger than the grounds for thinking killing innocents is always wrong.*

This, however, raises the immediate question: Does the biblical theist have adequate grounds for thinking that God on these unique occasions issued such an exemption? Wesley Morriston has recently argued that the biblical theist cannot have adequate grounds for thinking this. Morriston appears to grant that God *could* command the killing of innocent people on rare occasions if doing so achieved some greater good. But, he continues, it is unlikely that God had some greater good in mind on the occasions recorded in Scripture:

The OT [Old Testament] texts themselves have quite a bit to say about what God's reasons were. So it will not be sufficient to make a blanket appeal to the transcendence of God and the cognitive limitations of human beings, arguing, that—for all we know—God may have had reasons for these commands which are too complicated or mysterious for us to understand. *The reasons actually given in the relevant OT texts* are not that complicated or mysterious, and they will have to be defended. If, relative to everything else we know, the reasons given in the OT are implausible and morally suspect, that will add strength to the prima facie case against the inerrancy of the OT.[1]

Morriston's claim is twofold. First, the relevant biblical texts explicitly state what God's reasons are for issuing the commands. Second, we have good grounds for thinking these reasons are inadequate ones for commanding the killing of innocent people. Morriston attempts to substantiate these claims by turning to what he takes to be the relevant texts: Deuteronomy 20:16; Deuteronomy 7:2; Numbers 31:15; and 1 Samuel 15:3. We will argue against Morriston's twofold claim as we unpack these texts.

Deuteronomy 20:16: "Save Alive Nothing That Breathes"

One text Morriston cites is Deuteronomy 20:16. "But in the cities of these peoples that the LORD your God is giving you for an inheritance, you shall save alive nothing that breathes" (ESV). Morriston asks why God would command such a thing. The rest of the text is quite explicit: "but you shall devote them to complete destruction, the Hittites and the Amorites, the Canaanites and the Perizzites, the Hivites and the Jebusites, as the LORD your God has commanded, that they may not teach you to do according to all their abominable practices that they have done for their gods, and so you sin against the LORD your God" (vv. 17–18 ESV). What are these "abominable practices"? Morriston wonders. "Two in particular have caught the eye of prominent Christian philosophers: Temple prostitution and child sacrifice."[2] Here Morriston cites one philosopher—Richard Swinburne—in his recent defense of these reasons. Morriston claims that this case fails:

> Citing these texts, Swinburne suggests that God's purpose in issuing the genocidal command was to preserve Israel "from lethal spiritual infection by the polytheism of the Canaanites." Swinburne assures us that "when monotheism had become more deeply rooted in Israel, such an extreme measure was not, according to the Old Testament, required again." The extermination program, he says, was "a defensive measure necessary to preserve the identity of the people of Israel."[3]

We must ask whether this is a morally acceptable explanation. Swinburne thinks it is. "Even today, and without a divine command," he says, many people would think it justified to kill people who had an infectious lethal disease and refused to be kept isolated from the rest of the population. Those who think that an infection that leads to spiritual death is as bad an evil as one that leads to natural death will think that there are reasons (though not of course adequate reasons) for the Israelites to kill the Canaanites even without a divine command.[4]

Morriston replies that these reasons for God's command to kill the Canaanites are clearly inadequate:

> The obvious worry is that this line of argument may have wider application than Swinburne intends it to have. After all, many persons carrying what he would presumably count as "spiritual infection" are amongst us today. What should be done about that? Should a law be passed silencing evangelical atheists of the Richard Dawkins type, or requiring that they isolate themselves from the rest of the population? If they refused to comply, would there be a prima facie reason to kill them? What if someone were to announce that God had commanded the assassination of such persons? I presume that Swinburne (like the rest of us) would regard such a person as a dangerous lunatic. But on what principled ground could he make that judgment?[5]

So, as Morriston sees it, God's reason for the command as cited in Deuteronomy 20:16–18 is inadequate.

In our view, there are three problems with Morriston's argument. First, contrary to what Morriston asserts, Deuteronomy 20:16–18 does not explicitly state that *God's* reason for issuing the command was to prevent the Israelites from being taught to follow the abhorrent practices of the Canaanite nations. What the text states is this: "but you shall devote them to complete destruction . . . as the LORD your God has commanded, that they may not teach you to do according to all their abominable practices that they have done for their gods, and so you sin against the LORD your God" (vv. 17–18 ESV). This does not state *God's* reasons for issuing the command; rather, it gives *the Israelites* a reason to obey a command God has already laid down.

This distinction is subtle but important. For example, the reason for legislators issuing a law is not always the same as the reason a citizen has for obeying their legislation. At a crude level, the existence of sanctions or punishments makes this obvious. One reason all of us citizens have to obey laws is to avoid punishment. But the legislators' reasons for passing these laws were not so that citizens should escape punishment, since prior to passing the law there was no punishment imposed for disobedience.

The point extends to reasons beyond the avoidance of punishment. Consider, for example, the institution of parenthood. There may be good, impartial reasons based on promoting general societal welfare for laying down clear rules to identify who parents are and to require them to adequately provide for their children. However, it doesn't follow that parents obey this rule for the sake of general societal well-being. Parents care for their children because they love their children; if the reason they care for their particular children is out of some general impartial concern for all, they probably won't enhance the general social welfare nearly as well. Rather, the general welfare requires that parents care for their children because they love those particular children. This illustrates how the reasons for issuing a command and the reasons why people should obey that command are not the same.

This distinction was noted by philosopher Richard Brandt.[6] He makes the point that *what justifies someone in promoting the acceptance of a code or set of rules* is not necessarily the same as *the motivation or reason people have for following those rules*. Given that humans are not all-knowing, if they attempt to do individual actions because those actions have the best overall consequences for society, they will in fact *fail* to bring about the best consequences for society. Yes, they can calculate the long-term effects of their actions and weighing the alternatives, but they will not benefit society by doing so. But what is the result if they try to avoid a certain behavior *for its own sake* rather than for the general good of society? The outcome is to bring general benefit to society! If people avoid killing because it harms others or refrain from breaking promises because it violates trust with others, this will in fact bring overall improved consequences to society even though this wasn't the goal of the actions.

Adam Smith drew on a similar distinction in his book *The Wealth of Nations*. There he argued that the common good is not necessarily opposed to self-interest. Society overall can benefit when *my* goods can benefit *you* and *your* goods can benefit *me*. However, *self-interest* is not identical to *selfishness*. It's a normal and healthy self-interest to feed and nourish our bodies, for example (cf. Eph. 5:29 NASB: "for no one ever hated his own flesh, but nourishes and cherishes it"). So if you are a baker, you provide a service that can benefit me (I can eat the bread you have made and feed my body), and you benefit, too (the payment you receive from me helps sustain you and your family). Attending to our mutual self-interest can actually bring benefit to society.[7]

In light of such distinctions, we can see more clearly that Morriston's argument is mistaken. The text he has cited does not provide an account of *God's* reasons for issuing the command. It gives *Israelites* a reason for obeying.

However, even if one ignores this point—one we consider substantial—a second problem emerges. Morriston simply does not provide grounds for thinking these reasons are inadequate. All his argument shows—if successful—is that Swinburne has failed to defend these reasons. However, the failure of one person to defend a position is a far cry from the claim that the position itself is problematic.

Third, Morriston's critique of Swinburne is unpersuasive because it misses some important disanalogies found in Swinburne's defense. (You will recall what we noted in chap. 10—namely, a whole crop of disanalogies in Morriston's comparison of the US president calling for an invasion of Iran.)

Morriston refers to Swinburne's comments about lethal infection. It's worth looking at what Swinburne says in full: "God's reason for issuing this command, according to the Old Testament, was to preserve the young monotheistic religion of Israel from lethal spiritual infection by the polytheism of the Canaanites, a religion which included child sacrifice and cultic prostitution. Such spiritual infection was without doubt a very real danger."[8] Swinburne does not simply mention "spiritual infection"; he refers to a specific type of spiritual infection—one that includes "child sacrifice." Moreover, Swinburne notes that it produced a threat to the "young monotheistic religion of Israel."

Swinburne emphasizes this point when he adds, "When monotheism had become more deeply rooted in Israel, such an extreme measure was not, according to the Old Testament, required again. It was a defensive measure necessary to preserve the identity of the people of Israel."[9] Moreover as Morriston notes, the passage *limits* the command, "to the nations the LORD your God is giving you as an inheritance" (Deut. 20:16). In other words, it emphasizes that the people who engaged in these practices were occupying land to which Israel had legal title.

These features of Swinburne's position call into question Morriston's analogies. For example, "evangelical atheists of the Richard Dawkins type" are *not* typically leading people to engage in human sacrifice, nor are they typically occupying church buildings and church lands without owner consent and refusing to leave. And while they might threaten to lead various individuals astray, they are not a threat to the existence of the whole community of believers.

If Morriston's analogy were changed to reflect these differences, it would cease to carry as much force. (1) Suppose, for example, the atheist Richard Dawkins was trespassing on church property, refusing to leave. (2) Imagine further he was leading people not just to apostasy but to a specific type of apostasy that involved human sacrifice of infants. (3) And, finally, assume that his doing so threatened the entire community of God's people—that his influence was threatening to lead almost all the churches in the world into those practices; in fact, his actions would, in principle, frustrate God's mission to bring salvation to the world. In such circumstances, "should a law be passed silencing evangelical atheists of the Richard Dawkins type, or requiring that they isolate themselves from the rest of the population?"

The answer is plausibly *Yes*. Under the laws of England, Dawkins's own country, human sacrifice is a form of murder, and a person who counsels a person to engage in murder is guilty of murder.[10] Hence, under present laws in England, a person who advocates this sort of spiritual infection will not only be silenced; he or she will be incarcerated—which of course involves isolating this person from the rest of the population.

If Dawkins engages in this activity to "aid and abet" murder, should he then be imprisoned or capitally punished by some authorized agency? Under the laws of Morriston's own state of Colorado, a person who commits murder with premeditation and has a history of violent offenses is guilty of a capital offense—a law that has been on the books since 1859.[11] No doubt capital punishment is controversial, but the claim that something is controversial is a far cry from the claim that only a "dangerous lunatic" would argue for capital punishment under these circumstances. Most ethics textbooks today contain articles from respected mainstream philosophers defending capital punishment. Are these people all "dangerous lunatics"?

Finally, under the laws of most Western jurisdictions today, a person who attempts to undermine the mission and identity of a group on their own property and refuses to leave commits an act of trespass and can be removed by force if necessary. Our point is that if Richard Dawkins were to threaten "spiritual infection" analogous to the sort Swinburne has in mind, then it's simply false that only a dangerous lunatic would advocate that he be stopped and silenced through imprisonment or a more severe form of punishment.

Deuteronomy 7:2: "Destroy Them Totally"

A further example Morriston cites is Deuteronomy 7:2, where God is reportedly commanding the Israelites to totally destroy the seven Canaanite nations. Morriston states:

> What we are concerned with, after all, is the character of the God of the Hebrew Bible, and its authors do not leave us in the dark about the reasons for genocide. It is said to be a way of preventing the Israelites from marrying the Canaanites and joining in the worship of their gods (Deut. 7:1–6). *This* reason is not beyond our ken. If anything it is only too humanly comprehensible, and it is not difficult to evaluate. We can think of any other number of ways an

omnipotent being might have inoculated the Israelites against apostasy without commanding them to engage in indiscriminate slaughter. Moreover, the biblical records make it abundantly clear that the chosen method did not get the job done. God's supposed plan simply did not pan out.[12]

Morriston makes two claims here. First, he asserts that Deuteronomy 7:1–6 teaches that God's reasons for commanding genocide were to prevent the Israelites from marrying Canaanites and worshiping other gods. Second, he offers an argument that this reason is inadequate. We think both moves are questionable.

What does Deuteronomy 7:1–6 actually say? Here is the text:

> When the LORD your God brings you into the land you are entering to possess and drives out before you many nations—the Hittites, Girgashites, Amorites, Canaanites, Perizzites, Hivites and Jebusites, seven nations larger and stronger than you—and when the LORD your God has delivered them over to you and you have defeated them, then you must destroy them totally. Make no treaty with them, and show them no mercy. Do not intermarry with them. Do not give your daughters to their sons or take their daughters for your sons, for they will turn your children away from following me to serve other gods, and the LORD's anger will burn against you and will quickly destroy you. This is what you are to do to them: Break down their altars, smash their sacred stones, cut down their Asherah poles and burn their idols in the fire. For you are a people holy to the LORD your God. The LORD your God has chosen you out of all the peoples on the face of the earth to be his people, his treasured possession.

First, as we have argued above, this text doesn't portray God as commanding genocide, which Morriston defines as "the deliberate and systematic extermination of a national or ethnic group."[13] Nor does this command commit Israel to killing people with the intention of physically destroying the whole or a substantial part of an ethnic or religious group. The text states that the Israelites must totally destroy the Canaanites *after* God had "drive[n] out" these Canaanite nations. God says he would deliver them over to Israel (v. 2)— that is, the remaining Canaanites who have not been driven out or fled from the field, but remained to fight and would have been subsequently defeated.

The author of the text does not say that God issued the command to totally destroy the Canaanites to prevent the Israelites from marrying Canaanites or worshiping their gods. True, the text juxtaposes the command to totally destroy the Canaanite nations alongside a series of other commands which include a command to "not give your daughters to their sons or take their daughters for your sons" (v. 3). The text doesn't cite this as the reason *God* issued the command. Contrary to what Morriston says, in this passage *God doesn't state explicitly what his reasons are at all.* The text does go on to warn the Israelites of some negative consequences if they intermarry with the Canaanites, make treaties with them, or fail to destroy their religious objects. Providing Israel with some reasons to obey one of these commands is not the same as showing the reasons God has for commanding them to totally destroy the Canaanites.

Morriston's second assertion is also problematic. He says that the prevention of intermarriage and apostasy does *not* constitute a sufficient reason for God to command such violence. Morriston provides two grounds for rejecting this purported reason for God's command: (1) *God had other (presumably less morally reprehensible) means of achieving this goal,* and (2) *this method failed to achieve the goal in question anyway.* However, neither argument seems compelling. Let's explore these one at a time.

With respect to 1, Morriston argues: "Assuming God's desire to destroy the Canaanite religion by destroying the Canaanites was a legitimate one, why would he choose such an inefficient means of accomplishing his aim? It is only too easy to imagine the Almighty using other more effective means to remove the Canaanites from the picture."[14]

This argument, however, proves too much. Morriston's argument makes this assumption: *A loving and just God would not command people to suppress some evil he desires to be suppressed if God has a more efficient means of suppressing that evil himself.* But this is clearly false. If it were true, then we would have to give up almost everything we take for granted about morality. Consider, for example, the existence of courts which suppress crimes such as theft and rape. It's clear that God could suppress the evils of crime far more efficiently without relying on human beings. God could, for example, exercise his causal powers to stop every thief or rapist, and he could punish each one immediately himself without relying on detectives, police forces, and courts. Does it follow, then, that a loving and just God would never permit human beings to set up courts that punish crime?

Here is another example—namely, a paradigm case of justified killing. A woman in self-defense kills a rapist who has attacked and tried to kill her. Obviously, God can prevent rapes and murders far more effectively than an attacked woman can; does it follow that God would never permit humans to kill in self-defense? In fact, Morriston's assumption would have the implication that God would never issue even a general command against homicide. If God desires that homicides never occur, he has much more effective means of stopping them than commanding human beings to not kill. Such examples could be multiplied.

Morriston's argument requires that a loving and just God would not command anyone to refrain from homicide or permit courts to punish thieves or permit women to defend themselves from lethal attack. This is clearly absurd.[15]

Similar problems afflict the second justification for Morriston's argument—that God's "chosen method did not get the job done." The biblical record shows that the Israelites did not follow God's command and that the Canaanite nations and religion were not destroyed. The problem is that this is again true of many actions which a loving and just God would plausibly prohibit. A loving and just God would command people not to rape. Nonetheless, history shows that people still rape, and the good God desires is unrealized. A loving and just God would command people not to harm each other through murder, assault, or theft. Yet throughout history people have continued to murder, steal, and cause harm. In doing so, they prevent the certain goods from being attained that would come through complying with such commands. Does this mean that God would not issue commands to refrain from rape, murder, theft, and assault?

Morriston is mistaken in claiming that Deuteronomy 7 spells out explicitly what God's reasons for the command were. And even if the text did so, the ground or justification Morriston provides for thinking God's reasons fail is itself problematic.

Numbers 31:15: "Have You Allowed All the Women to Live?"

The third example Morriston cites to make his point is the defeat of Midian as recorded in Numbers 31. In this passage, the Israelites "fought against Midian, as the LORD commanded Moses, and killed every man" (v. 7). After the battle, however, Moses commanded Israel to ". . . kill all the boys. And kill every woman who has slept with a man, but save for yourselves every girl who has never slept with a man" (vv. 17–18). Morriston states: "The reason for all this is quite explicit. Once again, the danger of 'spiritual infection' by foreign religious practices is the issue. Yahweh was angered by the fact that some young Israelite men had worshiped Baal alongside their new Midianite brides. Not only must the Israelites be punished, but *the Midianites must be punished for causing the Israelites to be punished.*"[16]

God's stated reasons, according to Morriston's thinking, are inadequate:

> Of course, none of this makes the slightest sense. Yahweh blames the Midianites, as if *they* had caused all the trouble, "harassing" the Israelites with their "wiles." What wiles? To what end? The Midianites could not have been *trying* to harm the Israelites by inviting them to participate in the worship of a god in whom

they obviously believed. Nor could they have known that Yahweh would become enraged and send a plague killing 24,000 Israelites. Why, then, does Yahweh tell Moses that the Israelites are to "avenge themselves" against the Midianites? I do not think there is a morally satisfying answer to that question.[17]

Morriston appears to have misread the text. First, consider his claim that the text explicitly states that God's reason for commanding the killing of the Midianite women and boys was "spiritual infection" because "some young Israelite men had worshiped Baal alongside their new Midianite brides." There are several problems with this.

First is the fact that, in the text Morriston cites (Num. 31:17–18), *God himself* does not explicitly command Israel to kill all the Midianite women and boys—which we pointed out in chapter 9. God's command to Moses regarding the Midianites is actually recorded in Numbers 25:17–18 and 31:1–2. Let's look at these. First, Numbers 25:17–18 states, "Be hostile to the Midianites and strike them; for they have been hostile to you with their tricks, with which they have deceived you in the affair of Peor and in the affair of Cozbi" (NASB).[18] Here God explicitly commands Israel to respond to the Midianites' spiritual subterfuge by fighting against the Midianites and defeating them. Nowhere does God state his reasons for issuing this command, though he does give some reasons why Israel should obey it. These reasons are not the "spiritual infection" of women Morriston talks about; rather, the reasoning has to do with the fact that Midian has been hostile toward and deceived Israel.

Let's move to God's specific command in Numbers 31:1–2. The text reads: "The LORD spoke to Moses, saying, 'Avenge the Israelites on the Midianites; afterward you shall be gathered to your people'" (NRSV). Here again God only commands that Israel go to war; his reasons for issuing this command are not cited. Furthermore, in verse 7 we read: "They fought against Midian, *as the LORD commanded Moses*, and killed every man." This suggests that the Israelites, by fighting and defeating Midian and killing all the male combatants, fulfilled God's explicit command.

The command to kill women and children cited by Morriston actually occurs *after* this—that is, after Israel had *already* carried out God's specific command. Interestingly, normally in the Torah when Moses utters a command on God's behalf, the passage begins with, "The LORD commanded Moses"; aside from Israel's carrying out God's command noted in 31:7, this preface is absent from the commands given by Moses in chapter 31. The text does not explicitly attribute this command to God at all. In fact, the text appears to make a differentiation between God's command and that of Moses.

Morriston acknowledges this later in his essay. However, he suggests three reasons why this observation "does not come to much": (1) "Moses is regularly characterized as being very close to Yahweh" (cf. Deut. 34:10–12), faithfully obeying his instructions—"except for the notable incident in which he strikes a rock instead of speaking to it" (Num. 20:2–13); (2) "Yahweh expresses no disapproval of anything Moses does in this story"; and (3) "Yahweh himself is the principal instigator of the attack on Midian."[19]

These responses, however, are inadequate. Let's begin with the last one (3) first. The fact that someone is the "principal instigator" of an attack and commands or permits someone to go to war does not entail that they command or approve every single action that takes place within the battle in question. Many people who believe England's decision to oppose Nazi aggression with force was justified do not likewise support the terror bombing of Dresden in February 1945. Similarly, many people who believed Japan's attack on Pearl Harbor (December 7, 1941) was justification for the United States to declare war on Japan did not, consequently, support the bombing of Nagasaki and Hiroshima (August 1945). Likewise, we can differentiate between the text in which God explicitly commands Israel to "be hostile" and "strike" Midian, and the text that says their actions of killing the men and sparing the women and children were done "as the LORD commanded Moses."

Similarly with 2: the lack of explicit disapproval in the text does not entail approval. For one thing, Morriston's argument here commits the logical fallacy of appealing to ignorance (*argumentum ad ignorantiam*). But as the dictum goes: *absence of evidence is not evidence of absence*. Just because we have no author's comment on action is not an argument for the author's endorsement of that act. The biblical narrative often recounts events where characters explicitly sin and yet no explicit disapproval is mentioned. Lot's daughters raping and conceiving through him (Gen. 19:31–38), for example, is passed over with no explicit disapproval. David's multiplication of wives is contrary to one of the laws governing kingship (Deut. 17:17)—and again, no expressed disapproval. We might also mention Abraham's disastrous mistake of taking Hagar as a secondary "wife" (Gen. 16:3) instead of trusting God to produce an heir through Sarah—or perhaps Samson's consorting with a prostitute (Judg. 16:1). It is not uncommon in biblical narratives for authors to describe sinful behavior without expressing explicit disapproval. In most cases, no doubt, the author *expects the reader to know* certain actions are right and wrong.

Finally, regarding 1, "Moses is regularly characterized as being very close to Yahweh," we can reply in this way:[20] the fact that someone is portrayed in the text as "close to God" or "faithful to him" does not mean that every action he is recorded as doing is commanded by or endorsed by God. For example, David is said to have been a man after God's own heart (1 Sam. 13:14); he was a king who was fully devoted to the Lord (1 Kings 15:3) and who "did what was right in the eyes of the Lord" (2 Kings 22:2). Yet even the most casual reader of the book of Samuel will be struck by David's many moral failures: multiplying wives (2 Sam. 5:13), murdering Uriah the Hittite and committing adultery with his wife (2 Sam. 11–12), taking a census (1 Chron. 21:1–17—an act likely motivated by David's pride in military might and indicating a failure to trust in God; cf. 1 Chron. 14:11; 16:8), inaction after the rape of his daughter Tamar (2 Sam. 13), inaction in the face of Absalom's rebellion (2 Sam. 14–18), and the list goes on.

Likewise, Abraham is held up as "the friend of God" (James 2:23 NASB; cf. 2 Chron. 20:7), a paradigm of faith. Yet the Genesis narrative records him failing on many points and making various mistakes. Again, the Scriptures declare that King Josiah "did what was right in the eyes of the Lord . . . not turning aside to the right or to the left" (2 Chron. 34:2). Yet Scripture candidly affirms that he showed bad judgment in his campaign against Pharaoh Neco and lost his life as a result (2 Chron. 35:20–23). Though an apostle, Peter was publicly rebuked by Paul for removing himself from table fellowship with gentile believers (Gal. 2:11–14). One simply cannot conclude that because a person is described as "close to God" or a "faithful servant" that everything that person does in the text is in accord with God's commands (cf. the disobedient "man of God" [1 Kings 13, esp. v. 26]). The biblical narrative provides numerous examples.

So in the Numbers 31 text, God does not explicitly command Israel to "kill all the boys. And kill every woman who has slept with a man." Moses commands this, and in this context, he appears to be speaking on his own behalf.

A second instance of Morriston's misreading of the text is that not only does he attribute Moses's reasons to God; he also *misstates* the reasons Moses *does* give in the text. Morriston suggests that "Yahweh was angered by the fact that some young Israelite men had worshiped Baal alongside their new Midianite brides." However, in the text Moses actually says this: "Have you allowed all the women to live? These women here, on Balaam's advice, made the Israelites act treacherously against the Lord in the affair of Peor, so that the plague came among the congregation of the Lord" (vv. 15–16 NRSV).

What is the real issue? The Midianite women had been following the devious advice of the pagan seer, Balaam, who had been explicitly commanded by God not to curse Israel (Num. 22–24). Balaam had led the Israelites into acting *treacherously* at Baal-Peor. *This* is the clearly stated issue (31:16).

The backdrop for this is contained in the larger context of the Pentateuch. Israel had been delivered from slavery in Egypt: during this time they witnessed the ten plagues, the parting of the Red (Reed) Sea, the leading of the pillar of fire and the cloud, the manna from heaven, various signs in the desert, and so on. At Mount Sinai (Horeb), they entered into a covenant with Yahweh (Exodus 24). Comparative historical studies of ancient documents strongly suggest that the covenant, as recorded in Exodus 20–24 (as well as Deuteronomy) takes the form of a suzerain-vassal treaty.[21] This was a treaty or covenant between two parties of unequal social status, normally a powerful ruler (suzerain) and weaker land holder (vassal). Occasionally, a small nation that was being threatened or oppressed by a neighboring king would enter into a treaty with a great king to free themselves from this oppression.

After freeing them, the king would offer protection to the vassal nation, guaranteeing them control over their own property. In exchange, the vassal nation would acknowledge the king as their sole legitimate ruler, swear exclusive loyalty and allegiance, agree to make no alliances with other kings, and promise to obey his laws. Under the legal conventions of the period, to violate this covenant was a form of *treason* (which we discussed in chap. 5). If the smaller nation did not keep its part of the agreement, then the great king would be free not to keep his part, and the smaller nation would no longer be protected from invading enemies.

It is in such a context that Numbers 31 is to be understood. Israel had seen firsthand miraculous proof that Yahweh is God (see chap. 19 in this book). The Israelites had voluntarily bound themselves in a vassal treaty to Yahweh; they had promised exclusive loyalty to him. Moses is concerned that Israel had acted *treacherously*—that is, knowingly committing treason and violating the oath they had made with Yahweh. The very act of treachery highlighted is the affair at Peor (Num. 25)—treachery instigated by the Moabite king Balak, who followed the seer Balaam's advice.

Balak purchased the services of the seer Balaam to "curse" the nation of Israel so that Balak could launch a military attack against this wandering nation to severely harm and even destroy them (Num. 22). Of course, modern readers are skeptical of the efficacy of cursing, but the characters in the narrative (not to mention the biblical authors) believed at least in its potential efficacy. In contemporary language, conspiracy to commit mass murder and attempted mass murder are being engaged in. Of course, Balak's problem is that God refuses to let Balaam curse Israel (cf. Gen. 12:3) and instead blesses them. By the end of Numbers 24, however, it is made clear to Balaam and Balak that God *will not curse* Israel because they are God's people.

Immediately following this (in Numbers 25), Israel deals "treacherously against the Lord in the affair of Peor" (Num. 31:16 NRSV). Contrary to Morriston, this is not a case of Israelites worshiping with "new Midianite brides." The Revised Standard Version, which Morriston uses, states, "the people began to *play the harlot* with the daughters of Moab" (25:1) and the Midianites (cf. 25:6, 18). The Hebrew verb here (*zanah*) is translated as "played the harlot" (NASB), "whore with" (ESV), or "indulge in sexual immorality," and it is used ninety-nine times in the Old Testament, typically regarding prostitution or adultery. What occurs, then, is not that some Israelites marry Midianite women, but rather these women use sex to seduce Israel into violating the terms of their covenant with God—an event that threatened Israel's very national identity, calling, and destiny. The text's mention that "Israel joined [*tsamad*] themselves to Baal of Peor" (Num. 25:3 NASB) gives further indication of covenant-breaking against Yahweh.

Moreover, the text states that this act was in fact deliberate: "These women here, *on Balaam's advice, made* the Israelites act treacherously against the LORD in the affair of Peor" (Num. 31:16 NRSV, emphasis added). And the New Testament commentary on this passage confirms the same picture: "Balaam, who taught Balak to put a stumbling block before the people of Israel, so that they would eat food sacrificed to idols and practice fornication" (Rev. 2:14 NRSV; cf. 2 Pet. 2:15; Jude 11).

Consequently, Morriston's comments are far off the mark when he insists that the "Midianites could not have been *trying* to harm the Israelites by inviting them to participate in the worship of a god in whom they obviously believed."[22] His other suggestion—that "they could not have known that Yahweh would become enraged and send a plague"—is similarly flawed. The whole point of the exercise was *to get God to curse Israel* so that a military attack could be launched by Moab and Midian (Num. 22:4, 7). The picture here is not of Israelites and innocent Midianite brides. It's more like that of the famous double agent Mata Hari (1876–1917), who seduced French men so she could then relay their secrets to the Germans during World War I—secrets used with the intention of bringing about France's military defeat. Or we could compare the picture of the Midianite sexual seduction to that of female KGB agents during the Cold War who used sex to persuade Americans to betray their country by passing on vital secrets.

The biblical narrative portrays a picture of a pagan prophet, Balaam, who knows that Yahweh will not curse the nation of Israel, with whom he has made a covenant. So Balaam suggests that women be sent into the Israelite camp for the purpose of seducing men into committing adultery and idolatry. This was done with the knowledge that these were—under the terms of ancient Near Eastern legal conventions—acts tantamount to treason. This subterfuge was carried out with the knowledge that God had delivered Israel from the hand of the mighty Egyptians (Num. 22:1–7), which filled king Balak with fear. So to induce this nation to commit treason against its king or suzerain—Yahweh—would result in this powerful deity no longer protecting them. This in turn would make them vulnerable to Moab's and Midian's military attack.

So for Morriston to suggest the concerns here are simply "spiritual infection" from foreign religious practices is false. Note that the problem wasn't God's opposition to Israelites marrying Midianites *per se*. Indeed, Moses married Zipporah, a Midianite, and he received wise counsel from his father-in-law, Jethro (or Reuel)—a Midianite priest (Exod. 2:15–21; 18:1–12).

Finally, as we noted, the text does not portray Yahweh as commanding the killing of Midianite women and children. God commands Israel to take Midian's actions as an act of war and meet them in battle. Again, the text specifically states that God's command had been fulfilled by Israel: "They warred against Midian, as the LORD commanded Moses, and killed every male" (Num. 31:7 ESV). They killed the combatants and spared the noncombatants. Only later does *Moses* order that the women who had deliberately seduced the Israelite men into treachery be executed alongside children. Contrary to Morriston's assertion, we do not actually read in the text that the Lord issued a command against noncombatants.

1 Samuel 15:3: "Do Not Spare Them"

Morriston's final example is the account of Saul's destruction of the Amalekites in 1 Samuel 15:

> Samuel said to Saul, ". . . now therefore listen to the words of the LORD. Thus says the LORD of hosts, 'I will punish [*paqad*] the Amalekites for what they did in opposing the Israelites when they came up out of Egypt. Now go and attack Amalek, and utterly destroy all that they have; do not spare them, but kill both man and woman, child and infant, ox and sheep, camel and donkey." (vv. 1–5 NRSV)

Morriston suggests this should be read alongside Deuteronomy 25:17–19:

> Remember what Amalek did to you on your journey out of Egypt, how he attacked you on the way, when you were faint and weary, and struck down all who lagged behind you; he did not fear God. Therefore when the LORD your God has given you rest from all your enemies on every hand, in the land that the LORD your God is giving you as an inheritance to possess, you shall blot out the remembrance of Amalek from under heaven; do not forget. (NRSV)

Juxtaposting these two texts leads Morriston to reject interpretations of the passage proposed by Eleonore Stump. Stump suggests that when God "made reckoning [*paqad*]" of what the Amalekites had done hundreds of years previously, he also made note of the fact that the Amalekites had long been on a very bad trajectory—that they had "progressively gotten worse and worse" as a nation.[23]

Now, Morriston dismisses this as "unsupported speculation," which fails to do justice to the text. Morriston states:

> In the "timeline" of the biblical narrative, the text in Deuteronomy describes a divine judgment that precedes the command to attack Amalek by many hundreds of years. According to the narrative, Yahweh was already—at that earlier time—determined to have Israel blot out Amalek on account of what it had done to "faint and weary" Israelites who "lagged behind" on their long march up out of Egypt. The implied reason for waiting a while to deal with the Amalekites has nothing to do with *future* Amalekite transgressions. It has instead to do with the urgent need to get the Israelites safely settled in Canaan. Once that has been accomplished, it will be time to *remember* and to *blot out*.[24]

However, Morriston's own claim that the reason for waiting a while to deal with the Amalekites has "nothing to do with *future* Amalekite transgressions" is refuted by the text. Morriston is correct that 1 Samuel 15:1–5 refers to *past* sins of the nation of Amalek—when they opposed defenseless Israel as they had just come out of Egypt (Exod. 17). But the text goes on to say: "Go and completely destroy *those wicked people*, the Amalekites; wage war against them until you have wiped them out" (1 Sam. 15:18). Despite the past, here the emphasis is on the *present wickedness* of the current Amalekites. A few verses later, when Samuel executes the Amalekite king Agag, he states, "*As your sword has made women childless*, so will your mother be childless among women" (v. 33). Samuel put Agag to death because of his personal involvement in aggressive wars.

Moreover, immediately prior to 1 Samuel 15, the narrator summarizes Saul's military achievements: "After Saul had assumed rule over Israel, he fought against their enemies on every side. . . . He fought valiantly and defeated the Amalekites, delivering Israel from the hands of those who had plundered them" (14:47–48). So just a few verses prior to God's command through Samuel to wipe out the Amalekites, we see evidence of Amalek's *present* aggression against Israel—and *a reason for Saul's military response*.

We suggest that the best way to understand this passage is not just to read it alongside Deuteronomy (25:17–19), but also alongside a passage like Jeremiah 18:7–10:

At one moment I might speak concerning a nation or concerning a kingdom to uproot, to pull down, or to destroy it; if that nation against which I have spoken turns from its evil, I will relent concerning the calamity I planned to bring on it. Or at another moment I might speak concerning a nation or concerning a kingdom to build up or to plant it; if it does evil in My sight by not obeying My voice, then I will think better of the good with which I had promised to bless it. (NASB)

Jeremiah makes clear that announcements of future judgment against a nation are conditional; they are contingent on the members of that nation not repenting. Notice that this applies to *any* nation ("if that nation…"), and this would include even the wicked Amalekites ("if that nation . . . turns from its evil, I will relent").

The book of Jonah makes a similar point. Jonah goes to Nineveh, the capital city of Israel's enemy to the north—Assyria. This important capital was a "three-day-visit" city ("it took three days to go through it" [Jon. 3:3]). That is, a state visitor to this diplomatic center had to follow the three-day protocol: locating and greeting appropriate officials, presenting credentials, giving gifts (day one); meeting and conducting the desired business (day two); and having a send-off with any government responses being delegated to emissaries (day three).[25] Significantly, on the very *first* day (v. 6), Jonah's message that seemed fraught with inevitable doom—"Forty more days and Nineveh will be overthrown" (v. 4)—struck its mark. It awakened the entire city—including King Asshur-dan III himself—to repentance. The king urged his people: "Let everyone call urgently on God. Let [all] give up their evil ways and their violence. Who knows? God may yet relent and with compassion turn from his fierce anger so that we will not perish" (vv. 8–9).

This announcement was explicitly said to be a prophetic utterance made on God's behalf. Yet the text goes further to state that the inhabitants of Nineveh repented, and so God did not bring the prophesied calamity. Judgment was not a guarantee. The king had no inkling of what God would do: "*Who knows*, God may yet relent and with compassion turn from his fierce anger so that we will not perish" (v. 9). By contrast, the prophet Jonah knew of God's gracious and compassionate character (cf. Exod. 34:6) and relenting from judgment is the very thing God readily does: "Please LORD, *was not this what I said while I was still in my own country?* Therefore in order to forestall this I fled to Tarshish, for I *knew* that You are a gracious and compassionate God, slow to anger and abundant in lovingkindness, and one who relents concerning calamity" (Jon. 4:2 NASB).

If prophetic pronouncements of doom are conditional, then this nicely explains what we see in 1 Samuel 15. True, Deuteronomy 25:17–19 reflects on how the ruthless Amalekites showed no concern for a weary, vulnerable Israelite population just after they had crossed the Red Sea. For this reason, God announced that the Amalekites would, at a future time, be "blotted out." This statement, however, was implicitly conditional. Judgment was contingent on Amalek's refusal to repent. But the biblical narrative shows that for nearly a millennium—from the Red Sea crossing (fourteenth/thirteenth century BC) to Haman the Agagite's attempt to wipe out the Jews under Ahasuerus in Persia (fifth century BC)—the Amalekites were unrelenting in their hostility toward Israel.[26] And we saw that at the time of Saul, the Amalekites attacked and "plundered" Israel (1 Sam. 14:48); they were described as "sinners" (15:18), led by Agag who continued "making women childless" with his sword (v. 33). These Amalekites hadn't repudiated the crimes of their ancestors, and so the original judgment stood.

Morriston contests such a reading of the text, noting threatened judgment for past wickedness even during the reign of the righteous king Josiah, which we quote in full:

> Before him [Josiah] there was no king like him who turned to the LORD with all his heart and with all his soul and with all his might, according to all the law of Moses; nor did any like him arise after him. However, the LORD did not turn from the fierceness of His great wrath with which His anger burned against Judah, because of all the provocations with which Manasseh had provoked Him. The LORD said, "I will remove Judah also from My sight, as I have removed Israel. And I will cast off Jerusalem, this city which I have chosen, and the temple of which I said, 'My name shall be there.'" (2 Kings 23:25–27 NASB)

Morriston comments: "While under the leadership of Josiah, the best and most obedient of Judah's kings, Yahweh decided to destroy Judah because of the crimes of Josiah's grandfather Manasseh."[27] He adds: "Josiah comes to a bad end—defeated and killed in a battle against Egyptian invaders, and replaced by a son, who once again 'did what was evil in the sight of the LORD' (2 Kings 23:37). Manasseh, by contrast, was not punished. He merely 'slept with his ancestors, and was buried in the garden of his house' (2 Kings 21:18), after a fifty-five year reign (2 Kings 21:1)."[28]

Morriston has again misread the text. Let's look first at Yahweh's decision "to destroy Judah because of the crimes of Josiah's grandfather, Manasseh." Morriston quotes from 2 Kings 23:27 in the New Revised Standard Version: "The LORD said, 'I will remove Judah also out of my sight, as I have removed Israel. . . .'" This, however, does not say God will destroy the southern kingdom of Judah *during the reign of Josiah*. Several lines of evidence make this clear.

First, the text refers to "removing Judah" *as* God had removed the northern kingdom of "Israel," which had gone into exile under Assyria (eighth century BC). Thus, the text most obviously is not a reference to Judah's military defeat by "Egyptian invaders" but to exile under Babylon in the sixth century BC—an event that occurs during the reign of Zedekiah, several kings after Josiah's rule (2 Kings 22–24).

Second, Morriston's citation omits the last sentence of the passage, which we include in italics: "I will remove Judah also out of my sight, as I have removed Israel; and I will reject this *city that I have chosen, Jerusalem, and the house of which I said, 'My name shall be there.'*" The reference here is to the fall of Jerusalem and the destruction of the temple. Neither occurred during Josiah's reign but ultimately under Zedekiah's, and God's instrument of judgment was Babylon, not Egypt.

We see this in the next chapter, where Judah's collapse begins because of its persistence in wickedness: "Surely these things happened to Judah according to the LORD's command, in order to *remove them from his presence* because of the sins of Manasseh and all he had done" (2 Kings 24:3). We read that Jehoahaz "did evil in the sight of the LORD, according to all that his fathers had done" (23:32 NASB). And he was followed by Jehoiakim, who "did evil in the sight of the LORD" (v. 37 NASB) and by Jehoiachin, who "did evil in the sight of the LORD" (24:9 NASB) and then by Zedekiah, who "did evil in the sight of the LORD" (v. 19 NASB). So while it is true that Josiah was "the best and most obedient of Judah's kings," as Morriston says, the members of the dynasty who followed him were not.

Finally, that the predicted judgment upon Judah would not occur in Josiah's reign is explicitly stated in the previous chapter. In 2 Kings 22:15–17, the narrator records how Josiah consulted the prophetess Huldah about the coming judgment on Judah:

This is what the LORD, the God of Israel, says: Tell the man who sent you to me, "This is what the LORD says: I am going to bring disaster on this place and its people, according to everything written in the book the king of Judah has read. Because they have forsaken me and burned incense to other gods and aroused my anger by all the idols their hands have made, my anger will burn against this place and will not be quenched."

Immediately, however, she adds:

Tell the king of Judah, who sent you to inquire of the LORD, "This is what the LORD, the God of Israel, says concerning the words you heard: Because your heart was responsive and you humbled yourself before the LORD when you heard what I have spoken against this place and its people—that they would become a curse and be laid waste—and because you tore your robes and wept in my presence, I also have heard you, declares the LORD. Therefore I will gather you to your ancestors, and you will be buried in peace. Your eyes will not see all the disaster I am going to bring on this place." (vv. 18–20)

Second Kings 23 simply doesn't show that judgment for Manasseh's sins fell during the reign of his innocent grandson Josiah. What we see is the principle of conditional judgment illustrated once again: when Josiah humbled himself and brought about spiritual reforms in Judah, the nation was not punished for Manasseh's sins. But when they revert to Manasseh's sins, the prophesied judgment falls. And Josiah's own death was not "at the hand of Egyptian invaders," as Morriston contends; rather, Pharaoh Neco was simply marching toward the Euphrates and was not looking for a fight with Judah, and the text matter-of-factly asserts that Josiah went to fight against him. But we see no indication that this was judgment on Josiah for Manasseh's sins. In fact, we read in 2 Chronicles that Josiah died because of his own failure to listen to God's voice speaking through Neco (35:20–22).

So we find that Morriston seriously misreads the biblical text at a number of points. He gets wrong what *God's reasons* actually are for issuing commands to kill innocent persons. We noted that the actual grounds for God's judgments against the Midianites, Canaanites, Amalekites, and others in the Old Testament are different than what Morriston alleges, and Morriston is misguided in downplaying those grounds.

Final Thoughts on Divine Judgment

A little earlier we referred to the book of Jonah, which emphasizes God's compassion for a wicked people. We want to say a bit more about the point raised there—namely, God's desire to turn from threats of judgment in light of human repentance and the spirit in which God's judgment comes.

It has been argued that Scripture indicates God would not have been all that disappointed if all the Canaanites had been wiped out.[29] After all, didn't God obliterate all but Noah and his family at the flood? Surely this was not hyperbole either! (Note: we are not claiming that this is hyperbolic, as we have textual reasons for thinking the contrary. We could say the same about the destruction of Sodom and Gomorrah, which is not hyperbolic either; all textual indicators point to this being literal.)

Or consider Ezekiel 14:12–23—a passage that refers to sweeping judgment on Judah for its wickedness. God states that if three righteous men—Noah,

Daniel, and Job—lived in the wicked land, he would deliver them. However, he would pour out his wrath on the land—through sword, famine, wild beasts, and pestilence—and there would be few survivors. Earlier in the book, God promised that wild beasts would even kill children (5:17; cf. Lev. 26:22). These are not metaphorical. Moreover, the argument goes, Judah is so wicked that God appears *indifferent* toward judgment.

How does this square with what we have just said about God's compassion and willingness to turn from judgment to show mercy? While the Scriptures portray a God who is just and does not shrink from punishment when it is necessary, this fails to see the larger picture—which includes *both* kindness and severity (Rom. 11:22). Although God judges a disobedient world (say, at the flood) or a nation, we often read that God does so with a heavy or grieved heart (Gen. 6:5–7)—not because he desires this outcome.[30] Likewise, God issues commands to "destroy them totally" with the heaviest of hearts. God not only *permits* certain conditions because of hardened human hearts (Matt. 19:8), but God also issues certain difficult *commands* because of the hardness of human hearts (Mark 10:2–5)—including the Canaanite command. Stephen Williams writes: "Compared to the command in creation, Moses' prescription is embedded in a concessionary, permissive context, overall. Mosaic command is contingent on a situation where things have badly broken down. In a fallen world, there are things which are, sadly, commanded; commanded sadly."[31] These commands do not so much reveal the glories of God's nature but rather the dreadfulness of human fallenness.

Even in the book of Ezekiel itself, in which God is allegedly indifferent to or unaffected by human wickedness, we see another picture. Though God is exasperated by his people's disobedience, he is also "hurt" by their adulterous hearts (6:9). Later in the book, God pleadingly asks: "Why will you die, O house of Israel?" (33:11 NRSV). He emphatically states that he does not take pleasure in punishing the wicked (18:31; cf. 33:11, 14–16). This is not a picture of indifference. Even at the very end of the reign of Judah's last king, Zedekiah, Jeremiah 27:13 indicates there is opportunity to repent, using the same language as Ezekiel: "Why will you die, you and your people, by sword, famine, and pestilence?" (NASB). After the destruction of Jerusalem, we read that God "does not afflict willingly" but reluctantly (Lam. 3:31–33 NASB).

Divine judgment cannot be characterized as indifference. Judgment is not opposed to God's love and compassion, but rather springs from the character of a loving, caring God. Yale theologian Miroslav Volf, who experienced the horrors of war in the former Yugoslavia, comments on the relationship between the two.

I used to think that wrath was unworthy of God. Isn't God love? Shouldn't divine love be beyond wrath? God is love, and God loves every person and every creature. That's exactly why God is wrathful against some of them. My last resistance to the idea of God's wrath was a casualty of the war in the former Yugoslavia, the region from which I come. According to some estimates, 200,000 people were killed and over 3,000,000 were displaced. *My* villages and cities were destroyed, *my* people shelled day in and day out, some of them brutalized beyond imagination, and I could not imagine God not being angry. Or think of Rwanda in the last decade of the past century, where 800,000 people were hacked to death in one hundred days! How did God react to the carnage? By doting on the perpetrators in a grandfatherly fashion? By refusing to condemn the bloodbath but instead affirming the perpetrators' basic goodness? Wasn't God fiercely angry with them? Though I used to complain about the indecency of the idea of God's wrath, I came to think that I would have to rebel against a God who *wasn't* wrathful at the sight of the world's evil. God isn't wrathful in spite of being love. God is wrathful *because* God is love.[32]

Summary

- We have given good reason to think the Crucial Moral Principle is not absolute. We have reason to think the grounds for thinking God issued such a command are stronger than the grounds for thinking killing innocents is always wrong.

- But does the biblical theist have grounds for thinking God has issued this exemption on rare occasions? Some critics claim that the biblical texts explicitly state God's reasons and that those reasons are inadequate.

- Temple prostitution and child sacrifice were abhorrent practices worthy of divine judgment, and the commands to "utterly destroy" the Canaanites were given to preserve Israel's identity from the lethal spiritual and moral infection (Deut. 20:16). So, the critic asks, should a law be passed to stop atheist Richard Dawkins from proclaiming his antitheistic message? Should he be isolated from others?

- Note that this text (Deut. 20:16–18) doesn't state *God's* reasons for issuing the command; rather, it gives *the Israelites* a reason to obey a command God has already laid down (e.g., the reasons legislators may have for drafting laws vs. the reasons citizens may have to obey them—perhaps to avoid punishment).

- What *justifies* someone in promoting the acceptance of a code or set of rules is not necessarily the same as the *motivation or reason* people have for following those rules. For example, avoiding a certain behavior *for its own sake* rather than for the general good of society—refusing to break promises because this violates trust—may actually have the happy side effect of benefiting society, even though this wasn't the goal of the action.

- People like Richard Dawkins don't engage in human sacrifice, refuse to leave church property, and threaten the very existence of God's people. If they did, they should be isolated from the rest of the population! This is the kind of "spiritual infection" we are talking about.

- The critic says the clear—but inadequate—reason to totally destroy the Canaanites (Deut. 7:2) was so that the Israelites wouldn't intermarry with them and be drawn into their worship. But couldn't God accomplish this another way rather than the method that, in the end, failed to achieve God's aim?

- Deuteronomy 7:1–6 doesn't portray national extermination; it assumes Canaanites will still be around and that Israel should not make covenants or intermarry with them. And Israel is told to totally destroy the Canaanites *after* God had driven them out of the land—even though any Canaanites refusing to leave could be killed.

- This text also doesn't explicitly state what *God's reasons* are at all; he tells the Israelites of the negative consequences if they do intermarry.

- This argument makes the faulty assumption that *a loving and just God would not command people to suppress some evil he desires to be suppressed if God has a more efficient means of suppressing that evil himself.* This goes against much of what we know about morality. Should God directly and immediately stop criminals from doing their deeds rather than relying on detectives, police, and law courts? Should God not permit (less-efficient) human courts to punish crimes?

- Israel failed to obey God in driving out the Canaanites—just as people fail to obey God's commands not to rape or murder. Does this mean that God would not issue commands to refrain from rape, murder, theft, and assault?

- In Numbers 31:15, Moses asks, "Have you allowed all the [Midianite] women to live?" The critic raises the question as to whether the Midianites must be punished for seducing the Israelites into sexual immorality and idolatry. Note: (1) God himself did not command killing the women and boys; he only commanded killing the men, which Israel accomplished (v. 7); only then did the command come from Moses to kill the women and children. (Consider the bombing of Dresden, Germany, during World War II—a wrong act in an overall just war.) (2) This is an argument from silence. We aren't told of God's approval or disapproval, which is common in many biblical narratives (e.g., Abraham's deception, Lot's daughters' incest). (3) Even though the Bible depicts faithful saints (Abraham, Josiah), we still see them disobeying God at certain times.

- The real problem here is Israel's treason ("treachery")—a violation of God's covenant with Israel and the undermining of Israel's national identity, calling, and integrity. (The problem is not hostility against another nation; Moses marries a Midianite, and his father-in-law, Jethro, offers wise advice to Moses.)

- The critic raises the question of the Amalekites (1 Sam. 15:3: "do not spare them"). He argues that this text should be read alongside Deut. 27:17–19—a call to remember what Amalek had done to Israel at the exodus and whose name should be blotted out. But isn't it unfair to hold this past event against future generations?

- Yet 1 Samuel 14:48 mentions that the Amalekites had "plundered" Israel; they are described as "sinners" (15:18); and their king had made women childless (15:33). Attacking the Amalekites was a matter of *present* aggression—the specific reason for Saul's military response.

- We should also read this Amalekite text alongside Jeremiah 18:7–10 and Jonah 3, where a compassionate God is willing to show kindness and mercy to a nation that turns from its wicked ways. Prophetic pronouncements of doom are conditional.

- But what about God's bringing judgment during the reign of Josiah (who is killed by Egypt's Pharaoh Neco) because of the wicked king Manasseh (2 Kings 23:26)? Actually, this judgment took place during the reign of Zedekiah and came from Babylon, as 2 Kings 24 makes clear (cf. 22:15–17). And the text tells us that the remaining kings Jehoahaz, Jehoiakim, Jehoiachin, and Zedekiah all "did evil in the sight of the LORD."

- God's judgment is not a reflection of divine indifference or lack of compassion. God punishes with a grieved, wounded heart. His commands regarding the Canaanites are the tragic result of human wickedness.

18

What If Someone Claimed God Commanded Killing the Innocent Today?

We have argued that it is rational to think that God could, on rare occasions, grant an exemption to the moral rule against taking innocent human life for the sake of some greater good. We also rejected arguments which purport to show that the biblical theist lacks adequate grounds for thinking that God did on certain occasions *recorded in Scripture* issue such an exemption. One important point noted in the last chapter is that the scriptural texts don't tell us much about God's reasons for issuing these commands. Scripture, however, does provide the Israelites with some reasons why they should follow the commands. But the Scriptures leave us largely in the dark as to why God issued the commands in the first place.

Skeptical Theism and God's Reasons for Issuing Commands

Some think this fact by itself creates a difficulty for the biblical theist. They argue that because the believer *knows of no reason* God would command the killing of innocent people, then the proper conclusion to draw is that *there is no such reason*. So they conclude God did not issue such an order. However, recent work on the problem of evil has shown that this is a flawed conclusion.

233

That is, simply not knowing how to explain something isn't grounds for concluding that there are no reasons. This is called a "noseeum inference"—that if you can't see 'em, they must not be there. Imagine being on a camping trip:

> I look inside my tent: I don't see a St. Bernard; it is then probable that there is no St. Bernard in my tent. That is because if there were one there, I would very likely have seen it; it's not easy for a St. Bernard to avoid detection in a small tent. Again, I look inside my tent: I don't see any noseeums (very small midges [i.e., two-winged flies] with a bite out of all proportion to their size); this time it is not particularly probable that there are no noseeums in my tent—at least it isn't any more probable than before I looked. The reason, of course, is that even if there were noseeums there, I wouldn't see 'em; they're too small to see. And now the question is whether God's reasons, if any, for permitting such evils . . . are more like St. Bernards or more like noseeums.[1]

Various philosophers have argued that any attempt to cross this bridge and offer a successful noseeum inference is refuted by what has been dubbed the stance of "skeptical theism." The skeptical theist is *one who both believes in God and is modestly skeptical about the ability of humans to know the reasons an omniscient being has for doing or permitting certain things*—a theme we see repeatedly emphasized in Scripture. "'For My thoughts are not your thoughts, nor are your ways My ways,' declares the LORD. 'For as the heavens are higher than the earth, so are My ways higher than your ways and My thoughts than your thoughts'" (Isa. 55:8–9 NASB; cf. Rom. 11:33–35).[2]

When we reflect on the cognitive limitations we human beings possess, it's clear that there is much we do not know. We are unaware of many of the possible goods and evils which may come about as a result of our acting or failing to act. As one philosopher puts it, central to this position is that we have "no good reason for thinking that the total moral value or disvalue we perceive in certain complex states of affairs accurately reflects the total moral value or disvalue they really have."[3]

As an example of the last point, consider this scenario: "On the night that Sir Winston Churchill was conceived, had Lady Randolph Churchill fallen asleep in a slightly different position, the precise pathway that each of the millions of spermatozoa took would have been slightly altered. As a result . . . Sir Winston Churchill, as we knew him, would not have existed, with the likely result that the evolution of World War II would have been substantially different."[4] The point to remember is that the total value that results from a fairly trivial action depends on a large number of factors of which we have no knowledge or awareness.

The thrust of skeptical theism connects to the theme of our book and the question of God's giving difficult and perhaps baffling commands. That is, how can humans—who *do not know* of any greater good gained or greater evil prevented by God's issuing a given command—justifiably conclude that *there are no* greater goods gained or evils prevented *known to an omniscient being* for issuing the command in question? We are simply *not in a position* to draw such conclusions—much as we are not in a position to spot nosee-ums in our tent. Simply because *we don't know the reasons why* God issued a particular command, it doesn't follow that *there are no reasons* and that therefore *God didn't command it.*

By contrast, it's quite plausible to maintain that God being a loving and just being would command people to refrain from killing innocent humans in normal situations. Yet the literature on the morality of killing shows that very few human beings know or are agreed on why killing is wrong. Here are some suggestions by philosophers. Killing is wrong because it contradicts a person's desire to live; it violates one's freedom of self-determination (autonomy); it contradicts an ideal desire to live; it deprives an individual organism of a valu-able future; it violates a rule which is part of a code, the acceptance of which would maximize happiness; it fails to appropriately respond to the natural good of life; and so on.

The debates abound, and each position has sophisticated advocates in the literature—yet each contradicts the other. Obviously at best only one is cor-rect, and most lay people would not find their way out of the philosophical labyrinth. Similar things can be said about many of the most fundamental and basic moral norms accepted in any credible moral code. While it is relatively uncontroversial *that* these things are wrong, *why* they are wrong is often a matter of considerable philosophical dispute. The problem this poses is obvi-ous: if we can't justifiably attribute a command to God unless we know *why* he commands it, then we won't be able to attribute *any* commands to God, even a general command to not kill.

Christian philosopher Eleonore Stump further illustrates the limitations of human thought and dimness of perspective in considering difficult divine commands. She offers a thought experiment of "an intelligent being Max from a far-distant world" in which all sentient beings never get seriously sick and none ever dies. Max is then enabled to view a video of "events inside a large city hospital on earth where the Chief of Staff is a surgeon." Upon seeing the video, "Max is filled with moral indignation at the doctors," who plunge sharp objects into human beings first to render them helpless and then to slice them open with sharp knives."[5] The patients appear to leave the hospital in far worse shape than when they came in. Stump compares this to the question of the killing of the Amalekites (so-called "genocide"), and she concludes:

> Genocide, like torture, is not properly defined without reference to some intention or motivation. Where the primary aim is healing, rescue from death, there is neither torture nor genocide. And just as it is possible to recognize what looks like torture as instead done in the interest of healing, however counter-intuitive such a recognition may seem to Max, it is also possible to recognize God's ending of the existence of civilizations, nations, and peoples [or, as noted above, driving them out of the Promised Land] as motivated by providential care.[6]

We discussed the definition of "genocide" in chapter 10, but Stump here reinforces the point that we finite humans are not properly positioned to know the mind of an omniscient God.

What If a Texas Governor Says, "God Commanded Me to Kill People"?

We have pointed out that we limited humans are not properly positioned to know whether the total moral value or disvalue *we perceive* in certain complex states of affairs accurately reflects the total moral value or disvalue *they really have*. What's more, we are not well positioned to know the reasons an all-good, all-knowing being has for issuing commands, let alone difficult commands.

Another question waiting to be addressed goes back to Raymond Bradley's claim: "The Bible tells us that God commands us to perform acts that violate the Crucial Moral Principle [of not killing innocent human beings]."[7] Wes Morriston proposes an objection along these lines: the skeptical theist's defense is inadequate because "we have no reason to think that God will not *again* command wholesale slaughter and no good reason to adopt such a dismissive attitude toward *new* reports of horrific divine commands."[8] To illustrate his point, Morriston refers to a 2008 event in which fifty-two children were rescued from a polygamist sect at the Yearning for Zion Ranch in west Texas amid allegations of forced marriages and sexual abuse.[9] He then asks us to imagine that upon hearing this, the governor of Texas "told reporters today that after praying for divine guidance, he received the following command. 'Thus says the LORD. The Fundamentalist Church of Jesus Christ of Latter Day Saints must be completely wiped out. Make no agreements with these people. Show no mercy. Kill them all, so that everyone will know that polygamy and forced marriage and child abuse are abominations in my sight.'"[10]

Morriston notes that even a proponent of skeptical theism would contend the governor here is "out of his mind."[11] It would be "far more likely that the

Governor is deluded than that God had issued such a command."[12] Morriston suggests, therefore, that "we should treat [Old Testament] reports of divinely mandated genocides in the same way."[13] This is because "divine communications are not generally thought to have ended with the closing of the canon. Christians in particular pray for divine guidance and they often receive what they take to be answers." And, he adds, there are recognized ways of forming beliefs of what God wants for us and ways of recognizing what would count against such beliefs ("defeaters"). What counts *against* the claim that God has spoken to the believer concerns "the moral character of the content of the beliefs that are the outputs of the [established] practice." So "prophets" or any believers who advocate cheating, mass murder, or child torture in God's name can be readily dismissed. Morriston continues: "No doubt an inventive philosopher could come up with a story. But to remove the grotesque implausibility of such claims about what God wants from us, a fanciful story is not enough. Nor is it sufficient to observe that God knows far more than we about the total value/disvalue of such things. Are things relevantly different when we turn our attention to divinely mandated genocides in the Bible?"[14] So what if someone *today*—like the fictitious governor of Texas in the scenario above—were to claim that God "told him" to "leave alive nothing that breathes" at the Yearning for Zion Ranch?

On What God Would(n't) Command Today

We can offer several responses to the kinds of charges Morriston makes above.

Prophets, Apostles, and a Closed Canon

Morriston states that plenty of believers today are convinced that God still speaks, guides, and reveals himself. We agree that divine revelation is not restricted to the biblical era; it did not end with the death of the apostles and the closing of the biblical canon. That said, the guidance believers receive is different from the authoritative utterances of divinely appointed prophets like Isaiah and Jeremiah ("thus says the LORD") and official apostles like Peter and Paul. To reject them was to reject God/Christ. So for example, John writes: "We are from God; he who knows God listens to us; he who is not from God does not listen to us. By this we know the spirit of truth and the spirit of error" (1 John 4:6 NASB; cf. Gal. 1:12). Yes, the New Testament refers to the revelatory and ongoing spiritual gift of prophecy—*the ability to report what God brings to mind.*[15] Paul wrote that those with the gift of prophecy were still subject to apostolic authority: "If anyone thinks he is a prophet or spiritual, let him recognize that the things which I write to you are the Lord's commandment. But if anyone does not recognize this, he is not recognized" (1 Cor. 14:37–38 NASB).

A generally accepted view within the three branches of Christianity—Roman Catholic, Eastern Orthodox, and Protestant—is that the closing of the biblical canon in the apostolic era rules out any new divinely authoritative utterance equal to that of Moses, Samuel, Isaiah, and Paul. And even though the church required time to recognize the inherent authority of the New Testament books, it can be argued that these authoritative books had been completed while a representation of the original apostolic witnesses remained alive.[16]

We have good reason to accept that the Scriptures are the sure and final authority for the believer and that, with the death of the apostles, there is no longer any authoritative revelation on the level of Moses or Paul. So we have good grounds for ruling out Morriston's suggestion about some purported divine command to the fictitious Texas governor who now speaks on God's behalf.

Recognizing Moral Defeaters

Another point Morriston raises has to do with recognized ways of forming beliefs. How do we recognize what God wants? How do we know when our belief is *not* what God wants? If we encounter a belief of which God would not approve, on what basis could such a belief be rejected or called into question? Morriston says that one way of making such a determination is by examining the moral content of the beliefs that emerge from practicing that particular faith or way of thinking. Two things about his argument need to be noted.

First, the established practices to which Morriston refers are practices recognized *within the Christian religious community*—a community that accepts certain religious doctrines. These would include the Bible as the Word of God, various theological beliefs about God, salvation, morality, and so on. These beliefs operate as background beliefs and presuppositions against which the established practice operates.[17] Morriston notes that "*Christians* would take [an impulse to mass killing] as a sure sign" that such an experience was false.[18] But Morriston's approach suggests that Christians holding such beliefs are unwarranted in doing so, as though atheism is the rational default position. But, of course, Morriston himself operates from within a certain community (atheists) who hold certain shared beliefs (God does not exist; miracles cannot occur; there is no afterlife; there is no just God who issues difficult commands for good reasons). The fact that a community has its own beliefs and established practices is not itself an argument. More important is the truth of the matter—namely, whether a good God exists who may occasionally issue difficult commands for an overriding good.

Second, Morriston raises the question of moral criteria within the recognized practices of the believing community—criteria that would shed light on whether a command could be issued by a good God. We have talked about general moral truths that properly functioning people can readily recognize (e.g., Amos 1–2), but we noted in chapters 15–16 of this book that in cases of supreme emergency, certain moral principles can be overridden, including the taking of innocent human lives. And we have also argued that practicing believers should not operate by rejecting a purported divine command simply because it contradicts a moral belief that they hold. Instead, we have suggested the following two guidelines regarding purported divine commands:

1 one should *dismiss* any purported divine command that violates a *non-negotiable moral belief* (i.e., it is intrinsically evil—raping or torturing babies for fun);

2 one should *reject* any purported divine command to do X that contradicts a *negotiable moral belief* when the claim "Action X is wrong" has greater plausibility or is more validly knowable than the claim that God commanded it.

Once these qualifications are noted, it's no longer clear that Morriston's argument holds. For example, Morriston approvingly cites Richard Swinburne, who says: "The prophet who commends cheating and child torture can be dismissed straight away."[19] However, this comment can be understood in different ways—that it is *generally* morally wrong to cheat or torture *or* that it is *always* morally wrong no matter what the circumstances. If taken the first way, Swinburne's comments refer only to what we call general moral beliefs.

In fact, this is the kind of distinction that Swinburne actually points out. It's not the true prophet of God who will be commanding people to do what is *"evidently* morally wrong."[20] He is, it appears, referring to *claims that are self-evidently morally wrong*. In some sense, they are not negotiable claims. Swinburne confirms this point: So "for example, a candidate revelation must not contain moral claims incompatible with any *clear intuitions* we have about what are the necessary moral truths of morality."[21] Furthermore, if "it tells us that rape and lying, murder and theft (*without exceptional divine permission*) are good, then that is good reason for supposing the candidate revelation not to be a genuine one," says Swinburne.[22] Furthermore, as we have seen in earlier chapters, God's difficult commands to the Israelites were not intrinsically evil—an impossibility for an all-good God; they did not contradict nonnegotiable moral truths.

Consider the fictional Texas governor scenario. Let's assume that Morriston believes the governor generally prohibits killing the innocent but in this particular scenario is claiming to have exceptional (divine) authorization for it. So his order does not violate a nonnegotiable moral belief. It still seems pretty obvious that, from within their community's established practices, biblical theists will consider the evidential situation regarding the Texas governor and the accounts of Moses or Joshua to be *very different*. By definition, biblical theists believe the Bible to be God's authoritative revelation and Moses to be a prophet. They will not have comparable reasons for thinking that the governor of Texas is a prophet. Believers will think that it's more likely that the governor is deluded than that Moses was when issuing the command to "utterly destroy." So it is false that we are required to treat Old Testament reports of "divinely mandated genocides in the same way."

Morriston anticipates this response and states "he does not know of any reason" for thinking that the "the genocide texts in the [Old Testament] are completely trustworthy" and challenges the biblical theist to come up with arguments for this conclusion.[23]

Notice, however, that Morriston has now changed the subject. We have emphasized in this book, for the sake of argument, that biblical theism is true and that the existence of a good, commanding God cannot be removed from the biblical narrative without doing serious damage to its coherence and significance. Also in framing his objection, Morriston recognizes that there exist within the Christian community certain established beliefs, such as the belief that the Old Testament is divinely authoritative and truthful in what it teaches. So the question is *not* whether biblical theists can provide people like Morriston—who is skeptical of biblical authority—a defense of its truthfulness.[24] Rather, it is whether biblical theists who accept the typical beliefs and assumptions of the Christian community can defensibly attribute these commands to God.

Other Criteria of Testing Prophets

It is worth noting that even if Christians can't appeal to a defeating argument based on the "moral character" of their (purported) revelation itself, they could still reject the Texas governor's statement on *other* grounds. Scripture suggests several potential points which would counter the governor's claim of purportedly receiving a divine command.

The first criterion has to do with *the nature of the medium*—that is, *how does the purported prophet obtain his information?* In the book of

Deuteronomy, God rejects certain occult practices such as "divination," "sorcery," "interpret[ing] omens" and "witchcraft" (Deut. 18:9–13; cf. 2 Chron. 33:6; Gal. 5:20). In contrast, God reveals his will through his commissioned prophets as he directs, "Surely the Lord God does nothing unless He reveals His secret counsel to His servants the prophets" (Amos 3:7 NASB).

Second is *the criterion of truth*—that is, *does the purported prophet's word come true?* In response to the question, "How can we know when a message has not been spoken by the Lord?," Moses replies: "If what a prophet proclaims in the name of the Lord does not take place or come true, that is a message the Lord has not spoken. That prophet has spoken presumptuously; so do not be alarmed" (Deut. 18:21–22). The same point is made about the prophet Samuel: "The Lord was with Samuel as he grew up, and he let none of Samuel's words fall to the ground" (1 Sam. 3:19). *Samuel had a consistent track record of accurate predictions through his ministry.* So by the time we get to the difficult command to totally destroy the Amalekites, Samuel had an established prophetic reputation with a history of making precise, testable claims.

The same goes for Moses. By the time he issued the harsh command to "utterly destroy" the Canaanites in Deuteronomy 7 and 20, *he had made numerous accurate predictions with accompanying displays of power* such as the ten plagues falling on Egypt, the parting of the Red Sea, and so on (more on this in the next chapter). Reflecting on Moses's life, a biblical editor gives this assessment of a towering prophetic career: "Since that time no prophet has risen in Israel like Moses, whom the Lord knew face to face, for all the signs and wonders which the Lord sent him to perform in the land of Egypt against Pharaoh, all his servants, and all his land, and for all the mighty power and for all the great terror which Moses performed in the sight of all Israel" (Deut. 34:10–12 NASB).

The Scriptures take the testing of truth claims very seriously, and prophetic claimants take standards of falsification quite seriously. If the word of a purported prophet fails, God has not sent him. And when a true prophet's status is challenged, the prophet typically responds with clear, verifiable indicators of authenticity. For example, Micaiah makes a specific prediction when challenged by Zedekiah the son of Chenaanah: "If you ever return safely, the Lord has not spoken through me." Then he added, "Mark my words, all you people!" (1 Kings 22:28). Or when the divinely bestowed authority of Moses and Aaron is challenged by Korah, Dathan, and Abiram, Moses announces that his claim to prophetic status could be falsified—or made abundantly clear:

> Moses said, "By this you shall know that the Lord has sent me to do all these deeds; for this is not my doing. If these men die the death of all men or if they

suffer the fate of all men, then the LORD has not sent me. But if the LORD brings about an entirely new thing and the ground opens its mouth and swallows them up with all that is theirs, and they descend alive into Sheol [i.e., the grave], then you will understand that these men have spurned the LORD." (Num. 16:28–30 NASB)

This is, of course, followed by an unambiguous divine endorsement of Moses:

As he finished speaking all these words, the ground that was under them split open; and the earth opened its mouth and swallowed them up, and their households, and all the men who belonged to Korah with their possessions. So they and all that belonged to them went down alive to Sheol; and the earth closed over them, and they perished from the midst of the assembly. (vv. 31–33 NASB)

Third, another important criterion is *consistency with previous revelation—* that is, *is the present purported revelation in accord with earlier revelations?* Here it is worth comparing Deuteronomy 18 (above) with Deuteronomy 13. In Deuteronomy 13, Moses instructs the people that a purported prophet *may* accurately predict the future, but if he leads Israel to disobey God's commands by worshiping other gods, they must not listen to him: "It is the LORD your God you must follow, and him you must revere. Keep his commands and obey him; serve him and hold fast to him" (13:1–4). So an accurate "prophet" is to be rejected if he counsels people to disobey God's revealed commands in Scripture.

The same point is applied by the apostles not just to God's *commands* but also to specific theological *doctrines*. For example, Paul writes: "Therefore I want you to know that no one who is speaking by the Spirit of God says, 'Jesus be cursed,' and no one can say, 'Jesus is Lord,' except by the Holy Spirit" (1 Cor. 12:3). Paul states here that any claimant to divine revelation must acknowledge Christ's lordship; no true prophet—whether of the stature of Moses or those who have the spiritual gift of prophecy—will repudiate this belief (cf. 14:37–38). Elsewhere Paul states that the message he originally gave to the Galatians was divinely given: "even if we or an angel from heaven should preach a gospel other than the one we preached to you, let them be under God's curse!" (Gal. 1:8). Notice how Paul says that even if *he himself* were to deviate from his original message, he should be condemned. Likewise, the apostle John states that anyone who denies the incarnation and the messiahship of Jesus of Nazareth is a false prophet (1 John 2:20; 4:2–3; cf. John 1:1, 14).

Fourth is the criterion of *moral character*—that is, *does the purported prophet exhibit a virtuous life?* In the Sermon on the Mount, Jesus warned against "false prophets" and suggested one could recognize them by their moral "fruit": "A good tree cannot bear bad fruit, and a bad tree cannot bear good fruit. Every tree that does not bear good fruit is cut down and thrown into the fire. Thus, by their fruit you will recognize them" (Matt. 7:16–20). Jesus is alluding to Old Testament texts like Isaiah's vineyard song, in which God expects Israel to bear the fruits of "justice" and "righteousness," although they bear only "worthless" fruit of "bloodshed" and "distress" (Isa. 5:7). Harking back to the Old Testament's anticipation of the moral fruitfulness of God's new covenant people, Paul takes up the same "fruit" metaphor in Galatians 5:22–23.[25] Here certain (primarily community) virtues—the fruit of the Spirit—are to characterize believers:[26] "love, joy, peace, forbearance, kindness, goodness, faithfulness, gentleness and self-control." Furthermore, a purported prophet who engages in the following behavior cannot rightly claim such a title: "sexual immorality, impurity and debauchery; idolatry and witchcraft; hatred, discord, jealousy, fits of rage, selfish ambition, dissensions, factions and envy; drunkenness, orgies" (Gal. 5:19–21). Along these lines, Jesus brings judgment on those who lay claim to his name in various demonstrations of power but are actually "evildoers": "Not everyone who says to me, 'Lord, Lord,' will enter the kingdom of heaven, but only the one who does the will of my Father who is in heaven. Many will say to me on that day, 'Lord, Lord, did we not prophesy in your name and in your name drive out demons and in your name perform many miracles?' Then I will tell them plainly, 'I never knew you. Away from me, you evildoers!'" (Matt. 7:21–23). So we have another test of prophetic genuineness—the moral test— that indicates a person is genuinely in communication with God, is obedient to Christ and his teaching, and is being transformed in his character through God's Spirit.

This moral criterion for prophetic authenticity is included with the three others we have discussed—(1) the source or medium of the purported prophet's information, (2) the truth or accuracy of what the prophet says (often accompanied by visible indicators to confirm this), and (3) the doctrinal or theological test.

So biblical theists would be alerted to questions about the Texas governor's purported revelation by examining to see, for example, whether he is a person of *fine moral character* with a history of obedience to God. Furthermore, biblical theists could test the governor's claims against their *moral intuitions*. Now, as we have noted, principles like the Crucial Moral Principle are not absolute and can be overridden in unique situations (e.g., cases of supreme emergency). And we noted that some of our moral intuitions may need revising and can be revised in light of further information.

Beyond this we could further appeal to any one or a combination of the other criteria we have listed concerning the alleged revelation. For example, has the governor received his message through some dubious occultic practice?

Does he have a long-standing track record of making accurate predictions on behalf of God? It would be difficult to claim that such a man is "out of his mind" if he meets all of these criteria.

Of particular significance, however, is the third criterion—consistency with previous revelation. A genuine prophetic message from God will not command us or counsel us to disobey the commands he has revealed in Scripture. This is important because a command to kill all polygamist Mormons would violate this command. As we noted in chapters 4 through 6, the command to "utterly destroy" the Canaanites is presented in Scripture as an *occasional* and *unique* command for a particular context. It is a command God gives *to ancient Israel in the unfolding of salvation history*, and it is *applied only to the nations occupying the land God had promised Israel*. He made this promise to the patriarchs before a nation was formed to take possession of the Promised Land. Furthermore, the rules that governed war outside the land of promise and that were meant to govern all war once Israel occupied the land *prohibited killing noncombatants*. So for a governor of Texas to kill polygamous Mormons would violate these commands.

Summary

- We have good reason for thinking that God did on certain occasions *recorded in Scripture* issue an exemption to the general prohibition against taking innocent human life.

- The "skeptical theist" points out that just because we *know* of no reason God would on a rare occasion command the killing of innocent people, this does *not* mean there *is* no such reason. We are not in a position to know the reasons an omniscient God has for doing or permitting certain things (cf. Isa. 55:8–9; Rom. 11:33–35). Consider the total value that results from trivial actions and events that depend on a large number of factors of which we have no knowledge or awareness (e.g., the odds concerning the conception of Winston Churchill).

- Philosophers will typically argue *that* killing is wrong, but the reasons they give for *why* killing is wrong are quite varied. The same is true for other basic moral norms that right-thinking humans accept.

- The problem this poses is obvious: if we can't justifiably attribute a command to God unless

we know *why* he commands it, then we won't be able to attribute *any* commands to God, even a command to not kill.

- What if God commanded the killing of the innocent *today*? What if a Texas governor claims that God commanded him to annihilate a polygamous, child-abusing sect in his state? Wouldn't we think he was out of his mind?

- In response to such prophet-like claims, we have excellent reason to think that the biblical canon is closed—and consequently any accompanying infallible "thus says the LORD" utterances. Indeed, the authoritative utterances from Isaiah and Paul are the measure by which we judge other purported divine revelations, including genuine revelatory spiritual gifts used today (cf. 1 Cor. 14:37–38; 1 John 4:6).

- We should reject whatever violates nonnegotiable moral beliefs (rape, torturing babies for fun), and we should *reject* any purported divine command to do X that contradicts a *negotiable moral belief* when the claim

"Action X is wrong" has greater plausibility or is more validly knowable than the claim that God commanded it.

- If prophets say murder and theft are good, or they command what is intrinsically evil, they should be rejected.

- What about the Texas governor? We have good reason for taking Moses and Joshua seriously as being God's representatives, whose commands were accompanied by remarkable signs and wonders; the same is not true of the Texas governor.

- We looked at four criteria of prophetic authenticity. (1) *The nature of the medium—how does the purported prophet obtain his information (sorcery, witchcraft)?* (2) *The criterion of truth—does the purported prophet's word come true?* Does he have a consistent track record of accurate predictions in his ministry (cf. Num. 16:28–30; 1 Sam. 3:19)? (3) *The criterion of consistency with previous revelation—is the present purported revelation in accord with earlier revelations (Deut. 13:1–4)?* (4) *The criterion of moral character—does the purported prophet exhibit a virtuous life (Matt. 7:16–20)?*

- Also, the command to "utterly destroy" the Canaanites is presented in Scripture as an *occasional* and *unique* command for a particular context. It is a command God gives *to ancient Israel in the unfolding of salvation history*, and it is *applied only to the nations occupying the land God had promised Israel*.

19

The Role of Miracles and the Command to Kill Canaanites

There is a further response to Morriston's worries that is worth discussing. His argument raises the question: If God decrees something at variance with universal commands by special revelation through a human representative, then how can the commandee know that this mouthpiece accurately speaks for God and that this command is neither a delusion nor a demon?

Imagine you are a skeptical soldier in Moses's or Joshua's army and that you ask yourself the question, "Why should I obey Moses's call to war against the Canaanites?" How would one *know* that a good, just God is behind such a command? And could one find *warrant* for condemning violence done in the name of God in the present? If a respected Christian leader tells us, "God wants us to go to war," how would we know God has revealed *that* to him? Of course, the mere *report* of a purported vision or heavenly voice is insufficient, as we have no way of distinguishing true revelations from mistaken ones. In such a case, as philosopher Søren Kierkegaard argued in *Fear and Trembling*, there would be no apparent difference between *the faithful man* and *the madman* claiming such a revelation, and, someone might argue, a person today could likewise claim personal divine revelation to justify something terrible.[1]

The concern here can be expressed as follows:

1 In very unusual circumstances in the past, God, by commanding people to kill the innocent (for the sake of some greater good), exempted them from a moral principle that otherwise would be binding on them.

2 But if God did this in the past, then he could theoretically do so again in the present.

3 Yet if the awareness of that exemption comes through one's mere inner (subjective) sensing of what one takes to be God's will, there would be no way for the individual or an onlooker to verify that this is God's will.

4 Thus there would be no way to know whether or not the individual was really commanded by God to kill innocent people.

Miracles and the Will of God

Matthew Rowley has written an essay on sacralized violence in the exodus under Moses and during the conquest under Joshua.[2] His argument, which we summarize in this chapter, addresses this concern. The argument above—points 1 through 4—shows that if the awareness of God's granting an exception comes through one's mere inner (subjective) sensing of what one takes to be God's will, then there would be no way to know whether or not the individual was really commanded by God to kill innocent people.

Rowley's key argument is that the biblical narrative suggests that in such situations, God desired to safeguard against the misunderstanding of his will; therefore, he chose to validate this new knowledge with clear displays of miracles. When a new revelation issues the extraordinary command of taking another's life (call it "life-taking obedience"), it does not come through one's mere inner subjective sensing. Rather, God chooses to unite this new knowledge with miracles.

So in light of the *concern* expressed above—statements 1 through 4—here is how the argument goes:

1 In very unusual circumstances in the past, God, by commanding people to kill the innocent (for the sake of some greater good), exempted them from a moral principle that otherwise would be binding on them.

2 But if God did this in the past, then he could theoretically do so again in the present.

3' However, in these unusual cases, the awareness of the exemption comes through the declaration of the messenger of God *and* is validated by individual and communal miracles (multiple, large-scale miracles).

4' Thus, the personal (and perhaps communal) sensing can be objectively verified by the individual or an onlooker (e.g., crossing of the Jordan on dry ground, thus validating Joshua's message in Josh. 3:7: "This day I will begin to exalt you [Joshua] in the sight of all Israel, that they may know that just as I have been with Moses, I will be with you" NASB).

Consequently, there is a solid foundation based on the pattern of the Bible that helps onlookers know whether the messenger was really "called by God" to command an exemption from a moral principle that otherwise would be binding on them.

Miracles in the Old Testament Narrative

In making his case, Rowley identifies several different categories of miracle, according to what we can know from God's activity in the world.

> *Category 1*: At a very basic level, God has created the universe out of nothing (itself a miracle) and through his divine action sustains a remarkable world in being, which operates according to natural laws. We can learn much from creation—namely, God's power, intelligence, and creativity. We don't learn from it, however, that Moses was God's chosen mouthpiece. *That* would be the stuff of Category 2.

> *Category 2*: These miracles can be placed on an "epistemic spectrum" (a spectrum of validating knowledge claims)—say, 2L (lesser), 2M (moderate), 2G (greater). The miracles can vary in their value, inspiring greater or lesser confidence in knowing. The 2L (lesser) kinds of miracles—a vision, dream, or small-scale event like a burning bush—are less weighty since they could be easily misinterpreted or faked. By contrast, Category 2G (greater) miracles (crossing the Red Sea, eating manna daily for decades) are harder to misinterpret and are impossible to fake. Such miracles "make God's presence more noticeable" and aid in arriving at a proper interpretation of God's will.[3] Category 2M (moderate) miracles are smaller miracles that go against the normal pattern of nature. They are private, local, spontaneous, single event, and single-sensory (e.g., *hearing* alone or *seeing* alone—not a combination of these sense experiences at one time). These miracles carry some weight but may be misinterpreted and are not as easy to validate—unlike large-scale Category 2G miracles (communal, multiethnic, widespread, multisensory, multi-event, prophesied in detail).

A chart on this may help:

Spectrum of the Epistemic Value of Miracle Claims

Category	2L	2M	2G
Claim	"God talked to me in a bush"	"God made bitter water sweet"	"God fed us for decades with bread from heaven"
Epistemic Value	Lesser	Moderate	Greater
Conclusion	I should doubt this claim	I should hold this experience loosely	I should trust this

Unlike private revelation claims made by Muhammad, Joseph Smith, and others that could not be checked or tested, such is not the case when we look at Moses and Joshua. When one turns to the book of Exodus, one finds that Moses's prophetic message is authenticated by Category 2G miracles. God is clearly confronting Pharaoh and Egypt's gods through the plagues and then grants Israel deliverance through the Red Sea. Thus Yahweh made it very clear to Egyptians, Israelites, and surrounding nations that *he* alone had worked redemption for his people: "For by now I could have stretched out my hand and struck you [Pharaoh] and your people with a plague that would have wiped you off the earth. But I have raised you up for this very purpose, that I might show you my power and that my name might be proclaimed in all the earth" (Exod. 9:15–16; cf. Rom 9:17). Through a barrage of Category 2G miracles, observers would know that Moses was Yahweh's mouthpiece and that Yahweh is the supreme God and that there is no one like Yahweh (Exod. 15:11–12).

Evidence, Miracles, and Moses's and Joshua's Believability

Suppose then we can imagine a skeptical soldier in Israel under Moses or Joshua who wonders whether a harsh command is truly from Yahweh. He thinks, "Why should I believe that you speak for God?" and is looking for reasons to doubt Moses or Joshua. But at the same time, he is open to evidence and for reasons to believe that Moses or Joshua truly speaks for God. The narrative suggests that Moses and Joshua *should have been believed* because of the confirming miracles God performed through them.

The Israelites, soldiers included, were to learn two chief lessons from the miracles surrounding the exodus out of Egypt: first, that Yahweh is supreme above all gods in power and authority and, second, that Moses was "like God"—God's representative—before Egypt and Israel (Exod. 7:1; cf. 4:16). And these lessons were to be communicated to future generations of Israelites.[4] Miracles validated that the God of Abraham was truly speaking through Moses (vv. 6–9). So no wonder that at the exodus itself, the people "believed in the LORD *and in his servant Moses*" (14:30–31 NASB; cf. 19:9; Deut. 34:10–12). The miracles of judgment on Egypt and her gods validated Moses and his message.[5] Many Egyptians came to esteem Moses (Exod. 3:21; 11:3), and a "mixed multitude" even attached themselves to Israel (12:36–38 NASB). Pharaoh and the Egyptians learned firsthand that *Moses was like God* to them.

Moses's unique role was further confirmed in the dreadful direct revelation at Sinai (Deut. 5:23–27), which the Israelites could *see* (smoke, fire), *hear* (thunder, trumpet, voice), and *feel* (earthquake) and which would be etched in

Israel's collective memory.[6] God spoke to Moses in a cloud "so that the people may hear when I speak with you and may also believe *in you forever"* (Exod. 19:9 NASB). Moses's words about Israel's eating, planting, judicial, and warfare practices were to be heeded because he had led the Israelites through the sea. Day and night by pillared cloud and fire, God's visible presence remained in their midst as a reminder of Moses's calling as a leader in the sight of Israel and of Israel's calling by God in the sight of the nations (33:15–16).

The Ten Commandments (the Decalogue) begin with the affirmation of the exodus miracle to confirm *both* Yahweh's and Moses's believability: "I am the LORD your God who brought you out of the land of Egypt, out of the house of slavery" (Exod. 20:2; Deut. 5:6 NASB). Moses should be believed as God's trusted mouthpiece because he actually led them out of the land of Egypt; this is a historical basis to ground Israel's moral obligation to keep the law of Moses, which carries over into the rest of the Old Testament.[7] Indeed, the construction "I am the LORD" or "who brought you out of the land of Egypt" appears about one hundred times in Exodus through Deuteronomy and is usually connected to a command. The cluster of exodus miracles—displays of God's grace and salvation—are grounds for Israel's grateful obedience in the present (Num. 14:11) and for Moses's believability as God's representative issuing commands.[8] In Leviticus, many commands are grounded by the phrase, "I am the LORD."[9] This is likely shorthand for the fuller statement that includes "who brought you out of Egypt" (cf. Lev. 19:35–37).[10] Later, Psalm 105:23–45 summarizes the exodus and wilderness wanderings: "He [God] turned . . . And he sent . . . And he gave . . . And he struck . . . And he brought . . ." At the end of this chain of verbs, the psalmist makes the connection between the history of the exodus miracles and obedience: "that they might keep his statutes and observe his laws" (NASB).

A large number of the commands in the Mosaic law are grounded in the exodus event. For example, the people should not fear the Canaanites since the God who triumphed over the Egyptians would also triumph over them (Deut. 7:17–26). The "questioning Israelite soldier" could trust Moses as Yahweh's messenger because of divine miraculous displays at the exodus. And he should trust Moses even when things have gone badly and Moses's authority is challenged by the likes of Korah or complaining Israelites—grumblings that were ultimately "against God" and not only "against Moses" (Exod. 16:8; Num. 16:11; 21:5). Any potential confusion created by rebellion was cleared up through miracles seen by the entire community (Num. 16:28–32, 35, 41, 48–49; 17; cf. 12:1–15). The questioning Israelite soldier doesn't simply have to "take Moses's word for it"; he is in a position to *see firsthand* God's miraculous actions—reports to be passed on to future generations (Exod. 12:26; 13:14;

Deut. 6:4–9, 20–25; 11:19–20; Josh. 4:21). Indeed, Exodus-Deuteronomy regularly appeals to what the Israelites physically *saw*[11]—not ahistoric myths—to anchor their knowledge of God.[12]

As for believing Joshua's commands, Scripture uses the same language as it does of Moses. As Israel is about to cross the Jordan, God says, "This day I will begin to exalt you [Joshua] in the sight of all Israel, *that they may know that just as I have been with Moses, I will be with you*" (Josh. 3:7 NASB; cf. 1:5, 9). After they crossed the Jordan, the people "revered [Joshua], just as they had revered Moses" (Josh. 4:14).

Beyond this, the *Israelites themselves and their enemies knew* that Yahweh was truly with Joshua: "Then the cloud covered the tent of meeting, and the glory of the LORD filled the tabernacle. . . . In all the travels of the Israelites, whenever the cloud lifted from above the tabernacle, they would set out; but if the cloud did not lift, they did not set out—until the day it lifted. So the cloud of the LORD was over the tabernacle by day, and fire was in the cloud by night, *in the sight of all the Israelites*" (Exod. 40:34, 36–38; cf. Num. 9:15–23).

Let us not miss two critical points here. First, *God's presence was highly visible—ever "in the sight" of Israel whether on the move or settled.* Second, *the tabernacle would continue to move until a more permanent house of God—the temple—was established where God would cause his name to dwell* (Deut. 12:11; 14:23; 16:2–11) *and where the glory of God would be visibly manifested* (2 Chron. 7:1–3; cf. 1 Kings 8:10–13). And if the pillar of cloud by day and fire by night was constantly at the center of Israel's camp and leading them to the next destination, then any non-Israelite nation surrounding them could have seen this miraculous manifestation of God's presence as the Israelites approached. Not only did the Canaanites and Philistines *hear reports* of Yahweh's miraculous activity, but they also could *see* the manifestation of Yahweh's presence as Israel camped or moved about (cf. Josh. 2:9–11; 1 Sam. 4:1). This means that both the Israelites and the inhabitants of Canaan saw the miraculous presence of God. The Scriptures make clear that the more abundant and clear the miracles, the greater the culpability of those who rejected them (e.g., Matt. 11:21–24). Consider how hard-hearted nations must have felt about going to war with Israel when they had seen with their own eyes God's presence clearly manifested. These enemies—both inside and outside Canaan—included the Egyptians (Exod. 13:17–22; 14:19–20), the Amalekites (17:8–16), the southern Canaanites (Num. 21:1–4), the king of Bashan (21:33–35), the Midianites (31:6–12), the inhabitants of Jericho (Josh. 6:1–27) and Ai (8:1–29), the inhabitants of Jerusalem and its allies (10:8–26), and the inhabitants of Libnah (vv. 29–30), Lacish (vv. 31–32), Gezer (v. 33), Eglon (vv. 34–35), Hebron (vv. 36–37), Debir (vv. 38–39), and Hazor and its allies (11:1–15). At any rate, the "questioning Israelite soldier" would have had strong evidence of God's miraculous presence.

The Storehouse of Divine Validation

In order for the Israelite soldier to engage in "life-taking obedience" in response to Moses's command, he needs a storehouse stocked with indicators of miraculous divine validation, which he has—*unlike* any person today who advocates violence in the name of God. The Israelite soldier has multisensory, highly public evidence of a Category 2G type. These experiences include seeing the miracles of the plagues and exodus; witnessing the trumpet sound, earthquake, fire, thunder, and lightning at Mount Sinai; observing the earth-splitting judgment on Korah and his family for their rebellion; following the pillar of cloud and fire—to name a few. By contrast, Moses's *private* burning bush experience would not be adequate proof for the questioning soldier to engage in life-taking obedience.

However, the large cluster of weighty miracles performed while Moses led Israel would *reinforce the believability of the less-weighty miracles* like the burning bush. Indeed, the less evidentially weighty, private, fading miracles of the Category 2L sort gain credibility within the context of the shock-and-awe sorts of Category 2G miracles—the Egyptian plagues, crossing the sea, the pillar of fire, and daily manna—that have an enduring quality and can't be easily faked. So even when our prospective Israelite soldier first heard Moses's report about a burning bush, he may not have been impressed. But this report was reinforced with the more impressive leprous hand and staff-into-snake miracles (Exod. 4:1–7, 29–31)—and later by plagues and crossing the sea. Looking back, the soldier can come to trust Moses's testimony about the burning bush because he is gazing at the pillar of fire in front of him. Such less evidentially weighty miracles become more believable because they are embedded in a broader context of more weighty, empirically verifiable ones.

Moses, Miracles, and the Ancient Near East

This kind of empirical, publicly accessible validation of miracles is much different from the impoverished epistemology (how we know) elsewhere in the ancient Near East. According to John Walton, "Divination produced the only divine revelation known in the ancient Near East. Through its mechanisms, the ancients believed not that they could know the deity, but that they could get a glimpse of the designs and will of the deity."[13] Yet such divination and magic were completely forbidden for Israelites—for they were a faulty attempt to gain divine guidance, often through highly subjective, manipulable means. One exception is the casting of lots; but lots produce an unambiguous, "entirely binary" answer. Unlike the ancient Near Eastern practice of consulting an animal liver to divine the mind of the gods, lots are not open to interpretation: God "did not 'write' his messages in the entrails of animals or in the movements of heavenly bodies." The practice of casting lots in Israel was established by a miraculously validated mouthpiece and typically carried out in the visible presence of the glory cloud.[14] Ancient Near Eastern religious leaders could claim divine authority without strong verifiability. The miracles recorded in Exodus through Joshua uniquely single out Moses and Joshua. It is the difference between saying, "I speak for God," and "I speak for the God who just dried up the sea, who is leading you by a pillar of fire, and who is feeding you daily with bread from heaven."

Prophetic Punctuated Equilibrium and Inheriting Ripples

The biblical narrative suggests a pattern—namely, large-scale miraculous activity and increased prophetic utterances are connected to a call to restore order from chaos through destruction. We do see a connection between evidentially weighty miracles and sacralized violence (e.g., divinely mandated wars)—what Rowley calls *prophetic punctuated equilibrium*; that is, spurts of miraculous "mutations" occurring within a short time—clustered around the old covenant (Moses and Joshua) and new covenant (Jesus and the apostles)—followed by longer periods when relatively fewer miracles take place (*stasis*). We see violence when Israel is being established as a nation, and again in a divine reversal, violence is done to the Messiah, who in turn overthrows the powers of evil. As theologian Henri Blocher writes, "At the cross, God turned evil against evil and brought about the practical solution to the problem [of evil]." "Evil is conquered as evil because God turns it back upon itself."[15]

The Old Testament's commands involving life-taking obedience (but evidentially buttressed by weighty signs and wonders) were unique and unrepeatable. The miraculous validations of Moses's commands are like a rock thrown into the waters of history. But for us in the present, they are like ripples in the water—the effects of God's activity in the world as recounted in Scripture. These ripples do not command "go and experience likewise" but "believe that this happened!" They serve as a reminder of God's clear and inimitable workings in the course of salvation history and a call to remember his faithfulness in bringing his purposes to fruition. We cannot engage in physical conquest as God's people any more than we can re-walk through the sea, be guided by a pillar of fire, or eat supernatural bread from heaven.

So for the skeptical soldier wondering whether God has really commanded war on the Canaanites, Rowley argues that Scripture connects the harsh command for life-taking obedience with large-scale, communal miracles that function as epistemological currency in the soldier's trust bank. Thus we stand on solid ground in rejecting the present-day leaders who say that Christians should engage in a Yahweh war and sacralized violence because "God told us so." They do not have the epistemological weight of large-scale, exodus-type miracles to support such a claim. Rowley writes, "Repeating the oath of office does not turn an unelected citizen into the President and give him the authority to sign laws or declare war. In the same way, invoking the Deity by saying that he declared violence does not say anything true about reality. Nothing like the claimed miracles surrounding the exodus and conquest has ever been historically repeated; therefore all comparisons are false comparisons."[16] Rowley concludes that divinely approved violence in the past is not justification for repeating it in the present. While "people in the present day can *borrow language* from the conquest," he notes, "they cannot *repeat the context* of the conquest."[17]

Conclusion

In a post-9/11 environment, Wes Morriston's arguments strike a significant chord. He asks us to consider the following question: *If biblical theists accept that God has in the past exempted people from the moral principle to not kill (for the sake of some greater good), then on what principled basis can they claim that God is not doing so today?*

We have addressed this concern in this chapter as well as the previous one. First, Morriston's argument wrongly assumes that prophetic utterances like those recorded in Scripture continue after the closing of the biblical canon. Second, we have noted that one can rationally attribute to God a command that under ordinary circumstances would be immoral to carry out only on two conditions: (1) *that the command does not contradict a nonnegotiable moral principle*, and (2) *that, on the background evidence accepted by a biblical theist, the claim that God issued the command is more likely than the claim that the action is wrong.* Third, even if the command meets these criteria, *further* tests must be passed—tests we've already seen were not met by the God-invoking Texas governor:

- alleged prophets must have a track record of true predictions and have proved themselves authentic;
- their message must not contradict previous revelation or commands recorded in Scripture;
- their character must show fruit of the Spirit in their life, and they must have a lifestyle of sincere obedience to God's commands;
- if prophets announce an exemption from the normal rules against killing, this message will be authenticated by Category 2G miracles.

Summary

- If God by special revelation through a human representative decrees something at variance with universal or general moral principles, then how can the commandee know that this mouthpiece accurately speaks for God? Perhaps it's the result of a delusion or a demon?

- Imagine you are a skeptical soldier in Moses's or Joshua's army and that you ask yourself the question, "Why should I obey Moses's call to war against the Canaanites?" How would one *know* that a good and just God is behind such a command?

- The biblical narrative suggests that in such situations, God desired to safeguard against the misunderstanding of his commands ("life-taking obedience"); therefore, he chose to validate this new knowledge with clear displays of miracles so as not to confuse it with one's mere inner subjective sensing (Matthew Rowley).

- The argument goes like this: (1) In very unusual circumstances in the past, God, by commanding people to kill the innocent (for the sake of some greater good), exempted them from a moral principle that otherwise would be binding on them. (2) But if God did this in the past, then he could theoretically do so again in the present. (3′) However, in these unusual cases, the awareness of the exemption comes through the declaration of the messenger of God *and* is validated by individual and communal miracles (multiple, large-scale miracles). (4′) Thus, the personal (and perhaps communal) sensing can be objectively verified by the individual or

an onlooker (e.g., crossing of the Jordan on dry ground, thus validating Joshua's message in Josh. 3:7: "This day I will begin to exalt you [Joshua] in the sight of all Israel, that they may know that just as I have been with Moses, I will be with you" NASB).

- When we observe the universe, we can learn of the miraculous power, intelligence, and creativity of God, who created and sustains the universe (Category 1 miracles). However, we don't learn from this observation that Moses was God's chosen mouthpiece.

- Miracles to support or validate such a claim (Category 2 miracles) can vary in their value, inspiring greater or lesser confidence in knowing (the epistemic spectrum)—ranging from a private burning bush experience (less weighty—Category 2L) to crossing the Red Sea and eating manna daily for decades (hard to misinterpret and impossible to fake—Category 2G).

- The latter would show that Moses is God's mouthpiece (Exod. 9:15–16; 15:11–12; cf. Rom. 9:17). Such miracles offer evidence that is communal, multiethnic, widespread, multisensory, multi-event, and prophesied in detail.

- The narrative suggests that Moses and Joshua *should have been believed* because of the confirming miracles God performed through them—that Moses was "like God" to Israel (Exod. 7:1; cf. 4:16).

- The questioning soldier should trust Moses even when things have gone badly and Moses's authority is challenged by the likes of

Korah or complaining Israelites (Exod. 16:8; Num. 16; cf. 12:1–15).

• Beyond this, *Israel's enemies themselves knew* that Yahweh was truly with Joshua, not only by the miracles in Egypt and the Red Sea crossing, but also by the pillar of cloud by day and fire by night (Exod. 40:34–38; cf. Num. 9:15–23). The Canaanites and Philistines had *heard reports* of God's miraculous activity (cf. Josh. 2:9–11; 1 Sam. 4:1).

• Consider how hard-hearted nations must be to go to war with Israel when they have seen with their own eyes God's presence clearly manifested. At any rate, the "questioning Israelite soldier" would have had strong evidence of God's miraculous presence.

• In order for the Israelite soldier to engage in "life-taking obedience" in response to Moses's command, he needs a storehouse stocked with indicators of miraculous divine validation, which he has—*unlike* any person today who advocates violence in the name of God.

• The large cluster of weighty miracles performed while Moses led Israel *reinforce the believability of the less-weighty miracles* like the burning bush.

• Unlike the impoverished methods of validating divine revelation in the ancient Near East (magic, divination, manipulation with "messages" on animal entrails or the movements of heavenly bodies), the miracles in Exodus-Joshua validate Moses and Joshua as God's spokesmen.

• We see a connection between evidentially weighty miracles and divinely mandated wars—spurts of miracles (*prophetic punctuated equilibrium*) clustered around the old covenant (Moses and Joshua) and new covenant (Jesus and the apostles)—followed by longer periods when relatively fewer miracles take place (*stasis*). These weighty miracles give the skeptical Israelite soldier the assurance that Moses is God's mouthpiece.

PART 4

RELIGION AND VIOLENCE

We have looked at some of the key questions surrounding the Old Testament war texts that many misconstrue as being "genocidal." We have addressed misunderstandings about the nature of divine commands, the meaning of "utterly destroy" and "leave alive nothing that breathes," and many classic and contemporary arguments these texts evoke—arguments that question and even challenge the goodness and the justice of God.

As we have pointed out, it seems that more work needs to be done to round out our discussion. We thought it important to address related questions that, in our experience, regularly accompany the topic of Old Testament warfare. These include whether "religion" inevitably leads to violence, whether Islamic jihad and Old Testament warfare make for a fair comparison, whether the Crusades were inspired by Old Testament warfare texts (along with other Crusades-related issues), and whether warfare is even morally permissible. It is to these issues that we now turn.

20

Does Religion Cause Violence?

Charles Kimball's book *When Religion Becomes Evil* declares that religion has caused more violence than any other "institutional force in human history."[1] He gives "five warning signs" of when religion is likely to turn evil and violent: when religions make absolute truth claims; when they require blind obedience; when they establish an "ideal time" to act in order that better times may come (e.g., setting up a theocracy); when they believe that the end justifies the means, including lying and murder; and when they make a declaration of holy war—such as Islamic clerics' fatwahs against Danish cartoonist Kurt Westergaard for his drawing of Muhammad and against Salman Rushdie for his *Satanic Verses*.

In his *Terror in the Mind of God*, Mark Juergensmeyer claims that religion is violent by its very nature because it tends to "absolutize and to project images of cosmic war."[2] This is true even if a religion's ultimate goal is peace and order. To stop violence to produce peace and harmony, Juergensmeyer recommends that religions adopt the softening influence of Enlightenment values such as "rationality and fair play."[3]

According to Regina Schwartz, the real problem is not simply "religion," but *monotheistic* religion—Judaism, Islam, and Christianity. In her book *The Curse of Cain*, she points to monotheism's "violent legacy." After all, if you believe in *one God* (monotheism), then you are making *exclusivistic* truth-claims. And those who do not agree are "other" or "outsiders." As a result of rejecting monotheism, these outsiders will be ostracized, abhorred, even obliterated because they fail to acknowledge "the one true God."[4] Monotheism inevitably leads to an us-versus-them mind-set. If monotheists are to preserve their distinctive religious identity, then the outsider threat must be removed. (We partially addressed this accusation in chap. 16.)

Curiously, the book title invokes the "curse of Cain" (cf. Gen. 4:11). The offering of Cain's brother Abel was accepted before God while Cain's was rejected. Here we have monotheism rearing its ugly head—Cain is excluded from God's blessing, and in anger he kills his brother. We see the same problem when God chose Jacob over Esau, which led to alienation between brothers and ongoing hostilities between Israel and Edom. And again, the Israelites are chosen and the Canaanites aren't; and so the Canaanites are eliminated. Alienation and murder are the predictable results of monotheism. The same us-versus-them mind-set flows from God's "election" of Christians out of "the world."[5] Terrorist attacks, social exclusion, bigotry, and coercion are some of the predictable results of monotheism. Schwartz recommends the "Enlightenment values" of tolerance, diversity, and pluralism; these values generously welcome outsiders and don't stifle creativity.

There is much wrong with this portrayal of "religion." In this chapter we explore some of the caricatures, mistakes, and even myths made by modern scholars and popular writers in their discussion of "religion."

Getting Clear on "Religion" and "Enlightenment Values"

What Is Religion?

Despite some scholars' efforts to weed out "religion" from society, it is truly impossible to remove the "cult" from "culture"—that is, the "religious" worldview that gives unity and shapes shared, learned behavior. When these scholars pit "Enlightenment values" against "religion," a number of ironies emerge.

One irony is that *the pro-Enlightenment advocates and/or "religion" attackers are not even clear on what "religion" is.* For example, Kimball is quick to point out the dangers of "religion," but he doesn't give any clear guidance in distinguishing between the religious and the nonreligious or secular. He simply assumes that "we all know [religion] when we see it."[6] The fact is, the meaning of "religion" is a much debated topic, and Kimball's attack on "religion" and its dangers actually backfires.

William Cavanaugh exposes the acknowledged fuzziness in defining "religion."[7] He illustrates this by pointing to historian of religion Martin Marty of the University of Chicago; Marty writes about the need to separate religion from politics, and he emphasizes how "religion divides." Yet he informs us of *seventeen* different ways religion can be defined and admits that "scholars will never agree on the definition of religion."[8] Cavanaugh comments on this: "If one is trying, as is Marty, to convince the reader that 'religion divides' and 'religion can be violent,' then one ought to be clear about what religion is."[9]

In light of this first irony, we should consider two points. (1) *As we look for a core set of beliefs, we don't really find much commonality across the traditional "religious" spectrum*: the nature of reality (e.g., God vs. no God), the human person, the human problem, the solution to this problem, the nature of the afterlife, and so on. If there is any overlap, it would be at the ethical level. Classical Buddhism, for example, rejects the existence of a Creator. Hinduism is perhaps united by the common belief in the existence of the soul and reincarnation—but not much else beyond this. And secular humanist groups in the United States even have 501(c)(3) tax-exempt status—just as their traditional "religious" counterparts do. We cannot neatly separate the religious and the secular, as moderns tend to do. Despite the modern attempt to distinguish between the religious and secular, such a distinction is rather unilluminating.

(2) *To spare us the repeated confusions and arbitrary distinctions, we would be wise to think in terms of an all-encompassing "worldview" or "philosophy of life" instead of the misused and abused term "religion."* Here we speak of a fundamental personal or heart commitment to certain basic beliefs of some grand story or metanarrative that shapes our lives and identities. And here we note that *everyone*—the traditional "religionist" as well as the "secular humanist"—has a worldview whose assumptions operate mostly at a subconscious level.[10]

Paul Griffiths refers to the inescapable *religious* or *worldview* perspective as being "a form of life that seems to those who inhabit it to be comprehensive, incapable of abandonment, and of central importance."[11] By *form of life*, Griffiths means a pattern of activity that appears to its practitioners to have boundaries and particular actions that are bound up with it. He describes the three basic characteristics this way:

- *Comprehensive*: It takes into account and is relevant to everything—a framework into which all the particularities of life can be placed—from how one dresses to the significance of marriage to moral actions.
- *Incapable of abandonment*: This religious stance/form of life defines the religionist's identity. Native English speakers, say, though they could learn another language, don't really think of themselves as those who could readily abandon their deeply embedded mother tongue.
- *Of central importance*: This form of life is no mere add-on or extra; it addresses issues of paramount importance: *What is real? What is to be valued? What is my purpose?*

So getting clear on our terminology and definitions would help clear away much misunderstanding in the modern-day discussion and criticism of "religion."

A second irony is this: *political visions—even allegedly secular ones—often take on strongly "religious" overtones.* Political leaders have been deified by the masses. For example, how does "religion" differ from Germany's National Socialism (Nazism)? The prominent philosopher Martin Heidegger, author of *Being and Time*, not only joined the Nazi Party in 1933, but he proudly wore the swastika, readily "heiled" Hitler, and sang Nazi songs with gusto. He reminded German students: "Do not let principles and ideas be the rulers of your existence. The Führer himself and he alone is the German reality of today, and of the future, and its law."[12] Or what about the "deification" of and reverential devotion to dictators such as Stalin or North Korea's Kim Jung Il? And in the Communist Chinese song "The East Is Red," Chairman Mao Zedong is called "the people's savior." Even in ancient Rome, emperors came to be deified as "the Son of God," "Lord," and "Savior of the World." It was the early Christians who were accused of being "atheists"—after all, in comparison to worshiping the variety of deities on offer in the Mediterranean world, worshiping just one God is close enough to atheism.[13] The line between the religious and the secular is quite clearly irrelevant when it comes to the phenomenon of exalting dictators. Humans are inescapably "religious," whether they believe in a Creator or are atheists, whether they worship God or tyrants.

A third and related irony is that *"secular" ideologies can readily compete with the most fanatical and dangerous elements found within traditional religion.* At this juncture, let's take up Kimball's "five warning signs." Cavanaugh asks why we cannot apply these warning signs to *secular* ideologies: "If the five warning signs also apply to secular ideologies why not frame the [Kimball's] book as an analysis of the circumstances under which *any* institution or ideology becomes evil?"[14] *Why single out religion?* And Juergensmeyer actually undermines his very argument against "religion" when he refers to the serial killer the "Unabomber," Ted Kaczynski. Kaczynski terrorized and harmed people through the use of pipe bombs, and he was *not* affiliated with any traditional religion. Juergensmeyer even admits to the existence of "secular nationalism," which embraces a "doctrine of destiny" and which he elsewhere says "*is* 'a religion.'"[15]

The same kind of intolerance and hostility of progressivism—a totalizing vision that leaves no part of life untouched, muzzles free speech, and bullies those who don't comply—has been well documented by Jonah Goldberg in *Liberal Fascism*.[16] He tracks the movement of progressivism starting with Woodrow Wilson who despised the Constitution and warned, "If you're not a progressive, watch it!" Wilson's Sedition Act suppressed any dissent against the presidency.

Though "totalitarianism" is a negative term to our minds, the idea was initially well received by Western intellectual elites. This word itself was actually invented by Benito Mussolini—a celebrity to American and European progressives, all of whom readily approved of the term "fascist." Early on, Hitler too was praised by many American progressives, and Hitler himself wrote a letter to Franklin Delano Roosevelt commending his "heroic effort" in sweeping social policies that were being followed with interest and admiration by the German people. Only in the aftermath of World War II and the "Final Solution" to destroy the Jews did many progressives distance themselves from Hitler; prior to Hitler, it was not assumed that fascism had anything to do with anti-Semitism. And even though many progressives such as John Dewey and H. G. Wells have been self-proclaimed secularists, they too advocated a totalitarian vision. Indeed, such secularists have not been exempt from hostility toward their opponents and from creating an us-versus-them mentality.[17]

As we end this section, we emphasize how *we cannot truly escape a "religious" point of view*. Cavanaugh's book *The Myth of Religious Violence* nicely dismantles the religious-secular (and even the religious-political) dichotomy put forward by the New Atheists, academics, and other members of the intelligentsia. Ideologies such as Marxism, socialism, liberalism, or nationalism can rival anything done in the name of "religion." Unfortunately, much current empirical research that delves into "religious violence" is hobbled by this flawed distinction, and this further contributes to Western caricatures and stereotypes of traditional religionists and serves as a post-Enlightenment propaganda tool.[18]

Cavanaugh refers to the "myth of religious violence" as part of the "folklore of Western societies."[19] He advises that people who write books entitled *When People Do Bad Things in the Name of Religion* be more economical—and accurate. Since "religion" can encompass *anything* that gives people purpose and meaning, he suggests a more appropriate title: *When People Do Bad Things.*[20]

Europe's "Religious Wars": Did the Enlightenment Make a Difference?

The three ironies we've just noted are further illustrated as we look at the "religious wars" of Europe during the sixteenth and seventeenth centuries. And given some of the views of leading, highly praised Enlightenment figures, we can call into question the uncritical praise of their "secular values."

Perhaps the most notable symbol of the shift from "religion" to "secular reason" was the French Revolution of 1789. Ironically, the barbarity of the Enlightenment's French Revolution and its pursuit of liberty, equality, and fraternity became a nightmare of inhumanity and cruelty. But even so, wasn't the "rational" and "tolerant" Enlightenment (1650–1800) opposed to Europe's religious wars and bigotry that had hitherto characterized religion? Didn't Enlightenment figures press for tolerance?

The first point to observe here is that with the onset of the Enlightenment, *the church's political power came to be replaced by the state's political power.* And as we noted above, the twentieth century showed how state power, sometimes in the name of atheism or nationalism, can be just as—or even more— tyrannical. Indeed, we cannot coherently separate politics from "religion." This tidy separation is the *invention* of the modern West.[21]

Second, *the "religious wars" were in fact not predictably divided along doctrinal lines but rather political ones.* Cavanaugh has carefully documented how Catholics, Lutherans, Zwinglians, and Calvinists were less driven by dogmatics than the pragmatics of strategic alliances and interests. No, it wasn't all about sects. Rather, the boundaries of these alleged "religious wars" were drawn primarily along *political* lines. Here is a sampling to illustrate this point:

- Shortly after Martin Luther posted his Ninety-Five Theses in 1517, the Catholic emperor Charles V fought not against Lutherans but against the very Catholic pope; his soldiers sacked Rome in 1527. The wars in the 1520s were political—between emperor and pope; they concerned territorial control over Italy and over the church in German territories.
- Catholic France frequently fought against the Catholic emperor Charles V in multiple wars extending from 1521 through 1552.
- In 1544, Protestant princes sided with Catholic emperor Charles V in wars against Catholic France.
- In 1531, Lutheran princes were allied with Catholic Bavaria in opposition to the Catholic Ferdinand's rule of the Romans.
- In 1556–57, Pope Paul IV fought against the devout Catholic Habsburg monarch, Philip II of Spain.
- The Catholic king Henry II of France attacked the Catholic emperor's forces in 1552. And most of Charles's soldiers were mercenaries, many of whom were Protestant.[22]

Much more of the same could be listed here to show that such mixed alliances were typically "political," including economic and territorial. In fact, a goodly number of historians describing these wars—including J.-H. Mariéjol, Lucien Romier, James Westfall Thompson, Henri Hauser, George Livet—viewed them as clearly "political," despite the religious veneer. It was Natalie Zemon Davis's 1973 article, "The Rites of Violence," that was considered to be the watershed article that reintroduced the religious factor into the study of the French wars.[23]

Prior to the Enlightenment, however, church and state had been bound together. The Enlightenment influenced the creation of the alleged sacred-secular or religious-secular dichotomy. Despite secularists laying claim to the influence of the "rational, tolerant Enlightenment" that stood in opposition to Europe's post-Reformation religious wars, this is a fabrication.

Third, *various celebrated Enlightenment figures had their own share of un-enlightened viewpoints—sometimes in contrast to their more enlightened "re-ligious" opponents.* Despite the sophisticated "enlightened" attitudes among this period's idea-shapers, many of them explicitly supported slavery—Thomas Hobbes, Voltaire, Baron Montesquieu, Comte de Mirabeau, Edmund Burke, David Hume—though some Enlightenment figures like Denis Diderot and Samuel Johnson did support abolition, and there certainly were "religionists" who supported slavery. However, as Rodney Stark notes,

> Most accepted slavery as a normal part of the human situation. It was not philosophers or secular intellectuals who assembled the moral indictment of slavery, but the very people they held in contempt: men and women having intense Christian faith, who opposed slavery because it was a sin. . . . It was the natural theologian William Paley, not his atheist [or at best deist] opponent David Hume, who condemned slavery as an "odious institution" and did so on the basis of Christian "light and influence."[24]

This is not all that surprising. Hume confidently declared that those who believe in the miraculous are "ignorant and barbarous" peoples.[25] And if we extend Hume's logic, we can draw parallels between his view on miracles and on white racial supremacy. For Hume, "ignorant and barbarous" peoples (who believed miracle claims) were basically nonwhites—people he believed to be of "naturally inferior" intelligence. The implication? Despite having heard reports of exceptions, Hume's experience would have found the existence of an intelligent nonwhite person to be just as unreasonable as expecting a miracle. His "enlightened" presumption was always *against* intelligent nonwhites. The point is this: as Hume had made up his mind about what is uniform—whether white superiority or miracles—then he could always dismiss any counterex-amples (of intelligent nonwhites or well-attested miracle claims) as going against probability.[26] So, given this mind-set, it is not not surprising to think that Hume would espouse slavery.

Overall, the intellectuals of the "Enlightenment" fell "far short of matching the extent and passion of abolitionist commitment spreading through religious circles at the same time."[27] The area of slavery is one of the many examples in which dedicated Christians have had a prophetic voice, standing against the tide of societal evils and serving as the clear influence for moral change. As we note later in the chapter, certain fundamental Enlightenment ideals touted by secularists were themselves largely influenced by Christian thought and action.[28]

Third, *prominent "enlightened" and "secular" voices denouncing "religion" as dangerous will themselves even advocate violence against traditional religionists.* Sam Harris engages in this double standard by advocating the "unthinkable crime" of a nuclear first-strike that could kill "tens of millions of innocent civilians in a single day" but which "may be the only course of action available to us, given what Islamists believe."[29] Christopher Hitchens says much the same thing—that the "enemies of civilization should be beaten and killed and defeated, and I don't make any apology for it."[30] And again: "We can't live on the same planet as them [*sic*]. . . . I don't want to breathe the same air as these psychopaths and murders [*sic*] and rapists and torturers and child abusers. It's them or me."[31]

So these New Atheists denounce the Israelites who, under divine orders accompanied by confirmatory signs and wonders, drove out or killed the Canaanites because of their criminal acts of infant sacrifice, incest, ritual prostitution, and other morally degraded practices. Yet they advocate something that sounds even harsher against, in this case, Muslims for their "anticivilizational" and "irrational" beliefs and practices. To kill in the name of religion is bad, but not in the name of secularism.

Bad—and Good—Religion: The Baby and the Bathwater

"Religion," we've seen, is a misleading and abused term—and some will dismiss wholesale anything labeled "religion." And to make matters worse, some traditional "religious" groups give other ones a bad name. Yes, some of them are destructive and harmful—think of Rajneesh's free-love commune in Oregon; David Koresh's community in Waco, Texas; or Jim Jones's group that participated in a mass suicide in Guyana. Statistically speaking, acts of terrorism are typically carried out by Muslim extremists, not Buddhists, Christians, or Jews—and 80 percent of religious persecution today is against Christians.[32] Lumping "all religions" together is as unhelpful and misleading as the religious-secular divide. The "enlightened" claims that "religion poisons everything" (Hitchens) or that it is "the root of all evil" (Dawkins) are shockingly ignorant generalizations, throwing out its positive effects along with abuses done in the name of religion. We note these clear and well-recognized effects.

First, *a growing number of scholars—including atheists—are documenting the remarkable benefit the Christian faith has brought to the world, and particularly in the West.* Consider what Europe's most prominent philosopher, Jürgen Habermas—an atheist—says about the influence of the biblical worldview in the West:

> Christianity has functioned for the normative self-understanding of modernity as more than a mere precursor or a catalyst. Egalitarian universalism, from which sprang the ideas of freedom and a social solidarity, of an autonomous conduct of life and emancipation, of the individual morality of conscience, human rights, and democracy, is the direct heir to the Judaic ethic of justice and the Christian ethic of love. This legacy, substantially unchanged, has been the object of continual critical appropriation and reinterpretation. To this day, there is no alternative to it. And in light of current challenges of a postnational constellation, we continue to draw on the substance of this heritage. Everything else is just idle postmodern talk.[33]

Another atheist intellectual—the postmodern thinker Jacques Derrida—acknowledges the powerful and positive influence of the biblical faith:

> Today the cornerstone of international law is the sacred, what is sacred in humanity. You should not kill. You should not be responsible for a crime against the sacredness, the sacredness of man as your neighbor . . . made by God or by God made man. . . . In that sense, the concept of crime against humanity is a Christian concept and I think there would be no such thing in the law today without the Christian heritage, the Abrahamic heritage, the biblical heritage.[34]

Time magazine's well-respected correspondent David Aikman reported the summary of one Chinese scholar's lecture to a group of foreigners:

> "One of the things we were asked to look into was what accounted for the success, in fact, the pre-eminence of the West all over the world," he said. "We studied everything we could from the historical, political, economic, and cultural perspective. At first, we thought it was because you had more powerful guns than we had. Then we thought it was because you had the best political system. Next we focused on your economic system. But in the past twenty years, we have realized that the heart of your culture is your religion: Christianity.

That is why the West has been so powerful. The Christian moral foundation of social and cultural life was what made possible the emergence of capitalism and then the successful transition to democratic politics. We don't have any doubt about this."[35]

The speaker was a representative of one of China's premier academic research organizations—the Chinese Academy of Social Sciences.

Noted British historian Niall Ferguson—another atheist—has marked the strong connection between Protestantism and a strong work ethic; he calls this one of the six "killer apps" that propelled the West forward as a civilization. The context of the biblical faith served as the cradle to other cultural benefits; these include civilizational competition, science, modern medicine, property rights, and a free market. Though an atheist, Ferguson claims that the decline in religion in Europe has led to Europeans becoming the "idlers of the world"—and that China's increasingly strong work ethic has been shaped by Protestantism in the West.[36]

The agnostic political philosopher Guenter Lewy acknowledges how in the Christian tradition, believers follow a suffering Savior, and thus they more readily identify with the less fortunate, disempowered, and suffering. He contrasts this Christian mind-set with the secularistic one:

> Adherents of [a secularistic] ethic are not likely to produce a Dorothy Day or a Mother Teresa. Many of these people love humanity but not individual human beings with all their failings and shortcomings. They will be found participating in demonstrations for causes such as nuclear disarmament but not sitting at the bedside of a dying person. An ethic of moral autonomy and individual rights, so important to secular liberals, is incapable of sustaining and nourishing values such as altruism and self-sacrifice.[37]

Second, *the influence of the Christian faith has made a clear impact in various non-Western settings as well*. Before he became a Christian, the then-agnostic journalist Malcolm Muggeridge spent many years in India and Africa, where he witnessed "much righteous endeavor undertaken by Christians of all denominations." By contrast, however, "I never, as it happens, came across a hospital or orphanage run by the Fabian Society or a Humanist leper colony."[38]

Political scientist Robert Woodberry of the National University of Singapore has marshaled impressive documentation—taking into account the wide range of variables—to show how "conversionary Protestant" Christians (i.e., missionaries) in particular have been responsible for remarkable gains in non-Western settings, including "the development and spread of religious liberty, mass education, mass printing, volunteer organizations, most major colonial reforms [abolishing slavery, widow-burning, female circumcision, pre-pubescent marriage of girls, etc.], and the codification of legal protections for nonwhites in the nineteenth and early twentieth centuries."[39] Protestant missionaries have been the driving force behind literacy and education for all (in order to read God's Word), mass printing and the print technology (in order to spread God's Word), and the spread of democracy/civil society (the result of educating all rather than merely social elites). Studies have consistently shown that the Reformation, not the Enlightenment, has been the well-spring for modern-day democracy.[40]

Incidentally, Robert Woodberry's study of the impact of Protestant missionaries throughout the world was summarized in the *American Political Science Review*, which required an additional 192 pages of supporting documentation. This article has received several awards, including the prestigious Luebbert Article Award in 2012 for the best article in comparative politics.[41]

Woodberry urges us to look at any map: wherever Protestant missionaries have established themselves, there you will find more printed books and more schools per capita. And you will discover that in Africa, the Middle East, and parts of Asia, "most of the early nationalists who led their countries to independence graduated from Protestant mission schools."[42]

Here is a summary of his findings:

Areas where Protestant missionaries had a significant presence in the past are on average more economically developed today, with comparatively better health, lower infant mortality, lower corruption, greater literacy, higher educational attainment (especially for women), and more robust membership in nongovernmental associations.[43]

Third, *attempts to attribute these democratizing gains to the influence of Greek democratic ideals or the Enlightenment are inadequate.* Woodberry notes that some might suggest that the Christian faith is not responsible for democracy and equality; rather, it is the result of ancient Greek democratic ideas. However, Greek ideas are quite different from modern democracy and still very much elitist. For example, Plato's *Republic* emphasizes the rule of philosopher-kings; ordinary citizens are not capable of ruling. And philosopher-kings should breed with intelligent women to create intelligent offspring (a kind of genetic-engineering program). As for Aristotle, he believed that some humans were slaves by nature ("animated tools"). And both thinkers considered manual labor to be undignified—a kind of semi-slavery ("banausic"; that is, not free).[44] And even though the writings of Greek thinkers like Aristotle were widely read and studied in the Muslim world, these works did not bring about democratizing effects.

Furthermore, these democratizing advances cannot be traced to the *Enlightenment*; for one thing, leading Enlightenment figures were themselves shaped by the Protestant Reformation. Key democratic theorists and practictioners such as Hugo Grotius, John Locke, Jean-Jacques Rousseau, Benjamin Franklin, John Adams, Patrick Henry, James Madison, and Alexander Hamilton had a Calvinist education or family background.[45] Even the US Constitution and Bill of Rights are modeled on previous colonial compacts utilizing theological and biblical terms—well before social contract theorists Thomas Hobbes (1588–1679) and John Locke (1632–1704). And Puritans and Protestant Nonconformists preceded these (more) secular social contractarians by arguing for the equality of all persons.[46]

Perhaps we should round out this section by considering the very positive social good the Christian faith has been and continues to be throughout the world. One powerful example of this is the Canadian Broadcasting Corporation journalist Brian Stewart, who had once been critical of "religion." But his mind changed—he eventually came to faith in Christ—because of his frontline journalistic experience. He saw Christians in quiet corners of the world, working faithfully, humbly, bravely—often away from the media's cameras and lights. We quote Stewart at length:

> I've found there is no movement, or force, closer to the raw truth of war, famines, crises and the vast human predicament, than organized Christianity in action. And there is no alliance more determined and dogged in action than church workers, ordained and lay members, when mobilized for a common good. It is these Christians who are right "on the front lines" of committed humanity today and when I want to find that front, I follow their trail.
>
> It is a vast front, stretching from the most impoverished reaches of the developing world to the hectic struggle to preserve caring values in our own towns and cities. I have never been able to reach these front lines without finding Christian volunteers already in the thick of it, mobilizing congregations that care, and being a faithful witness to truth, the primary light in the darkness, and so often the only light.
>
> Now this is something the media and government officials rarely acknowledge, for religion confuses many and anyway, we all like to blow our own horns. So front line efforts of Christianity do not usually produce headlines, and unfortunately this feeds the myth that the church just follows along, to do its modest bit.
>
> Let me repeat, I've never reached a war zone, or famine group or crisis anywhere where some church organization was not there long before me sturdy, remarkable souls, usually too kind to ask "What took you so long?"
>
> I don't slight any of the hard work done by other religions or those wonderful secular NGOs [nongovernmental organizations] I've dealt with so much

over the years. They work closely with church efforts, they are noble allies. But no, so often in desperate areas it is Christian groups there first, that labour heroically during the crisis and continue on long after all the media and the visiting celebrities have left.

Now I came to this admiring view slowly and reluctantly. At the start of my career, I'd largely abandoned religion for I, too, regarded the church as a rather tiresome irrelevance. What ultimately persuaded me otherwise and I took a lot of persuading was the reality of Christianity's mission, physically and in spirit, before my very eyes. It wasn't the attraction of great moments of grandeur although I admit covering this Pope on six of his early trips abroad, including his first one to Mexico and then epic returns to Poland, certainly shook any assumptions I had of Christianity as a fading force. . . .

I'm often asked if I lost belief in God covering events like Ethiopia, then called "the worst hell on earth." Actually, like others before me, it was precisely in such hells that I rediscovered religion. I saw so many countless acts of human love and charity, total respect for the most forsaken, for all life.[47]

The "secularist" opponent or critic of "religion" should take note of such observations.

Is Monotheism the Problem?

We've seen that the category of "religious," as opposed to "secular," is both an invention as well as a flawed distinction. So we are all the more skeptical that monotheism is the culprit, as Schwartz claims. Let's get back to Schwartz's claim that monotheism in particular leads to violence.[48] There are several problems with her argument.

First, *why think God's oneness could lead to violence in itself?* For one thing, Schwartz ignores Old Testament references to God's grace, compassion, patience, and mercy (e.g., Exod. 34:6–7). Theologian Miroslav Volf rightly insists that *if one gets rid of monotheism*, "the division and violence between 'us' and 'them' hardly disappears."[49] After all, the stronger picking on the weaker happens on the school playground or in the world of nations with competing interests.

Second, *history (in addition to tomorrow's headlines) is littered with plenty of polytheistic tribes warring against each other—or this Communist government attacking that "religious" group.* As we pointed out earlier, singling out "religion"—monotheistic or not—is unhelpful. "Religion" may simply be a label masking ethnic tribalism that may lead to a justification of hostility and violence—as in the former Yugoslavia. *Complex sociological and historical factors* can contribute to conflict—as well as alienation, poverty, disempowerment, racism/tribalism, power structures, long-standing feuds, and animosity.

Third, *even if monotheistic "religion" could be partly blamed for certain wrongs like the Inquisition or the Salem witch trials, it should not be considered the sole factor.* The notion that monotheistic religion "causes" violence or harm typically obscures a complexity of factors involved. Consider an article in the *American Psychologist* titled "Dangerous Ideas" that analyzes five beliefs that "propel groups toward conflict." Nothing specifically "religious"—let alone "monotheistic"—is listed as one of those beliefs. Rather, the beliefs cut across all worldviews and ethnopolitical conflicts; they are *superiority, injustice, vulnerability, distrust,* and *helplessness.*[50]

Mark Smith, a scholar of the ancient Near East, observes that ancient Israel was hardly a major force for violence, and he makes clear that the connection between monotheism and violence is out of touch with history:

> In short, ancient Near Eastern cultures, both polytheistic and monotheistic, associate violence with various gods and goddesses. In the history of the ancient Near East, violence is not inherent in either monotheism or polytheism. It is not a function of the form of theism, whether polytheism or monotheism; it is a function of power and the capacity to wield it. In this respect critics of Israel's monotheism tend to view it in the abstract and disembed it from its cultural and political context. For these reasons, it is finally time to put to rest this canard about monotheism and violence.[51]

The Problem of "Unchosen" Cain?

What of Schwartz's "problem of Cain"? She suggests the danger and injustice of God's electing Abel over Cain—something like an "Abel I have loved and Cain I have hated" scenario (which is comparable to Malachi 1:2–3, where God favors Jacob over Esau). Let us make a few comments on this point.

First, *God didn't choose Abel at the expense of Cain.* Schwartz, unfortunately, picked the *wrong text* for her book title! As we look more closely at the biblical text, we see that God took pains to warn Cain of his sinful attitude: "If you do well, will not your countenance be lifted up? And if you do not do well, sin is crouching at the door; and its desire is for you, but you must master it" (Gen. 4:7 NASB). Just as God would present Israel with a choice between life and death (Deut. 30:19), God presents Cain with life and death as well. Cain *could have* offered an acceptable sacrifice *if* his resentment had turned to humility. His condition wasn't inevitable. God's disapproval of Cain was due to Cain's anger and his becoming a murderer—not because God elected

Abel. Ironically, it wasn't the "religious" or "monotheistic" Abel who resorted to violence because God approved of his sacrifice; God would have accepted Cain's own sacrifice if he would "do well" (Gen. 4:7). And even *after* Cain killed Abel, the one true God still granted a protective grace for Cain (4:15).

Second, *the same opportunity applies to Jacob and Esau*. Though Esau didn't receive the inheritance rights, he was still reconciled to his trickster brother at story's end (Gen. 33:4). Esau succeeded while Cain failed. In either scenario, God shouldn't be blamed for playing favorites. And when it comes to Israel and the nations, God's choosing Israel didn't exclude gentiles from salvation (e.g., Rahab, Ruth, and Nineveh). Indeed, God's desire is to include all who will come to him.

Third, *Israel's election—the result of God's grace—was nothing to brag or feel superior about*: "Know, then, it is not because of your righteousness that the LORD your God is giving you this good land to possess, for you are a stubborn people" (Deut. 9:6 NASB). And Israel was chosen not for her own sake, but that she might bring blessing and the light of God's glory to the nations (Gen. 12:1–3; 22:18; Isa. 42:6; 49:6). What's more, Schwartz takes a wrong turn by assuming that election begins with Abel over Cain. The story of election begins with Abraham in Genesis 12—though this election is to bring blessing to all the families of the earth (v. 3). And the election required Abraham's *response* to the divine calling and command: "And Abram went . . ." (v. 4).[52]

Fourth, *Schwartz fails to distinguish between the nonelect and the antielect.* The vast majority of Old Testament texts affirm the existence of *non*elect peoples and that Israel is to engage in cordial relations with them, even though Israel should not adopt their spiritual habits. In fact, some among the nonelect receive lavish divine blessings right alongside the elect! Consider what the nonelect Ishmael is promised: "I will bless him, and will make him fruitful and will multiply him exceedingly. He shall become the father of twelve princes, and I will make him a great nation" (Gen. 17:20 NASB). Or consider this text that lumps Israel together with other nonelect nations: "'Are you not as the sons of Ethiopia to Me, O sons of Israel?' declares the LORD. 'Have I not brought up Israel from the land of Egypt, and the Philistines from Caphtor [i.e., Crete] and the Arameans [i.e., Syrians] from Kir?'" (Amos 9:7 NASB).

In contrast to the *non*elect, only three groups fit the *anti*elect category—the Amalekites, the Canaanites, and the Midianites (Num. 25, 31). As it turns out, the Midianites don't quite fit. Yes, the Midianites deliberately attempt to lead the Israelites astray into adultery and idolatry—and thus treachery and treason—at Baal-Peor (chap. 25), which provokes a divinely mandated battle against them. And the Midianites engage in attacking Israel during the time of the judges (Judg. 6–8). But there is another side: Moses marries a

Midianite woman and carries on cordially with his father-in-law, Jethro (Exod. 2:15–22; 18:1; Num. 10:29). As we've seen, the Canaanites are another mixed bag. Although the Canaanites would eventually become extremely wicked (Gen. 15:16), they are actually viewed more positively throughout Genesis: Jacob seeks to get along with them (chap. 34); both peoples generally interact peacefully (chaps. 23 and 38); and Judah even marries a Canaanite (chap. 38). The only consistently antielect people are the Amalekites, who are provocative and hostile to the people of God and seek their eradication for nearly a thousand years—from the crossing of the Red Sea (Exod. 17) to Haman the Agagite (Agag had been the king of the Amalekites [1 Sam. 15]) who sought to exterminate the Jews during the Persian Empire, as recounted in the book of Esther.[53] The us-versus-them (or Israel-versus-non-Israelites) charge is fallacious and fails to properly track the biblical data.

As we bring this chapter to a close, we see just how spot-on is William Cavanaugh's observation that the notion that religion causes violence is one of the most prevalent myths in the West. The problem is certainly not that "religion poisons everything" or that monotheism inevitably leads to violence. Nor do we read in the Old Testament of some high-minded us-versus-them theological theme—rather we read of God's grace as well as national Israel's liability to divine curse and punishment, as with the other nations. The proposed "secular" solution is not that we need the promotion of "Enlightenment values"—as though (1) there is a tidy distinction between sacred and secular or between religious and political, or (2) the Enlightenment was not shaped in large part by the Protestant Reformation. Such "nonreligious" solutions are both simplistic and misguided. We have seen that matters of violence are much broader than what many academics and the mainstream media would lead us to believe. To reinforce the argument against the "religion poisons everything" thesis, we can point to the historical facts: the power of the gospel—the biblical faith lived out by individuals and communities throughout the world—has been responsible for a wide array of moral reforms and positive democratizing gains for humanity.

Summary

• A common accusation is that religion causes more violence than any other institutional force in human history. Religion is violent by its very nature—especially the us-versus-them mind-set propounded by monotheism. The outsider, it is argued, must be removed.

Allegedly, this begins with God accepting Abel's sacrifice but rejecting Cain's.

• Those who point to religion as the culprit are very imprecise about how religion is to be defined. "Religions" may have similar features when it comes to ethics (love, kindness, compassion) but not in terms of their view of reality (metaphysics), the nature of the human problem (anthropology), its solution (soteriology), and the afterlife (eschatology). Perhaps "worldview" or "philosophy of life" would be more suitable. "Religion" is "a form of life that seems to those who inhabit it to be comprehensive, incapable of abandonment, and of central importance" (Paul Griffiths).

• Philosopher Martin Heidegger swore ultimate allegiance to Hitler ("The Führer himself, and he alone is the German reality of today, and of the future, and its law"). Other "secular" rulers have been virtually deified by some of their citizenry (North Korea's Kim Jung Il, China's Chairman Mao Zedong).

• Many of the criticisms launched at "religion" by secularists can be applied to secular ideologies themselves. *Any* institution can become evil or violent. In fact, we frequently see an us-versus-them mentality—a hostility toward outsiders—and even a totalitarian tendency in secularist progressivists like John Dewey and H. G. Wells (as Jonah Goldberg has argued). People do all sorts of bad things, and not just in the name of traditional "religion."

• Despite the charge that "religion" is behind Europe's religious wars, this is inaccurate. The Enlightenment attempted to introduce a religious-versus-secular dichotomy—a modern invention—but this was simply a period when the *church's political power* came to be replaced by the *state's political power*. We cannot coherently separate politics from religion.

• Europe's "religious wars" were *not* predictably divided along *doctrinal* lines of Catholics, Lutherans, Zwinglians, and Calvinists, but along *political* lines.

• Even atheists like Christopher Hitchens and Sam Harris engage in the kind of hostile

language toward Islamists that they accuse religionists of, often advocating violence themselves ("it's them or me").

• Various leading atheist intellectuals (Habermas, Derrida, Ferguson) have acknowledged the profound culture-shaping influence of the Christian faith on human rights, education/literacy for all, moral reforms, democracy, and equality before the law.

• Why think monotheistic religion is the culprit? Wasn't it polytheists who persecuted the earliest Christians during the time of the Roman Empire? Even if religion is partly to blame for violence in certain cases, why think this is the *sole* factor?

• The "Cain"/"monotheism" argument is inaccurate. First, election begins not with Abel but with Abraham who was to bring blessing to the nations. Also, God gave Cain ample opportunity to resist sin and obey (Gen. 4:7); he could choose between life and death. Furthermore, Israel's election was not based on prior righteousness (Deut. 9:6) but on divine grace.

• Another problem with Schwartz's idea is the failure to distinguish between the *non*elect and the *anti*elect. In fact, the vast majority of Old Testament texts affirm the existence of *non*elect people and that Israel is to engage in cordial relations with them; the nonelect may even receive God's blessing (Gen. 17:20). Even with the *anti*elect category (the Amalekites, the Canaanites, and the Midianites [Num. 25, 31]), the Midianites don't quite fit (Exod. 2:15–22; 18:1; Num. 10:29), and only later would the Canaanites become extremely wicked; but the patriarchs and the Canaanites lived peaceably side by side for the most part. The only consistently *anti*elect people are the Amalekites, who remained hostile to the people of God for hundreds of years.

21

Are Yahweh Wars in the Old Testament Just like Islamic Jihad?

Preliminary Claims

Karen Armstrong, a popular writer on religion, claims, "There is far more violence in the Bible than in the Qur'an; the idea that Islam imposed itself by the sword is a Western fiction, fabricated during the time of the Crusades when, in fact, it was Western Christians who were fighting brutal holy wars against Islam."[1]

Religion scholar Philip Jenkins asserts that Scripture is even more violent than the Qur'an:

> Commands to kill, to commit ethnic cleansing, to institutionalize segregation, to hate and fear other races and religions . . . all are in the Bible, and occur with a far greater frequency than in the Koran. At every stage, we can argue what the passages in question mean, and certainly whether they should have any relevance for later ages. But the fact remains that the words are there, and their inclusion in the scripture means that they are, literally, canonized, no less than in the Muslim scripture.[2]

As we'll see in the next chapter, Armstrong's claims about the Crusades are misleading and misguided.

What of the claims of Philip Jenkins? He is a fine and gracious scholar, but it seems that some of the "dark texts" or "terror texts," as he calls them, could use further qualification and precision. Descriptions such as "commit ethnic cleansing," "institutionalize segregation," and "hate and fear other races and religions" do not truly capture the spirit of the Old Testament Scriptures.

Although we have touched on such challenges in other chapters, it might be good to take this opportunity to review briefly some of these themes:

- "ethnic cleansing": This would be better termed "*moral* cleansing"— or more specifically, long-awaited moral *judgment* on a wicked people whose time had finally come (Gen. 15:16). Also, the same severe "anti-Canaanite" language is the very same as the "anti-Israelite" language that fills the Old Testament, particularly in the prophets. These threats serve as a warning to Israel, and they include the identical hyperbolic "utterly destroy" language (Jer. 25:9; cf. Isa. 43:28)—judgments God eventually brings down on his own people. In sobering parallel, God threatens, "As I plan to do to them, so I will do to you" (Num. 33:56 NASB; cf. Lev. 18:26–30; 20:22–23). Furthermore, the Canaanite Rahab (Josh. 2 and 6) and Canaanite "foreigners" who are apparently Shechemites (Josh. 8:33, 35) are included in the blessing of God because they responded to the one true God. From the outset, the Old Testament represents a God whose salvation is intended to affect all the peoples of the world (Gen. 12:1–3), which includes the enemies of Israel—Assyria, Egypt, Babylon, Philistia (Ps. 87:4–6; Isa. 19:23–25)—and even the Canaanites themselves, who will become part of the true people of God (Zech. 9:6; cf. Matt. 15:22). Finally, the Hebrew prophets used vehement, anti-Semitic-sounding language against God's people, calling them "Sodom" and "Gomorrah" and "harlot" (Isa. 1:9–10; Ezek. 16; Hosea).
- "institutionalize segregation": Israel was to be distinct morally and spiritually from the peoples around them so that they could ultimately bring blessing to the nations (Ps. 67). However, Israelites were repeatedly commanded to care for the alien and sojourner in their midst since they too had been aliens in the land of Egypt (e.g., Exod. 22:21; 23:9; Lev. 19:34; 25:6; etc.). And God promises to bless *any* nation that repents (Jer. 18:7–10; cf. Jon. 3–4).
- "hate and fear other races and religions": We have seen that the charge of hating and fearing other races is clearly false. But what about hating and fearing *other religions*? The Bible is, of course, opposed to idolatry—creating God-substitutes which end up only harming their worshipers. And we have observed that God brings severe judgment on ancient Israel—God's *very own chosen people*—for engaging in idolatry and breaking covenant with him after promising to love, cling to, and obey him (Exod. 24:3; Deut. 10:12; 11:1, 13, 22; etc.).

Let's take a closer look at the question of Old Testament warfare and Islamic jihad. How do they compare?

The Biblical and Qur'anic Texts

We see many Qur'anic references to warfare, and this warfare is not simply defensive but offensive as well. Here is a sampling:[3]

- "And those who are slain in the way of God, He will not send their works astray. . . . And He will admit them to Paradise, that He has made known to them" (47:4, 6).
- "So let them fight in the way of God who sell the present life for the world to come; and whosoever fights in the way of God and is slain, or conquers, We shall bring him a mighty wage. . . . The believers fight in the way of God, and the unbelievers fight in the idols' way. Fight you therefore against the friends of Satan" (4:74, 76).
- "Such believers as sit at home—unless they have an injury—are not the equals of those who struggle in the path of God with their possessions and their selves. God has preferred in rank those who struggle with their possessions and their selves over the ones who sit at home" (4:95).
- "Then, when the sacred months are drawn away, slay the idolaters wherever you find them, and take them, and confine them, and lie in wait for them at every place of ambush. But if they repent, and perform the prayer, and pay the alms, then let them go their way; God is All-forgiving, All-compassionate" (9:5).
- "This is the recompense of those who fight against God and His Messenger, and hasten about the earth, to do corruption there: they shall be slaughtered, or crucified, or their hands and feet shall alternately be struck off; or they shall be banished from the land. That is a degradation for them in this world; and in the world to come awaits them a mighty chastisement, except for such as repent, before you have power over them" (5:33, 34).
- "Fight them [unbelievers], till there is no persecution and the religion is God's entirely; then if they give over, surely God sees the things they do" (8:39).
- "O Prophet, urge on the believers to fight. If there be twenty of you, patient men, they will overcome two hundred; if there be a hundred of you, they will overcome a thousand unbelievers, for they are a people who understand not" (8:65).
- "Fight those who believe not in God and the Last Day and do not forbid what God and His Messenger have forbidden—such men as practise not

the religion of truth, being of those who have been given the Book—until they pay the tribute out of hand and have been humbled" (9:29).

As for the Scriptures, we have reviewed the language in a number of warfare texts in the Old Testament—language of "no survivors," "utterly destroy," leaving "nothing that breathes," "drive out," "dispossess"—and we have attempted to put these texts in their proper ancient Near Eastern historical context. Jenkins states that the Bible's "terror texts" are "canonized" within the Bible just as they are within the Qur'an. But the word "canonized" is quite misleading. No matter how much we stack up biblical texts next to Qur'anic ones, clear differences between them emerge as we peel back the layers and explore the notable differences at various levels.

First, *military events captured in a biblical canon are merely descriptive of a unique part of the unfolding of salvation history.* It has been clear to most Jewish and Christian readers that these warfare texts lay no enduring normative claim on believers—no more than God's commanding Abraham to slay his son becomes the basis for the practice of human sacrifice. Indeed, Jews throughout their history have not relied on war texts to justify subsequent or ongoing warfare in the name of God, and the same is generally true for Christians throughout history. We've noted these matters in previous chapters.

Second, *whereas the biblical texts offer descriptions of unique history, the Qur'anic texts, by contrast, appear to be issuing enduring commands.* In fact, these texts have been taken by many Muslims throughout history to justify an ongoing jihad to bring non-Muslims in the realm of war (*dar al-harb*) into the realm of Islam (*dar al-islam*).[4] This division is reflected in the history of Islam as well as its treatment of subordinate and often humiliated *dhimmis* (e.g., Jews and Christians) under its rule.[5] While we can be grateful that many peace-loving Muslims exist, and we are grateful to know and have friendships with loving, hospitable Muslims. But "facts are stubborn things,"[6] as American President John Adams once said. One of these facts is that Islam has exhibited a militaristic aggressiveness from the beginning, and this aggressiveness has been fed by Qur'anic texts that many Muslims throughout history have taken as normative or binding, enduring throughout history, and worldwide in applicability. Indeed, this is assumed in Muhammad's own global vision; as he told his followers in his farewell address: "I was ordered to fight all men until they say, 'There is no God but Allah.'"[7]

Third, *the distinctions between divinely commanded wars in the Old Testament and Islamic jihad are much more pronounced than their similarities.* The Scriptures emphasize the uniqueness of these war texts embedded within one portion of Israel's long history—and part of the unfolding of salvation history.

In addition to being *unique* and *unrepeatable* events within Scripture itself, these wars are restricted to a *relatively small portion of land* (Canaan)—approximately the size of New Jersey. Indeed, the Israelites were commanded to *avoid* certain lands such as Edom, Ammon, and Moab. Furthermore, we find in Scripture *an overwhelming display of divine signs and wonders* for both Israel and its opponents to see. By contrast, the "revelations" to Muhammad were *private* and not publicly available for scrutiny or reinforced by dramatic signs and wonders. What's more, Israel was an instrument of divine judgment on wicked people—unlike Muhammad, who attacked and overtook even those who were "People of the Book" (Jews and Christians)—part of the global reach to which Muhammad and his followers aspired.

Muhammad's Example

Adding weight to the Qur'anic texts is Muhammad himself, who is the supreme human example for Muslims to follow. As we saw, his goal was "to fight all men until they say, 'There is no God but Allah.'" Would his followers not take such a charge seriously? Indeed they did.

Muhammad died in AD 632 with his own plans for attacking neighboring nations unfulfilled. His immediate successors carried on in the same spirit, advancing to Syria, Palestine, Persia, Egypt, islands in the Mediterranean, and beyond. Exactly one hundred years after Muhammad's death, Charles Martel would be fighting off Muslim warriors in Tours, France—a decisive clash of civilizations whose significance is typically overlooked or downplayed by contemporary historians. But we are getting ahead of ourselves.

Perhaps it would help to give a bit of context to look at the career of Muhammad, whom Muslims "canonize" as their norm and role model. In his career, Muhammad fought in an estimated eighty-six military campaigns.[8] The first authoritative biography of Muhammad—and even now published by Oxford University Press—was written by Ibn Ishaq (d. 763) and covers Muhammad's battles in 75 percent of its 813 pages.[9] This biography also includes depictions of assassination, rape, and cruelty that met with Muhammad's approval.

Let's take a look at some of these events. In one instance, the "Apostle Muhammad" said, "Kill any Jew that falls into your power." Thereupon, one of his followers "leapt upon Ibn Sunayna . . . a Jewish merchant with whom they had social and business relations, and killed him."[10] Muhammad sent his companion and adopted son Zayd on a raid in Banu Fazara, and "a very old woman" Umma Qirfa was captured. Zayd ordered she be killed by Qays b. al-Musahhar, "and he killed her cruelly . . . by putting a rope to her two legs and to two camels and driving them until they rent her in two."[11]

In another episode, Muhammad sent a force commanded by Abu Ubayda, who encountered a one-eyed man who did not submit to Islam. While this half-blind man was snoring in his sleep, Abu Ubayda put the end of his bow "in his sound eye," he recounted, and "then I bore down on it until I forced it out at the back of his neck." Abu Ubayda recounted to Muhammad what had happened, and "he blessed me."[12]

In addition, here is an incident of torture commanded by Muhammad:

> Kinana b. al-Rabi`, who had the custody of the treasure of B. al-Nadir, was brought to the apostle [Muhammad] who asked him about it. He denied that he knew where it was. A Jew came . . . to the apostle and said that he had seen Kinana going round a certain ruin every morning early. When the apostle said to Kinana, 'Do you know that if we find you have it I shall kill you?' he said Yes. The apostle gave orders that the ruin was to be excavated and some of the treasure was found. When he asked him about the rest he refused to produce it, so the apostle gave orders to al-Zubayr b. al-`Awwam, 'Torture him until you extract what he has,' so he kindled a fire with flint and steel on his chest until he was nearly dead. Then the apostle delivered him to Muhammad b. Maslama and he struck off his head, in revenge for his brother Mahmud.[13]

According to the Qur'an and to the traditions about Muhammad (Hadith), he permitted his soldiers to have sex not only with their wives (obviously), but also with female captives and female slaves—which is the meaning of the phrase "those whom your right hand possesses" (4:24; 23:5, 6; 70:22–30; etc.). Though this practice would be outlawed shortly after the time of Muhammad, this practice of "temporary marriage" persists in Islam, most notably in Shia Islam (called *mutah*).[14]

We could say more here.[15] Instead, we refer you to this ancient, authoritative biography of Muhammad by Ibn Ishaq. We have seen a number of sample passages from the Qur'an that endorse an aggressive militancy, and these are illustrated and reinforced by the expansionist military vision of Muhammad—the ideal for all Muslims. Unfortunately, Muslim dialogue with Christians frequently ignores the strident verses of the Qur'an, the life of Muhammad, and—as we'll see below—the history of Islamic aggression, conquest, and rule of non-Muslims.

The Early History of Islam and Its Ongoing Encounters with the Non-Muslim World

Yet another layer differentiates biblical battle depictions from examples of the Qur'an and Muhammad—namely, the early expansion of Islam and its ongoing encounters with the non-Muslim world. This should also be considered as part of the ongoing story line of Islam.

Although the Qur'an affirms that there should be "no compulsion in religion" (2:256),[16] this verse that is taken by many today to endorse religious tolerance actually is contradicted by other passages within the Qur'an.[17] It is also contradicted by the example of Muhammad himself—as we noted above and who is quoted in the traditions (or *Hadith*) as saying, "Whoever changed his Islamic religion, then kill him."[18]

In our discussion of the Crusades in the next chapter, we briefly recount the early and rapid spread of Islam carried out by Muhammad's successors. They carried forward the militaristic spirit of Muhammad, whose own instruments of war are now on display in the Topkapi Palace in Turkey.[19] In addition to hair from Muhammad's beard and his extracted teeth and soil from his grave, the "Chamber of the Sacred Relics" contains Muhammad's bamboo bow and his swords, which are decorated in precious stones. Also found therein are the swords of the first four caliphs and other Islamic leaders. And the "Standard of Muhammad" that would be displayed on battlefields as Muslim armies moved into Turkey is now threadbare but is preserved in a chest at the Topkapi Museum. The earliest spirit of Islam under Muhammad was carried forward by his followers in an aggressive military expansion.

We should say something about the word "jihad" ("struggle"), which traditionally has had militaristic connotations. According to the *Encyclopedia of Islam*: "In law, according to general doctrine and in historical tradition, the jihad consists of military action with the object of the expansion of Islam and, if need be, of its defense."[20] It continues that the "spread of Islam by arms is a religious duty upon Muslims in general. . . . Jihad must continue to be done until the whole world is under the rule of Islam."[21] The Qur'an has a place for an "internal" sense of spiritual *struggling* or *exerting* within oneself for Allah (8:72), which is called "greater jihad," but the Qur'an also clearly indicates military struggle and connects jihad to physical fighting (what is called "lesser jihad").[22] As David Cook indicates in his book *Understanding Jihad*, there is little support in the Qur'an and Hadith for the notion of jihad as internal struggle.[23]

In the Qur'an, *jihad* includes physical *fighting* (*qitāl*), a strong militaristic impulse, and a general and nonrestrictive reach: "whosoever fights in the way of God and is slain, or conquers, We shall bring him a mighty wage" (4:74); "those who struggle in the path of God with their possessions and their selves [lives]" (4:95); "fight those who believe not in God" (9:29). It also includes *terror*: "We will cast into the hearts of the unbelievers terror" (3:151); "I shall cast into the unbelievers' hearts terror; so smite above the necks, and smite every finger of them!" (8:12). The Qur'an emphasizes *martyrdom* through fighting: "Those who believe, and have emigrated, and have struggled [or 'fought'] in the way of God with their possessions and their selves [lives] are mightier in rank with God" and will receive "lasting bliss" (9:20–21; cf. 9:111; 57:19).

Not only did early Islamic history continue the militaristic spirit of its founder; Islam's history reveals an oppressive stance toward non-Muslims under Islamic rule. Jewish Egyptian scholar Bat Ye'or has thoroughly documented the history of "dhimmitude"—the condition of Christians, Jews, and other non-Muslims (*dhimmis*) under Islamic law—in Muslim-dominated areas.[24] She argues that, yes, Muslims in the past have shown tolerance to Jews and Christians in their midst (Muslim apologists emphasize this picture). However, the condition of dhimmitude involved tribute (*jizya*) being paid to the reigning Muslims who compelled allegiance in the ongoing spirit of *jihad*: that is, any such tolerance was always under threat of Muslim jihad if tribute wasn't paid, and tribute was paid in ceremonies attempting to humiliate the subjugated non-Muslim. Ye'or makes a strong case for the oppression and even "open extermination of Christian populations and the disappearance of Eastern Christian culture."[25]

Generally (though there were exceptions), non-Muslims could not freely practice their religion. They could not repair synagogues or church buildings; nor could they observe their religion in public. Despite Islam's "protection" of "People of the Book," so many humiliations and conditions were attached to their "legal standing" that dhimmitude took on the status of "oppression, deprivation and insecurity."[26]

Even Cordoba, Spain—which has been highlighted by many as a city of Muslim tolerance and center for Jewish, Christian, and Muslim philosophers, artists, and poets such as Maimonides, Ibn Hazm, and Averroës—was not all that tolerant. Even the Islamophile historian Reinhart Dozy (1820–83) acknowledges how the chief cathedral would be turned into a mosque:

> *All the churches in that city had been destroyed except the cathedral, dedicated to Saint Vincent*, but the possession of this fane [cathedral] had been guaranteed by treaty. For several years the treaty was observed; but when the population of Cordova was increased by the arrival of Syrian Arabs [Muslims], the mosques did not provide sufficient accommodation for the newcomers, and the Syrians considered it would be well for them to adopt the plan which had been carried out at Damascus, Emesa [Homs], and other towns in their own country, *of appropriating half of the cathedral and using it as a mosque.* The [Muslim] Government having approved of the scheme, the Christians *were compelled* to hand over half of the edifice. *This was clearly an act of spoliation, as well as an infraction of the treaty.* Some years later, Abd-er Rahman I requested the

Christians to sell him the other half. *This they firmly refused to do, pointing out that if they did so they would not possess a single place of worship. Abd-er Rahman, however, insisted, and a bargain was struck* by which the Christians ceded their cathedral. [27]

What's more, the Muslim poet Ibn Hazm instigated persecution against Jews in Granada, Spain, which killed four thousand Jews in 1066. The Muslim philosopher Averroës was also a strong anti-Semite. The Jewish philosopher Maimonides eventually had to flee persecution. The Islamic conquest and rule of Spain was marked by regular massacres, raids, persecutions, and humiliations of the subjugated *dhimmis*. The "Golden Age of Islam" in Spain is a myth.[28]

In fact, according to Ye'or, the "myth of Muslim toleration" didn't exist before the twentieth century: "It is largely a modern creation. The West's obfuscation [of Islamic intolerance] was a result of the political and cultural difficulties of colonialism." She adds: "France had North Africa, Algeria, Morocco, Tunisia, Syria, and Lebanon after World War I. England had a huge Islamic population in India and also in Egypt and Sudan, Iraq and Palestine. They didn't want to confront this population. They didn't want to protect the Christian minorities in these lands because they wanted to have an economically beneficial pro-Arab, pro-Islamic policy."[29]

So after colonial rule, Christians (predominantly) in these areas were forced to try integrating into Muslim cultures. They had no protection from the colonial powers who, for political and economic (mostly oil-related) reasons, didn't want to upset these Muslim countries: "As a result, they developed a whole literature praising Islamic tolerance toward Jews and Christians."[30] Even though we read in the Qur'an, "Let there be no compulsion in religion" (2:256), compulsion was embodied in Muhammad's military career, the expansion of Islam after his death, and life under the rule of Islam.

Conclusions

The claim that the Bible's warfare texts are "just like" the Qur'an's is incorrect. Further consideration should be given to the teaching of Muhammad (e.g., in the *Hadith*), the example of Muhammad in his military campaigns, the rapid expansion of Islam under his successors, and the life of the *dhimmis* under Islam over the centuries.

The Hebrew Scriptures portray unique, unrepeatable events of Israelite warfare—unlike the ongoing and normative aspect of jihad in the Qur'an and under the leadership of Muhammad. Unlike the biblical text that stresses God's *judgment* against *specific* people (Canaanites, Amalekites), the Qur'an and

Muhammad placed no such limitations on jihad, as the opponents of Islam are non-Muslims remaining in the "abode of war" (*dar al-harb*) rather than the "abode of Islam." Even the lands of Christians and Jews would be overrun in the Middle East, North Africa, Turkey, Spain, and other parts of Europe. And while the Scriptures emphasize a limited geographical area of military engagement, the Qur'an and Muhammad placed no such limit (e.g., "I was ordered to fight all men until they say, 'There is no God but Allah'"). While the biblical warfare commands are reinforced by very obvious, public, dramatic, and repeated signs and wonders, Muhammad's revelation is private and utterly unverifiable.

Another point of contrast is the nature of God in the Qur'an and the Bible. The Qur'an portrays a deity who loves only those who love him. Yes, Allah is merciful and compassionate, but he only loves those who love him: "God loves not unbelievers" (3:32; 30:45); "God loves not the prodigal" (6:141) or the "aggressors [or 'transgressors']" (2:190)[31] and is "an enemy to the unbelievers" (2:98). Those who reject Islam are "the worst of creatures" (98:6). Here God's love is *conditional*, depending on the response of human beings.

The love of the biblical God is unconditional. He does not merely love those who love him. Rather, God loves all people and even his enemies (cf. Matt. 5:44–48; John 3:16; Rom. 5:6–10; 1 John 2:2). He seeks to make salvation available to all, including the very enemies of his people Israel (e.g., Gen. 12:1–3; Ps. 87:4–6; Isa. 19:23–25; Zech. 9:7).

When we contrast Canaanite warfare and Islamic jihad, the differences are quite pronounced.

Yahweh War in the Old Testament	Islamic Jihad
Geography: War was geographically limited to the Promised Land.	There are no geographic limitations to jihad. The non-Muslim world is the "abode of war."
Historical length/limit: War was limited to roughly one generation (around the time of Joshua)—though minor conflicts continued with persistent enemies of Israel.	There are no historical/temporal limitations to jihad.
Objects of warfare: The Israelites were God's instrument to punish a hostile enemy (the Amalekites) or a deeply morally corrupted culture—not because they were non-Israelites or even because they didn't worship Yahweh. This punishment came after a period of over 400 years, waiting for the Canaanites' sin to ripen fully (Gen. 15:16).	Aggression/war is indiscriminate, directed toward all non-Muslims, even Christians and Jews ("People of the Book"). The Qur'an is fairly universal ("Slay the idolaters wherever you find them" [9:5]). It is indiscriminate concerning the objects of jihad: all non-Muslims, including Jews and Christians ("People of the Book" [9:29]). The Qur'an leaves matters open-ended without historical specificity.

Yahweh War in the Old Testament	Islamic Jihad
Objects of God's love: Yahweh loves even his enemies/those who don't love him (cf. Gen. 12:3; Jon.). His redemptive plan encompasses the traditional enemies of Israel (Babylon, Assyria, Egypt), incorporating them into the people of God.	God loves only those who love and obey him. "God loves not unbelievers" (3:32; 30:45); "God loves not the prodigal" (6:141) or the "aggressors [or 'transgressors']" (2:190) and is "an enemy to the unbelievers" (2:98).
Standard of morality: God's "compassionate and gracious" *nature* is the source of God's commands. God cannot command what is intrinsically evil (cf. Jer. 19:4–5).	The Qur'an stresses God as sheer *will* (as opposed to a morally good nature) who commands indiscriminately.
Signs and wonders: A continuous series of miracles (plagues in Egypt, parting of the Red Sea, pillar of cloud/fire, manna, crossing the Jordan, etc.) clearly indicate the presence of God, his superiority over all other deities, and his authority to judge the Canaanites.	Islam is noticeably lacking in signs and wonders. We only have private, unverifiable revelations to Muhammad.
Normativity of war: The passages about fighting against Canaanites are *descriptive*—they describe a unique and unrepeatable event that was to pave the way for the coming of the Messiah and salvation to all the world.	The Qur'an's warfare passages are *prescriptive*, prescribing what Muslims should do, illustrated by the military aggression of Muhammad (Islam's founder and moral ideal) and the early spread of Islam; its ongoing history of expansion and aggression continues the story line begun by Muhammad himself.

Summary

- A commonly heard claim is that the Bible is more violent that the Qur'an and that Islam's imposing itself by the sword is a fiction. Moreover, a common assertion is that the Old Testament promotes "ethnic cleansing," "institutionalize[s] segregation," and promotes "hate and fear [of] other races and religions."

- As for "ethnic cleansing" and hating and fearing other races, note that the "anti-Canaanite" language is the same kind of "anti-Israelite" language that fills the Old Testament when God is judging his people. This includes the hyperbolic "utterly destroy" language (Jer. 25:9; cf. Isa. 43:28); the Hebrew prophets calling God's people "Sodom" and "Gomorrah" and "harlot" (Isa. 1:9–10; Ezek. 16; Hosea); and God's warning Israel: "As

I plan to do to them, so I will do to you" (Num. 33:56; cf. Lev. 18:26–30; 20:22–23). And included in God's people are Canaanites like Rahab (Josh. 2 and 6) and the Canaanite "foreigners" in Shechem (Josh. 8:33, 35).

- As for institutionalizing segregation, Israel was to be distinct morally and spiritually, but ultimately to bless the nations (Ps. 67); they were to care for the alien and sojourner in their midst (e.g., Exod. 22:21; 23:9; Lev. 19:34; 25:6; etc.). And God promises to bless *any* nation that repents (Jer. 18:7–10; cf. Jon. 3–4).

- As for hating and fearing "other . . . religions," Yahweh opposes other gods and idolatry, which only harm their worshipers. As we saw earlier, for the Israelites to align themselves with other deities through sexual immorality and idolatry was an act of treason.

- As for comparing the Qur'an and Old Testament texts, the Old Testament's divinely commanded war texts are notably hyperbolic, whereas we have good reason to think that the Qur'an's warring passages are not, given what we know of the military career of Muhammad.

- While the Scriptures speak *descriptively* about unique events that happened, the Qur'an's passages sound *prescriptive*; indeed, the history of Islam from the time of Muhammad onward seems to indicate that these are enduring commands.

- The Old Testament's Yahweh wars were not only *unique* and *unrepeatable*, but they are accompanied by *an overwhelming display of divine signs and wonders* for both Israel and its opponents to see. By contrast, the "revelations" to Muhammad were *private* and not publicly available for scrutiny.

- In the Old Testament, the objects of God's judgment were *limited* and *localized* to a small portion of real estate in the ancient Near East (Deut. 20:16–17)—and not against Israel's other enemies such as the Edomites, Ammonites, and Moabites; this was quite different from the kind of global reach to which Muhammad and his followers aspired.

- In his farewell address, Muhammad told his followers: "I was ordered to fight all men until they say, 'There is no God but Allah.'" His followers took this charge seriously. Exactly one hundred years after Muhammad's death, Charles Martel would be fighting back Islamic warriors in Tours, France.

- Muhammad's first authoritative biography by Ibn Ishaq (d. 763) covers Muhammad's battles in 75 percent of its 813 pages. It includes depictions of assassination, rape, and cruelty that met with Muhammad's approval ("Kill any Jew that falls into your power"; a very old woman, Umma Qirfa,

was pulled in two by camels; Muhammad permitted soldiers to have sex with female captives and female slaves—a practice still continued in Shia Islam [*mutah*]; Muhammad commanded torture—kindling a fire on a man's chest—until he disclosed the location of the treasure).

- Yet another layer differentiates biblical battle depictions from examples of the Qur'an and Muhammad—namely, the early expansion of Islam and its ongoing encounters with the non-Muslim world. This should also be considered as part of the ongoing story line of Islam.

- From the very beginning, "jihad" ("struggle") has had militaristic connotations; there is little support for its early meaning of "inner struggle."

- Bat Ye'or has documented the history of "dhimmitude" (the condition of Christians, Jews, and other non-Muslims [*dhimmis*] under Islamic law) in Muslim-dominated areas. She documents the oppression and even "open extermination of Christian populations and the disappearance of Eastern Christian culture."

- Even in Cordoba, Spain—though highlighted as a place of Muslim tolerance and a center for Jewish, Christian, and Muslim philosophers, artists, and poets—all the churches of that city had been destroyed except one, which would eventually be appropriated as a mosque, first in part, then entirely.

- The Muslim poet Ibn Hazm instigated persecution against Jews in Granada, Spain, which killed four thousand Jews in 1066. The Muslim philosopher Averroës was also a strong anti-Semite. The Jewish philosopher Maimonides eventually had to flee persecution. The "Golden Age of Islam" in Spain is a myth.

- Ye'or observes that the "myth of Muslim toleration" didn't exist before the twentieth century and is largely a modern creation.

22

Did Old Testament War Texts Inspire the Crusades?

Perhaps after our comparison of the Canaanite situation and Islamic jihad, we could pause to take a true or false quiz. Here are five statements. Are they true or false?

- The Crusades were a completely morally unjustified military campaign against peaceable Muslims initiated by the church.
- The Crusades were an attempt to gain riches for Christendom by plundering Muslim lands.
- The Crusades were an effort to gain Muslim conversions to Christianity by force.
- Muslims have held the Crusades against Christians since the Middle Ages.
- The Crusades were inspired by Canaanite warfare texts in Deuteronomy and Joshua.

The answer to each of these is *false*.

However, when you read much of the popular literature on the Crusades, you don't get this impression at all. For example, the former-nun-turned-religious-writer Karen Armstrong has denounced the Crusades in the roundest of terms. Although they "answered a deep need in the Christians of Europe," she asserts, "today most of us would unhesitatingly condemn the Crusades as wicked and unchristian. After all, Jesus had told his followers to love their enemies, not to exterminate them. He was a pacifist and had more in common with Gandhi, perhaps, than with Pope Urban." But the Crusades, she claims, are understandable since "Christianity had an inherent leaning toward violence" despite Jesus's pacifism.[1] Earlier, we cited Armstrong's confident assertion: "There is far more violence in the Bible than in the Qur'an; the idea that Islam imposed itself by the sword is a Western fiction, fabricated during the time of the Crusades when, in fact, it was Western Christians who were fighting brutal holy wars against Islam."[2]

This flawed criticism is not new. Enlightenment-era critics who denounced the Crusades included Voltaire, David Hume, and Denis Diderot who considered these military episodes to be cruel, debauched, foolish, and treacherous. The noted eighteenth-century historian Edward Gibbon claimed that the Crusaders went to the Holy Land in pursuit of "mines of treasures, of gold and diamonds, of palaces of marble and jasper, and of odoriferous groves of cinnamon and frankincense."[3] And beyond this, the notable Yale church historian Roland Bainton claimed that the Crusades were inspired by warfare texts in Deuteronomy and Joshua.[4]

Is it true that the book of Joshua was the inspiration for the Crusades? Were the Crusades attempting to replicate the killing of the Canaanites? Were the Crusades comparable to Islamic jihad, which expanded the territory of Islam across North Africa, Asia, and into Europe? In the first section of this chapter, we'll briefly respond to the first four myths. Then we'll look at the fifth myth in more depth.

A Brief Response to Some Myths of the Crusades

Myth #1: The Crusades were an unjustified military campaign against peaceable, tolerant Muslims.

The year was 1095, the date November 27. Pope Urban II spoke to a crowd outside Clermont, France, after receiving a letter from Byzantium's emperor, Alexius Comnenus, requesting assistance from the Count of Flanders. Constantinople was at risk of falling to the Seljuk Turks who raped, tortured, and killed Christians and who desecrated Christian pilgrimage sites and other sacred places. Though the Great Schism of 1054 divided Eastern Orthodoxy and Roman Catholicism, the pope believed that much was at stake and that fellow believers should be protected from such assaults and degradations:

They [the Seljuk Turks] destroy the altars, after having defiled them with their uncleanness. They circumcise the Christians, and the blood of the circumcision they either pour on the altars or pour into the vases of the baptismal font. When they wish to torture people by a base death, they perforate their navels, and dragging forth the extremity of the intestines, bind it to a stake; then with flogging they lead the victim around until the viscera having gushed forth the victim falls prostrate on the ground. . . . What shall I say about the abominable rape of women? To speak of it is worse than to be silent. On whom therefore is the labor of avenging these wrongs and recovering this territory incumbent, if not upon you?[5]

Historian Bat Ye'or points out further provocations:

In Antioch around 1058, Greeks and Armenians were converted by force, torture being used to persuade the recalcitrants. After the defeat of the Mongols by the Mamluks in Syria (1260), the Christians of Damascus were pillaged and slaughtered, others were reduced to slavery, and churches were destroyed and burned down. . . . In 1261, the slaves of Malik Salih, governor of Mosul, looted the Christians and killed anyone who did not become a Muslim. In 1264, Jews and Christians in Cairo paid heavy ransoms to escape being burned alive.[6]

The Crusades were a *response to* aggression, not *acts of* aggression—a defensive war. As we've seen, the first Crusade (1095) was a response to the recent Turkish takeover of Christianized Asia Minor—like the previous Muslim conquest of Christianized Palestine. The second Crusade was a response to the Muslim conquest of Edessa—now southern Turkey (1144). The third was a response to the conquest of Jerusalem and other Christianized lands east of there (1187).[7]

In her response to the Crusades, Karen Armstrong, in our view, assumes false alternatives: in reaction to Islamic aggression, Christendom's leaders could either (1) embrace "pacifism" or (2) "unhesitatingly condemn [the possibility of] the Crusades as unchristian." Armstrong's view ignores a third alternative, however: these leaders could (3) invoke the just war tradition which Augustine, for instance, developed and advocated (which we address in the next chapter). For starters, the Crusades involved a *just cause* (the Crusades were defensive and an attempt to protect Christendom's citizens as well as reclaim Christianized lands overrun by Muslims), *just intent* (to secure a just and fair peace), and legitimate authority (involving pope and state authorities in Christendom).

Matters of self-defense, the protection of Christian communities, the recovery of largely Christianized lands overrun by Muslim armies during and shortly after the time of Muhammad (d. 632),[8] and the high stakes in the "clash of civilizations" are all part of the picture, and these are the stuff of just war considerations.[9] Crusades scholar Thomas Madden writes:

> The crusades were in every way a *defensive war*. They were the West's belated response to the Muslim conquest of fully two-thirds of the Christian world. While the Arabs were busy in the seventh through the tenth centuries winning an opulent and sophisticated empire, Europe was defending itself against outside invaders and then digging out from the mess they left behind. Only in the eleventh century were Europeans able to take much notice of the East. The event that led to the crusades was the Turkish conquest of most of Christian Asia Minor (modern Turkey). The Christian emperor in Constantinople, faced with the loss of half of his empire, appealed for help to the rude but energetic Europeans. He got it.[10]

We are not arguing that all the Crusaders were even Christians. We recognize, too, that not all actions in the Crusades were morally justifiable. Crusaders brought harm to Jews and Muslims, and they even fought amongst themselves. And the slaughter of 3,000 people in Jerusalem (1099) is the chief example of troops losing control in their bloodlust. On the other hand, one observer's description of blood running up to the Crusaders' knees and to the bridles of horses is clearly an exaggeration—indeed, a physical impossibility—and perhaps an allusion to the apocalyptic text of Revelation 14:20.[11] As we note in the next chapter, we consider just war to be a defensible Christian position and that the general impulse of the Crusades is in line with these principles.

While there was no clear line between the Christian church and the state during this time, the authorities within Christendom were rightly concerned to protect pilgrims as well as their own Christian citizens from the physical threat of Islam in the Middle East and in Europe. Muslims had made many early attempts to colonize the West—efforts compounded by attacks on Christian pilgrims in Palestine and on Christian holy sites. And since the rise of Islam, it is a general, well-documented fact that the ruling Muslims have intentionally humiliated and punished the *dhimmis*—Jews, Christians, and other non-Muslims who lived under Islam.[12]

We've already observed how swiftly Christianized areas fell to Islamic rule. Thomas Madden writes: "Muslim conquerors who swept through all of Christian North Africa also crossed the Strait of Gibraltar and established their rule over Spain. By the eighth century, Muslim expeditionary forces were crossing the Pyrenees and marching into the heart of Catholic Europe."[13]

When it comes to the Crusades, the foremost Western scholar of Islam, Bernard Lewis, puts the matter into perspective:

For almost a thousand years . . . Europe was under constant threat from Islam. In the early centuries it was a double threat—not only of invasion and conquest, but also of conversion and assimilation. All but the easternmost provinces of the Islamic realm had been taken from Christian rulers, and the vast majority of the first Muslims west of Iran and Arabia were converts from Christianity. North Africa, Egypt, Syria, even Persian-ruled Iraq, had been Christian countries, in which Christianity was older and more deeply rooted than in most of Europe. Their loss was sorely felt and heightened the fear that a similar fate was in store for Europe.[14]

Noted British historian Paul Johnson writes something similar:

The history of Islam has essentially been a history of conquest and reconquest. The 7th-century "breakout" of Islam from Arabia was followed by the rapid conquest of North Africa, the invasion and virtual conquest of Spain, and a thrust into France that carried the crescent to the gates of Paris. It took half a millennium of reconquest to expel the Moslems from Western Europe. The Crusades, far from being an outrageous prototype of Western imperialism, as is taught in most of our schools, were a mere episode in a struggle that has lasted 1,400 years, and were one of the few occasions when Christians took the offensive to regain the "occupied territories" of the Holy Land.[15]

Myth #2: The Crusades were an attempt to gain riches for Christendom by plundering peaceful Muslim lands.

Contrary to the historian Edward Gibbon, the Crusades were not an attempt to accumulate wealth. While Pope Urban II's speech appealed to "making spoil of their treasures," this was an incidental motivation. The actual motive was religious and moral, not material, and medieval/Crusade historians have thoroughly documented this.[16] Church leaders "had to persuade their listeners to commit themselves to enterprises that would disrupt their lives, possibly impoverish and even kill or maim them, and inconvenience their families, the support of which they would . . . need if they were to fulfill their promises."[17]

The Crusades were an expensive undertaking, and wealthy European families sank much money into the Crusade effort without any presumption that they would recover their losses. According to estimates, the average Crusader had to raise four to five times his annual income before he could venture forth on the journey. True, a number of eager peasants and villagers embarked on this pursuit without counting the financial cost, but at a material level, this expedition toward the Holy Land was no romantic or idealized venture. Nor was it an attempt at colonization and imperialism. They were acts of self-renunciation and sacrifice, of laying down one's life for another.

If Crusaders wanted to get rich quickly, they should have gone to the very wealthy Moorish Spain. The reason they did not pursue that course was because Spain was not all that religiously meaningful compared to Jerusalem, Bethlehem, Galilee, Antioch, and other biblically significant places. Furthermore, many made great monetary sacrifices to sustain the effort. For example, in 1096, Robert the Duke of Normandy pawned his duchy of Normandy to his brother, the king of England (William II), for 10,000 marks to pay for 2,500 ship captains for a year and which required William to impose a new tax on his people.

The flow of money was from West to East rather than East to West, and many bankrupted themselves in this Crusade endeavor.[18] Indeed, no Crusader became wealthy through the Crusades, and any wealth he may have accumulated would be used to sustain his military endeavors and then to return home.[19]

Myth #3: The Crusades were an effort to gain Muslim conversions to Christianity by force.

The simple truth is that the Crusaders had no program for converting Muslims. Even though the pope called for a response against an aggressive Muslim threat, the Crusades simply did not have a view to force or pressure Muslims to change their faith. Rulers in Christendom were concerned about protecting Christianized lands and their citizens as well as protecting Christian pilgrims and the shrines they were visiting.[20] Even so, while Christendom was attempting to protect its citizens during the Crusades, others like Francis of Assisi were attempting to do important bridge-building work. In 1219, he sought out the Egyptian sultan Malik al-Kamil to converse with and preach to him.[21] Both "just protection" and "just peacemaking" are important responses to this type of conflict. Such endeavors can be simultaneous rather than mutually exclusive.

Myth #4: Muslims have held the Crusades against Christians since the Middle Ages.

Movie producer Ridley Scott's *Kingdom of Heaven* depicted the Crusades as a brutal, deranged attempt to overrun the lands of peace-loving Muslims who were only trying to defend themselves.[22] This film expresses the same point made by Sir Walter Scott's classic *The Talisman* (1825) which impacted the thinking of Europeans and eventually Muslims. This is a common accusation—along with the notion that today's Islamic terrorism represents the backlash of those Crusades. This is not the case.

For one thing, the Crusaders' fighting was basically limited to the Holy Land, and this fighting was viewed by Muslims as more localized, intermittent fighting—much like other battles that Muslims had fought since the time of Muhammad. The Muslim world at this time did not fear any cataclysmic threat from the Crusades.[23] Secondly, Cambridge scholar Jonathan Riley-Smith rebuts the claim that the Crusades have been a long-standing point of Muslim hostility against Christians. He argues that Muslims had pretty much forgotten about the Crusades since they had won. As it turns out, however, the history of the Crusades became an opportunity for Arab nationalists like Sayyid Qutb (d. 1966), particularly in the wake of Israel's nationhood, to denounce "crusaderism" as an attempt to subvert Islam and destroy Muslims.[24] Riley-Smith views such revisionism as a means of placing "the exploitation they believe they have suffered in a historical context and to satisfy their feelings of both superiority and humiliation."[25]

Likewise, Rodney Stark writes: "Claims that Muslims have been harboring bitter resentments about the Crusades for a millennium are nonsense: Muslim antagonism about the Crusades did not appear until about 1900, in reaction against the decline of the Ottoman Empire and the onset of actual European colonialism in the Middle East. And anti-crusader feelings did not become intense until after the founding of the state of Israel."[26]

Joshua Texts and the Crusades

Here we come to our fifth myth—that the "terror texts" of Joshua inspired the Crusaders toward genocidal action. While we should not ignore or underestimate the potential misuse of Scripture, Old Testament scholar John Goldingay reminds us that we should not "overestimate the influence of Scripture in causing people to make war."[27] In fact, a review of Israel's history reminds us that they themselves have not taken their own Hebrew texts to serve as the basis for initiating warfare: "Israel managed to tell these stories without being turned into a people who were always making war. . . . Jews have always been among the least war-making peoples in the world."[28]

Yes, some Christians have abused the Scriptures. Puritans who came to the New World believed they were preserving the Protestant Reformation—that they were the new Israel and the "city set on a hill" modeled after John Calvin's "Holy Commonwealth" in Geneva. The spread of the Reformation would, it was hoped, bring the gospel to the world and usher in the second coming of Christ.

Some Puritans in colonial America took the Manifest Destiny idea to the extreme when they mistreated or even slaughtered American Indians. For example, Richard Mather considered the Pequot Indians of Connecticut to be the "cursed seeds of Canaan" and promoted a "holy war" against the Pequots in 1636–37.[29] Other Puritans in colonial America, like Jonathan Edwards and David Brainerd, treated Indians kindly and sought to evangelize them. Some would establish educational institutions like Dartmouth College to bring the gospel to them.

While Canaanite texts can be misused by Christians, one would think that if any group could most justifiably appeal to such texts, it would be ethnic Jews. Yet even Israel throughout much of the Old Testament appears to take for granted that these divinely commanded wars were unique and unrepeatable. Indeed, different stages of Israel's history brought differing demands and moral obligations:[30]

Stage 1: Ancestral wandering clan (*mishpachah*): Genesis 10:31–32

Stage 2: Theocratic people/nation ('*am*, *goy*): Genesis 12:2; Exodus 1:9; 3:7; Judges 2:20

Stage 3: Monarchy, institutional state, or kingdom (*mamlakah*): 1 Samuel 24:20; 1 Chronicles 28:5

Stage 4: Afflicted remnant (*sheerith*): Jeremiah 42:4; Ezekiel 5:10

Stage 5: Post-exilic community/assembly of promise (*qahal*): Ezra 2:64; Nehemiah 13:1

During the first stage, Abraham and other patriarchs are only incidentally involved in political or military affairs—for example, when Abraham rescued his nephew Lot after he was kidnapped during a raid (Gen. 14). Abraham knew that God would eventually—hundreds of years later—judge the Canaanites but only when their sins had reached maximum levels (15:16). Yet during the Babylonian exile, God's people were commanded not to rebel and fight. In Babylon, they were to handle their situation very differently: they were to build gardens, settle down, have children, and pray for the welfare of Babylon—the very enemy that had displaced them by carrying them into exile (Jer. 29:4–7). Israel's obligations and relationship to gentile nations hardly remained fixed or static.

What we want to address here is the commonly made claim that the texts of Joshua inspired the Crusades. Roland Bainton, the church historian most noted for his biography of Martin Luther, *Here I Stand*, wrote a chapter "The Origins of the Crusading Idea in the Old Testament" in his *Christian Attitudes toward War and Peace*. There Bainton makes a tight connection between the Crusades and various "crusading" texts from Deuteronomy and Joshua. He says that the "architects of the Christian crusade . . . drew their warrant from the books of the conquest and of the Maccabean revolt."[31] In her book *War in the Hebrew Bible*, Susan Niditch cites Bainton in her assertion that "European Christians were encouraged to join in the crusading wars against the Saracens [Muslims] by religious leaders quoting Hebrew Scriptures. . . . It comes as no surprise that modern students of war trace a trajectory of justified crusade back to the Hebrew Scriptures."[32] The problem with Bainton's assertion—and consequently Niditch's citing him for support—is that he offers no evidence at all for his statement. He does mention a couple of verses connected to the Crusades: Jeremiah 48:10 (the one who keeps back his hand from blood is cursed) and Psalm 118:24 (rejoicing in the day the Lord made).[33] Despite this noted historian's claims, he fails to justify his assertions.

British Old Testament scholar Douglas Earl indicates that neither ancient Israel nor the early church read Joshua as a text demanding ongoing conquest and "genocide."[34] Nor was it a text used by the Crusaders of the Middle Ages. For example, one French text from the thirteenth century cites Joshua's entrance into Jericho and the destruction that ensued after the trumpets were blown (Josh. 6). And how was this passage interpreted? "That the sons of Israel sounded their trumpets and carried the ark and the walls fell signify the Apostles who spread their preaching through the world and carried the Holy Church, and the Jews and the miscreants and their idols fell and came to nothing."[35] Nothing is said about justifying the Crusades. For many during the period of the Crusades, the book of Joshua was understood "more in terms of a typology of the church than as a manifesto for conquest or crusade."[36]

Furthermore—and here is a startling irony—the primary motivating texts for the Crusades were the Gospels and the words of Jesus in particular. They made mention of love for God and of Christ's words to forsake everything—family, wealth, security—in order to be a faithful disciple. It was not Old Testament texts of warfare and conquest, but rather *Jesus's own words*, that promoted the Crusades' cause. One should forsake all; one should not love father and mother more than Christ; one should take up one's cross and follow Christ; one should love one's spiritual brothers and sisters.[37] It was not bloodlust or greed but *love* for God and neighbor that prompted the Crusaders to lay down their lives for others.

So it was the *Gospels*, Earl writes, that "played a far more prominent role in justifying the Crusades than the book of Joshua, which is conspicuous by its absence."[38] He points out that, contrary to Bainton, Joshua is of little significance for the Crusades.[39]

Concluding Remarks

Bishop Kenneth Cragg—an expert on Islam and Islamic-Christian relations—has nevertheless chastised Europe for having sparked "Islamic reprisals against Christians by resisting Muslim invaders," Bat Ye'or points out. She continues:

"By constantly reexamining European guilt for the Crusades, Bishop Cragg minimizes the causes: the destruction of churches in the Holy Land, the assassinations, abductions, and forced conversions of pilgrims, and the *jihad* ravages in Armenia. In 1998, this assumption of guilt for the Crusades even moved groups of repentant Christians to travel through the Middle East—former Christian lands—to ask Muslim forgiveness."[40] So continues the typically unchallenged narrative concerning the Crusades.

One historian of the Crusades, Thomas F. Madden, writes of the despairing attitude that characterizes a group of capable and learned—but, alas, typically ignored—scholars in this field: "So we continue to write our scholarly books and articles, learning more and more about the Crusades but scarcely able to be heard. And when we are heard, we are dismissed as daft. I once asked Riley-Smith [whom we have cited above] if he believed popular perceptions of the Crusades would ever be changed by modern scholarship. 'I've just about given up hope,' he answered."[41] And as we have attempted to put the Crusades in clearer perspective, albeit briefly, we hope we have contributed to dispelling these leading Crusade myths, one being that the book of Joshua inspired these events. In doing so, however, we are not thereby advocating trust in military might over the power of God. We are not commending the advancement of the kingdom of God by the sword. We are not attempting to justify all actions carried out by the Crusaders.

Legitimate governments have a God-given obligation to protect their citizens from threats within and without—to "bear the sword" (cf. Rom. 13:1–7). In the Christendom of the Middle Ages, there was no clear separation of religion and state. Indeed, as we argue in chapter 20, these are inescapably intermingled today, as secularism in modern democracies is not neutral but has its own set of deeply embedded worldview commitments—very much like traditional religion. However, given the overlap of church and state power in the Middle Ages, the rulers of Christendom were no less obligated to protect their citizens from harm than they would be in modern nation-states. Protection of citizens, stopping aggressors, righting wrongs, and justly punishing evildoers are duties God has assigned to human governments—the very thinking on which the Crusades were founded. And this brings us to our next chapter.

Summary

- According to one critic, "Christianity has an inherent leaning toward violence" and "the idea that Islam imposed itself by the sword is a Western fiction, fabricated during the time of the Crusades when, in fact, it was

Western Christians who were fighting brutal holy wars against Islam."

- These are the common Crusade myths: Crusades were unjustified military campaigns on peaceable and tolerant Muslims; they were undertaken to pursue treasures; they were an attempt at forcing Muslim conversions; Muslims have held the Crusades against Christians for centuries; the Crusades were inspired by warfare texts of Deuteronomy and Joshua.

• Were the Crusades comparable to Islamic jihad, which expanded the territory of Islam across North Africa, Asia, and into Europe?

• Crusades were provoked by Muslim atrocities against Christians—torture of Christian pilgrims, rape of women, forced conversions, pillaging and slaughter, and burning of churches. While not everything done during the Crusades was justifiable, the Crusades were not acts of aggression but a response to Muslim aggression.

• The first Crusade (1095) was a response to the recent Turkish takeover of Christianized Asia Minor—like the previous Muslim conquest of Christianized Palestine. The second Crusade was a response to the Muslim conquest of Edessa—now southern Turkey (1144). The third was a response to the conquest of Jerusalem and other Christianized lands east of there (1187).

• While there was no clear line between the Christian church and the state during this time, the authorities within Christendom were rightly concerned to protect pilgrims as well as their own citizens from the physical threat of Islam in the Middle East and in Europe.

• Riches were an incidental motivation. The actual motive was religious and moral, not material, and medieval historians have thoroughly documented this. Indeed, the Crusades were an expensive undertaking, and wealthy European families sank much money into the Crusade effort without

any presumption that they would recover their losses. If Crusaders wanted to get rich quickly, they should have gone to the very wealthy Moorish Spain.

• The Crusaders had no program for converting Muslims. Rulers in Christendom were concerned about protecting Christianized lands and their citizens as well as Christian pilgrims and the shrines they were visiting.

• The Crusaders' fighting was basically limited to the Holy Land, and this fighting was viewed by Muslims as more localized, intermittent fighting—much like other battles that Muslims had fought since the time of Muhammad. The Muslim world at this time did not fear any cataclysmic threat from the Crusades.

• Cambridge scholar Jonathan Riley-Smith has rebutted the claim that the Crusades have been a long-standing point of Muslim hostility against Christians. He argues that Muslims had pretty much forgotten about the Crusades since they had won.

• Some Puritans in colonial America took the Manifest Destiny idea to the extreme and mistreated or even slaughtered American Indians (the "cursed seeds of Canaan").

• Some scholars have claimed that European Christians were encouraged to join in the crusading wars against Muslims by citing Hebrew Scriptures. But there is no noteworthy evidence for this. Actually, it was the Gospels and the words of Jesus himself that were most often used to encourage self-sacrifice, love for fellow believers, and taking up one's cross to follow Christ. Joshua is of little significance for the Crusades.

• Crusades historians seem to be fighting a losing battle to correct the misperceptions about the Crusades.

23

Turning the Other Cheek, Pacifism, and Just War

We have argued that divinely commanded wars for Israel were unique and unrepeatable. So we do not regard such wars as the basis for discussing the principles and framework for just warfare for any given nation. On the other hand, we should keep in mind that warfare in the ancient Near East was a way of life, both for monotheistic Israel and its surrounding polytheistic cultures. Typically, a nation would have to protect itself against aggressors or face extinction. So it might be worth asking whether we can say something more general about warfare, moving beyond divinely commanded fighting.

For example, could certain conditions become so intolerable that justified force may be the only recourse? One biblical scholar observes: "Although one might argue that the Bible often rationalizes forms of violence that are unacceptable today, one must acknowledge that there are certain times when it is morally imperative to use violent means against those who represent injustice."[1]

Biblical scholar N. T. Wright takes the view that force—yes, even lethal force—may be necessary to stop criminals from doing their worst.[2] He makes an important observation about the imprecatory (prayer-curse) psalms, which don't sound all that nice to modern ears: "Part of our reaction to the so-called 'cursing Psalms' is that we think the modern world basically has the problem of evil solved. The Psalms bring us up short and say, 'No, evil is real, and some people are so wicked that we simply must wish judgment upon them.'"[3]

Is it possible that sometimes physical force is a justifiable means to thwart certain evils? Croatian theologian and Yale professor Miroslav Volf affirms the compatibility of loving one's neighbor and using force to protect the neighbor: "I do think that a military response may be appropriate in cases of intolerable aggression. I shifted from the pacifism of my childhood and early adulthood to the position I am taking now by extending the obligation to love my neighbor when that neighbor's life is threatened by a third party." He adds: "I find that I'm not as far from just-war theory as I thought I was."[4]

As we see below, Romans 13 affirms that God does not always carry out divine wrath directly but has partly delegated this task to human governments. This point has a bearing on just war and the use of force, which we explore below. First we will review the relevant biblical texts and then discuss historical questions about pacifism in the early church and reflect on just warfare.

Biblical Considerations

The Teaching of Jesus

"What would Jesus do?"[5] On the one hand, we are commanded to "walk in the same manner as [Jesus] walked" (1 John 2:6 NASB) and "put on the new self"—that is, Christ and the virtues he exemplifies (Eph. 4:24; Col. 3:10–15). On the other hand, Jesus's calling involved dying for the sins of the world and taking the curse of our exile and alienation from God upon himself. Even if we are to lay down our lives for others and even for Christ in martyrdom, can something more be said about the use of human force as an expression of divine justice? Yes, Jesus stormed into the temple—his Father's house—to cleanse it because he had the authority to do so; this was an act unique to his mission and calling. But would Jesus prohibit his followers from working for the FBI or as local law enforcement officers—or from supporting the Normandy invasion in an effort to stop Hitler?

As we review some of the biblical material below, we refer back to material in chapter 3, although we apply it to the use of force and the ethics of Jesus. Also, just as Jesus did not address abortion, pornography, and gay marriage, we can still make a public case to show that these are morally problematic as well as detrimental to society. Likewise, even though Jesus did not comment on the matter of just warfare, it seems we can make appropriate inferences to support it by looking at the breadth of the New Testament material. Although many Christians and non-Christians alike take for granted that Jesus absolutely prohibits any use of force, we have our doubts.

Of course, the starting point for most discussions is Jesus's command to turn the other cheek after being slapped (Matt. 5:39 NASB). So let's begin there: "But I say to you, do not resist an evil person; but whoever slaps you on your right cheek, turn the other to him also."

As it turns out, this admonition to "turn the other cheek" is not the response to an act of *violence*, rather, to a gross insult. This is so whether one strikes with the back of the hand (Matt. 5:39) or with the palm of the hand (possible in Luke 6:29, though the specific cheek isn't specified). The language of Lamentations suggests this: "Let him give his cheek to the one who strikes, and let him be filled with insults" (3:30 ESV). Notice, too, that when Jesus was slapped in the face while on trial, he did not actually "turn the other cheek" but challenged this (John 18:23). In the Sermon on the Mount, Jesus is prohibiting returning insult for insult. He is exhorting his followers to break the vicious cycle of exchanging insults and to move toward reconciliation and peacemaking with our personal enemies—even with Roman soldiers who might commandeer Jewish citizens to carry their loads for them for a mile (Matt. 5:41).

We should take careful note at this point: *Jesus does not absolutize loving one's enemies* (Matt. 5:44). He denounces his opponents in very harsh—even damning—terms in Matthew 23. As we just observed, Jesus did not absolutize turning the other cheek (cf. John 18:23) any more than he abolished the judicial principle of proportionality ("an eye for an eye and a tooth for a tooth") or all oath-taking.[6] Jesus exemplifies a spirit of remarkable forgiveness on the cross (Luke 23:34), and he calls on us to have a generous spirit of forgiveness as well. Yet even so, it is not absolute. First, for forgiveness to be complete, it presupposes the offender's repentance ("if they repent, forgive them" [Luke 17:3–4]). Second, even when Christ instructs his disciples to forgive extravagantly—"seventy times seven" (Matt. 18:22 NASB)—he continues saying that those refusing to forgive will incur the wrath of their master and be "handed . . . over to the torturers" (v. 34 NASB). To make the point clear, Jesus says, "My heavenly Father will also do the same to you, if each of you does not forgive his brother from your heart" (v. 35 NASB). He uses strong words of *unforgiveness* when he says of Judas that it would have been better for him not to have been born (Mark 14:21) and when he says that the "blasphemy against the Spirit" (Matt. 12:31) can never be forgiven. Third, it can be a misguided sentimentality—and a gross injustice—for Christians to call for the forgiveness of the likes of Osama bin Laden and other terrorists. We must ask: Is that our rightful place? Unlike the Son of God (Mark 2:5), how can we simply forgive the offenses of others? What about the *victims* of their assaults? Should we forgive terrorists *while* they are planning another attack? And does forgiveness require that we no longer use force to stop them?

Or rather than intervening, do we wait till terrorists and rapists have carried out their evil acts before we extend forgiveness to them?[7] Finally, we note below, the state—though ordained by the God and Father of our Lord Jesus Christ—has a different role in God's economy. Its business is not to forgive rapists or murderers but rather to punish evildoers—though tempered with mercy when appropriate. When Jesus says "turn the other cheek," he is not referring to the responsibility of civil authorities toward criminals.

What about not resisting the evil person (Matt. 5:39)? For one thing, Jesus himself is constantly resisting evil. Consider his harsh rebuke of religious leaders (Matt. 23) as well as his temple-cleansing activity, for instance. Second, Matthew 5:39 is better translated as not resisting *"by evil means"* rather than *"the evil one/person."*[8] And this is precisely how other New Testament writers interpret Jesus's words: we are not to return evil for evil but overcome evil with good (Rom. 12:17–21; 1 Pet. 2:21–24). Third, even if we take this passage in the traditional way, once again we do not have an absolute prohibition of resisting evil persons. Jesus is routinely driving out evil spirits. We see Peter resisting Simon Magus (Acts 8:18–24) and Paul standing up to Elymas (Acts 13:9–11). The God-ordained state is called to resist evildoers (Rom. 13).

Let's go back to the temple cleansing, which Jesus likely undertook twice, not just once (Mark 11:15–17; John 2:14–15).[9] He "drove out" or "cast out" the moneychangers from the temple (Matt. 21:12). This is indeed a curious incident for those taking a Christian pacifist stance. Would Jesus make a whip and drive moneychangers from the temple—and stop people from entering the temple? This looks like a clear use of force and the resisting of evildoers.

While Jesus welcomes sinners and forgives them, he also threatens judgment on his opponents: the vineyard owner will "come and destroy the vine-growers, and will give the vineyard to others" (Mark 12:9 NASB)—or to use the words of his perceptive audience, "he will bring those wretches to a wretched end" (Matt. 21:41). He threatens judgment on Bethsaida, Chorazin, and Capernaum (11:21–24), which would take place in AD 70. And those who lead the least of his followers astray should have a millstone fastened to their neck and be drowned in the depths of the sea (18:6)—very imprecatory! Jesus says that his opponents' "father" is "the devil" (John 8:44). Jesus pronounced judgment on the false prophetess "Jezebel" and on the Nicolaitans (Rev. 2:16, 21–23). And we see Jesus himself coming at the end of history—John uses the imagery of a military conqueror on a white horse (19:11)—to bring final judgment to the world. Repeatedly, we see that Jesus himself doesn't absolutize forgiving enemies.

Other Voices in the New Testament

Elsewhere in the New Testament, we see the imprecatory psalms reenacted. This is because when people become so utterly wicked, what can one do but pray for judgment? For example, when the Eleven are seeking a replacement for the treacherous Judas, they cite two imprecatory psalms as their justification: "LET HIS HOMESTEAD BE MADE DESOLATE, AND LET NO ONE DWELL IN IT" and "LET ANOTHER TAKE HIS OFFICE" (Acts 1:20 NASB; quoting Pss. 69:25; 109:8). Paul calls Elymas "you son of the devil" (Acts 13:10 NASB); John refers to false prophets as "the children of the devil" (1 John 3:10). Paul is confident that Alexander, who brought Paul much harm, will be justly repaid for it (2 Tim. 4:14). And the martyred saints in Revelation cry out with a loud voice: "How long, O Lord, holy and true, will You refrain from judging and avenging our blood on those who dwell on the earth?" (Rev. 6:9–10 NASB). They recognized that justice cannot be ignored, and they called on God to set matters right.

Now, sometimes divine "wrath" is carried out by the state. Consider late evangelical statesman John Stott, who had joined the Anglican Pacifist Society at the start of World War II, as he thought this was his Christian obligation. But he came to reject this view in favor of a just war perspective. The Sermon on the Mount, he claimed, is not justification for total pacifism, moral compromise, or political anarchy. "Instead, what Jesus here demands of his followers is a personal attitude to evildoers which is prompted by mercy not justice, which renounces retaliation so completely as to risk further costly suffering, which is governed never by the desire to cause them harm but always by the determination to serve their highest good."[10]

Stott distinguished between *person* and *office*, between personal relationships and the authority of the state. At times the authorities require the violation of conscience, in which case we "must obey God rather than men" (Acts 5:29 NASB). Otherwise, the disciple may faithfully serve in the God-ordained state, which may require the use of force to oppose evildoers.

Romans 12 and 13 illustrate the complementarity of the personal and the official. In Romans 12, Paul follows Jesus's commands from the Sermon on the Mount about breaking the vicious cycle of personal animosity to work toward reconciled relationships—of turning enemies into friends. Rather than taking personal "revenge," believers are to leave room for the "wrath of God" (v. 19 NASB). Paul exhorts his readers to bless, forgive, serve, and show kindness toward their enemies rather than to return unkindness with unkindness and evil with evil (v. 21).

Then in Romans 13, we read of the state officials whose role has been ordained of God to *protect* the innocent, to *preserve* the peace (cf. 1 Tim. 2:1–2), and to *punish* evildoers. To do this, these officials bear the "sword"—an image of potentially lethal force. It is not the equivalent of a police officer's ticket book! The sword implies force in order to protect the defenseless and to punish or take "vengeance" on evildoers (Rom. 13:4). Paul picks up on the "revenge" and "wrath of God" from 12:19, stating that the state is the "avenger" of evil to bring "wrath" on evildoers (13:4 NASB). Some pacifists will downplay the word "sword" (*machaira*), claiming it is a simple short sword not meant for slaying. However, the New Testament indicates that this "sword" is very much a *lethal instrument* (cf. Acts 12:2; Heb. 11:37; Rev. 13:10). This same word can be used of a sword of larger size—a "*great* sword"—like the one given to the rider of the red horse, which symbolizes death/bloodshed (Rev. 6:4).

Others will claim that the "sword" in Romans 13 is what tax gatherers carried about with them—and that Paul was admonishing believers not to rebel against Rome's demand for taxes. Again, this seems strained. The language of "avenge" and "bring wrath" in Romans 13 is not the language of tax gathering; it is something much more severe and sobering.

This is illustrated very nicely in Acts 23, where Paul's life has come under threat. When Paul's nephew reports that some thugs had hatched a plot to kill Paul, he appeals to his right to be protected as a Roman citizen. Paul receives the protection of two hundred spearmen and seventy horsemen who, if necessary, would have used force ("the sword")—precisely what Paul was hoping they would do. Paul was not depending on unbelievers to do the "dirty work" of protection that Christians aren't allowed to do; rather, Paul's situation is an excellent illustration of the complementarity of Romans 12 and 13—that Christians could likewise serve in a God-ordained role to protect innocent citizens, by lethal force if necessary.

We also encounter general biblical passages that lend support to the idea of a just war. There is a "time for war" (cf. Eccles. 3:8). Proverbs advises the reader to "make war by wise guidance" (20:18 NASB). And again: "For by wise guidance you will wage war, and in abundance of counselors there is victory" (24:6 NASB). Jesus himself seems to suggest this in Luke 14:28–32 when using two mundane illustrations about counting the cost as a disciple: counting the cost before building a tower and counting the cost before a king goes to battle. Jesus asks: "Or what king, when he sets out to meet another king in battle, will not first sit down and consider whether he is strong enough with ten thousand men to encounter the one coming against him with twenty thousand? Or else, while the other is still far away, he sends a delegation and asks for terms of peace" (vv. 30–32 NASB). And although Old Testament battles are unique and unrepeatable events in the history of national Israel, it is interesting to note that Stephen, Paul, and the author of Hebrews affirm and commend Israel for fighting in those divinely commissioned battles (Acts 7:45; 13:19; Heb. 11:33–34).

Another point: soldiers and centurions are treated quite favorably in the New Testament. One biblical scholar, Richard Hays, maintains that a Christian's serving as a soldier—and by extension, a police officer—is morally equivalent to prostitution.[11] Yet this is not what we see in the biblical text. These soldiers are not told to repent of their soldierly ways; that is, their station in life is not presented as inherently immoral. Indeed, one such military officer has more faith than any Israelite (Matt. 8:10; Acts 10:1–2). Military men coming for baptism are told by John the Baptist to be fair in their dealings, content with their wages, and not extort money (Luke 3:14). Now, if Hays is correct that a disciple's soldiering is equivalent to prostitution, then should we expect John to tell a prostitute not to charge too much for her "services"? No, soldiers are not told, "Go and sin no more."

Again, the Scriptures exhibit a complementarity between being a disciple of Christ and involvement in the God-ordained state: "There is nothing anomalous about Christians serving in the police force or the prison service, as politicians or magistrates or town councillors. Christians worship a God who is just and are, therefore, committed to the quest for justice. The Christian community should not stand aloof from the secular community, but should seek to penetrate it for Christ."[12]

We see the qualities of love and justice in governing illustrated in the presidential career of Abraham Lincoln. Presidential historian Doris Kearns Goodwin's book *Team of Rivals* documents the remarkably wise, virtuous, courageous, and magnanimous character of this president.[13] Though he used force to preserve the Union and put down rebellion, he exhibited Christlike humility and graciousness toward his opponents, forgiving and restoring enemies rather than trying to humiliate them. This spirit is expressed in his Second Inaugural Address. "With malice toward none, with charity for all, with firmness in the right as God gives us to see the right, let us strive on to finish the work we are in, to bind up the nation's wounds, to care for him who shall have borne the battle and for his widow and his orphan, to do all which may achieve and cherish a just and lasting peace among ourselves and with all nations." Lincoln's public and personal life was marked by integrity. He grew in his Christian faith during his presidency.[14] And he very much exemplified the teachings of the Sermon on the Mount (Matt. 5–7) and Jesus's own mission statement (Luke 4:18–19). He did not initiate war, and he always held out an olive branch to his enemies (he sought to go and first be reconciled to them). He did not seek to crush or humiliate his opponents (he loved his enemies and prayed for them). He did not return insult for insult in order to maintain his honor (he turned the other cheek). He was honest in his dealings (his yes was yes and his no, no). He was modest about his accomplishments (he did not attempt to display his righteousness before others). He recognized that he was accountable to God (he was seeking God's kingdom first). He sought to protect American citizens from harm and worked to free slaves (proclaiming release to the captives).[15]

Though the data of the New Testament on the issue of the Christian's participation in war is not direct nor abundant, the basic principles are clear: To be godlike is to make a sacrificial, loving response to maintain a nonvindictive, magnanimous, reconciling attitude in all personal relationships when one's own rights or honor are at stake; and human government is responsible with accountability to God to use force when necessary to reinforce righteous behavior for its citizenry while never putting our trust in military might or earthly kingdoms. Those who do so will likewise "perish by the sword" (Matt. 26:52).

Historical Considerations: Constantinianism and Christian Soldiering

Before Constantine

Scholars such as historian Roland Bainton and theologian John Howard Yoder have maintained that the church was uniformly nonmilitary ("pacifistic") from the second century till the rise of Constantine (AD 312).[16] Citing church fathers such as Tertullian (160–225) and Origen (ca. 185–254), they claim that the early church refused any part in political power or the military violence of the Caesars' wars.[17] It is the spirit of Constantinianism, so the argument goes, that has given rise to the church's compromising entanglement with the state.

The evidence for this uniform pacifism, however, is not all that tidy. For one thing, the New Testament itself is not nonmilitaristic. As we have just pointed out, it speaks favorably of soldiers and centurions, including their conversions and seeking baptism (Matt. 8:5–13; 27:54; Luke 3:14; Acts 10–11; 23:16–22). Jesus himself used force to drive out moneychangers from the temple (e.g., John 2:14–15). Stephen and Paul matter-of-factly endorsed the dispossession of the Canaanites (Acts 7:45; 13:19). Paul taught that the God-ordained minister of the state bears a sword to punish evildoers (Rom. 13:4). And the author of Hebrews commended those who "conquered kingdoms," "became mighty in war," "put foreign armies to flight" (11:33–34 NASB).

What about beyond the New Testament? After the New Testament and up to the mid-second century, we have silence on Christian soldiers. But just after this time, we have clear evidence of Christian soldiers in the Roman army. The Christian historian Eusebius records that when Emperor Marcus Aurelius was fighting the Germans and Sarmatians, his troops had no water; so Christian soldiers knelt down and prayed, and water came from the heavens to refresh them. We also have tomb inscriptions of Christian soldiers before Constantine, and St. Sebastian and many other Christians served in the army under Emperor Diocletian (early fourth century). And we have evidence of Christians fighting in Syria a whole century prior to Constantine and in Armenia just before the rise of Constantine.

Furthermore, the nonmilitaristic perspective of several church fathers does not necessarily represent a uniformly held, empire-wide Christian belief during this time. In fact, we have indications in Tertullian's own writings that there were Christians everywhere—in "fortresses [*castella*]" and in the "military camp [*castra*]." Tertullian appears to shift from a more tolerant attitude toward the military to a more negative one as more and more Christians were making military life into a career. And Origen argues that Christians can better fight for the emperor through prayers than with weapons; this suggests the possibility of a just war.

Beyond this, questions remain. If early Christians did reject fighting for *Caesar*, did this imply a rejection of *any* possible military involvement whatsoever? Or was fighting for Caesar different from fighting to stop, say, Nazi aggression? And could the fact that Caesars at particular times or places required idolatrous practices of soldiers be a major reason for Christians abstaining from military service? And as Rome had no police force, many soldiers served in police-like functions, keeping order within the calmer empire—unlike the fiercer fighting at the borders. At any rate, early Christian military involvement didn't require assistance from Constantine.

The Advent of Constantine

With the ascent of Emperor Constantine (312), the Christian outcast minority would become part of "the establishment." Though various Christian critics have spoken negatively of Constantine, we should recognize his historical significance and the fact that his presence was a blessing to many Christians. Surely Constantine's rule was a huge relief to a once persecuted minority. Indeed, believers *do* have a duty to pray for rulers who will, it is hoped, enable believers to lead peaceable and quiet lives—instead of their being harassed and persecuted (1 Tim. 2:1–4; cf. Rev. 6:10). So these previously harassed believers were rightly grateful for a ruler who kept other Romans from killing Christians! Jesus himself came to deliver people from all manner of oppression and bondage (Luke 4:18–19). And we should remember that political (or even cultural) power is not inherently evil but is ordained by God (Rom. 13).

Christians under Constantine began to wrestle with what it meant to have "dual citizenship" in a heavenly kingdom *and* an earthly one. This was a totally new experiment. Paganism was waning, and Christians were trying to fill the vacuum and figure out how to run things. What's more, Constantine was not an oppressor of pagans. And he actually brought about many positive moral reforms—banning gladiatorial games and the abandonment of children, as well as requiring segregated prison cells for men and women, for instance. He also encouraged charitable ministries that benefited everyone, not just Christians. This isn't to deny that the church would make some grievous mistakes with the temporal power it had (e.g., the Inquisition many centuries later).

Constantine has been portrayed negatively by thinkers like John Howard Yoder (who adopts an Anabaptist perspective). He refers to the "heresy" of "Constantinianism"—a term referring to the church's taking a dominant cultural place in the Roman Empire. Allegedly, the church fell from its "pristine" existence as a dynamic, though politically disempowered, community. It capitulated and compromised as it came to operate according to the idolatrous machinery of political power, including Christian involvement in the military. Although we can't address Yoder's argument here, his reference to the church's "Constantinian shift" is highly questionable; it is both historically flawed and theologically inaccurate. For example, as noted earlier, the New Testament speaks quite positively of Roman centurions, and Christians were involved in the military in some capacity before the time of Constantine, not simply after he came to power.[18]

A Brief Discussion of Just War

After the rise of Constantine, Ambrose of Milan (340–397) and then his disciple Augustine (354–430) would advocate principles for a just war—a view that held sway until the twentieth century. In the wake of the Reformation, Anabaptists took a nonresistance position. Even so the Anabaptist *Schleitheim Confession* (article 6) affirms that the sword in the hands of government is "ordained of God outside the perfection of Christ" and "punishes and puts to death the wicked, and guards and protects the good." The sword is "ordained to be used by the worldly magistrates." Contrary to many Christian pacifists in this tradition, this Confession observes that not all worldly power is inherently evil.

Can there be a just war? Mahatma Gandhi once asked whether fighting for liberty and democracy was better than fighting for totalitarianism when *both* leave behind the dead, the orphan, and the homeless. Is the right stance that of a presumption against war, as pacifists commonly assert?

Gandhi and Martin Luther King Jr. have been highlighted by pacifists as examples of those who brought about change nonviolently. Indeed, we can admire their courage, boldness, and inner strength. But perhaps it is worth pointing out here that their nonviolent resistance succeeded only because the governments to which they appealed were fairly humanitarian and better informed by biblical values than the vast number of ruthless regimes that have existed over time. These may be misleading role models for those living under brutal and unprincipled totalitarian regimes such as Soviet or Chinese Communism. In these systems, the likes of Gandhi, King, and their followers would have simply "disappeared" in the middle of the night and never heard from again.

Furthermore, we can rightly wonder whether those promoting pacifism in the West during the 1930s and 1940s played into the hands of Stalin and Hitler, encouraging the expansion of his oppressive tyranny and encouraging greater evils. This is no idle curiosity.[19] C. S. Lewis rightly observed that a pacifistic nation will not remain one for long. Totalitarianism and evil will oppress good people who do not protect themselves and future generations from oppression. And is not the use of force (even lethal force) to protect an innocent victim from a homicidal maniac an expression of love for neighbor?[20] Is it not a greater injustice to "resist not the one who is evil"?

Principles of Just War

After World War I, in which France lost 1.3 million of its men, pacifism came to dominate Europe. War came to be viewed as *inherently evil* as well as tragic and pointless—without heroes and villains. France's pacifism was not lost on the observant Hitler. Nor was Britain's mistaken notion of "peace in our time"—inspired by Prime Minister Neville Chamberlain's meeting with Hitler in Munich in the wake of Germany's invasion of the Sudetenland (Czechoslovakia) in 1938. It took Hitler six weeks to overpower a weak-willed but militarily superior France in 1940, and he assumed that Britain would similarly lack the will to defend itself.[21] It seems that pacifism, however well motivated, actually encouraged further aggression.

The just war theorist attempts to deal realistically with unpreventable violent aggression against the vulnerable. These just war principles are applicable to both the *military* and the *police* force (remember that in ancient Rome, soldiers were involved in local policing). Just war theory recognizes the justice of protecting innocent nations from thugs, bullies, and tyrants. A nation may not need to fire a shot so long as it has a stronger military than thug nations so that they can be held in check. The just war concept recognizes that attempts at negotiation and peacemaking with ruthless tyrants will often be fruitless (e.g., the Munich Agreement of 1938) and that "trust" may be nothing more than gullibility.

Against Gandhi, it does make a difference whether one is defending tyranny or freedom. One may engage in sacrificial fighting so that future generations might have greater opportunity, freedom, security, and the protection of rights. Military historian Victor Davis Hanson reminds us that war or military strength has helped bring an end to chattel slavery in America, Nazism, Fascism, and Soviet Communism. More often than not, wars break out not because of failure of communication or misunderstanding—or from poverty or inequality. Rather, they begin from malicious intent and the absence of deterrence—or because of unresolved disagreements from an earlier war or lack of a clear resolution. Often nations become accomplices to evil through inaction.[22] On the other hand, Jews who survived in concentration camps and citizens of European nations under Nazi Germany's oppression rejoiced greatly at the arrival of Allied troops to liberate them from tyranny. On this side of the fall and before Christ's second coming, war will be with us.

When it comes to articulating what just war involves, there are seven standard criteria, although they should not be weighted equally (a common mistake made by critics of the just war theory). The first three take priority as essential conditions, whereas the last four are more prudential and should not override the first three.[23]

1 *Just Cause*: All unprovoked aggression is condemned. A war for self-defense and protection (including defense of other vulnerable nations) is morally legitimate. Following this first criterion alone would eliminate all war and aggression.

2 *Just Intent*: The only legitimate intention is to secure a just or fair peace for friend and foe alike, ruling out revenge, conquest, economic gain, or ideological supremacy. Ultimately, greater good than harm should result from war: "Vengeance, subjugation, and conquest are unjustifiable purposes."[24] Sometimes there may be "unintentional effects" (killing civilians) which accompany the intended effect of restraining violence.

3 *Lawful Declaration*: Only a lawful government has the right to initiate war. Only the state—not individuals or parties within the state—can legitimately exercise this authority.

4 *Last Resort*: "War should be pursued only when negotiation, arbitration, compromise, and all other paths fail; for as a rational being man

should, if possible, settle disputes by reason and law, not force."[25] Of course, this doesn't mean negotiations should go on indefinitely while gross injustices continue with no end in sight. Last resort is a prudential, secondary consideration, as are the remaining criteria.

5 *Immunity of Noncombatants*: Since war is an official act of government, only those who are officially agents of government may fight, and individuals not actively contributing to the conflict (including POWs, medical personnel, and casualties, as well as civilian nonparticipants) should be immune from attack—although this is not always possible. For example, troops may be embedded in civilian-populated areas.[26] Note that simply because noncombatants are killed does not by itself render an otherwise just war unjust.

6 *Limited Objectives*: The goal of a just war is peace; it is not the utter destruction of an enemy nation's people, economy, or political institutions.

7 *Limited/Proportionate Means*: The weaponry and the force used should be limited to what is needed to repel the aggression and deter future attacks, that is to say, to secure a just peace: "only sufficient force should be used to resist violence and restore peace."[27] "Sufficient" does not necessarily mean overwhelming victory.

Let's elaborate a bit. First, in the context of just war principles, which are universally applicable and rooted in God's general revelation to all people, it may be helpful to *distinguish between "force" and "violence."* While all violence is force, not all force is violence. Appropriate force is motivated by both justice and love of neighbor; it is aimed at restoring peace; it is carried out by a proper authority. Violence is not inspired by justice and love but by greed and hatred; it is not aimed at restoring peace but at destruction and evoking terror; it is often carried out by those without proper authority—though those in authority can also overstep their bounds. The issue is not violence versus no violence, but a legitimate use of force versus an illegitimate one.[28]

Second, a nation or group of nations may engage in a truly just war, but *the fact that missteps may be made does not undermine the overall justice of the war*. Even if certain powers veer off course—out-of-control soldiers who engage in rape or kill noncombatants or a misguided plan that causes more destruction than necessary—this does not negate the *overall* justice of the cause. The fact that missteps or moral violations may be made, say, on the part of the Allies in their attempt to stop the Nazis and the Japanese does not put the Allies and Axis powers on equal moral footing.

Or some might suggest that what some call a just war may not have been a truly *last* resort; after all, maybe one or two further attempts could have averted war. We can talk about giving principled diplomacy a strong or reasonable chance, but we should also consider the track records of thugs and tyrants who have had a history of breaking one promise after another. Well-grounded trust is one thing; gullibility or misguided optimism is another.

Third, a war that is just should ultimately *exhibit love for one's neighbor*. In the Old Testament, God commanded love for one's neighbor (Lev. 19:18), but this love was not in opposition to capital punishment in the law of Moses; such punishments were a protective measure to guard the spiritual and moral integrity of the community of God's people. Similarly, while it is true that Jesus is the crucified Messiah who died in weakness for the sake of lost humanity, he is also coming in triumph to punish those who have opposed his kingdom purposes. Likewise, just wars show concern for the victims of unjust aggression. But, one might ask, should we not show love to the perpetrators as well? Are they not also our neighbors as well? We must take care here not to confuse what love requires. Love for the victim may require *removing* the source of harm and, lest we forget Romans 13:1–7, *punishment* as well from the God-ordained minister of the state. And the perpetrator and the victim cannot sit down at the table together without the perpetrator's repentance.

Fourth, the pacifistic understanding of "turn the other cheek" raises questions about *protecting the innocent* from injustice when it is in our power to do so. What if a believer's wife is about to be raped or children kidnapped by a criminal who breaks into his home? Would it be sinful to lethally resist? Are children not entrusted to parents for protection from would-be rapists and kidnappers? It would be wrong and irresponsible rather than virtuous not to step in with force to protect them even if it means the regrettable taking of the perpetrator's life. It would seem that, for pacifists in such a situation, to call the police for protection on their behalf would be making allowance for another to potentially carry out the sinful act for them. And we must remember Paul did just that! He made the equivalent of a 911 call, appealing to the Roman military for protection when thugs were plotting to take his life, and they were thoroughly prepared to use lethal force to protect him (Acts 23).

The believer can justifiably physically resist a dangerous criminal but at the same time show love to him by visiting him in prison, praying for him, and showing concern for his struggling family. We know Christians in law enforcement who may even harm criminals to protect innocent civilians, yet they visit these criminals in prison, show kindness to them, and tell these prisoners about the love of Christ.

Finally, we should *simultaneously support "just peacemaking" efforts to build bridges of understanding and partnership between nations and communities while not neglecting the appropriate use of force against thugs and tyrants when necessary*. These are not mutually exclusive, as some theologians suggest. That is, we should not ignore the realities on the ground while pursuing the ideal. Showing good will and wise diplomacy where differences and disagreements exist is laudable. But as history has repeatedly shown, tyrants typically engage in thuggery and aggression where they have opportunity—unless they encounter the deterring effect of a superior military.[29] Even the mere *possession* of military strength—without needing to fire a shot—can prevent rogue nations from bullying or invading weaker ones. The same applies to police preserving order and protecting the vulnerable. The world's realities require being shrewd as serpents and innocent as doves (Matt. 10:16). A strong military (or, at a local level, a citizen's brandishing of a registered handgun)—even without its being utilized—can help prevent aggression and protect the innocent.

As beneficial as military strength or a police force may be, however, this by itself is insufficient to secure lasting peace without some deeper social and moral transformation. We noted in chapter 20 that one of the leavening effects of the gospel has been to help promote human rights, stable democracies, moral and social reforms, education, and many other societal gains. But the pacifistic refusal to use—indeed, the denunciation of—serious, potentially lethal force against tyrants to protect the innocent only encourages the tyrants to do their worst, exposing many innocents to their oppression.

Conclusion

Like John Stott, Dietrich Bonhoeffer had been a pacifist, but he came to revise his view in light of the horrific evils being perpetrated by Hitler. And as we saw, the same is true of Miroslav Volf who shifted from pacifism to a just war view after seeing the devastation of his own Croatia, its women raped, and many of its people killed or displaced. Taking up a just war position in the face of "intolerable aggression" is an extension of the obligation to love one's neighbor "when that neighbor's life is threatened by a third party."[30] We find this an apt summary of the stance we are taking in this chapter.

Summary

- Certain conditions—aggression and oppression—may become so intolerable that justified force is the only recourse to deal with them.
- Romans 13 affirms that God does not always carry out divine wrath directly but has partly delegated this task to human governments.

- Jesus's command to "turn the other cheek" does not refer to an act of *violence* but an insult (cf. Lam. 3:30). And Jesus himself didn't literally turn the other cheek when struck (John 18:23). Jesus prohibits returning insult for insult in personal relationships but rather calls us to work toward reconciliation. He is not referring to the responsibility of civil authorities toward criminals.

- We should take careful note at this point: *Jesus does not absolutize loving one's enemies.* He denounces his opponents in very harsh—even damning—terms in Matthew 23. And despite the call to extravagant forgiveness (Matt. 18:22), this is not absolute (18:34—being "handed over to the torturers").

- Do we forgive terrorists? Is that our rightful place? What about the victims and their families? Does forgiveness require abandoning the use of force as they prepare to launch another attack? The state has a different role in God's economy. Its business is not to forgive rapists or murderers but rather to punish evildoers—though tempered with mercy when appropriate. This does not mean we don't pray for terrorists, but we must make efforts to stop them from doing their worst.

- In Matthew 5:39, Jesus tells us not to resist "by evil means" (not "*the evil one/person*")—since evil persons are resisted by Jesus, Peter, and Paul. And God ordains the states to resist evildoers.

- Jesus's own temple cleansing (apparently twice!) is an example of the use of force.

- Jesus threatens judgment on his opponents (Mark 12:9; cf. Matt. 21:41: "he will bring those wretches to a wretched end").

- We must distinguish between *person* and *office*, between personal relationships and the authority of the state. At times the authorities require the violation of conscience, in which case we "must obey God rather than men" (Acts 5:29). Otherwise, the disciple may faithfully serve in the God-ordained state, which may require the use of force to oppose evildoers.

- Romans 13 asserts that the state official has the God-ordained role to *protect* the innocent, to *preserve* the peace (cf. 1 Tim. 2:1–2), and to *punish* evildoers. To do this, these officials bear the "sword"—an image of potentially lethal force ("wrath" and "vengeance" do not describe a Roman tax gatherer who carried a sword).

- In Acts 23, when Paul's life came under threat, Paul received the protection of two hundred spearmen and seventy horsemen, who, if necessary, would have used lethal force—precisely what Paul was hoping they would do.

- We also encounter general biblical passages that lend support to the idea of a just war (cf. Prov. 20:18; 24:6; Eccles. 3:8; Luke 14:30–32). Stephen, Paul, and the author of Hebrews affirm and commend Israel for fighting in those divinely commissioned battles (Acts 7:11; 13:9; Heb. 11:33–34).

- In the New Testament, soldiers are not told to repent of their soldierly ways; that is, their station in life is not presented as inherently immoral. Indeed, Jesus says one such military officer has more faith than any Israelite (Matt. 8:10; Acts 10:1–2). Military men coming for baptism are simply told by John to be fair in their dealings, content with their wages, and not extort money (Luke 3:14).

- Consider Abraham Lincoln, who exhibited Christlike humility and graciousness toward his opponents, forgiving and restoring enemies rather than trying to humiliate them.

- It is doubtful that the early church was uniformly pacifistic (contra Roland Bainton). The New Testament itself is not nonmilitaristic (Matt. 8:5–13; 27:54; Luke 3:14; Acts 10–11; 23:16–22; cf. John 2:14–15; Acts 7:45; 13:19; Rom. 13:4; Heb. 11:33–34).

- After the New Testament, we have ample evidence of Christian soldiers in the Roman army from the mid-second century onward (historical accounts, tomb inscriptions, mention of Christians in "fortresses" and in the "military camp," etc.).

- Beyond this, questions remain: If early Christians did reject fighting *for Caesar*, did this imply a rejection of *any* possible military involvement whatsoever? Or was fighting for Caesar different from fighting to stop, say, Nazi aggression? And could the fact that Caesars at particular times or places required idolatrous practices of soldiers be a major reason for Christians abstaining from military service?

- Surely Constantine's rule was a massive relief to a once persecuted minority. Christians under Constantine began to wrestle with what it meant to have "dual citizenship" in a heavenly kingdom *and* an earthly one.

- The notion of the church's "Constantinian shift" (John Howard Yoder) is historically flawed and theologically problematic.

- Can there be a just war? Had Mahatma Gandhi and Martin Luther King Jr. lived under Chinese or Soviet communism, they would have simply "disappeared" in the middle of the night and never been heard from again.

- The pacifistic nation will not remain one for long, and pacifists historically have emboldened tyrants and the spread of totalitarianism (e.g., pacifism in France and Britain after World War I).

- The theory of just war attempts to deal realistically with unpreventable violent aggression against the vulnerable. These just war principles are applicable both to the *military* and a *police* force (remember that in ancient Rome, soldiers were involved in local policing).

- War or military strength has helped bring an end to chattel slavery in America, Nazism, Fascism, and Soviet Communism. Wars typically begin from malicious intent and the absence of deterrence—or because of unresolved disagreements from an earlier war or lack of a clear resolution. Often nations become accomplices to evil through inaction.

- The criteria for a just war (the first three being essential, the last four being prudential) are *just cause, just intent, lawful declaration, last resort, immunity of noncombatants, limited objectives,* and *limited/proportionate means.*

- We should distinguish between "force" and "violence." Unlike violence, force is motivated by both justice and love of neighbor; it is aimed at restoring peace; it is carried out by a proper authority.

- A nation or group of nations may engage in a truly just war, but *the fact that missteps may be made does not undermine the overall justice of the war.*

- Regarding *last* resort, a nation doesn't have to exhaust literally all diplomatic options. We can make judgments based on the track records of thugs and tyrants who have a well-established history of promise-breaking.

- A war that is just will ultimately *exhibit love for one's neighbor.* Love for the victim may require *removing* the source of harm.

- We should *simultaneously* support "just peacemaking" efforts to build bridges of understanding and partnership between nations and communities while not neglecting the appropriate use of force against thugs and tyrants when necessary to keep them at bay and protect the vulnerable.

Afterword

The question of God's command to kill the Canaanites is considered to be the most problematic question of all the ethical challenges raised in the Old Testament Scriptures. We have undertaken the task of showing that the charge, "Yahweh commanded genocide," is false. We have examined the relationship of divine and human authorship in Scripture as this relates to divine commands to "utterly destroy" and "leave alive nothing that breathes." We noted how Jesus and New Testament authors see themselves anchored in the Old Testament Scriptures; they do not at all shrink from identifying with its depictions of divine wrath and judgment of human wickedness.

As we look at the nature of these war texts in the setting of the ancient Near East, a clearer picture emerges—namely, that these texts, like so many others of that day, are properly understood as exaggerations or hyperbole. But we can look at the biblical texts themselves to see that "utter destruction" is always accompanied by an abundance of survivors who "could not be driven out" and "are there to this day."

As for divine commands, we have pointed out that while killing the innocent is generally wrong, this "Crucial Moral Principle" is not, strictly speaking, absolute. A loving and just God could, in rare circumstances, exempt people from this principle for the sake of some greater good. Challenges to divine command theory are, more often than not, misunderstandings and misrepresentations. God's issuing difficult (though not intrinsically evil) divine commands is not an incoherent notion; divine commands are neither arbitrary nor without content but can be philosophically, theologically, and ethically defended.

What if a Texas governor claimed that "God told me to 'utterly destroy' a bizarre sect in my state"? We have argued that such claims can be challenged on a number of fronts—including lack of prophetic and character qualifications, absence of supporting divine signs and wonders, and the like. And the questioning Israelite soldier, wondering whether he should listen to Moses or Joshua about driving out or killing Canaanites, would have had ample evidence to see the divine stamp of approval on these leaders of Israel.

Finally, we address miscellaneous issues that often emerge when discussing this weighty topic: Does religion lead to violence? Are Yahweh wars just like Islamic jihad? Did the biblical war texts inspire the Crusades? Does Jesus's command to turn the other cheek rule out just warfare and advocate pacifism? While some of these questions can be contentious, we hope that crucial misunderstandings are clarified and that false assumptions are challenged and even corrected.

We trust that this book will bring insight and moral understanding to an issue that continues to vex many people. We hope sufficient light has been shed on the central issues, even though there may be disagreement at the margins.

Notes

Introduction

1. Richard Dawkins, *The God Delusion* (Boston: Houghton Mifflin, 2006), 51.

2. Dawkins spells out the contradiction: "As an academic scientist, I am a passionate Darwinian, believing that natural selection is, if not the only driving force in evolution, certainly the only known force capable of producing the illusion of purpose which so strikes all who contemplate nature. But at the same time as I support Darwinism as a scientist, I am a passionate anti-Darwinian when it comes to politics and how we should conduct our human affairs." *A Devil's Chaplain: Reflections on Hope, Lies, Science, and Love* (New York: Houghton Mifflin, 2003), 10–11.

In another place, he admits to the *logic* of his own determinism (that people cannot be held responsible for their actions), but *emotionally* he cannot accept this. See the Dawkins interview by Logan Gage, "Who Wrote Richard Dawkins's New Book?," *Evolution News* (website), October 28, 2006, http://www.evolutionnews.org/2006/10/who_wrote_richard_dawkinss_new002783.html.

3. For example, Paul Copan and William Lane Craig, eds., *Contending with Christianity's Critics: Answering New Atheists and Other Objectors* (Nashville: B&H Academic, 2009); Greg Ganssle, *A Reasonable God: Engaging the New Face of Atheism* (Waco, TX: Baylor University Press, 2009); Alister McGrath, *The Dawkins Delusion?* (Downers Grove, IL: InterVarsity, 2007); Chad Meister and William Lane Craig, eds., *God Is Great, God Is Good: Why Believing in God Is Reasonable and Responsible* (Downers Grove, IL: InterVarsity, 2009); Alvin Plantinga, *Where the Conflict Really Lies: Science, Religion, and*

Naturalism (New York: Oxford University Press, 2011); Paul Copan, *Is God a Moral Monster? Making Sense of the Old Testament God* (Grand Rapids: Baker Books, 2011).

4. From the cover of McGrath's book, *Dawkins Delusion?*

5. These accusations come from Dawkins, *God Delusion*, 280–81.

6. This is taken from the *Oxford English Dictionary* (2010). This definition is standardly used in the skeptical literature on this topic. For example, Wesley Morriston, "Ethical Criticism of the Bible: The Case of Divinely Mandated Genocide," *Sophia* 51, no 1 (2012): 117; and Edwin Curley, "The God of Abraham, Isaac and Jacob," in *Divine Evil? The Moral Character of the God of Abraham*, ed. Michael Bergmann, Michael J. Murray, and Michael C. Rea (New York: Oxford University Press, 2010), 62.

7. Tooley's argument defines God as "an appropriate object of worship"; God is also an appropriate object of other human concerns—that good will triumph over evil and that justice will be done, for example. What characteristics should such an appropriate object of worship—"God"—possess? Tooley answers that "a being, to be characterizable as God in that sense, should be a personal being, should be a being that is morally perfect, a being that is omnipotent, and a being that is omniscient." See Michael Tooley, "Does God Exist?," in *Knowledge of God*, ed. Alvin Plantinga and Michael Tooley (Malden, MA: Blackwell, 2008), 72. See also Michael Tooley, "Opening Statement," transcript of a debate with William Lane Craig, "Does God Exist?," University of Colorado Boulder, November 1994, *Reasonable*

Faith (website), http://www.reasonablefaith.org /does-god-exist-the-craig-tooley-debate.

8. Tooley, "Does God Exist?," 74.

9. Walter Sinnott-Armstrong, *Morality without God* (New York: Oxford University Press, 2009), 91.

10. Louise Antony, "Atheism as Perfect Piety," in *Is Goodness without God Good Enough? A Debate on Faith, Secularism, and Ethics*, ed. Robert K. Garcia and Nathan L. King (Lanham, MD: Rowman & Littlefield, 2008).

11. See "Did God Mandate Genocide?" issue of *Philosophia Christi* 11, no. 1 (2009). See in particular these critical articles: Wesley Moriston, "Did God Command Genocide? A Challenge to the Biblical Inerrantist," *Philosophia Christi* 11, no. 1 (2009): 8–26; Randal Rauser, "'Let Nothing that Breathes Remain Alive': On the Problem of Divinely Commanded Genocide," *Philosophia Christi* 11, no. 1 (2009): 27–41; Clay Jones, "We Don't Hate Sin So We Don't Understand What Happened to the Canaanites: An Addendum to Divine Genocide Arguments," *Philosophia Christ* 11, no. 1 (2009): 53–72; Paul Copan, "Yahweh Wars and the Canaanites: Divinely-Mandated Genocide or Corporate Capital Punishment? Responses to Critics," *Philosophia Christi* 11, no. 1 (2009): 73–90.

12. The proceedings of this conference were later published in Bergmann, Murray, and Rea, *Divine Evil?*

13. David T. Lamb, *God Behaving Badly: Is the God of the Old Testament Angry, Sexist and Racist?* (Downers Grove, IL: InterVarsity, 2011); Paul Copan, *Is God a Moral Monster? Making Sense of the Old Testament God* (Grand Rapids: Baker Books, 2011); Jeremy Evans, Heath Thomas, and Paul Copan, eds., *Holy War in the Bible: Christian Morality and an Old Testament Problem* (Downers Grove, IL: IVP Academic, 2013); Christopher Wright, *The God I Don't Understand: Reflections on Tough Questions of Faith* (Grand Rapids: Zondervan, 2008); Eric Seibert, *Disturbing Divine Behavior* (Minneapolis: Fortress Press, 2009); Eric Seibert, *The Violence of Scripture: Overcoming the Old Testament's Troubling Legacy* (Minneapolis: Fortress Press, 2012); Iain Provan, *Seriously Dangerous Religion: What the Old Testament Really Says and Why It Matters* (Waco, TX: Baylor University Press, 2014).

14. Paul Copan, *Is God a Moral Monster?*; Paul Copan and Matthew Flannagan, "Was Israel Commanded to Commit Genocide?," *Christian Research Journal* 34, no. 5 (2011): 6–7; Paul Copan and Matthew Flannagan, "The Ethics of 'Holy War' for Christian Morality and Theology," in *Holy War in the Bible: Christian Morality and*

an Old Testament Problem, ed. Jeremy Evans, Heath Thomas, and Paul Copan (Downers Grove, IL: IVP Academic, 2013), 199–237. Matthew Flannagan and Paul Copan, "Does the Bible Condone Genocide?," in *In Defense of the Bible*, ed. Steven Cowan and Terry Wilder (Nashville: B&H Academic, 2012); Matthew Flannagan and Paul Copan, "Old Testament Ethics," *Lexham Bible Dictionary* (an online dictionary) at http://www.lexhambibledictionary.com/. Again, we are thankful to IVP Academic and to B&H Academic for permission to revise and expand on previously published material with them— particularly Copan and Flannagan, "The Ethics of 'Holy War'"; Flannagan and Copan, "Does the Bible Condone Genocide?"; and Matthew Flannagan, "Did God Command the Genocide of the Canaanites?," in *Come Let Us Reason: New Essays in Christian Apologetics*, ed. Paul Copan and William Lane Craig (Nashville: B&H Academic, 2012). Thanks also to *Dialogue* journal (UK), which granted permission to revise material from Matthew Flannagan, "Defending Divine Commands," *Dialogue* 37 (November 2011).

Chapter 1: The Problem Clarified: An Atheistic Philosophical Argument

1. Raymond Bradley, "A Moral Argument for Atheism," in *The Impossibility of God*, ed. Michael Martin and Ricki Monnier (Amherst, NY: Prometheus Books, 2003), 144. Similar arguments have been made in Wesley Moriston, "Did God Command Genocide? A Challenge to the Biblical Inerrantist," *Philosophia Christi* 11, no. 1 (2009): 8–26; Randal Rauser, "'Let Nothing that Breathes Remain Alive': On the Problem of Divinely Commanded Genocide," *Philosophia Christi* 11, no. 1 (2009): 27–41; Michael Tooley, "Does God Exist?," in *The Knowledge of God*, ed. Michael Tooley and Alvin Plantinga (Malden, MA: Blackwell, 2008), 73–77; Evan Fales, "Satanic Verses: Moral Chaos in Holy Writ," in *Divine Evil? The Moral Character of the God of Abraham*, ed. Michael Bergmann, Michael J. Murray, and Michael C. Rea (New York: Oxford University Press, 2010); Edwin Curley, "The God of Abraham, Isaac and Jacob," in *Divine Evil?*; Walter Sinnott-Armstrong, "Why Traditional Theism Cannot Provide an Adequate Foundation for Morality," in *Is Goodness without God Good Enough? A Debate on Faith, Secularism, and Ethics*, ed. Robert K. Garcia and Nathan L. King (Lanham, MD: Rowman & Littlefield, 2008); and Louise Antony, "Atheism as Perfect Piety," in *Is Goodness without God Good Enough?*

2. Bradley, "A Moral Argument for Atheism," 144.

3. Ibid., 132.

4. Ibid., 137. Here we insert the term "Crucial Moral Principle" into Bradley's argument.

5. Ibid., 144.

6. Ibid., 132.

7. Ibid., 131.

8. Raymond Bradley, "Opening Statement," in a debate with Matthew Flannagan, "Is God the Source of Morality? Is It Defensible to Ground Right and Wrong in the Commands of God?," Auckland University, Auckland, New Zealand, August 2, 2010. Transcript available at http://www.mandm.org.nz/2010/08/raymond-bradleys-opening-statement-bradley-v-flannagan-debate.html.

9. Bradley, "A Moral Argument for Atheism," 144.

10. Ibid., 130. Here Bradley cites Peter van Inwagen, "Genesis and Evolution," in *Reasoned Faith*, ed. Eleonore Stump (Ithaca, NY: Cornell University Press, 1993), 97.

11. Bradley, "A Moral Argument for Atheism," 130. Bradley cites Alvin Plantinga, "When Faith and Reason Clash: Evolution and the Bible," *Christian Scholar's Review* 21, no. 1 (September 1991): 12.

12. Alvin Plantinga, *Warranted Christian Belief* (Oxford: Oxford University Press, 2000), 396.

13. Bradley, "Moral Argument for Atheism," 144.

14. Alvin Plantinga, "Evolution, Neutrality, and Antecedent Probability: A Reply to McMullin and Van Till," *Christian Scholar's Review* 21, no. 1 (September 1991): 93–94.

15. Plantinga, *Warranted Christian Belief*, 400.

16. Ibid., 401.

17. Ibid., 396, 397.

18. William Lane Craig, "Doctrine of Revelation (Part 4)," transcript of a class lecture, Reasonable Faith (website), http://www.reasonablefaith.org/defenders-2-podcast/transcript/s2-4, accessed March 5, 2014.

19. Ibid.

20. Ibid.

21. See Paul Copan, "Hateful, Vindictive Psalms?," *Christian Research Journal* 31, no. 5 (2008): 50–51. Available at http://www.equip.org/articles/hateful-vindictive-psalms/. For more on this topic, see N. T. Wright, *The Case for the Psalms: Why They Are Essential* (New York: HarperOne, 2013). See also Kit Barker, "Divine Illocutions in Psalm 137: A Critique of Nicholas Wolterstorff's 'Second Hermeneutic,'" *Tyndale Bulletin* 60, no. 1 (2009): 1–14.

Chapter 2: What Does It Mean to Say the Bible Is the Word of God?

1. William Lane Craig, "'Men Moved by the Holy Spirit Spoke from God' (2 Peter 1.21): A Middle Knowledge Perspective on Biblical Inspiration," *Philosophia Christi* 1, no. 1 (1999): 45–82.

2. See William Lane Craig, "A Molinist Perspective on Biblical Inspiration," *Reasonable Faith* (website), http://www.reasonablefaith.org/a-molinist-perspective-on-biblical-inspiration, accessed March 5, 2014.

3. Ibid., emphasis added.

4. Ibid.

5. What follows summarizes and elaborates the account spelled out in much more depth in Nicholas Wolterstorff, *Divine Discourse: Philosophical Reflections on the Claim that God Speaks* (Cambridge: Cambridge University Press, 1995).

6. Ibid., 54.

7. Ibid., 295.

8. Richard Swinburne, "What Does the Old Testament Mean?," in *Divine Evil? The Moral Character of the God of Abraham*, ed. Michael Bergmann, Michael J. Murray, and Michael C. Rea (New York: Oxford University Press, 2010), 212.

9. This was expressed in dialogue at Auckland University between Raymond Bradley and Matthew Flannagan (August 10, 2010).

10. Wolterstorff, *Divine Discourse*, 204, emphasis added. The fuller quotation is this:

> The most fundamental principle, I submit, is this: the interpreter takes the stance and content of my appropriating discourse to be that of your appropriated discourse, unless there is good reason to do otherwise—such "good reason to do otherwise" consisting, at bottom, of its being improbable, on the evidence available, that by my appropriation in this situation, I would have wanted to say that and only that. At those points where the interpreter does have good reason to do otherwise, he proceeds by selecting the illocutionary stance and content which have the highest probability of being what I intended to say in this way. If the most probable of those is nonetheless improbable, then he adopts some such fall-back option as that I didn't really appropriate the discourse but only appeared to do so, that in appropriating it I said something I never intended to say, that I misunderstood the discourse I appropriated—or that *he* has misunderstood the appropriated discourse.

11. Ibid.

12. Ibid., 205.

13. Ibid.

14. See ibid., 236–38.

15. William Lane Craig, "What Price Biblical Errancy?," *Reasonable Faith* (website), http://www.reasonablefaith.org/what-price-biblical-errancy, accessed October 23, 2013.

16. Ibid., 212.

17. Ibid., 213.

18. Ibid., 214. It is important to emphasize that while a narrative may be told to make a point or even appropriated to make a point, this does not entail that it is presented as true or even asserted as true; at the same time, people can and do use real historical events to teach moral lessons (e.g., 1 Cor. 10).

19. Alternatively, one can give up the moral belief in question and conclude the command is not immoral. We discuss this option in part 3.

20. For further explorations of these themes, see Steve Cowan and Terry Wilder, eds., *In Defense of the Bible* (Nashville: B&H Academic, 2013); Craig Blomberg, *Can We Still Believe the Bible?* (Grand Rapids: Brazos Press, 2014).

21. William Lane Craig, "The Slaughter of the Canaanites," *Reasonable Faith* (website), http://www.reasonablefaith.org/slaughter-of-the-canaanites, accessed October 31, 2013.

Chapter 3: The God of the Old Testament versus the God of the New?

1. René Girard, *Things Hidden Since the Foundation of the World*, trans. Stephen Bann and Michael Metteer (Stanford, CA: Stanford University Press, 1987), 157–58.

2. Peter C. Craigie, *The Problem of War in the Old Testament* (Grand Rapids: Eerdmans, 1978), 43.

3. Ibid., 54.

4. Thomas W. Mann, *Deuteronomy* (Louisville: Westminster John Knox, 1995), 149.

5. Peter Enns, "Is Peter Enns a Marcionite?," *Rethinking Biblical Christianity* (blog), January 17, 2014, http://www.patheos.com/blogs/peterenns/2014/01/is-pete-enns-a-marcionite/. Thanks to Eric Seibert for his helpful comments on an earlier draft of this chapter (email to Paul Copan dated January 26, 2014) and also for his pointing us to Enns's blog post.

6. Eric Seibert, *The Violence of Scripture: Overcoming the Old Testament's Troubling Legacy* (Minneapolis: Fortress Press, 2012); and *Disturbing Divine Behavior* (Minneapolis: Fortress Press, 2009).

7. Eric Seibert, "When the 'Good Book' Is Bad," *Rethinking Biblical Christianity* (blog), February 1, 2013, http://www.patheos.com/blogs

/peterenns/2013/02/when-the-good-book-is-bad-challenging-the-bibles-violent-portrayals-of-god/.

8. Seibert, *The Violence of Scripture*, 9.

9. Ibid., 26, emphasis in original.

10. Ibid., 8.

11. Ibid., 9, emphasis in original.

12. Ibid., 117.

13. Eric Seibert, *Disturbing Divine Behavior*, 253; see also appendix A in Seibert's book.

14. Ibid., 57.

15. Ibid., 119.

16. Ibid., 127.

17. See Rodney Stark's *The Victory of Reason: How Christianity Led to Freedom, Capitalism, and Western Success* (New York: Random House, 2006); Alvin Schmidt, *How Christianity Changed the World* (Grand Rapids: Zondervan, 2004); Robert D. Woodberry, "The Missionary Roots of Liberal Democracy," *American Political Science Review* 106, no. 2 (2012): 244–74; Andrea Palpant Dilley, "The World the Missionaries Made," *Christianity Today* (January/February 2014): 34–41.

18. Peter Enns, "Inerrancy, However Defined, Does Not Describe What the Bible Does," in *Five Views on Biblical Inerrancy*, ed. J. Merrick and Stephen M. Garrett (Grand Rapids: Zondervan, 2013), 105.

19. Seibert, *Disturbing Divine Behavior*, 120.

20. On this theme, see Gordon Wenham, *Psalms as Torah: Reading Biblical Song Ethically* (Grand Rapids: Baker Academic, 2012), 167–79, 197–201.

21. John Stott, *Favorite Psalms* (Chicago: Moody, 1988), 121.

22. Ibid.

23. John Goldingay, *Joshua, Judges & Ruth for Everyone* (Louisville: Westminster John Knox, 2011), 3.

Part 2: Occasional Commands, Hyperbolic Texts, and Genocidal Massacres

1. Edwin Curley, "The God of Abraham, Isaac, and Jacob," in *Divine Evil? The Moral Character of the God of Abraham*, ed. Michael Bergmann, Michael J. Murray, and Michael C. Rea (New York: Oxford University Press, 2011), 62–63. See also Evan Fales, "Satanic Verses: Moral Chaos in Holy Writ," in *Divine Evil?*

2. Randal Rauser, "'Let Nothing that Breathes Remain Alive': On the Problem of Divinely Commanded Genocide," *Philosophia Christi* 11, no. 1 (2009): 27–41; and Wesley Morriston, "Did God Command Genocide? A Challenge to the Biblical Inerrantist," *Philosophia Christi* 11, no. 1 (2009): 8–26.

3. Louise Antony and Evan Fales are also contributors to *Divine Evil?*

4. Louise Antony, "Atheism as Perfect Piety," in *Is Goodness without God Good Enough? A Debate on Faith, Secularism, and Ethics*, ed. Robert K. Garcia and Nathan L. King (Lanham, MD: Rowman & Littlefield, 2008), 79.

5. Peter Millican in his debate with William Lane Craig, "Does God Exist?" University of Birmingham, United Kingdom, October 21, 2011. Available at https://www.youtube.com/watch?v =fEw8VzzXcjE.

6. Morriston, "Did God Command Genocide?," 8.

7. Raymond Bradley, "A Moral Argument for Atheism," in *The Impossibility of God*, ed. Michael Martin and Ricki Monnier (Amherst, NY: Prometheus Books, 2003), 135.

8. Christopher Hitchens, *God Is Not Great: How Religion Poisons Everything* (New York: Hachette Book Group, 2007), 101, 102.

Chapter 4: Does the Bible Command *Us* to Kill Innocent Human Beings?

1. Richard Mouw, "Biblical Revelation and Medical Decisions," in *On Moral Medicine*, ed. Stephen E. Lammers and Allen Verhey (Grand Rapids: Eerdmans, 1987), 56.

2. Alan Donagan, *The Theory of Morality* (Chicago: University of Chicago Press, 1979), 4–5.

3. The term found in 1 Cor. 6:9–10 and 1 Tim. 1:9–11 is *arsenokoitēs* (a man who has sexual relations with another man). This word *arsenokoitēs* derives from a combination of *arsenikos* ("male") and *koitē* ("bed"). This term is taken from the Greek translation of Lev. 18:22. See David F. Wright, "Homosexuals or Prostitutes? The Meaning of ΑΡΣΕΝΟΚΟΤΑΙ (1 Cor. 6:9; 1 Tim. 1:10)," *Vigiliae Christianae* 38 (1984): 126–29. See a fuller discussion of this topic in chap. 18 of Robertson McQuilkin and Paul Copan, *Introduction to Biblical Ethics* (Downers Grove, IL: InterVarsity, 2014).

4. Some contend that the Hebrew word *abomination* (*to'ebah*) in Lev. 18 applies not only to homosexual acts (v. 22; cf. 20:13) but sex with a menstruating woman (18:19), and sex during menstruation means one can be "cut off" from the people of Israel (20:18). Does this mean homosexuality is on the same level as sex with a menstruating woman? Note that apart from the constant rejection of homosexual acts in Scripture, the term *abomination* itself occurs about 112 times in the Old Testament and denotes all sorts of things and practices. It first appears as a mere description in Gen. 43:32: the Egyptians wouldn't eat with the Hebrews (something that is neither

religious nor sexual) because such a thing was *detestable* to them. The same general sense of detestability is connected to the term *abomination*. In Lev. 18:26–30, the term describes the general acts just identified, but in 18:22 and 20:13 it happens to "flag" homosexuality specifically. Furthermore, these passages concerning menstruating build on Lev. 15:19–20, 24, where any contact with a menstruating woman renders one unclean. So sexual contact would logically seem to be all the more a cause of uncleanness. And we should note that in the Mosaic law, the emission of semen and the menstruation of blood render male and female unclean because it "wastes" those fluids specifically created to give and nurture life. Arguably the prohibition against sex during a woman's period is a *protective* measure for the woman so that she does not have to submit constantly to the man's sexual demands. From Richard Hess's email correspondence with Paul Copan, August 30, 2013.

5. At this point, some critics may appeal to the teaching of Jesus in the Sermon on the Mount:

> Do not think that I have come to abolish the Law or the Prophets; I have not come to abolish them but to fulfill them. . . . Anyone who sets aside one of the least of these commands and teaches others accordingly will be called least in the kingdom of heaven, but whoever practices and teaches these commands will be called great in the kingdom of heaven. For I tell you that unless your righteousness surpasses that of the Pharisees and the teachers of the law, you will certainly not enter the kingdom of heaven. (Matt. 5:17, 19–20)

However, citing Christ's reference to the fulfillment of the law of Moses in his own person and ministry does nothing to establish that the entire law of Moses is binding on gentiles.

6. Joe M. Sprinkle, *Biblical Law and Its Relevance: A Christian Understanding and Ethical Application for Today of the Mosaic Regulations* (Lanham, MD: University Press of America, 2006), 177. Thanks to Joe Sprinkle for kindly forwarding to Matthew Flannagan a copy of the relevant chapter.

7. Ibid., 178.

8. The New Testament equivalent of peace vs. judgment is found in Jesus's words in Luke 10:5–16: for those towns refusing to receive the disciples in peace, it will be more tolerable for the divinely judged cities of Sodom, Tyre, and Sidon in the final day.

9. Sprinkle, *Biblical Law*, 176.

10. Some critics might cite God's command to Saul to "totally destroy" the Amalekites in

1 Sam. 15 as counterexamples to this claim. This, however, is mistaken. Though it is true that the command to "totally destroy" the Amalekites applies to a nation outside the Promised Land (Amalek) and is followed by centuries of provocation of Israel once it had settled in the land, this is *not* held up as a norm for the nations to follow; rather, it is a specified exception to the command God had already issued to Israel. Moreover, this exception is explicitly spelled out in the Torah alongside the laws of Deut. 20:10–15 (cf. Deut. 25:17–19).

Chapter 5: Does the Bible Portray the Canaanites as Innocent?

1. Note that it is the Creator of the world (Gen. 1–2) who creates an earthly temple, a divine-human meeting place with gold, bdellium, and onyx (2:11–12), and is the one who meets with his covenant people, a kingdom of priests (Exod. 19:6) in an earthly tabernacle. Eden's sanctuary had watery boundaries—the Euphrates and Tigris Rivers as well as rivers in "Cush" (or Ethiopia), which borders Egypt (Gen. 2:13–14). And the author of Genesis connects this same stretch of land to the place within which Abram is to settle (15:18, which mentions the Nile "river of Egypt" and "the great" Euphrates river, NASB). In general, we see a clear connection between creation and covenant: the Creator of the world is identical to the God who chooses Abraham, whose offspring become the nation of Israel, through whom salvation will come to the world. This is pointed out in chap. 4 of John Sailhamer, *Genesis Unbound: A Provocative New Look at the Creation Account* (Portland, OR: Multnomah Books, 1996).

2. We will examine below the fact that the land was possessed for a purpose.

3. David Lamb, *God Behaving Badly: Is the God of the Old Testament Angry, Racist, and Sexist?* (Downers Grove, IL: InterVarsity, 2011), 78.

4. Christopher Wright, *Old Testament Ethics for the People of God* (Downers Grove, IL: InterVarsity, 2004), 473.

5. Gary Anderson, "What about the Canaanites?," in *Divine Evil? The Moral Character of the God of Abraham*, ed. Michael Bergmann, Michael J. Murray, and Michael C. Rea (New York: Oxford University Press, 2010), 289.

6. Ibid., 281n17.

7. Ibid., 289.

8. Peter Williams, "Moral Objections to the Old Testament: Part 1: Genocide," Southeastern Seminary, Wake Forest, NC, September 2013, http://thegospelcoalition.org/blogs/justintaylor/2013/09/26/answering-moral-objections-to-the-old-testament/.

9. Lamb, *God Behaving Badly*, 78.

10. Wright, *Old Testament Ethics*, 475.

11. Anderson, "What About the Canaanites?," 280.

12. Deut. 12:29–31: "The LORD your God will cut off before you the nations you are about to invade and dispossess. But when you have driven them out and settled in their land, and after they have been destroyed before you, be careful not to be ensnared by inquiring about their gods, saying, 'How do these nations serve their gods? We will do the same.' You must not worship the LORD your God in their way, because in worshiping their gods, they do all kinds of detestable things the LORD hates. They even burn their sons and daughters in the fire as sacrifices to their gods."

13. See Jer. 7:31–32; 19:5–6; Ezek. 16:20–21; 20:31. Kings who engaged in this were roundly criticized (cf. 2 Kings 23:10); Ps. 106:38 condemns this practice as murder.

14. For a discussion, see Victor P. Hamilton, *Exodus: An Exegetical Commentary* (Grand Rapids: Baker Academic, 2011), 202–4. God demanded that the firstborn be dedicated to the Lord (Exod. 22:29). They were to be "set apart" (Exod. 13:2; Lev. 27:26; Deut. 15:19; cf. Num. 3:13). Mic. 6:7 reads: "Shall I present my firstborn for my rebellious acts, the fruit of my body for the sin of my soul?" (NASB). Although kings during Micah's time were making their children "pass through the fire," which was condemned (e.g., 2 Kings 16:3; 2 Chron. 33:6), this passage is rhetorical. As Hans Walter Wolff comments, the questioner goes from the *excessive* ("thousands of rams" and "ten thousand rivers of oil") to the *obscene* ("Shall I present my firstborn . . . ?"). What God requires is neither *excessive* nor *outrageous*. He uses a reductio ad absurdum (reducing the argument to absurdity) to show that "Yahweh does not make these kinds of demands upon his people"; rather, God has already revealed what he requires (v. 8; cp. Deut. 10:12). See Wolff, *Micah: A Commentary*, Continental Commentary (Minneapolis: Augsburg, 1990), 179; see also, Bruce K. Waltke, *A Commentary on Micah* (Grand Rapids: Eerdmans, 2007), 385–90. Yes, firstborn animals *were* sacrificed and died. But is there any indication that Israelites used to sacrifice firstborn children because Yahweh commanded and approved of it? True, the firstborn was to be set apart for God (Exod. 22:29), but this didn't imply infant sacrifice to Yahweh. Jesus himself as the firstborn (male child) was dedicated at the temple, and Luke 2:23 cites Exod. 13:2: "Every firstborn male is to be consecrated to the Lord." Furthermore, God very clearly distances himself from this practice in Jer.

7:31: "They have built the high places of Topheth, which is in the valley of the son of Hinnom, to burn their sons and their daughters in the fire, which I did not command, and it did not come into My mind" (NASB). It would seem odd to claim here that Yahweh approved such practices in his name—just not in the name of another deity. And we saw from Micah that God makes no such outrageous demands.

Some interpreters will argue that infant sacrifice to Yahweh—not pagan gods—*is* approved. Some claim that Ezek. 20:25–26 affirms this: God literally gave harmful ("not good") statutes by which Israel could not "live"—commands involving sacrificing the firstborn child in the fire. In response, first, the text indicates that God gave the *Sinai* generation "statutes [feminine plural, *huqqot*]" (e.g., Sabbath commands) by which an Israelite might "live" (20:12–13)—although Israel *rejected* these laws (v. 21). So God "withdrew [His] hand" (v. 22). The text continues with how God responded to the second (or *wilderness*) generation, giving them over to their own desires: he "gave them other statutes that were not good and laws through which they could not live" (v. 25). These "statutes" are inferior, as distinguished by the shift from the *feminine* to the *masculine* plural (*chuqqim*); this is evidenced by the sarcastic command in this context: "Go, serve everyone his idols" (20:39); to put it another way, "Go, sacrifice your children." This sarcastic "statute" to stubborn Israel to continue in idolatry and infant sacrifice is comparable to God's sarcasm in Amos 4:4: "Go to Bethel and sin; go to Gilgal and sin yet more" (cf. Micaiah's sarcastic comment to the disobedient king of Israel in 1 Kings 22:15: "Go up and succeed, and the LORD will give it into the hand of the king" (NASB). These are the kind of sarcastic "commands" that aren't "good" and by which Israel can't "live"! See John Goldingay, *Old Testament Theology: Israel's Life*, vol. 3 (Downers Grove, IL: InterVarsity, 2009), 796; also Daniel I. Block, *The Book of Ezekiel: Chapters 1–24* (Grand Rapids: Eerdmans, 1997), 636–41.

Some point to Jephthah, who sacrifices his own daughter—another example of the morally and spiritually impoverished climate portrayed in the book of Judges. Jephthah's practice reflects the influence of pagan sacrifice of children (cf. 2 Kings 3:27), particularly practices connected with the god Molech and the place of sacrifice, Topheth (Lev. 18:21; 20:2–5; 2 Kings 23:10; Jer. 32:35; cf. 2 Kings 11:1 [Ammonites]; Jer. 7:31–32; 19:5–6, 11–13). Despite his valor in battle, in the end Jephthah turns out to be more like a devout Canaanite in his worship! See Trent C. Butler,

Judges, Word Biblical Commentary 8 (Nashville: Thomas Nelson, 2009), 288–89; also David Janzen, "Why the Deuteronomist Told about the Sacrifice of Jephthah's Daughter," *Journal for the Study of the Old Testament* 29, no. 3 (2005): 339–57.

Some suggest that Mesha, the king of Moab, who sacrifices his firstborn son in battle with Israel, causes Israel to withdraw because the "fury against Israel was great" (2 Kings 3:27). Was it God's fury or fury of another sort—maybe the Moabite god Chemosh or perhaps human fury? It can't be *Chemosh* since we read a few chapters earlier of "Chemosh the detestable idol" as well as "Molech the detestable idol" (1 Kings 11:7 NASB); this doesn't square with the author's theological stance. Others claim it is the wrath of *Yahweh*, who responds positively when humans are sacrificed to him—though not to other gods. In this scenario, some claim that because Mesha sacrificed his son to Yahweh, Israel withdrew because of *God's* wrath toward Israel. This too is problematic: (a) Human sacrifice is portrayed as abhorrent in 2 Kings (16:3; 17:17; 21:6). This ritual is not divinely approved. (b) The anger or fury is better understood as human wrath. The term used here is *qetseph* ("fury, wrath"). The cognate verb of this word (*qatsaph*) is used elsewhere in 2 Kings to refer to *human* wrath or fury, not God's (5:11: "Naaman *was furious*"; 13:19: "the man of God *was angry* with him"). The scenario is that, in desperation, Mesha sacrifices his son. The result? "His troops respond to this desperate act with an [intensified fury] that leads them to victory" (Iain Provan, *1 and 2 Kings*, New International Biblical Commentary [Peabody, MA: Hendrickson, 1995], 186).

15. Rob Barrett, "Understanding Yhwh's Threats through Modern Politics—and Vice Versa," *Political Theology* 11, no. 3 (2010): 364.

16. Wesley Morriston, "Did God Command Genocide? A Challenge to the Biblical Inerrantist," *Philosophia Christi* 11, no. 1 (2009): 13.

17. Richard Hess, *Joshua: An Introduction and Commentary*, Tyndale Old Testament Commentary (Downers Grove, IL: InterVarsity, 1996), 83.

18. Ibid.

19. Ibid., 91–92.

20. Douglas S. Earl, "Reading Joshua as Christian Scripture" (PhD thesis, Durham University, 2008), 52, http://etheses.dur.ac.uk/2267/1/2267_277.pdf?UkUDh:CyT.

21. Ibid., 117.

22. Douglas Earl, *The Joshua Delusion? Rethinking Genocide in the Bible* (Eugene, OR: Cascade, 2010), 76

23. This contrasts with the pile of stones left after Achan's death that remain "to this day" (Josh. 7:26).

24. See the section on Rahab immediately above.

25. Joe M. Sprinkle, "Just War in Deuteronomy 20 and 2 Kings 3," in *Biblical Law and Its Relevance: A Christian Understanding and Ethical Application for Today of the Mosaic Regulations* (Lanham, MD: University Press of America, 2005), 180.

26. Louise Antony, "Comments on Reading Joshua," in *Divine Evil? The Moral Character of the God of Abraham*, ed. Michael Bergmann, Michael J. Murray, and Michael C. Rea (New York: Oxford University Press, 2010), 262.

27. Louise Antony, "Atheism as Perfect Piety," in *Is Goodness without God Good Enough? A Debate on Faith, Secularism, and Ethics*, ed. Robert K. Garcia and Nathan L. King (Lanham, MD: Rowman & Littlefield, 2008), 79.

28. As we discuss in the next chapter, the language of the *herem* ("utter destruction") was applied to Judah in a hyperbolic manner. For example, in Jer. 25:9, God promises: "I will bring them against this land and its inhabitants and against all the surrounding nations. I will *completely destroy* them and make them an object of horror and scorn, and an everlasting ruin." The text of Jeremiah affirms that the inhabitants who have been "completely destroyed [*haram*]" will be restored from exile after seventy years (vv. 11–12; 29:10).

Chapter 6: Thrusting Out, Driving Out, and Dispossessing the Canaanites—Not Annihilating Them

1. This also explains, as we mention later, that after Israel attacked various cities and regions, the "utterly destroyed" inhabitants reappear a few chapters later in seemingly repopulated areas.

2. See Exod. 6:1: "Then the Lord said to Moses, 'Now you will see what I will do to Pharaoh: because of my mighty hand he will let them go; because of my mighty hand he will drive them out of his country.'"

3. Glenn Miller, "How Could a God of Love Order the Massacre/Annihilation of the Canaanites?," *A Christian Think Tank* (website), February 8, 1997, updated January 2013, http://christianthinktank.com/qamorite.html, emphasis in original.

4. William Lane Craig, "Argument from Morality," *Reasonable Faith* (website), http://www.reasonablefaith.org/argument-from-morality, accessed December 20, 2013.

5. William Lane Craig, "The 'Slaughter' of the Canaanites Revisited," *Reasonable Faith* (website), http://www.reasonablefaith.org/the-slaughter-of-the-canaanites-re-visited#ixzz2SxyQPlHN, accessed May 11, 2013, emphasis in original.

6. Richard Dawkins, "Why I Refuse to Debate with William Craig," *The Guardian* (October 20, 2011), at http://www.theguardian.com/commentisfree/2011/oct/20/richard-dawkins-william-lane-craig.

7. Joe M. Sprinkle, "Just War in Deuteronomy 20 and 2 Kings 3," in *Biblical Law and Its Relevance: A Christian Understanding and Ethical Application for Today of the Mosaic Regulations* (Lanham, MD: University Press of America, 2005), 180. Sprinkle says here: "Thus the goal of *herem* was not genocide, but ethnic cleansing in which most Canaanites would have survived as refugees outside the promise [*sic*] land." We should note that the term "ethnic cleansing" has a range of connotations and associations. Sprinkle here refers to the technical distinction between ethnic cleansing and genocide. Genocide involves the intent to physically destroy a whole ethnic or religious group. Ethnic cleansing, on the other hand, attempts to render an area ethnically homogeneous by using force or intimidation to remove from a given area persons of another ethnic or religious group.

Hence, if a person forcibly expels all members of a particular religious group from a region, they do something that falls under the definition of ethnic cleansing but not genocide. Note also that by this definition, it's not actually true that ethnic cleansing is *always* wrong. A country that forcibly deported all members of the terrorist group Al Qaeda would be, strictly speaking, engaging in ethnic cleansing. See further our discussion of genocide and international law in chap. 10.

8. Ibid., 180.

Chapter 7: The Question of Genocide and the Hyperbolic Interpretation of Joshua

1. Raymond Bradley, "A Moral Argument for Atheism," in *The Impossibility of God*, ed. Michael Martin and Ricki Monnier (Amherst, NY: Prometheus Books, 2003), 137.

2. Walter Sinnott-Armstrong, "Why Traditional Theism Cannot Provide an Adequate Foundation for Morality," in *Is Goodness without God Good Enough? A Debate on Faith, Secularism, and Ethics*, ed. Robert K. Garcia and Nathan L. King (Lanham, MD: Rowman & Littlefield, 2008), 110; Richard Dawkins, *The God Delusion* (Boston: Houghton Mifflin, 2006), 292.

3. Nicholas Wolterstorff, "Reading Joshua," in *Divine Evil? The Moral Character of the God of Abraham*, ed. Michael Bergmann, Michael J. Murray, and Michael C. Rea (New York: Oxford University Press, 2010), 249.

4. Ibid.

5. Joshua comes after Deuteronomy and before Judges. These books should be read as a single narrative—a connected literary unit. For example, Josh. 24:28–31 mentions Joshua's death and burial place at Timnath-serah "in the hill country of Ephraim" (NASB), and then Judges 2:6–9 refers to Joshua's death and burial place at Timnath-heres "in the hill country of Ephraim" (NASB). That is, Joshua and Judges are literarily connected in their mention of Joshua's (a) death and (b) burial. (a) Both books state that "Joshua the son of Nun, the servant of the LORD, died" at the age of "one hundred and ten" (Josh. 24:29; Judg. 2:8). (b) Then a deliberate literary connection is made on the burial place of Joshua, using the Hebrew letter-substitution cipher known as *atbash*, in this case reversing the first and last consonants of the burial place from "-*serah*" to "-*heres*." Compare "they buried him in the territory of his inheritance in *Timnath-serah*, which *is* in the hill country of Ephraim, on the north of Mount Gaash" (Josh. 24:30 NASB) with "they buried him in the territory of his inheritance in *Timnath-heres*, in the hill country of Ephraim, north of Mount Gaash" (Judg. 2:9 NASB).

Not only this, Judges connects to 1 (and 2) Samuel (the next book in the Hebrew canon) with its reference to "the hill country of Ephraim." (Note this phrase in Josh. 17:15; 19:50; 20:7; 24:30, 33; then in Judg. 2:9; 3:27; 4:5; 7:24; 10:1; 17:1, 8; 18:2, 13; 19:1, 16, 18; and then in 1 Sam. 1:1; 9:4. The linkage of Judg. 17:1 and 19:1 with 1 Sam. 1:1 is connected by the general threefold pattern of (a) "There was a (certain) man . . ."; (b) "from the hill country of Ephraim"; (c) "and his name was _____."

6. In addition to these general claims about exterminating populations, Josh. 11:21 states, "Joshua came and wiped out the Anakim from the hill country, from Hebron, from Debir, from Anab, and from all the hill country of Judah" (NRSV). This happened *after* Joshua is already said to have killed the inhabitants in these areas in Josh. 10:30–40. Joshua 11:21 states that no Anakites were left living in Israelite territory after this campaign. In Judges 1:20 the text explicitly states that *Anakites* ("the three sons of Anak") are in Hebron.

7. While Gregory K. Beale questions the hyperbolic interpretation we have followed, we think that this approach can be sustained in light of the expanded case we have made here and throughout this portion of the book. Cf. the appendix to his booklet *The Morality of the God of the Old Testament* (Phillipsburg, NJ: P&R, 2013).

8. John Goldingay, "City and Nation," in *Old Testament Theology: Israel's Life*, vol. 3 (Downers Grove, IL: InterVarsity, 2009), 570.

9. Brevard Childs, *An Introduction to the Old Testament as Scripture* (Philadelphia: Fortress Press, 1979), 247.

10. See our discussion on this below.

11. Kenneth Kitchen, *On the Reliability of the Old Testament* (Grand Rapids: Eerdmans, 2003), 161–62, emphasis in original.

12. See Josh. 11:13: "But Israel burned none of the towns that stood on mounds except Hazor, which Joshua did burn" (NRSV).

13. Kitchen, *Reliability of the Old Testament*, 162, emphasis in original.

14. Ibid., emphasis in original.

15. Wolterstorff, "Reading Joshua," 251.

16. See Tremper Longman III, *The Book of Ecclesiastes*, New International Commentary on the Old Testament (Grand Rapids: Eerdmans, 1997).

17. Another problem with this objection is that it assumes the tensions in question are between different sources than the sources that those who edited the final form into a single sequence used. This, however, is false. Several of the same tensions Wolterstorff notes occur within literary units which source critics attribute to a single source. Consider three examples: (a) Josh. 10:20 [ESV] states that Joshua and the sons of Israel had "finished striking" and "wiped out" their enemies. Immediately thereafter, however, the text affirms that "the remnant that remained of them had entered into the fortified cities." In this context, the language of total destruction is clearly hyperbolic. (b) In the account of the battle of Ai, Joshua's troops feign a retreat; the text states that "all the men of Ai" are pressed to chase them. "Not a man was left in Ai or Bethel who did not go out after Israel. They left the city open and pursued Israel" (Josh. 8:17 ESV). Joshua lures the pursuers into a trap "so they were in the midst of Israel, some on this side, and some on that side. And Israel struck them down, until there was left none that survived or escaped" (v. 22 ESV). Then the text immediately following states: "When Israel had finished killing all the inhabitants of Ai in the open wilderness where they pursued them, and all of them to the very last had fallen by the edge of the sword, all Israel returned to Ai and struck it down with the edge of the sword" (v. 24 ESV). (c) Joshua 11:21 states: "Joshua came and wiped out the Anakim from the hill country, from Hebron, from Debir, from Anab, and from all the

hill country of Judah" (NRSV). This happened *after* Joshua is already said to have killed the inhabitants in these areas in 10:30–40. All these tensions are within the block material that makes up chapters 1–12 which typically are attributed to the same source. Further examples could be supplied.

Chapter 8: Genocide and an Argument for "Hagiographic Hyperbole"

1. Nicholas Wolterstorff, "Reading Joshua," in *Divine Evil? The Moral Character of the God of Abraham*, ed. Michael Bergmann, Michael J. Murray, and Michael C. Rea (New York: Oxford University Press, 2010), 252–53.

2. Ibid., 251.

3. Ibid., 252.

4. Ibid. The ritualized nature of the narration is also stressed by Duane L. Christensen, *Deuteronomy 1:1–21:9* (Nashville: Thomas Nelson, 2001).

5. Wolterstorff, "Reading Joshua," 252, emphasis in original.

6. Ibid., 251.

7. K. Lawson Younger Jr., *Ancient Conquest Accounts: A Study in Ancient Near Eastern and Biblical History Writing* (Sheffield: Sheffield Academic Press, 1990).

8. Ziony Zevit, *The Religions of Ancient Israel: A Synthesis of Parallactic Approaches* (London: Continuum, 2001), 114.

9. Younger, *Ancient Conquest Accounts*, 200–204.

10. Ibid., 216.

11. Ibid., 258–60.

12. Ibid., 220–25.

13. Kenneth Kitchen, *On the Reliability of the Old Testament* (Grand Rapids: Eerdmans, 2003), 170, emphasis added.

14. Ibid., emphasis added.

15. Ibid., 172. These letters are 185 and EA 186.

16. Ibid., 174–75. For further details, see Kitchen.

17. Younger states, "As the ancient historian (ancient Near Eastern, biblical, or otherwise) reconstructed 'historical' referents into a coherent description, he produced a figurative account, a 're-presenting representation.'" Younger suggests such a historian functioned as "a literary artist." He goes on to state: "Ancient Near Eastern conquest accounts are figurative in three ways: (1) the structural and ideological codes that are the apparatus for the text's production, (2) the themes or motifs that the text utilizes; and (3) the usage of rhetorical figures in the accounts." K. Lawson Younger Jr., "Judges 1 in Its Near Eastern Literary

Context," in *Faith, Tradition, and History: Old Testament Historiography and Its Ancient Near Eastern Context*, ed. A. R. Millard, J. K. Hoffmeier, and D. W. Baker (Winona Lake, IN: Eisenbrauns, 1994), 207.

18. Younger, *Ancient Conquest Accounts*, 208–11.

19. Ibid., 217.

20. Ibid., 219. For further discussion of the relationship between Joshua's long day and other ancient Near Eastern texts, see John Walton, "Joshua 10:12–15 and Mesopotamian Celestial Omen Texts," in *Faith, Tradition, and History*, 181–90.

21. Younger, *Ancient Conquest Accounts*, 211.

22. Some critics suggest that all this text states is that the army they fought that day was utterly destroyed; it doesn't mean Mitanni didn't have other forces to draw on, and total destruction of an army sometimes happens. The complete text, however, states:

The great army of Mitanni,
it is overthrown in the twinkling of an eye.
It has perished completely,
as though they never existed,
Like the ashes.

This text states that the army was overthrown in the twinkling of an eye (that is, instantaneously) and that the entire army was annihilated as though it never existed. While an army can be destroyed in a battle, for it to be instantaneously vaporized so that all trace of it, including all memories of it, ceases to exist making it like ash, is not credible in literal terms. This is clearly hyperbolic language. In fact, Younger notes that the phrase "as though they never existed" appears to be a common hyperbole—figure of speech—in Egyptian writings. See *Ancient Conquest Accounts*, 190–92. Younger also documents linguistic similarities between this hyperbole and the language in Joshua.

23. Kitchen, *Reliability of the Old Testament*, 174.

24. Younger, *Ancient Conquest Accounts*, 227.

25. Ibid., 228.

26. Ibid.

27. Kitchen, *Reliability of the Old Testament*, 174.

28. Younger, *Ancient Conquest Accounts*, 227.

29. Ibid., 245, emphasis in original.

30. Ibid., 234.

31. In Joshua, however, the object one is to fear and obey is God; in the other accounts the object is human rulers. We think this makes a substantive moral difference, the unqualified allegiance to an all-knowing, all-powerful, all-good God is very

different from unqualified obedience to a flawed and finite human ruler.

32. Younger, *Ancient Conquest Accounts*, 235.

33. Ibid., 234.

34. Ibid., 253, emphasis added.

35. Ibid., 234.

36. Ibid., 228.

37. Ibid., 246.

38. Kitchen, *Reliability of the Old Testament*, 174.

39. Ibid., emphasis in original.

40. Daniel M. Fouts, "A Defense of the Hyperbolic Interpretation of Numbers in the Old Testament," *Journal of the Evangelical Theological Society* 40, no. 3 (1997): 377–87. Another example of hyperbole in Joshua occurs in 10:2, which uses "all," stating that "all its men were mighty."

41. Richard S. Hess, "The Jericho and Ai of the Book of Joshua," in *Critical Issues in Early Israelite History*, ed. Richard S. Hess, Gerald A. Klingbeil, and Paul J. Ray Jr. (Winona Lake, IN: Eisenbrauns, 2008), 35, 42.

42. Colin Humphreys makes the suggestion that the total number of men, women, and children who left Egypt at the exodus was 20,000 rather than 2 million. Confusion comes with the term '*eleph*, he claims. The total number of Israel's fighting men (in Num. 2:32) was written as 598 + 5 *eleph* (meaning "military division" or "unit," which we take to mean a thousand). We have mixed numbers in Num. 1:46:

598 military divisions (*eleph*)
5 thousand (*eleph*) and
5 hundred and 50 men

On this interpretation, the number of military men over twenty years of age was not 603,550 but around 6,000. Humphreys arrives at this number by adding 598 men (not 598 *eleph*) to 5 *eleph*, which is 5,598; he can also read the last line, "5 hundred and 50 men," as saying "the final tally adds up to 550 men" and adds this to the 5 *eleph* getting 5,550 men. (For example, a number like 74,600 [in Num. 2:4] could be read as 74 military divisions *adding up to* 600 men.) Humphrey argues that the 603,550 number was conflated by a later scribe or editor (adding 598 *eleph* + 5 *eleph* + 550 = 603,550 men), and the original meaning of *eleph* was overlooked or forgotten.

Consider again, Humphreys argues, that "three thousand" go and fight Ai, and "thirty-six" Israelites are killed, frightened, and routed (Josh. 7:5). This would be strange if 3,000 went to fight Ai. See Colin J. Humphreys, "The Numbers in the Exodus from Egypt: A Further Appraisal," *Vetus Testamentum* 48 (1998): 196–213; and "The Numbers in the Exodus from Egypt," *Vetus Testamentum* 50, no. 3 (2000): 323–28.

Of course, Humphreys's explanation does not undermine the overall hyperbolic interpretation.

43. Iain Provan, V. Philip Long, and Tremper Longman III, *A Biblical History of Israel* (Louisville: Westminster John Knox, 2003), 281–85.

44. Kitchen, *Reliability of the Old Testament*, 174.

45. Wolterstorff, "Reading Joshua," 251.

46. K. Lawson Younger Jr., "Joshua," in *The IVP Bible Background Commentary: Old Testament*, ed. John H. Walton, Victor H. Matthews, and Mark W. Chavalas (Downers Grove IL: InterVarsity, 2000), 227.

47. Younger, *Ancient Conquest Accounts*, 227.

48. Wolterstorff, "Reading Joshua," 252.

49. Kitchen, *Reliability of the Old Testament*, 174.

50. Richard S. Hess, "The Jericho and Ai of the Book of Joshua," in *Critical Issues in Early Israelite History*, 39.

51. K. Lawson Younger Jr., *Judges/Ruth*, NIV Application Commentary (Grand Rapids: Zondervan, 2002), 26–77.

52. Nicholas Wolterstorff, "Reply to Antony," in *Divine Evil?*, 263.

53. Wolterstorff, "Reading Joshua," presented at the "My Ways Are Not Your Ways" conference (September 2009; Notre Dame, IN); this paragraph was in the paper presented at the conference but was omitted from the published version in *Divine Evil?*

Chapter 9: Objections from the Biblical Text to the Hyperbolic Interpretation

1. Wesley Morriston, "Did God Command Genocide? A Challenge to the Biblical Inerrantist," *Philosophia Christi* 11, no 1 (2009): 12.

2. Morriston refers to this passage in a footnote in ibid., n12.

3. Kenneth Kitchen, *On the Reliability of the Old Testament* (Grand Rapids: Eerdmans, 2003), 162, emphasis in original.

4. Ibid., 174.

5. Note in this regard that Saul's crime is said explicitly to be taking plunder—that is, he took livestock that was left behind by fleeing Amalekites and kept it rather than destroyed it.

6. Kitchen, *Reliability of the Old Testament*, 162.

7. See Richard A. Gabriel, *The Great Armies of Antiquity* (Westport, CT: Praeger, 2002), 6.

8. See Matthew Flannagan and Paul Copan, "Did God Really Command Genocide?," in *In Defense of the Bible*, ed. Steve Cowan and Terry Wilder (Nashville: B&H Academic, 2013). See endnote 42 in the previous chapter for details.

9. For a general overview, see Daniel M. Fouts, "Numbers, Large Numbers," in *Dictionary of Old Testament Historical Books*, ed. Bill Arnold and H. G. M. Williamson (Downers Grove, IL: InterVarsity, 2003), 750–54. The quotation cited is found on page 753.

10. James K. Hoffmeier, *Israel in Egypt: Evidence for the Authenticity of the Exodus Tradition* (New York: Oxford University Press, 1997), 41.

11. Cited in ibid.

12. Cited in ibid.

13. Ibid., 42.

14. Ralph W. Klein, *1 Samuel*, Word Biblical Commentary 10 (Waco, TX: Word, 1983), 150.

15. See Paul Copan, *Is God a Moral Monster? Making Sense of the Old Testament God* (Grand Rapids: Baker Books, 2011), 174.

16. David G. Firth, *1 & 2 Samuel* (Downers Grove, IL/Nottingham, UK: InterVarsity/Apollos, 2009), 173.

17. Hoffmeier, *Israel in Egypt*, 41–42.

18. Ibid., 42; cf. 50n148.

19. Morriston, "Did God Command Genocide?," 13, emphasis in original.

20. Aside from official theological and moral differences between Israelites and Canaanites, Israelites distinguished themselves by identifying their tribal (or village) and regional connections, for example, "Ehud the son of Gera, the Benjamite" (Judg. 3:15), "Elon the Zebulunite" (Judg. 12:11), and "Izban of Bethlehem" (Judg. 12:8). See Alan R. Millard, "Were the Israelites Really Canaanites?," in *Israel: Ancient Kingdom or Late Invention?*, ed. Daniel I. Block (Nashville: B&H Academic, 2008), 156–68.

21. Prior to the battle, the Lord tells Judah to go up first, but God doesn't promise victory (Judg. 20:18). They badly lose the battle, and God says to go up against the Benjamites again (20:23). After the second defeat, God promises that he will give Benjamin into their hands (20:28). The upshot is that *God intentionally allows Israel to lose as a judgment on the general moral decay throughout the land*. Lawson Younger notes that the tone of Yahweh is sarcastic and ultimately disapproving. See K. Lawson Younger Jr., *Judges and Ruth*, NIV Application Commentary (Grand Rapids: Zondervan, 2002), 370–76; and Daniel I. Block, *Judges, Ruth*, New American Commentary 6 (Nashville: B&H Academic, 1999), 342–45, 567–69, 570.

22. Philosopher Evan Fales interprets the command "kill all the women but save for yourselves every girl who has never slept with a man" as commanding rape—a reading he also ascribes to Deut. 21. See Evan Fales, "Satanic Verses: Moral

Chaos in Holy Writ," in *Divine Evil? The Moral Character of the God of Abraham*, ed. Michael Bergmann, Michael J. Murray, and Michael C. Rea (New York: Oxford University Press, 2010). As it turns out, a glance at the immediate context shows that the reference to a woman not sleeping with a man in the former passage was mentioned to distinguish the women in question from those who had seduced Israelite men into idolatry and adultery; it is not there to emphasize their availability for sex. Deuteronomy 21, in fact, protects female captives from being raped or sold as concubines. See Paul Copan, *Is God a Moral Monster? Making Sense of the Old Testament God* (Grand Rapids: Baker Books, 2011), 118–21, 180.

23. Jacob Milgrom, *Numbers* (Philadelphia: Jewish Publication Society, 1990), 490–91.

24. Ibid., 490.

25. Ibid.

26. Robert Alter, *The Five Books of Moses: A Translation with Commentary* (New York: W. W. Norton, 2008), 843.

27. John Goldingay, *Numbers and Deuteronomy for Everyone* (Louisville: Westminster John Knox, 2010), 84.

28. Kitchen, *Reliability of the Old Testament*, 173–74, emphasis in original.

Chapter 10: Legal and Theological Objections concerning Genocide

1. Article 2 from the Convention on the Prevention and Punishment of the Crime of Genocide, December 9, 1948, available at http://www .preventgenocide.org/law/convention/text.htm.

2. See *Prosecutor v. Goran Jelisic* Trial Judgement, sec. 62 of the ICTY proceedings at: United Nations High Commissioner for Refugees, http:// www.refworld.org/docid/4147fe474.html, accessed January 3, 2014.

3. *Jorgic v. Germany*, sec. 36, October 12, 2007. European Court of Human Rights (HUDOC), http://hudoc.echr.coe.int/sites/eng/pages/search .aspx?i=001–81608#{"itemid":["001–81608"]}, emphasis added.

4. *Prosecutor v. Krstic,* Judgement, para. 580, International Criminal Tribunal for the former Yugoslavia, August 2, 2001, http://www.icty .org/x/cases/krstic/tjug/en/krs-tj010802e-3.htm. The judgment continued: "An enterprise attacking only cultural or sociological characteristics of a human group in order to annihilate these elements which give to that group its own identity distinct from the rest of the community would not fall under the definition of genocide." See also *The Criminal Law of Genocide: Comparative and*

Contextual Aspects, ed. Ralph J. Henham and Paul Behrens (Burlington, VT: Ashgate, 2007), 83, emphasis added.

5. *Prosecutor v. Krstic*, Appeal Judgement, April 19, 2004, sec. 25, http://www.icty.org/x/cases /krstic/tjug/en/krs-tj010802e-3.htm, cited in ibid., emphasis added.

6. Cited in ibid.

7. *Prosecutor v. Kupreskic*, sec. 751, January 14, 2000, http://www.icty.org/x/cases/kupreskic /tjug/en/kup-tj000114e.pdf, emphasis added.

8. *Prosecutor v. Radislav Krstic*, Appeals Chamber, para. 8–9, April 19, 2004, emphasis added, cited in *Genocide, War Crimes, and Crimes Against Humanity* (New York: Human Rights Watch, 2006), 158.

9. Ibid., 159.

10. Eric Seibert, *The Violence of Scripture: Overcoming the Old Testament's Troubling Legacy* (Minneapolis: Fortress Press, 2012), 96.

11. Ibid., 107–8. More specifically, he highlights Paul Copan, Christopher Wright, and David Lamb.

12. See *Jorgic v. Germany*, sec. 47.

13. *Prosecutor v. Kupreskic*, sec. 751.

14. Ibid.

15. *Bosnia and Herzegovina v. Serbia and Montenegro*, 2007, available at http://www.icrc.org /customary-ihl/eng/docs/v2_cha_chapter38_rule 129_sectionc, accessed April 18, 2014.

16. *Prosecution v. Milomir Stakic*, United Nations International Tribunal, July 31, 2003, sec. 519, available at http://www.icty.org/x/cases/stakic /tjug/en/stak-tj030731e.pdf, emphasis added.

17. Cited in Henham and Behrens, *Criminal Law of Genocide*, 86.

18. Here is a sampling of such a charge by Norman Bacrac in an audio debate with Paul Copan in "Is God a Moral Monster?" *Unbelievable!*, hosted by Justin Brierley, *Premier Christian Radio* (website), April 9, 2011, http://www.premierradio.org .uk/listen/ondemand.aspx?mediaid={BD4A5C6A -9C16-417C-8C3D-5D833B5F654C}.

19. For excellent commentary on interpreting Revelation, for example, see G. K. Beale, *Revelation*, New International Greek Testament Commentary for the New Testament (Grand Rapids: Eerdmans, 2013). For a general approach to the genres of literature in Scripture, see Gordon Fee and Douglas Stuart, *How to Read the Bible for All Its Worth* (Grand Rapids: Zondervan, 2003).

20. For further discussion of the historicity of the exodus, see James K. Hoffmeier, *Israel in Egypt: Evidence for the Authenticity of the Exodus Tradition* (New York: Oxford University Press, 1997), and his *Ancient Israel in Sinai: The Evidence for the Authenticity of the Wilderness*

Tradition (New York: Oxford University Press, 2005).

21. Raymond Bradley, "Opening Argument," in a debate with Matthew Flannagan, "Is God the Source of Morality? Is It Defensible to Ground Right and Wrong in the Commands of God?," Auckland University, Auckland, New Zealand, August 2, 2010. Transcript available at http:// www.mandm.org.nz/2010/08/raymond-bradleys -opening-statement-bradley-v-flannagan-debate .html.

22. Peter van Inwagen, "Reply to Curley," in *Divine Evil? The Moral Character of the God of Abraham*, ed. Michael Bergmann, Michael J. Murray, and Michael C. Rea (New York: Oxford University Press, 2010), 84.

23. Wesley Morriston, "Did God Command Genocide? A Challenge to the Biblical Inerrantist," *Philosophia Christi* 11, no 1 (2009): 8.

24. Again, see Alan R. Millard, "Were the Israelites Really Canaanites?," in *Israel: Ancient Kingdom or Late Invention?*, ed. Daniel I. Block (Nashville: B&H Academic, 2008), 156–68.

25. For details on Canaanite theology and moral practices, see Clay Jones, "We Don't Hate Sin So We Don't Understand What Happened to the Canaanites: An Addendum to 'Divine Genocide' Arguments," *Philosophia Christi* 11, no. 1 (2009): 53–71.

Chapter 11: Divine Command Theory: Preliminary Considerations

1. One might cite the case of the Amalekites in 1 Sam. 15 as an exception to this. However, even here the law of Moses (Torah) itself appears to warrant this exception when Moses tells Israel: "When the LORD your God gives you rest from all the enemies around you in the land he is giving you to possess as an inheritance, you shall blot out the name of Amalek from under heaven" (Deut. 25:9). In other words, this exception is implicit in the Torah itself. The case of the Amalekites, therefore, was not the norm laid down in Deut. 20. It is an explicit exception to it, laid down in the text itself.

2. Kenneth Kitchen, *On the Reliability of the Old Testament* (Grand Rapids: Eerdmans, 2003), 161–62.

3. Ibid.

4. William Lane Craig, "The 'Slaughter' of the Canaanites Re-visited," *Reasonable Faith* (website), http://www.reasonablefaith.org/the -slaughter-of-the-canaanites-re-visited, accessed January 1, 2014.

5. Raymond Bradley's reply to Matthew Flannagan in "Is God the Source of Morality? Is It

Rational to Ground Right and Wrong in Commands Issued by God? A Debate between Raymond Bradley and Matthew Flannagan," Auckland, New Zealand, August 2, 2010. Bradley's reply has been published at MandM (website), August 8, 2010, http://www.mandm.org.nz/2010/08/bradleys-reply-to-matt-bradley-v-flannagan-debate.html.

6. Raymond Bradley, "A Moral Argument for Atheism," in *The Impossibility of God*, ed. Michael Martin and Ricki Monnier (Amherst, NY: Prometheus Books, 2003), 136.

7. Randal Rauser, "'Let Nothing that Breathes Remain Alive': On the Problem of Divinely Commanded Genocide," *Philosophia Christi* 11, no 1 (2009): 34.

8. Ibid.

9. Richard Dawkins, *The God Delusion* (Boston: Houghton Mifflin, 2006), 246.

10. See sec. 21 of William Lane Craig, "Post Debate Comments," in *The Craig-Curley Debate: The Existence of the Christian God*, University of Michigan, February 5, 1998, available at *Reasonable Faith* (website), http://www.reasonablefaith.org/the-existence-of-the-christian-god-the-craig-curley-debate#ixzz2haglBRhU. Philip Quinn has documented (and what Craig here reflects) a long and distinguished line of Christian interpretation. See his "The Recent Revival of Divine Command Ethics," *Philosophy and Phenomenological Research* 50 (Fall 1990): 345–65.

11. Craig, "Post Debate Comments."

12. Craig has presented his position largely in popular writings and debates; the argument given here is a reconstruction of what we believe is the argument in these writings and debates.

13. William Lane Craig and J. P. Moreland, *Philosophical Foundations of a Christian Worldview* (Downers Grove, IL: IVP Academic, 2003), 531.

14. Quinn, "Recent Revival of Divine Command Ethics."

15. Stephen J. Grabill, *Rediscovering Natural Law in Reformed Theological Ethics* (Grand Rapids: Eerdmans, 2006), 172–74.

16. William Lane Craig, "The Craig-Curley Debate: The Existence of the Christian God" (Post-Debate Comments, sec. 21). Available at: http://www.leaderu.com/offices/billcraig/docs/craig-curley12.html.

17. Consider, for example, the cessationist view that prophetic utterances ceased with the close of the apostolic period held by people like B. B. Warfield, J. Gresham Machen, F. N. Lee, Richard B. Gaffin Jr., John F. MacArthur, and Daniel B. Wallace.

18. In discussion of the morality of terrorism, Igor Primoratz uses language stating that it is *almost absolutely wrong* to kill noncombatants. By this he means that, while it is possible in principle for there to be extreme cases where deliberately killing noncombatants is morally permissible, in practice these situations are so rare or unlikely to occur that in practice no case of terrorism so far has been morally justified—and that any resort to it in the future is extremely unlikely to be. In practice, this means Primoratz's view does not differ from an absolute prohibition.

19. Craig and Moreland, *Philosophical Foundations*, 531.

Chapter 12: The Divine Command Theory of Obligation: What It Is—and Is Not

1. Robert M. Adams, *The Virtue of Faith* (New York: Oxford University Press, 1987), 145.

2. Peter Geach, "The Moral Law and the Law of God," in *God and the Soul*, ed. Peter Geach (London: Routledge, 1969), 117.

3. See, for example, Glenn Peoples, "Is There an Echo in Here? Critiques of God-based Ethics," *Right Reason* (website), http://www.rightreason.org/articles/philosophy/echo.pdf, accessed January 1, 2014.

4. Mark C. Murphy, "Theological Voluntarism as a Degenerating Research Program," Australasian Philosophy of Religion Association Conference, Auckland, New Zealand, July 2011.

5. Philip L. Quinn, *Divine Commands and Moral Requirements* (Oxford: Oxford University Press, 1978); "An Argument for Divine Command Theory," in *Christian Theism and the Problems of Philosophy*, ed. Michael Beaty (Notre Dame, IN: University of Notre Dame Press, 1990), 289–302; "The Recent Revival of Divine Command Ethics," *Philosophy and Phenomenological Research* 50 (Fall 1990): 345–65; "The Primacy of God's Will in Christian Ethics," *Philosophical Perspectives* 6 (1992): 493–513; "Divine Command Theory," in *Blackwell Guide to Ethical Theory*, ed. Hugh LaFollette (Cambridge: Blackwell, 2000), 53–73; "Theological Voluntarism," in *The Oxford Handbook of Ethical Theory*, ed. David Copp (New York: Oxford University Press, 2006), 63–90.

6. Robert Adams, "Divine Command Meta-Ethics Modified Again," *Journal of Religious Ethics* 7, no. 1 (1979): 66–79; *Finite and Infinite Goods* (New York: Oxford University Press, 1999).

7. John Hare, *God's Call: Moral Realism, God's Commands, and Human Autonomy* (Grand Rapids: Eerdmans, 2001); *God and Morality: A Philosophical History* (Oxford: Blackwell, 2007).

8. William Alston, "Some Suggestions for Divine Command Theorists," in *Christian Theism and the Problems of Philosophy*, 303–26.

9. William Lane Craig, "This Most Gruesome of Guests," in *Is Goodness without God Good Enough? A Debate on Faith, Secularism, and Ethics*, ed. Robert K. Garcia and Nathan L. King (Lanham, MD: Rowman & Littlefield, 2008), 172; *Philosophical Foundations of a Christian Worldview* (Downers Grover, IL: InterVarsity, 2003), 529–32.

10. C. Stephen Evans, *Kierkegaard's Ethic of Love: Divine Commands and Moral Obligations* (New York: Oxford University Press, 2004).

11. Edward Wierenga, *The Nature of God: An Inquiry into the Divine Attributes* (Ithaca, NY: Cornell University Press, 1989), 215–27; "Utilitarianism and the Divine Command Theory," *American Philosophical Quarterly* 21 (1984): 311–18; "A Defensible Divine Command Theory," *Nous* 17 (1983): 387–408.

12. Matthew Carey Jordan, "Theistic Ethics: Not as Bad as You Think," *Philo* 12, no. 1 (Spring/Summer 2009): 31–45.

13. Janine Marie Idziak, "Divine Commands Are the Foundation of Morality," *Contemporary Debates in Philosophy of Religion* (Malden, MA: Blackwell, 2004), 290–98.

14. William Wainwright, *Religion and Morality* (Aldershot: Ashgate, 2005).

15. William Mann, "Theism and the Foundations of Ethics," in *The Blackwell Guide to Philosophy of Religion*, ed. William Mann (Oxford: Blackwell, 2005).

16. Thomas Carson, *Value and the Good Life* (Notre Dame, IN: Notre Dame University Press, 2000).

17. Alvin Plantinga, "Naturalism, Theism, Obligation and Supervenience," Faith and Philosophy 27, no. 3 (2010): 247–72.

18. David Baggett and Jerry L. Walls, *Good God: The Theistic Foundations of Morality* (New York: Oxford University Press, 2011).

19. Mark C. Murphy, "Theism, Atheism, and the Explanation of Moral Value," in *Is Goodness without God Good Enough?*, 127; see also Craig's response, "This Most Gruesome of Guests," in *Is Goodness without God Good Enough?*, 169.

20. In a discussion of "the definition of God" on his website, Craig states: "The best definition of God *as a descriptive term* is, I think, St. Anselm's: the greatest conceivable being. As Anselm observed, if you could think of anything greater than God, then *that* would be God! The very idea of God is of a being than which there cannot be a greater," "Defining 'God'," *Reasonable Faith*, http://www.reasonablefaith.org /defining-god#ixzz2cYiEQtoz, accessed March 20, 2014. Craig goes on to state that in his defenses of a divine command theory, he is using this definition.

21. In a debate with William Lane Craig, atheist Michael Tooley agrees to a similar definition: "I want to begin by briefly indicating how I'm going to understand the term 'God' in this next discussion. My view is that the question one should ask is, 'What characteristics should an object possess in order to be an appropriate object of religious attitudes?' I think that the answer to that is that a being, to be characterizable as God in that sense, should be a personal being, should be a being that is morally perfect, a being that is omnipotent, and a being that is omniscient." "Does God Exist? The Craig-Tooley Debate." Available at http://www.reasonablefaith.org/does-god-exist -the-craig-tooley-debate. See also Michael Tooley, "Does God Exist?" in *The Knowledge of God*, by Michael Tooley and Alvin Plantinga (Malden, MA: Blackwell, 2008), 72.

22. "Does God Exist? A Debate between William Lane Craig and Stephen Law," Westminster Central Hall, London, United Kingdom, October 2011. Transcript available at http://www.reason ablefaith.org/does-god-exist-the-craig-law-debate #ixzz2bw6oJM1x. The quotation from Peter Millican comes from "The Devil's Advocate," *Cogito* 3 (1989): 193, emphasis in original.

23. William Lane Craig, "Closing Statement," in "Is the Foundation of Morality Natural or Supernatural? A Debate between Sam Harris and William Lane Craig," University of Notre Dame, Notre Dame, IN, April 7, 2011. Transcript available at MandM (website), http://www.mandm .org.nz/2011/05/transcript-sam-harris-v-william -lane-craig-debate-%E2%80%9Cis-good-from -god%E2%80%9D.html, accessed July 29, 2013.

24. Below, we note Erik Wielenberg's argument in particular. He insists that a divine command theory entails the (false) claim that God could arbitrarily command something unjust. We respond to him in chap. 14, and we deal with a range of arbitrariness objections in chaps. 13 and 14.

25. The term "modified divine command theory" is used to distinguish these divine command theories from traditional versions, which identified the *good* (value) with God's commands (the *right*)—that is, duty or obligation—but didn't emphasize God as loving and just by nature. Calling this the "so called" modified divine command theory is because it is debatable whether anyone has ever held a "traditional divine command theory." Janine Marie Idziak notes that historical defenders of divine command theories typically

limited their theories to the obligatory, though these thinkers still believed God to be loving and just in his character. See Idziak's essay, "In Search of Good Positive Reasons for an Ethics of Divine Commands: A Catalogue of Arguments," *Faith and Philosophy* 6, no. 1 (1989): 60.

26. Robert Adams, *Finite and Infinite Goods* (New York: Oxford University Press, 1999); "Divine Command Meta-Ethics Modified Again"; "Divine Commands and the Social Nature of Obligation," *Faith and Philosophy* 4 (1987): 262–75. See also Alston, "Some Suggestions for Divine Command Theorists."

27. Adams, "Divine Command Meta-Ethics Modified Again," 76, emphasis in original.

28. The similarities to Craig are obvious, and are borne out by the fact that Craig himself claims that he is defending the divine command theory as proposed and defended by William Alston. See William Lane Craig, "This Most Gruesome of Guests," 186. Alston himself claims to be defending a version of the divine command theory "presented in Robert Adams's latest paper on the subject": "What Euthyphro Should Have Said," in *Philosophy of Religion: A Reader and Guide*, ed. William Lane Craig (Edinburgh: Edinburgh University Press, 2002), 284.

It should be noted that Craig's formulation does differ from Adams's in some respects. None of these are relevant to our discussion. While both identify wrongness with the property of being contrary to God's commands, Adams adds the qualification that these commands come from a loving God. In some places, Craig follows a formulation similar to Adams's, claiming that "our duties are constituted by the commands of a loving and just God"; but in other places he speaks solely of God. This difference is, however, not terribly significant when one realizes that Craig uses the word "God" as a title for "the greatest conceivable being," and Craig understands any being which meets this title to be essentially loving and just.

Another difference is that Craig understands God's commands as flowing "necessarily" from God's nature. Adams, on the other hand, grants that "some conclusions about what [God] would not command follow logically or analytically from the concept of a loving God"—the command that one ought "not practice cruelty for its own sake," for instance. But in other cases, some of God's commands are not necessary but contingent on particular and diverse "preferences" and purposes God has, though still compatible with love and certainly with an intrinsically authoritative deity. See Robert Adams, "Moral Arguments for Theistic Belief," in *Rationality and Religious Belief*,

ed. C. F. Delaney (Notre Dame, IN: University of Notre Dame Press, 1979), 116–21. As far as we can tell, little of what we discuss in this book turns on these differences.

29. These specifications or qualifications are those used by Adams, Alston, and Evans in both points mentioned in this section.

30. Quinn, "Argument for Divine Command Theory," 291.

31. Evans uses this example in his *Kierkegaard's Ethic of Love*, 16.

32. William Lane Craig, "Opening Statement," in "Is the Foundation of Morality Natural or Supernatural? A Debate between Sam Harris and William Lane Craig," University of Notre Dame, Notre Dame, IN, April 7, 2011. Transcript available at MandM (website), http://www.mandm .org.nz/2011/05/transcript-sam-harris-v-william -lane-craig-debate-%E2%80%9Cis-good-from -god%E2%80%9D.html, accessed July 29, 2013.

33. The thinkers Craig has in mind are Hilary Putnam, "The Meaning of Meaning," in *Mind, Language, and Reality: Philosophical Papers*, vol. 2, ed. Hilary Putnam (Cambridge: Cambridge University Press, 1975), 215–75; Keith Donnellan, "Reference and Definite Descriptions," *Philosophical Review* 75 (1966): 281–304; Saul Kripke, "Naming and Necessity," in *The Semantics of Natural Languages*, ed. Donald Davidson and Gilbert Harman (Dordrecht: Reidel, 1972), 253–355, 763–69.

34. For example Louise Antony writes, "'Good' for the divine command theorist is synonymous with 'commanded by God'; we are supposed to lack any conception of what it would be for an act to be good or bad that's independent of our knowledge of what God has commanded." "Atheism as Perfect Piety," in *Is Goodness without God Good Enough?*, 72. Interestingly, Antony provides no citation of any divine command theorist, contemporary or historical, who has said this.

35. Harry Gensler, *Ethics: A Contemporary Introduction* (London: Routledge, 1988), 39.

36. Patrick H. Nowell-Smith, "Morality: Religious and Secular," in *Christian Ethics and Contemporary Philosophy*, ed. Ian T. Ramsey (London: SCM Press, 1966), 97.

37. James W. Cornman and Keith Lehrer, *Philosophical Problems and Arguments* (New York: Macmillan, 1979), 429.

38. Antony, "Atheism as Perfect Piety," 67–84.

39. Walter Sinnott-Armstrong writes: "The divine command theory makes morality unknowable [because such theories entail that] we cannot know what is morally wrong, if we cannot know what God commanded . . . [and] we have no sound way to determine what God commanded." "Why

Traditional Theism Cannot Provide an Adequate Foundation for Morality," in *Is Goodness without God Good Enough?*, 109. For a fuller elaboration and critique of Sinnott-Armstrong's conflation of the question of whether one can believe something is wrong without first believing in God, and the question of whether moral obligations are constituted or identified with divine commands, see Matthew Flannagan, "Is Ethical Naturalism More Plausible than Supernaturalism? A Reply to Walter Sinnott-Armstrong," *Philo* 15, no. 1 (2012): 19–37.

40. Paul Kurtz, "The Kurtz/Craig Debate: Is Goodness without God Good Enough?" in *Is Goodness without God Good Enough?*, 26.

41. Ibid., 33. Note the obvious slippage in Kurtz's statement: he goes from the claim that *belief in God* is unnecessary to live a moral life, to the claim that *God* is unessential to morality. This is like arguing that because many people can fly successfully in planes without knowing about or believing in the laws of aerodynamics that the laws of aerodynamics are not essential for flight.

42. William Lane Craig, "The Indefensibility of Theistic Meta-Ethical Foundations for Morality," *Foundations* 5 (1997): 9.

43. Craig, "This Most Gruesome of Guests," 168.

44. Craig, "The Kurtz/Craig Debate," 29, emphasis in original.

45. Mark Murphy, a critic of divine command theories, notes this oddity: "If Kurtz wants to say that the moral goodness that is available to humans even without belief in God is good enough for leading generally morally decent lives, lives that morally sensible human beings would look upon with some admiration, then we should acknowledge the truth of what Kurtz says and move on. (This is what Craig rightly recommends, several times, though without seeming effect.)" See Murphy, "Theism, Atheism, and the Explanation of Moral Value," 119.

46. Jerry Coyne, "As Atheists Know, You Can Be Good without God," *USA Today* website, August 1, 2011, http://usatoday30.usatoday.com/news/opinion/forum/2011-07-31-atheism-morality-evolution-religion_n.htm. It is also worth noting that the claim that atheists display more moral behavior (statistically) than theists has been carefully discussed by Walter Sinnott-Armstrong, *Morality without God* (New York: Oxford University Press, 2009). Sinnott-Armstrong suggests these claims are, at best, inconclusive.

One misleading factor in surveys that "show" more moral behavior from secularists is that terms such as "religious believer" or "Christian" are mere labels for many. Further clarification is needed (e.g., looking at regular church attendance—not something many nominal Christians are engaged in). See Bradley Wright, *Christians Are Hate-Filled Hypocrites. . . and Other Lies You've Been Told* (Minneapolis: Bethany House, 2010). On the huge difference that religious (primarily Christian) devotion makes in the lives of America's youth today, see Christian Smith and Melina L. Denton, *Soul Searching: The Religious and Spiritual Lives of American Teenagers* (Oxford: Oxford University Press, 2009). We should add, too, that many "secularists" live in places strongly influenced by the Jewish-Christian tradition; it is difficult to separate the *benefits* of the Christian faith from the historical Christian roots. See Alvin Schmidt, *How Christianity Changed the World* (Grand Rapids: Zondervan, 2004); Robert D. Woodberry, "The Missionary Roots of Liberal Democracy," *American Political Science Review* 106, no. 2 (May 2012): 244–74.

47. See, for example, Philip Quinn, "Religious Obedience and Moral Autonomy," *Religious Studies* 11 (1975): 265–81.

48. William Paley, *The Principles of Moral and Political Philosophy* (Indianapolis: Liberty Fund, 2002), 33–61; C. D. Broad, "Berkeley's Theory of Morals," *Revue Internationale de Philosophie*, vols. 23–24 (1953): 72–86; Stephen Darwall, "Berkeley's Moral and Political Philosophy," in *The Cambridge Companion to Berkeley*, ed. Kenneth P. Winkler (Cambridge: Cambridge University Press, 2005), 311–38.

49. Alvin Plantinga suggests something like this in his "Reason and Belief in God," in *Faith and Rationality*, ed. Alvin Plantinga and Nicholas Wolterstorff (Notre Dame, IN: University of Notre Dame Press, 1983), 80; also Alvin Plantinga, *Warranted Christian Belief* (New York: Oxford University Press, 2000), 148.

50. Wesley Morriston, "God and the Ontological Foundations of Morality," *Religious Studies* 48 (2012): 16.

51. Wesley Morriston, "The Moral Obligations of Reasonable Non-believers: A Special Problem for Divine Command Meta-ethics," *International Journal for Philosophy of Religion* 65, no. 1 (2009): 3, emphasis in original.

52. Elsewhere in the article, Morriston distinguishes between a "divine will" version of divine command theory (right and wrong are identified with God's will) and Adams's divine command theory which involves "speech acts." Morriston accepts that the divine will version is immune from the objection he raises. However, later in the same article Morriston suggests that a divine will account of divine command theory involves the idea that God's will is known to human beings,

even if it is not known as God's will. The problem with Morriston's view is this: it is unclear to us how a theory holding that morality is identified with God's will and where God's will is known to all actually differs from Adams's divine command theory. After all, *Adams himself* affirms that when he speaks of a *divine command*, he means *God's revealed will*. See Adams, "Divine Command Meta-Ethics Modified Again," 76.

53. Morriston puts the word "heard" in scare quotes because he recognizes, quite correctly, that a divine command theory does not require—nor does it typically affirm—that people must hear an audible divine voice in order to receive a divine command. On many accounts, one knows what God commanded through the normal methods by which people become aware of moral obligations and duties. To "hear" a divine command, one *only need become aware* that one is morally prohibited from doing something.

54. Cited in Eusebius, *Ecclesiastical History* 6.25.14.

55. Morriston, "Moral Obligations of Reasonable Non-believers," 5–6.

56. This example is inspired by Matthew Flannagan's experience of living with Canadian tourists in the 1980s. They continually mistakenly referred to the Ministry of Transport as the police.

57. For a fuller critique of Morriston's argument along similar lines, see Glenn Peoples, "The Epistemological Objection to Divine Command Ethics," *Philosophia Christi* 13, no 2 (2011): 389–401.

Chapter 13: Arbitrary Divine Commands? The Euthyphro Dilemma

1. We say "typically," as some of the more recent criticisms of divine command theories seem to acknowledge that the Euthyphro dilemma has been addressed adequately by divine command theorists. Mark Murphy, for example, criticizes Adams's theory not in terms of the Euthyphro dilemma; rather, he argues that a theory of non-moral obligation that Adams relies on is false. See Mark Murphy, *God and the Moral Law: On the Theistic Explanation of Morality* (Oxford: Oxford University Press, 2011), 124–33, 166–72. Wolterstorff emphasizes a version of the prior duties objection. See Nicholas Wolterstorff, *Justice: Rights and Wrongs* (Princeton: Princeton University Press, 2010), 264–84.

2. Plato, *Euthyphro* 10a; also 4e. See Nicholas P. White, "Plato's Metaphysical Epistemology," in *The Cambridge Companion to Plato*, ed. Richard Kraut (Cambridge: Cambridge University Press, 1992), 278.

3. Plato, *Euthyphro* 10d–11b. See T. H. Irwin, "Plato: The Intellectual Background," in *Cambridge Companion to Plato*, ed. Richard Kraut (Cambridge: Cambridge University Press, 1992), 54.

4. James Rachels and Stuart Rachels, *The Elements of Moral Philosophy*, 5th ed. (New York: McGraw Hill, 2007), 56, emphasis in original. Note: James Rachels died in 2003, and the fifth edition of his work was published posthumously, edited by his son; hence, we use the reference to only James Rachels in the text, as he was the sole author of the original edition.

5. Ibid.

6. Ibid., emphasis in original.

7. Ibid.

8. This division is suggested by Mark C. Murphy, "Theological Voluntarism," in the *Stanford Encyclopedia of Philosophy*, August 12, 2012, http://plato.stanford.edu/entries/voluntarism-theological/.

9. Russ Shafer-Landau, "Introduction to Part IV," in *Ethical Theory: An Anthology*, ed. Russ Shafer-Landau (Malden, MA: Blackwell, 2007), 237.

10. Ibid., 238, emphasis added.

11. Some of the points here come from Stephen Sullivan, "Arbitrariness, Divine Commands, and Morality," *International Journal of Philosophy of Religion* 33, no. 1 (1993): 37–39; see also William Wainwright, *Religion and Morality* (Aldershot: Ashgate, 2005), 91.

12. These points are made cogently by Sullivan, "Arbitrariness, Divine Commands, and Morality." See also Matthew Flannagan, "Is Ethical Naturalism More Plausible than Supernaturalism? A Reply to Walter Sinnott-Armstrong," *Philo* 15, no. 1 (2012): 19–37.

13. We thank Graham Oppy for drawing our attention to this line of response.

14. Shafer-Landau, "Introduction to Part IV," 237.

15. C. Stephen Evans, *God and Moral Obligation* (Oxford: Oxford University Press, 2013), 9.

16. Robert Adams, *Finite and Infinite Goods: A Framework for Ethics* (New York: Oxford University Press, 1999), 238.

17. J. L. Mackie, *The Miracle of Theism* (New York: Oxford University Press, 1982), 114–15.

18. See Ralph Cudworth, *A Treatise concerning Eternal and Immutable Morality; with, A Treatise of Freewill*, Cambridge Texts in the History of Philosophy (Cambridge: Cambridge University Press, 1996).

19. This response comes from Mark Schroeder, "Cudworth on Normative Explanations,"

Journal of Ethics and Social Philosophy 1, no. 3 (October 2005): 1–27.

20. Ibid., 3.

21. Schroeder explains: "So if the Cudworth argument successfully shows that not all obligations can be explained by God's commands, then it looks like it must also show that not all obligations can be explained by self-interest, by hypothetical contracts, by what would maximize the good, by what is in accordance with rules no one could reasonably reject, or any other source. If this implication of the Cudworth argument does not grip you, then I do not know what could." Ibid.

22. This is argued by Schroeder in ibid., 5–7.

23. Ibid., 6.

24. Robert Merrihew Adams, "Prospects for a Metaethical Argument for Theism: A Response to Stephen J. Sullivan," *Journal of Religious Ethics* 21, no. 2 (1993): 318.

25. Michael Tooley, "Opening Statement," "A Classic Debate on the Existence of God"— a debate between Michael Tooley and William Lane Craig, University of Colorado, Boulder, CO, November 1994. Transcript available at *Reasonable Faith* (website), http://www.reasonablefaith.org/does-god-exist-the-craig-tooley-debate#section_2, accessed March 21, 2009.

26. Robert K. Garcia and Nathan L. King, "Introduction," in *Is Goodness without God Good Enough? A Debate on Faith, Secularism, and Ethics*, ed. Robert K. Garcia and Nathan L. King (Lanham, MD: Rowman & Littlefield, 2008), 11, emphasis in original.

27. David O. Brink, "The Autonomy of Ethics," in *The Cambridge Companion to Atheism*, ed. Michael Martin (Cambridge: Cambridge University Press, 2007), 152.

Chapter 14: Other Euthyphro-Related Objections

1. Wesley Morriston, "What If God Commanded Something Terrible? A Worry for Divine-Command Meta-ethics," *Religious Studies* 45 (2009): 251.

2. This acknowledgment of the compatibility of omnipotence and essential goodness comes from both the atheistic side and the theistic side. Erik Wielenberg, "Omnipotence Again," *Faith and Philosophy* 17, no. 1 (2000): 26–47; Thomas Morris, *Anselmian Explorations: Essays in Philosophical Theology* (Notre Dame, IN: University of Notre Dame Press, 1987), 70–75.

3. Thomas Flint and Alfred J. Freddoso, "Maximal Power," in *The Existence and Nature of God*, ed. Alfred J. Freddoso (Notre Dame, IN: University of Notre Dame Press, 1983).

4. Wesley Morriston, "Omnipotence and Necessary Moral Perfection: Are They Compatible?" *Religious Studies* 37 (2001): 158.

5. Ibid.

6. Morriston, "What If God Commanded Something Terrible?," 252.

7. Walter Sinnott-Armstrong, "Why Traditional Theism Cannot Provide an Adequate Foundation for Morality," in *Is Goodness without God Good Enough? A Debate on Faith, Secularism, and Ethics*, ed. Robert K. Garcia and Nathan L. King (Lanham, MD: Rowman & Littlefield, 2008), 110.

8. Ibid., 106.

9. Walter Sinnott-Armstrong, *Morality without God* (New York: Oxford University Press, 2009), 104.

10. Here is the fuller quotation: "In standard modal logics, any counterfactual with an impossible antecedent is true. . . . Results like this are widely regarded as regrettable, insofar as one looks to formal modal logic to reconstruct ordinary reasoning with counterfactuals. I'm going with ordinary intuitions, which do not treat all counterfactuals with impossible antecedents as true." Louise Antony, "Atheism as Perfect Piety," in *Is Goodness without God Good Enough?*, 82.

11. This has been recently argued by Alexander R. Pruss, "Another Step in Divine Command Dialectics," *Faith and Philosophy* 26, no. 4 (October 2009): 432–39.

12. Morriston has recently argued that the following counterfactual is true. Just as it is true that "if—per impossibile—a completely truthful and omniscient being said that two-plus-two is five then two-plus-two would be five," then God could also command moral atrocities.

If that is understood, then it really doesn't matter to Craig's position whether it's impossible for a perfect being to command such a thing. Why? Because if a perfect being commanded it, the being would have a morally sufficient reason for doing so; and if—per impossibile, perhaps—a perfect being had a morally sufficient reason for commanding us to eat our children, we should do it. If I am right about this, then Craig's divine command theory escapes refutation—not for the reason he gives, but rather because the alarming-sounding counterpossibles implied by it turn out to be true! Wesley Morriston, "God and the Ontological Foundation of Morality," *Religious Studies* 48 (2012): 20–21.

13. Erik J. Wielenberg, *Value and Virtue in a Godless Universe* (Cambridge: Cambridge University Press, 2005), 49. In brackets we insert

"though impossible" for the Latin *per impossibile* ("as is impossible"), which is rendered by Wielenberg as "per impossible."

14. Sam Harris, "First Rebuttal," in "Is the Foundation of Morality Natural or Supernatural? A Debate between Sam Harris and William Lane Craig," University of Notre Dame, Notre Dame, IN, April 7, 2011. Transcript available at MandM (website), http://www.mandm.org.nz/2011/05/transcript-sam-harris-v-william-lane-craig-debate-%E2%80%9Cis-good-from-god%E2%80%80%9D.html, accessed July 29, 2013; the debate transcript can also be found here at William Lane Craig's Reasonable Faith website: http://www.reasonablefaith.org/is-the-foundation-of-morality-natural-or-supernatural-the-craig-harris.

15. Ibid.

16. Ibid.

17. This exchange occurred during the Q&A of the debate, "Is the Foundation of Morality Natural or Supernatural?" The Q&A of this debate is not available with the online transcripts, but the videotaped version can be viewed online at "The God Debate II: Harris vs. Craig," YouTube (website), April 12, 2011, http://www.youtube.com/watch?v=yqaHXKLRKzg.

18. James Rachels and Stuart Rachels, *The Elements of Moral Philosophy*, 5th ed. (New York: McGraw Hill, 2007), 56.

19. It should also be noted that the claim that God does not have obligations has been defended on grounds other than a divine command theory. See, for example, William Alston, "Some Suggestions for Divine Command Theorists," in *Christian Theism and the Problems of Philosophy*, ed. Michael Beaty (Notre Dame, IN: University of Notre Dame Press, 1990).

20. William Lane Craig, *Philosophical Foundations of a Christian World View* (Downers Grove, IL: InterVarsity, 2003), 529. Similarly, in an essay, William Alston defends the claim that God has no obligations. He notes: "We can hardly suppose that God is obliged to love his creatures because he commands himself to do so." William Alston, "Response to Zagzebski," *Perspectives on the Philosophy of William P. Alston*, ed. Heather D. Battaly, Michael P. Lynch, and William P. Alston (Lanham, MD: Rowman & Littlefield, 2005), 204.

21. Peter van Inwagen, *The Problem of Evil* (Oxford: Oxford University Press, 2008), 161n6. This phrase *aliquid quo nihil maius cogitari possit* is Anselm's famous definition of God in his work, the *Proslogion*.

22. Mark Murphy notes this in his essay on divine command theory, "Theological Voluntarism" (*Stanford Encyclopedia of Philosophy*,

August 12, 2012, http://plato.stanford.edu/entries/voluntarism-theological/, #3.1):

Granting to some extent the force of the objection, we can say, on this view, that God's moral goodness cannot consist in God's adhering to what is morally obligatory. But there are other ways to assess God morally other than in terms of the morally obligatory. Adams, for example, holds that God should be understood as benevolent and as just, and indeed concedes that his theological voluntarist account of obligation as the divinely commanded is implausible unless God is thus understood (Adams 1999 [*Finite and Infinite Goods: A Framework for Ethics* (Oxford: Oxford University Press)], pp. 253–255). The ascription to God of these moral virtues is entirely consistent with his theological voluntarism, for his theological voluntarism is not meant to provide any account of the moral virtues. One can hold that God's moral goodness involves supereminent possession of the virtues, at least insofar as those virtues do not presuppose weakness and vulnerability. God is good because God is supremely just, loyal, faithful, benevolent, and so forth. It seems that ascribing to God supereminent possession of these virtues would be enough to account for God's supreme moral goodness: it is, after all, in such terms that God is praised in the Psalms.

23. Ibid.

24. Peter van Inwagen, *The Problem of Evil*, The Gifford Lectures Delivered in the University of St Andrews in 2003 (New York: Oxford University Press, 2006), 161.

25. Harris, "First Rebuttal."

26. William Lane Craig, "Opening Speech," in "Is the Foundation of Morality Natural or Supernatural? A Debate between Sam Harris and William Lane Craig," University of Notre Dame, Notre Dame, IN, April 7, 2011. Transcript available at MandM (website), http://www.mandm.org.nz/2011/05/transcript-sam-harris-v-william-lane-craig-debate-%E2%80%80%9Cis-good-from-god%E2%80%80%9D.html, accessed April 2, 2014.

27. For a discussion and rebuttal of the standard objections to divine command theories, see the following by Philip L. Quinn: *Divine Commands and Moral Requirements* (Oxford: Oxford University Press, 1978); "Divine Command Theory," in *Blackwell Guide to Ethical Theory*, ed. Hugh LaFollette (Cambridge: Blackwell, 2000), 53–73; "Theological Voluntarism," in *The Oxford Handbook of Ethical Theory*, ed. David

Copp (New York: Oxford University Press, 2006), 63–90. See also the following by Edward Wierenga: *The Nature of God: An Inquiry into the Divine Attributes* (Ithaca, NY: Cornell University Press, 1989), 215–27; "Utilitarianism and the Divine Command Theory," *American Philosophical Quarterly* 21 (1984): 311–18; "A Defensible Divine Command Theory," *Nous* 17 (1983): 387–408. See also David Baggett and Jerry L. Walls, *Good God: The Theistic Foundations of Morality* (New York: Oxford University Press, 2011); Matthew Flannagan, "The Premature Dismissal of Voluntarism," *Colloquium: The Australian and New Zealand Theological Review* 42 (2010): 38–66.

Chapter 15: Can One Coherently Claim That God Commanded the Killing of Innocents?

1. C. S. Cowles, "Response to Eugene H. Merrill," in *Show Them No Mercy: Four Views on God and Canaanite Genocide*, ed. Stanley N. Gundry (Grand Rapids: Zondervan, 2003), 100.
2. Eric Seibert, *Disturbing Divine Behavior* (Minneapolis: Fortress Press, 2009), 74.
3. Raymond Bradley, "A Moral Argument for Atheism," in *The Impossibility of God*, ed. Michael Martin and Ricki Monnier (Amherst, NY: Prometheus Books, 2003), 143.
4. Robert M. Adams, *Finite and Infinite Goods: A Framework for Ethics* (New York: Oxford University Press, 1999), 250.
5. Ibid., 256.
6. Raymond Bradley, "Opening Statement," in "Can a Loving God Send People to Hell?," debate with William Lane Craig, Simon Fraser University, Vancouver, BC, 1994; transcripts available at http://www.reasonablefaith.org/site/News2?page=NewsArticle&id=5301, accessed January 14, 2011.
7. Adams, *Finite and Infinite Goods*, 256, emphasis added.
8. Here is the full quotation by Robert Adams: "The property that is wrongness should belong to those types of action that are thought to be wrong—or at least it should belong to an important central group of them. It would be unreasonable to expect a theory of the nature of wrongness to yield results that agree perfectly with pre-theoretical opinion. One of the purposes a metaethical theory may serve is to give guidance in revising one's particular ethical opinions. But there is a limit to how far those opinions may be revised without changing the subject." "Divine Command Meta-Ethics Modified Again," *Journal of Religious Ethics* 7, no. 1 (1979): 74.

9. Adams calls this the "transcendence" of the good: "All of God's commands and judgments are right; God is the ethical standard. But our beliefs (even the most cherished) about them must be distinguished from God's commands and judgments themselves. To fail to make that distinction is idolatry. We express our respect for the distinction between God and us by maintaining a critical stance toward ethical and theological beliefs, being ready in principle to consider arguments against any of them, though we may quite rightly be strongly attached to some of them." Robert M. Adams, "Responses," *Philosophy and Phenomenological Research* 64, no. 2 (2002): 485.
10. Adams, *Finite and Infinite Goods*, 256.
11. Ibid., 256–57.
12. Ibid., 256.
13. Ibid., 256–57.
14. David Baggett and Jerry L. Walls, *Good God: The Theistic Foundations of Morality* (New York: Oxford University Press, 2011), 135.
15. Rissler explains this: "In such an instance, obedience requires that one give up everything one previously believed about morality. . . . One has been commanded to relinquish everything one understands about the nature of goodness, one will have no concept of the good with which to identify God's command, there will be complete breakdown between everything one currently affirms about goodness and everything one is asked to believe about goodness." James Rissler, "A Psychological Constraint on Obedience to God's Commands: The Reasonableness of Obeying the Abhorrently Evil," *Religious Studies* 38 (2002): 140–41.
16. Ibid.
17. See Michael Walzer, *Just and Unjust Wars: A Moral Argument with Historical Illustrations*, 3rd ed. (New York: Basic Books, 2000), especially chap. 16. See also Igor Primoratz, "The Morality of Terrorism," *Journal of Applied Philosophy* 14 (1997): 221–33.
18. Raymond Bradley, "Reply to Matthew Flannagan," University of Auckland, Auckland, New Zealand, August 2, 2010, transcript available at http://www.mandm.org.nz/2010/08/bradleys-reply-to-matt-bradley-v-flannagan-debate.html.
19. Randal Rauser, "'Let Nothing that Breathes Remain Alive': On the Problem of Divinely Commanded Genocide," *Philosophia Christi* 11, no. 1 (2009): 31.
20. C. A. J. Coady, "Terrorism, Just War and Supreme Emergency," in *Terrorism and Justice: Moral Argument in a Threatened World*, ed. C. A. J. Coady and M. O'Keefe (Melbourne: Melbourne University Press, 2002), 19–20.

21. We referred to Walzer's position earlier in this chapter in reference to cases of "supreme emergency."

22. Stephen Nathanson, *Terrorism and the Ethics of War* (New York: Cambridge University Press, 2010), where Nathanson takes a rule-utilitarian perspective; Alan Donagan, *The Theory of Morality* (Chicago: University of Chicago Press, 1979).

23. Here is Alan Donagan's full quotation: "The only difference between the consequences of the general acceptance of traditional morality, and the consequences of its general acceptance when supplemented by an escape clause, will be that, in cases which observing it in its unsupplemented form would be a calamity, that calamity would be avoided, together with the good educational consequences of perceiving that fact. And the chief objection to it is that, since nearly everybody's judgement is disturbed by the anticipation of calamity, it is probable that much of what is done on the ground of such escape clauses will be mistaken." *Theory of Morality*, 207.

24. This does raise epistemological (knowledge) questions about whether human beings could be justified in believing that God has commanded them to violate such a rule today. We will discuss this issue in chap. 18.

Chapter 16: Can One Rationally Believe God Commands a Violation of Innocent Human Beings?

1. Immanuel Kant, "Religion within the Boundaries of Mere Reason" (1793), in *Religion and Rational Theology*, trans. A. W. Wood and G. Di Giovanni (Cambridge: Cambridge University Press, 1996), 203–4.

2. Immanuel Kant, "The Conflict of the Faculties" (1798), in *Religion and Rational Theology*, 283.

3. Philip Quinn, "Religion and Politics," in *The Blackwell Guide to Philosophy of Religion*, ed. William Mann (Malden, MA: Blackwell, 2005), 316.

4. Ibid., 318.

5. It's worth noting here that Kant's general position about knowledge (epistemology) in his book *The Critique of Pure Reason* is that one cannot have knowledge by speculative reason of that which transcends our empirical categories; hence, one cannot have knowledge of God by theoretical reason, such as arguments for God's existence from design (teleological) or causality (cosmological). God is known rather through moral or practical reasoning. In his book *The Critique of Practical Reason* Kant argues that

God is a necessary presupposition or postulate of practical reasoning. That is, if we don't *assume* God exists, then our commitment to morality will be rationally unstable. Hence, for Kant one can only know claims about God through *moral*—not theoretical—reasoning.

6. For further discussion, see chap. 28 in Robertson McQuilkin and Paul Copan, *Introduction to Biblical Ethics: Walking in the Way of Wisdom* (Downers Grove, IL: InterVarsity, 2014).

7. Quinn, "Religion and Politics," 319.

8. This has been persuasively argued by Christopher Eberle in *Religious Convictions in Liberal Politics* (Cambridge: Cambridge University Press, 2002), 234–87. That the skeptical challenges to moral beliefs are the same type of challenges as those raised against theological beliefs is also noted by Russ Shafer-Landau, "Moral and Theological Realism: The Explanatory Argument," *Journal of Moral Philosophy* 4, no. 3 (2007): 311–29.

9. These criteria are noted by Eberle in *Religious Convictions*.

10. Kant's own reasoning suggests a more nuanced picture. As noted above, Kant contends we can never be certain that God has commanded an action because "the revelation reached the inquisitor only through the intermediary of human beings and their interpretation, and even if it were to appear to him to have come from God himself (like the command issued to Abraham to slaughter his own son like a sheep), yet it is at least possible that on this point error has prevailed" (*The Conflict of the Faculties*, 283). But this is equally true of many moral beliefs. A good amount of what people believe with regard to morality has been mediated or filtered through human beings and their interpretation of the world. Most Westerners' beliefs in classical liberal ideals (as distinct from modern liberalism) such as equality, human rights, the equality of women, opposition to slavery, and so on, have been passed on through human beings and traditions our parents bequeathed to us—indeed, have been given shape by the biblical tradition. See Alvin Schmidt, *How Christianity Changed the World* (Grand Rapids: Zondervan, 2004); Robert D. Woodberry, "The Missionary Roots of Liberal Democracy," *American Political Science Review* 106, no. 2 (May 2012): 244–74. Moreover, even if we can make moral judgments based on moral intuitions, it is possible that we are mistaken or that those intuitions need refining. Human moral judgments are not infallible, and we must often acknowledge the possibility of error.

11. Remember that the Crucial Moral Principle is proposed as a universal norm.

12. These schools include threshold deontology, act-utilitarianism, rule-utilitarianism, situation ethics, and Rossian deontology.

13. Randal Rauser, "'Let Nothing that Breathes Remain Alive': On the Problem of Divinely Commanded Genocide," *Philosophia Christi* 11, no. 1 (2009): 35.

14. Ibid., 33, emphasis in original.

15. Barbara Coloroso, *Extraordinary Evil: A Brief History of Genocide* (New York: Viking Canada, 2007), xvi cited in ibid., 34.

16. Ibid.

17. Ibid.

18. J. D. Greene, R. M. Sommerville, L. E. Nystrom, J. M. Darley, and J. D. Cohen, "An Investigation of Emotional Engagement in Moral Judgment," *Science* 293 (2001): 2105–8; cited by Peter Singer, in "Reply to Jan Narveson," in *Peter Singer under Fire*, ed. Jeffery A Schaler (Chicago: Open Court Publishers, 2009), 491.

19. Rauser, "'Let Nothing that Breathes Remain Alive,'" 35.

20. Marilyn McCord Adams, *Horrendous Evils and the Goodness of God* (Ithaca, NY: Cornell University Press, 2000), 26, cited in Rauser, "'Let Nothing that Breathes Remain Alive,'" 30.

21. Randal Rauser affirms: "Yes, I think there are conditions where a state is justified in going to war." He notes this in the comments section of his blog post, "Urinating on Corpses and Other Costs of War," Randal Rauser (website), January 13, 2012, http://randalrauser.com/2012/01/urinating-on-corpses-and-other-costs-of-war/.

22. A. A. Howsepian, "Moral Damage and Spiritual Repair in Posttraumatic Stress Disorder," *Christian Research Journal* 36, no. 2 (2013): 20.

23. The reasoning here is analogous to that by which we know it is justified to have PTSD counselors: the good brought about to other people (PTSD sufferers) is sufficiently great that one can legitimately permit (and even in some circumstances require) people to engage in such counseling, despite the risks involved. Similarly the pressing need to identify victims justifies permitting and requiring people to do the horrific task of examining charred human remains even if we know that doing so can cause PTSD.

24. Noam Chomsky, *Failed States: The Abuse of Power and the Assault on Democracy* (New York: Macmillan, 2007), 3; cited in Rauser, "'Let Nothing that Breathes Remain Alive,'" 37.

25. Rauser, "'Let Nothing that Breathes Remain Alive,'" 37.

26. Ibid.

27. Ibid., emphasis added.

28. This is a common point in the literature discussing the justification for self-defense.

29. See, for example, the traditional common law right to self-defense in William Blackstone's *Commentaries on the Laws of England*. Blackstone appeals to the law of nature: "In the next place, such homicide, as is committed for the prevention of any forcible and atrocious crime, is justifiable by the law of nature." He then cites the Old Testament for reinforcement: "If a thief be found breaking up, and he be smitten that he die, no blood shall be shed for him: but if the sun be risen upon him, there shall blood be shed for him; for he should have made full restitution [Ex. 22:2–3]." See Sir William Blackstone and St. George Tucker, *Blackstone's Commentaries*, 5 vols. (Union, NJ: Law Exchange, 1996), 4.14.3, 180.

Or consider John Locke on the right to self-defense in the *Second Treatise of Civil Government* (3.16):

I should have a right to destroy that which threatens me with destruction: for, by the fundamental law of nature, man being to be preserved as much as possible, when all cannot be preserved, the safety of the innocent is to be preferred: and one may destroy a man who makes war upon him, or has discovered an enmity to his being, for the same reason that he may kill a wolf or a lion; because such men are not under the ties of the common law of reason, have no other rule, but that of force and violence, and so may be treated as beasts of prey, those dangerous and noxious creatures, that will be sure to destroy him whenever he falls into their power. *The Second Treatise of Government and A Letter Concerning Toleration* (Mineola, NY: Courier Dover, 2012), 8.

Here Locke appeals to the law of nature, which he identifies as the law of God and hence a transcendent warrant for his view. He also appeals to the injustice perpetrated by the assailant. Furthermore, he suggests that, in attacking another, perpetrators put themselves in the position of a "beast of prey" and thus place themselves outside the "common law of reason." Thus, Locke is appealing to the superior status of the defender— one grounded in transcendent reality. Again, all of the features to which Rauser refers—(1), (2), and (3)—are present in such ordinary legal and philosophical treatises.

30. Rauser, "'Let Nothing that Breathes Remain Alive,'" 39.

31. Cited in ibid., 40. From John Howard Yoder, "Texts that Serve or Texts that Summon? A Response to Michael Walzer," *Journal of Religious Studies* 20 (1993): 230.

342

32. Cited in ibid. From Jeremy Cott, "The Biblical Problem of Election," *Journal of Ecumenical Studies* 21 (1984): 201.

33. Evan Fales, "Comments on 'Canaan and Conquest,'" in *Divine Evil? The Moral Character of the God of Abraham*, ed. Michael Bergmann, Michael J. Murray, and Michael C. Rea (New York: Oxford University Press, 2010), 312.

34. Susan Niditch, *War in the Hebrew Bible: A Study in the Ethics of Violence* (New York: Oxford University Press, 1993), 4. Niditch claims that "European Christians were encouraged to join in the crusading wars against the Saracens by religious leaders quoting Hebrew Scriptures." And here she refers to Roland Bainton as a source. We challenge Bainton's claims not only here but also in chap. 22.

35. Daniel Heimbach, "Distinguishing Just War from Crusade: Is Regime Change a Just Cause for Just War?," in *War in the Bible and Terrorism in the Twenty-First Century*, ed. Richard S. Hess and Elmer A. Martens (Winona Lake, IN: Eisenbrauns, 2008), 79–92.

36. Augustine, *The City of God*, vol. 1 (Edinburgh: T&T Clark, 1871), 4.14, 152.

37. Cited in Thomas Aquinas, *Summa Theologica* I-II, q. 40, a. 1, c. Taken from *The Summa Theologica of St. Thomas Aquinas*, trans. Fathers of the English Dominican Province, 5 vols. (New York: Benzinger Brothers, 1948).

38. Isidore of Seville, *Etymologiarum*, 58, 1, 2, cited in Frederick H. Russell, *Just War in the Middle Ages* (Cambridge: Cambridge University Press, 1977), 62.

39. Thomas Aquinas, *Summa Theologica* II-II, q. 64, a. 6.

40. Francisco Vitoria, "On the Indians, or, on the Law of War Made by the Spaniards on the Barbarians" (secs. 35 and 36). Available online at http://www.constitution.org/victoria/victoria_5.htm, accessed May 29, 2013. Also, Vitoria's document addresses the question of "whether it is lawful in war to kill the innocent." Vitoria recognizes that only by divine commands—"by the authority and at the bidding of God"—is this ever permitted, but not in "the present day" (sec. 34).

41. Ibid., sec. 36.

42. Douglas Earl, "Joshua and the Crusades," in *Holy War in the Bible: Christian Morality and an Old Testament Problem*, ed. Heath A. Thomas, Jeremy Evans, and Paul Copan (Downers Grove, IL: IVP Academic, 2013), 19–43. Earl finds some references to Rahab's ribbon as an allegory for Christ, and discussion on the battle of Ai is cited in debate about the morality of ambushes. But neither is cited as a normative model for killing noncombatants, which canon law forbade.

43. Rauser, "'Let Nothing That Breathes Remain Alive,'" 39, emphasis added.

44. See, for example, chapter 2 of Eric Seibert, *The Violence of Scripture: Overcoming the Old Testament's Troubling Legacy* (Minneapolis: Fortress Press, 2012).

45. We owe this example to Glenn Peoples.

46. Terrence Cuneo and Christopher Eberle, "Religion and Political Theory," in *Stanford Encyclopedia of Philosophy*, October 2, 2008, http://plato.stanford.edu/entries/religion-politics/. Quote is from Luis N. Rivera, *A Violent Evangelism: The Political and Religious Conquest of the Americas* (Louisville: Westminster John Knox, 1992), 50.

47. Aquinas wrote: "For it is a much graver matter to corrupt the faith which quickens the soul, than to forge money, which supports temporal life. Wherefore if forgers of money and other evil-doers are forthwith condemned to death by the secular authority, much more reason is there for heretics, as soon as they are convicted of heresy, to be not only excommunicated but even put to death." *Summa Theologica* II-II, q. 11, a. 3.

48. For example, see Thomas Sowell, *Intellectuals and Society*, rev. ed. (New York: Basic Books, 2012); Jonah Goldberg, *Liberal Fascism: The Secret History of the American Left, from Mussolini to the Politics of Change* (New York: Three Rivers Press, 2009).

Chapter 17: Is It Rational to Believe God Commanded the Killing of Innocents?

1. Wesley Morriston, "Did God Command Genocide? A Challenge to the Biblical Inerrantist," *Philosophia Christi* 11, no. 1 (2009): 9, emphasis in original.

2. Wesley Morriston, "Ethical Criticism of the Bible: The Case of Divinely Mandated Genocide," *Sophia* 51, no. 1 (2012): 120. In a footnote he states that "abhorrent practices" refer to various sexual practices (such as bestiality, incest, homosexual conduct, bigamy, and ritual prostitution) and infant sacrifice.

3. Morriston is citing Richard Swinburne, "What Does the Old Testament Mean?," in *Divine Evil? The Moral Character of the God of Abraham*, ed. Michael Bergmann, Michael J. Murray, and Michael C. Rea (New York: Oxford University Press, 2010), 224.

4. Swinburne, "What Does the Bible Mean?," quoted in Morriston, "Ethical Criticism of the Bible," 120.

5. Morriston, "Ethical Criticism of the Bible," 121.

6. Here is Richard Brandt's specific statement, which is in the context of the ethical theory of utilitarianism. This specific variety—act utilitarianism—affirms that the rightness of an act is determined by which act will likely produce the best consequences:

> For to have an act utilitarian code is to be motivated (basic motivations) to do what one thinks will have the best consequences, so that doing what one is thus motivated to do is not at all necessarily to do what will have the best consequences, assuming that agents are not omniscient. Whereas persons commited to an ideal code are motivated (basic motivations) to do what they think will be the keeping of a promise, the avoidance of causing injury, etc., and in doing what they are thus motivated to do, will be to do what in the long run will have the best consquences even if some such acts do not. (*A Theory of the Good and the Right* [Oxford: Oxford University Press, 1979], 296–97.)

7. For further discussion on this point, see Jay Wesley Richards, *Money, Greed, and God: Why Capitalism Is the Solution, Not the Problem* (New York: HarperOne, 2010).

8. Richard Swinburne, "What Does the Old Testament Mean?," in *Divine Evil?*, 224.

9. Ibid.

10. See, for example, sec. 8 of *The Accessories and Abettors Act 1861*: "Whosoever shall aid, abet, counsel, or procure the commission [of any indictable offence], whether the same be [an offence] at common law or by virtue of any Act passed or to be passed, shall be liable to be tried, indicted, and punished as a principal offender." Http://www.legislation.gov.uk/ukpga/Vict/24-25/94/crossheading/as-to-abettors-in-misdemeanors, accessed May 1, 2014.

11. See "Colorado and Capital Punishment" available Office of the Colorado State Public Defender (website), http://pdweb.coloradodefenders.us/index.php?option=com_content&view=article&id=150:death-penalty-information&catid=66:capital-punishment.

12. Wesley Morriston, "Comments on 'God Beyond Justice,'" in *Divine Evil?*, 168.

13. Note that Morriston is citing the *Oxford English Dictionary* ("Ethical Criticism of the Bible," 118n3).

14. Morriston, "Did God Command Genocide?," 13.

15. Eleonore Stump makes a similar point in "The Problem of Evil and the History of Peoples: Think Amalek," in *Divine Evil?*, 187–88.

16. Morriston, "Ethical Criticism of the Bible," 122, emphasis in original.

17. Ibid.

18. In chaps. 1 and 2 of this book, we discuss the distinction between divine and human authorship; in addition, we note the distinction between the human voice and the divine voice. For instance, Paul's distinctive voice is clear when he states that "beyond that, I do not know whether I baptized any other" (1 Cor. 1:16 NASB) or, "I assure you before God that I am not lying" (Gal. 1:20). The divine author's voice is also distinctively expressed in assertions such as "thus says the LORD." In Numbers 31, we see God's command and the fulfillment of that command—namely, to kill the Midianite men (31:2–3, 7). Moses's further command in 31:17–18 goes beyond what God had mandated.

19. These three criticisms are taken from Morriston, "Ethical Criticism of the Bible," 122.

20. Morriston is incorrect about the nature of Moses's failure. The wrongdoing was not in striking a rock instead of speaking to it—as is made clear by the fact that Aaron is guilty as well, not simply Moses. The text explicitly attributes unbelief to Moses and Aaron. Of course, Moses had struck a rock before, and water came from it (Exod. 17:6). Moses (along with Aaron, apparently) cried out in frustration and *unbelief*: "Listen, you rebels, must we bring you water out of this rock?" (Num. 20:10 NIV). The Hebrew text makes clear that *both Moses and Aaron* displayed a failure of faith. At Meribah, God rebukes *both Moses and Aaron*: "Because you [Moses *and* Aaron*; the Hebrew pronoun is *plural*] have not believed Me, to treat me as holy before Israel, you will not bring this community into the land I give them" (v. 12 NASB). And in case this is not clear enough, verse 24 makes this abundantly clear: "Aaron will be gathered to his people; for he shall not enter the land which I have given to the sons of Israel, because you rebelled [plural: *meriytem*] against My command at the waters of Meribah" (NASB). Throughout this narrative, God continues to address *both* Moses and Aaron, who had failed to trust in God. At the end of the Pentateuch (Deut. 32:51), we read again that at Meribah in Kadesh, Moses "broke faith" with God. Psalm 106:32–33 reinforces this theme of Moses's *unbelief*; the rebellion of the people prompted Moses to *speak rashly* (not *act* rashly): "rash words came from Moses' lips." As a result of this failure of faith, Moses along with Aaron could not enter the Promised Land.

21. See K. A. Kitchen and P. J. N. Lawrence, *Treaty, Law, and Covenant in the Ancient Near East*, 3 vols. (Wiesbaden: Harrassowitz, 2012).

22. Morriston, "Ethical Criticism of the Bible," 122, emphasis added.

23. Stump, "Problem of Evil," 185.

24. Morriston, "Ethical Criticism of the Bible," 123.

25. Douglas Stuart, *Hosea–Jonah*, Word Biblical Commentary 31 (Waco, TX: Word Books, 1987), 820; Joyce Baldwin, "Jonah," in *The Minor Prophets*, vol. 2, ed. Thomas McComiskey (Grand Rapids: Baker, 1993), 576–77.

26. For example, Judg. 3:13; 6:3–5, 33; 7:12; 10:12; 1 Sam 15; 27; 30; 1 Chron. 4:43; Esther 3:1; etc.

27. Morriston, "Ethical Criticism of the Bible," 124.

28. Ibid.

29. Thanks to Clay Jones for putting forward these comments in Facebook correspondence, November 16–17, 2013.

30. Stephen N. Williams, "Could God Have Commanded the Slaughter of the Canaanites?," *Tyndale Bulletin* 63, no. 2 (2012): 161–78.

31. Ibid., 172–73.

32. Miroslav Volf, *Free of Charge: Giving and Forgiving in a Culture Stripped of Grace* (Grand Rapids: Zondervan, 2006), 138–39, emphasis in original; see also Volf's *Exclusion and Embrace: A Theological Exploration of Identity, Otherness, and Reconciliation* (Nashville: Abingdon, 1996).

Chapter 18: What If Someone Claimed God Commanded Killing the Innocent Today?

1. Alvin Plantinga, *Warranted Christian Belief* (New York: Oxford University Press, 2000), 466.

2. For further reading on this topic, see the following essays from *The Evidential Argument from Evil*, ed. Daniel Howard-Snyder (Bloomington, IN: Indiana University Press, 1996): Stephen John Wykstra, "Rowe's Noseeum Arguments from Evil"; Peter van Inwagen, "The Problem of Evil, the Problem of Air, and the Problem of Silence," and "Reflections on the Chapters by Draper, Russell, and Gale"; William P. Alston, "The Inductive Argument from Evil and the Human Cognitive Condition," and "Some (Temporarily) Final Thoughts on Evidential Arguments from Evil"; Daniel Howard-Snyder, "The Argument from Inscrutable Evil."

3. Michael Bergmann, "Skeptical Theism and the Problem of Evil," in *The Oxford Handbook of Philosophical Theology*, ed. Thomas P. Flint and Michael C. Rea (Oxford: Oxford University Press, 2009), 379.

4. Kirk Durston, "The Consequential Complexity of History and Gratuitous Evil," *Religious Studies* 36 (2000): 66.

5. Eleonore Stump, "Reply to Draper," in *Divine Evil? The Moral Character of the God of Abraham*, ed. Michael Bergmann, Michael J. Murray, and Michael C. Rea (New York: Oxford University Press, 2010), 204.

6. Ibid., 207.

7. This is a modification of Raymond Bradley's formulation in "A Moral Argument for Atheism," in *The Impossibility of God*, ed. Michael Martin and Ricki Monnier (Amherst, NY: Prometheus Books, 2003), 135.

8. Wesley Morriston, "Ethical Criticism of the Bible: The Case of Divinely Mandated Genocide," *Sophia* 51, no. 1 (2012): 131.

9. Ralph Blumenthal, "52 Girls Are Taken from Polygamist Sect's Ranch in Texas," *New York Times*, April 5, 2008, http://www.nytimes.com/2008/04/05/us/05jeffs.html?_r=0.

10. Morriston, "Ethical Criticism of the Bible," 131–32.

11. Ibid., 132.

12. Ibid.

13. Ibid.

14. Here is the full quotation from Morriston (in ibid.), from which we have quoted various portions:

> Divine communications are not generally thought to have ended with the closing of the canon. Christians in particular pray for divine guidance and they often receive what they take to be answers. . . . There are recognized ways of forming beliefs about what God wants and recognized classes of defeaters for those beliefs. One obvious class of defeaters concerns the moral character of the content of the beliefs that are the outputs of the practice. As Richard Swinburne himself puts it, "the prophet who commends cheating and child torture can be dismissed straight away" (Swinburne 1992: 86). William Alston—who did as much as anyone to defend the epistemic credentials of religious experience—once wrote that if he reported that God wanted him to kill all phenomenologists, Christians would take this as a sure sign that his experience was non-veridical . . . (Alston 1982: 6). Indeed. Can we imagine defeaters for these defeaters? Something that would convince us that God had, after all, commanded cheating or child torture or the extermination of all phenomenologists? No doubt an inventive philosopher could come up

with a story. But to remove the grotesque implausibility of such claims about what God wants from us, a fanciful story is not enough. Nor is it sufficient to observe that God knows far more than we about the total value/disvalue of such things. Are things relevantly different when we turn our attention to divinely mandated genocides in the Bible?

15. For a discussion of the gift of prophecy, see Wayne Grudem, *The Gift of Prophecy in the New Testament and Today*, rev. ed. (Wheaton, IL: Crossway, 2007); Max Turner, *The Holy Spirit and Spiritual Gifts in the New Testament and Today* (Grand Rapids: Baker Academic, 1997).

16. For a brief discussion of the formation of the biblical canon, see Paul Copan, *"How Do You Know You're Not Wrong?" Responding to Objections that Leave Christians Speechless* (Grand Rapids: Baker, 2005).

17. In an endnote, Morriston cites Christian philosopher William Alston, who wrote that if he reported that God wanted him to kill all phenomenologists, Christians would take this as a sure sign that his experience was false. Yet Alston himself defends the epistemic credentials of Christian mystical practice, which is socially accepted within the Christian community.

18. Morriston, "Ethical Criticism of the Bible," 132.

19. Cited in ibid., 132. This is taken from Richard Swinburne, *Revelation: From Metaphor to Analogy* (Oxford: Clarendon Press, 1992), 86.

20. Richard Swinburne, *Revelation: From Metaphor to Analogy* (Oxford: Clarendon Press, 1992), 86.

21. Richard Swinburne, *Revelation: From Metaphor to Analogy*, 2nd ed. (Oxford: Oxford University Press, 2007), 110, emphasis added. Note that this is the *second* edition.

22. Ibid., emphasis added.

23. Morriston, "Ethical Criticism of the Bible," 132.

24. In fact, as Alston has pointed out, it is unlikely that a practitioner of recognized Christian mystical practices can provide a noncircular argument for its reliability that would persuade someone skeptical of the practice. That said, the *same* feature is true of many recognized rational practices such as believing things on the basis of perception, memory, deductive reasoning, and so on. So the failure to provide someone who is skeptical of another's practice with reasons for accepting it does not come to much.

25. Paul views the Spirit's fruit as the fulfillment of Isaianic prophecies—*righteousness, peace, confidence* (Isa. 32:10–18); *humility, praise,*

peace (Isa. 57:15–19). See G. K. Beale, "The Old Testament Background of Paul's Reference to 'the Fruit of the Spirit' in Galatians 5:22," *Bulletin for Biblical Research* 15, no. 1 (2005): 1–38.

26. See Gordon D. Fee, *God's Empowering Presence* (Peabody, MA: Hendrickson, 1994), 421–54. *Self-control* is, of course, carrying out what one intends to do, despite influences and appetites to the contrary, and this is the only virtue listed here that is more individual than communal. As for the others, *love* is a self-giving, self-sacrificing commitment to others (cf. Gal. 2:20). *Joy* is characteristic of life together (Rom. 14:17; 15:13). Joy is often linked with a well-ordered *peace* among believers (rather than dissension)—another community matter (Rom. 14:17; 15:13; Eph. 2:14–17). *Patience* deals with showing forbearance toward others (1 Cor. 13:4: "love is patient"). *Kindness* actively pursues the good of the other (1 Cor. 13:4: "love is kind"; cf. Eph. 2:7). *Goodness* is related to kindness but is more all-embracing; when we practice goodness, it takes the form of "doing good to all" (Gal. 6:9–10). *Faithfulness* is trustworthiness toward God and others (e.g., 1 Cor. 4:1–2; 2 Cor. 1:18; Col. 1:7); this flows from our faith in God, having entrusted ourselves to God's utterly faithful character (cf. Rom. 3:3). *Gentleness* refers to strength under control—like a well-trained horse—that places the interests of others ahead of oneself (cf. Matt. 11:29; Col. 3:12). Adapted from chap. 7 in Robertson McQuilkin and Paul Copan, *Introduction to Biblical Ethics: Walking in the Way of Wisdom* (Downers Grove, IL: InterVarsity, 2014).

Chapter 19: The Role of Miracles and the Command to Kill Canaanites

1. Søren Kierkegaard, *Fear and Trembling and The Sickness unto Death*, trans. Walter Lowrie (Garden City, NY: Doubleday, 1954), 41.

2. Thanks to Matthew Rowley, who has let us borrow very heavily from his paper, "The Epistemology of Sacralized Violence in the Exodus and Conquest." The paper has since been published in *The Journal of the Evangelical Theological Society* 57, no. 1 (March 2014): 63–83.

3. C. John Collins, *Genesis 1–4: A Linguistic, Literary and Theological Commentary* (Phillipsburg, PA: P&R, 2006), 273.

4. See Exod. 6:7; 7:5, 17; 8:10, 22; 9:14, 29; 10:2; 11:7; 14:4, 18; 16:6, 12; 18:10–11; 29:46; 31:13; Lev. 23:43; Num. 12:4–8; 14:31–34; 16:28–30; Deut. 4:9, 35, 39; 7:7–11, 15; 8:3–6; 9:2–8; 11:2; 29:4–6, 16; 31:11–13.

5. Craig Keener, *Miracles: The Credibility of the New Testament Accounts* (Grand Rapids: Baker Academic, 2011), 57–64.

6. Christopher J. H. Wright, *Knowing God the Father through the Old Testament* (Downers Grove, IL: IVP Academic, 2007), 43.

7. James K. Hoffmeier, "These Things Happened," in *Do Historical Matters Matter to Faith?*, ed. James K. Hoffmeier and Dennis Magary (Wheaton, IL: Crossway, 2012), 114–32.

8. Here is a sampling of texts: Exod. 12:17, 42; 13:7–9, 14–18; 16:6–8; 20:2; 22:21; 23:9, 15; 29:46; Lev. 11:45; 19:34, 36; 22:31–33; 23:43; 25:42, 55; 26:13; Num. 3:13; 8:17; 15:40–41; Deut. 1:29–33; 4:19–20, 32–40; 5:6, 15; 6:12, 21–25; 8:14; 10:19; 11:1–7; 13:10; 15:15; 16:1–6; 20:1; 24:22; 26:1–10; 29:1–9.

9. For instance, see Lev. 18:5, 30; 19:4, 12, 14, 25, 28, 30. Cf. Num. 3:13, 41, 45; 10:10.

10. One example is in Leviticus 18–19. Obedience is repeatedly grounded in "I am the LORD" (18:2, 4, 5, 6, 21, 30; 19:3, 4, 10, 12, 14, 18, 25, 28, 31, 32), and this section concludes with the full statement "I am the LORD your God, who brought you out of the land of Egypt" (19:36).

11. For example, Exod. 4:30–31; 6:1; 7:20; 9:8; 10:23; 14:13, 30–31; 16:5–9, 15, 32; 17:6; 19:4, 11; 20:18, 22; 24:10–17; 33:10; 34:10, 30, 35; 40:38; Lev. 9:24; 26:45; Num. 11:23–25; 14:14, 22–23; 20:8; 21:8; 32:11; Deut. 1:30, 35–36; 3:21; 4:3, 9, 12, 15, 34–36; 5:24; 6:22; 7:19; 10:21; 11:2, 7; 29:2–4; 34:10–12.

12. Wright, *Knowing God the Father*, 44.

13. John Walton, *Ancient Near Eastern Thought and the Old Testament: Introducing the Conceptual World of the Hebrew Bible* (Grand Rapids: Baker Academic, 2006), 267.

14. Ibid., 271, 273. Walton notes Scripture's historical *uniqueness* when "Moses performs signs to establish his credibility" (274). See also Jeffrey Niehaus, *Ancient Near Eastern Themes in Biblical Theology* (Grand Rapids: Kregel, 2008), 56, 82.

15. Henri Blocher, *Evil and the Cross: An Analytical Look at the Problem of Pain* (Grand Rapids: Kregel, 1994), 104, 132.

16. Rowley, "Epistemology of Sacralized Violence," 25.

17. Ibid., 1 (quotation found in abstract of unpublished paper).

Chapter 20: Does Religion Cause Violence?

1. Charles Kimball, *When Religion Becomes Evil* (San Francisco: Harper Collins, 2002), 1. Some material from this chapter is an expansion and adaptation from a portion of chap. 18 in Paul

Copan, *Is God a Moral Monster? Making Sense of the Old Testament God* (Grand Rapids: Baker Books, 2011).

2. Mark Juergensmeyer, *Terror in the Mind of God* (Berkeley: University of California Press, 2000), 242, 159, 243.

3. Ibid., 159, 243.

4. Regina Schwartz, *The Curse of Cain* (Chicago: University of Chicago Press, 1997), 63.

5. For a helpful understanding of election, see William Klein, *The New Chosen People: A Corporate View of Election* (Eugene, OR: Wipf and Stock, 2001).

6. Kimball, *When Religion Becomes Evil*, 15.

7. William Cavanaugh, *The Myth of Religious Violence: Secular Ideology and the Roots of Modern Conflict* (New York: Oxford University Press, 2009).

8. Ibid., 27.

9. Ibid., 28.

10. Michael W. Goheen and Craig G. Bartholomew, *Living at the Crossroads: An Introduction to Christian Worldview* (Grand Rapids: Baker Academic, 2008), 23.

11. Paul J. Griffiths, *Problems of Religious Diversity* (Oxford: Blackwell, 2001), 7; see also 2–12.

12. Cited in Ian Ward, *Introduction to Critical Legal Theory*, 2nd ed. (Portland, OR: Cavendish, 2004), 165.

13. In the *Letter to the Smyrneans*, the instigation of St. Polycarp's death included a call, "Away with the atheists."

14. Cavanaugh, *Myth of Religious Violence*, 24.

15. Mark Juergensmeyer, *The New Cold War? Religious Nationalism Confronts the Secular State* (Berkeley: University of California Press, 1993), 15.

16. The following comments are taken from Jonah Goldberg, *Liberal Fascism: The Secret History of the American Left, From Mussolini to the Politics of Change* (New York: Three Rivers Press, 2009).

17. Ibid., 26. Incidentally, the letter Hitler sent to Roosevelt was March 14, 1934. See History-of-the-Holocaust.org: http://www.yarok.biz/icons-multimedia/ClientsArea/HoH/LIBARC/ARCHIVE/Chapters/Forging/Foreign/Message.html.

18. Cavanaugh, *Myth of Religious Violence*, 226–27.

19. Ibid., 226.

20. Ibid., 26.

21. Ibid., 61.

22. For many more examples, see ibid., 142–51.

23. Ibid., 153–54. Natalie Zemon Davis's article is "The Rites of Violence: Religious Riot in

Sixteenth-Century France," *Past and Present* 59 (May 1973): 51–91.

24. Rodney Stark, *For the Glory of God: How Monotheism Led to Reformations, Science, Witch-Hunts, and the End of Slavery* (Princeton: Princeton University Press, 2003), 360.

25. Of course, from Abraham to Zacharias in the Scriptures, we encounter a crop of doubters in the face of miracle claims (Gen. 17:17; Matt. 1:18–21; Luke 1:13–20; 24:10–11; John 20:19–28; Acts 12:13–15)—though exploring this and the broader topic of miracles is a topic for another day. But see the magisterial defense of miracles by Craig Keener, *Miracles*, 2 vols. (Grand Rapids: Baker Academic, 2011).

26. See Charles Taliaferro and Anders Hendrickson, "Hume's Racism and His Case against the Miraculous," *Philosophia Christi* 4, no. 2 (2002): 427–41.

27. Ibid.

28. See Robert D. Woodberry, "The Missionary Roots of Liberal Democracy," *American Political Science Review* 106, no. 2 (2012): 244–74.

29. Sam Harris, *The End of Faith: Religion, Terror, and the Future of Reason* (New York: Norton, 2004), 128–29.

30. Christopher Hitchens said this in a debate with Chris Hedges. See Chris Hedges, *When Atheism Becomes Religion: America's New Fundamentalists* (New York: Free Press, 2008), 23. Also cited in Cavanaugh, *Myth of Religious Violence*, 219.

31. See "An Interview with Christopher Hitchens ('Moral and Political Collapse' of the Left in the US)," *Washington Prism* (June 16, 2005). Available at the *Free Republic*: http://www.free republic.com/focus/f-news/1457374/posts. This is also cited in Cavanaugh, *Myth of Religious Violence*, 219.

32. John L. Allen Jr., "The War on Christians," *The Spectator*, October 5, 2013. Available at: http://www.spectator.co.uk/features/9041841/the-war-on-christians/.

33. Jürgen Habermas, *Time of Transitions*, ed. and trans. Ciaran Cronin and Max Pensky (Cambridge: Polity, 2006), 150–51.

34. Jacques Derrida, "To Forgive: The Unforgivable and Imprescriptable," in *Questioning God*, ed. John D. Caputo et al. (Bloomington, IN: Indiana University Press, 2001), 70.

35. David Aikman, *Jesus in Beijing: How Christianity Is Transforming China and Changing the Global Balance of Power* (Washington, DC: Regnery, 2003), 5.

36. Niall Ferguson, *Civilization: The West and the Rest* (New York: Penguin, 2012). This work ethic was also historically connected to the values

of *reading books* and *saving money*. Thanks to Peter Copan for calling this book to our attention.

37. Guenter Lewy, *Why America Needs Religion* (Grand Rapids: Eerdmans, 1996), 137.

38. Malcolm Muggeridge, *Jesus Rediscovered* (New York: Pyramid Publications, 1969), 157.

39. Robert D. Woodberry, "The Missionary Roots of Liberal Democracy," *American Political Science Review* 106, no. 2 (2012): 244–45.

40. Ibid., 245.

41. Andrea Palpant Dilley, "The Surprising Discovery about Those Colonialist, Proselytizing Missionaries," *Christianity Today* (January/February 2014), 41. Note that Dilley's article explores the recent groundbreaking work of Robert Woodberry.

42. Cited in ibid.

43. Ibid, 39, emphasis in original.

44. See Plato's *Republic*, Bk. V. Aristotle's *Politics* 1.3–6 declares that slaves are such by nature; his *Nicomachean Ethics* 8.11 affirms that "a slave is an animated tool, and a tool an inanimate slave, whence there is nothing in common" between the master and the slave (see also his *Politics*, 1.14).

45. Woodberry, "Missionary Roots," 248.

46. Ibid.

47. See Brian Stewart, "Christians Are on the Front Lines of Compassion," Knox College convocation, Toronto, Ontario, May 12, 2004, transcript available at http://www.reformedevan gelism.com/library/library03-article-cbc.html.

48. The material in this section has been reworked from its original version in chap. 18 of Paul Copan, *Is God a Moral Monster?* Here we follow insights from Mirsoslav Volf, "Christianity and Violence," in *War in the Bible and Violence in the Twenty-First Century*, ed. Richard S. Hess and Elmer A. Martens (Winona Lake, IN: Eisenbrauns, 2008); R. W. L. Moberly, "Is Monotheism Bad for You? Some Reflections on God, the Bible, and Life in the Light of Regina Schwartz's *The Curse of Cain*," in *The God of Israel* (Cambridge: Cambridge University Press, 2007), 94–112; and Joel S. Kaminsky, *Yet I Loved Jacob: Reclaiming the Biblical Concept of Election* (Nashville: Abingdon, 2007)—the seeds of whose book are found in Joel S. Kaminsky, "Did Election Imply the Mistreatment of Non-Israelites?" *Harvard Theological Review* 96, no. 4 (October 2003): 397–425.

49. Volf, "Christianity and Violence," 8.

50. R. J. Eidelson and J. I. Eidelson, "Dangerous Ideas: Five Beliefs that Propel Groups toward Conflict," *American Psychologist* 58 (March 2003): 182–92.

51. Mark S. Smith, *God in Translation: Deities in Cross-cultural Discourse in the Biblical World* (Grand Rapids: Eerdmans, 2010), 29.

52. Patrick Miller makes this point in his "Review of Joel S. Kaminsky, *Yet I Loved Jacob*," *Review of Biblical Literature* (website), March 2008, http://www.bookreviews.org/pdf/6201_6898.pdf; http://www.bookreviews.org/rblsearch.asp?Code Page=2405,1310,8027,8402,6201,7662

53. Comments on *non*elect versus *anti*elect are taken from Kaminsky, "Did Election Imply Mistreatment?"

Chapter 21: Are Yahweh Wars in the Old Testament Just like Islamic Jihad?

1. Andrea Bistrich, "Discovering the Common Grounds of World Religions," interview with Karen Armstrong, *Share International* 26, no. 7 (September 2007): 19–22, available at http://www.unaoc.org/repository/armstrong_interview.pdf.

2. Philip Jenkins, "Dark Passages," *Boston Globe*, March 8, 2009, available at http://www.boston.com/bostonglobe/ideas/articles/2009/03/08/dark_passages/. See also Jenkins's book *Laying Down the Sword: Why We Can't Ignore the Bible's Violent Verses* (New York: HarperOne, 2011).

3. Unless otherwise noted, all Qur'anic translations are from Arthur John Arberry. For this and other parallel English translations of the Qur'an, see "The Quranic Arabic Corpus" available at: http://corpus.quran.com/.

4. Norman Anderson, "Islam," in *The World's Religions*, 4th ed. (Downers Grove, IL: InterVarsity, 1975), 128.

5. See referenced works of Bat Ye'or below.

6. Quoted in Margaret Miner and Hugh Rawson, eds., *The Oxford Dictionary of American Quotations*, 2nd ed. (Oxford: Oxford University Press, 2006), 245.

7. Cited in Efraim Karsh, *Islamic Imperialism: A History* (New Haven: Yale University Press, 2006), 3.

8. This tally of eighty-six battles comes from J. M. B. Jones, "The Chronology of the *Maghazi*: A Textual Survey," *Bulletin of the School of Oriental and African Studies* 19 (1957): 245–80.

9. Ibn Ishaq, *The Life of Muhammad*, trans. A. Guillaume (Karachi: Oxford University Press, 1955).

10. Ibid., 369.

11. Ibid., 665.

12. Ibid., 674–75.

13. Ibid., 515.

14. This is documented by Silas (a pseudonymn), "Muhammad and the Female Captives," *Answering Islam: A Christian-Muslim Dialog* (website), http://www.answering-islam.org/Silas/female captives.htm, accessed March 25, 2014. See also

www.mutah.com for a wide array of resources and documentation on the topic, with a "Mutah Chat" feature for single Muslims to meet a "like-minded Mutah partner," as well as the vows (*woman*: "I married myself to you for the known period and the agreed upon dowry"; *man*: I [have] accepted").

15. Thanks to Joshua Lingel for his insights. See also his "When Muslims Attack . . . the Faith," *Charisma*, September 20, 2011, http://www.charismamag.com/site-archives/1463–online-exclusives/september-2011/14468–when-muslims-attack-the-faith.

16. Here we use the more noted Yusuf Ali translation.

17. Here is a sampling of quotations from the Qur'an: "O Prophet, struggle with the unbelievers and hypocrites, and be thou harsh with them" (9:73). "O believers, fight the unbelievers who are near to you; and let them find in you a harshness . . ." (9:123). "Say to the Bedouins who were left behind: 'You shall be called against a people possessed of great might' to fight them, or they surrender" (48:16).

18. "Appendix E: Qur'an 2:256," *Answering Islam: A Christian-Muslim Dialog* (website), http://answering-islam.org/Hahn/mappe.html, accessed March 25, 2014. The traditions (*Hadith*) of Islam reinforce this theme: "Some Zanadiqa (atheists) were brought to 'Ali and he burnt them. The news of this event, reached Ibn 'Abbas who said, 'If I had been in his place, I would not have burnt them, as Allah's Apostle forbade it, saying, "Do not punish anybody with Allah's punishment [fire]." I would have killed them according to the statement of Allah's Apostle, "Whoever changed his Islamic religion, then kill him."'" *Hadith*, vol. 9, bk. 84, no. 57, from http://www.usc.edu/org/cmje/religious-texts/hadith/bukhari/084-sbt.php.

19. For more details, see the Topkapi Palace Museum website at http://www.ee.bilkent.edu.tr/~history/topkapi.html.

20. *Encyclopedia of Islam*, ed. Jane Dammen McAuliffe (Leiden: Brill, 1960–2003), s.v. "Djihad"; cited in David Cook, *Understanding Jihad* (Berkeley: University of California Press, 2005), 213n1.

21. Cited in ibid.

22. See David Cook, *Understanding Jihad*; also *The Oxford Encyclopedia of the Modern Islamic World*, ed. John L. Esposito (Oxford: Oxford University Press, 2001), s.v. "Jihād," 2:369–73.

23. Cook, *Understanding Jihad*, chap. 3.

24. For thorough documentation on this and other phenomena related to Muslim rule over Christians and Jews, see Bat Ye'or's excellent book *The Decline of Eastern Christianity under*

Islam: From Jihad to Dhimmitude (Teaneck, NJ: Fairleigh Dickinson University Press, 1997).

25. Cited in Michael Cromartie, interview with Bat Ye'or, "The Myth of Islamic Tolerance," in *Books and Culture* 4, no. 5 (September/October 1998): 38, http://www.christianitytoday.com/bc/8b5/8b5038.html.

26. Bat Ye'or, "Persecution of Jews and Christians: Testimony vs. Silence," lecture given at the Ethics and Public Policy Center, Washington, DC, April 2, 1998, http://www.dhimmi.org/LectureE4.html, accessed April 12, 2014.

27. Reinhart Dhozy, *Spanish Islam: A History of the Moslims in Spain*, repr. ed. (Bloomington, IN: Indiana University Press, 2008), 239, emphasis added.

28. Andrew G. Bostom, "The Cordoba House and the Myth of Cordoban 'Ecumenism,'" *PJMedia*, September 2, 2010, http://pjmedia.com/blog/the-cordoba-house-and-the-myth-of-cordoban-ecumenism/?singlepage=true; see also Bat Ye'or, "Andalusian Myth, Eurabian Reality," *Jihad Watch* (April 21, 2004), http://www.jihadwatch.org/2004/04/andalusian-myth-eurabian-reality.

29. Ye'or cited in Cromartie, "Myth of Islamic Tolerance."

30. Ibid.

31. The translations of Muhammad Sarwar, Yusuf Ali, and Marmaduke Pickthall use "transgressors" here.

Chapter 22: Did Old Testament War Texts Inspire the Crusades?

1. Karen Armstrong, *Holy War: The Crusades and Their Impact on Today's World*, 2nd ed. (New York: Random House, 2001), 4.

2. Andrea Bistrich, "Discovering the Common Grounds of World Religions," interview with Karen Armstrong, *Share International* 26, no. 7 (September 2007): 19–22. Available at http://www.unaoc.org/repository/armstrong_interview.pdf.

3. Edward Gibbon, *The History of the Decline and Fall of the Roman Empire*, vol. 10 (Basil: J. J. Tourneisen, 1789), 257, cited in Rodney Stark, *God's Battalions: The Case for the Crusades* (New York: HarperOne, 2009), 3.

4. Roland H. Bainton, *Christian Attitudes toward War and Peace: A Historical Survey and Critical Re-evaluation* (Nashville: Abingdon, 1960), 52, cf. 111.

5. Cited in Stark, *God's Battalions*, 3.

6. Bat Ye'or, *The Decline of Eastern Christianity under Islam: From Jihad to Dhimmitude* (Teaneck, NJ: Fairleigh Dickinson University Press, 1997), 89–90.

7. Thomas F. Madden, "Inventing the Crusades," *First Things*, June/July 2009, http://www.firstthings.com/article/2009/05/inventing-the-crusades-1243195699.

8. Muhammad, we noted, engaged in eighty-six military battles. Immediately after his death in 632, his followers continued to advance the "abode of Islam" into Syria (633–635), Persia (636), Palestine (636–638), Egypt (639–641), and beyond.

9. For a response to these myths, we refer the reader to Stark, *God's Battalions*.

10. Thomas F. Madden, "Crusade Propaganda," *National Review Online* (November 2, 2001), emphasis in original. Available at http://www.nationalreview.com/articles/220747/crusade-propaganda/thomas-f-madden.

11. For a tempered discussion of the Jerusalem killing, see Benjamin Kedar, "The Jerusalem Massacre of July 1099 in the Western Historiography of the Crusades," *Crusades* 3 (2004): 15–75.

12. For documentation on Islam's track record, see Bat Ye'or, *The Decline of Eastern Christianity under Islam: From Jihad to Dhimmitude* (Teaneck, NJ: Fairleigh Dickinson University Press, 1997); *The Dhimmi: Jews and Christians under Islam* (Teaneck, NJ: Fairleigh Dickinson University Press, 1985); *Islam and Dhimmitude: Where Civilizations Collide* (Teaneck, NJ: Fairleigh Dickinson University Press, 2002); Mark Durie, *The Third Choice: Islam, Dhimmitude and Freedom* (n.p.: Deror Books, 2010).

13. Thomas F. Madden, *A Concise History of the Crusades* (Lanham, MD: Rowman & Littlefield, 2013), 4.

14. Bernard Lewis, *Islam and the West* (New York: Oxford University Press, 1993), 13.

15. Paul Johnson, "Relentlessly and Thoroughly: The Only Way to Respond," *National Review*, October 15, 2001, http://www.nationalreview.com/articles/225632/relentlessly-and-thoroughly/paul-johnson.

16. For example, Jonathan Riley-Smith, *What Were the Crusades?*, 4th ed. (San Francisco: Ignatius Press, 2009); Thomas F. Madden, *The New Concise History of the Crusades* (Lanham, MD: Rowman & Littlefield, 2013).

17. Jonathan Riley-Smith, *The Crusades, Christianity, and Islam* (New York: Columbia University Press, 2008), 36.

18. See chap. 5 in Stark, *God's Battalions*.

19. Madden, "Inventing the Crusades."

20. Ibid., 8.

21. See John V. Tolan, *Saint Francis and the Sultan: The Curious History of a Christian-Muslim Encounter* (Oxford: Oxford University Press, 2009).

22. *Kingdom of Heaven*, directed by Ridley Scott (Los Angeles: Twentieth Century Fox, 2005).

23. Efraim Karsh, *Islamic Imperialism: A History* (New Haven: Yale University Press, 2006), 70–74.

24. Riley-Smith, *Crusades, Christianity, and Islam*, 74. See also the work of Elizabeth Sibbery, *The New Crusaders* (Burlington, VT: Ashgate, 2000).

25. Riley-Smith, *Crusades, Christianity, and Islam*, 76.

26. Stark, *God's Battalions*, 8–9.

27. John Goldingay, *Old Testament Theology*, vol. 3, *Israel's Life* (Downers Grove, IL: IVP Academic, 2009), 555.

28. Ibid., 582. Goldingay adds that Christians have been more inclined to make war.

29. Bruce Elliott Johansen, *The Praeger Handbook on Contemporary Issues in Native America: Linguistic, Ethnic, and Economic Revival* (Westport, CT: Greenwood, 2007), 123.

30. This section is slightly adapted from chap. 3 in John Goldingay, *Theological Diversity and the Authority of the Old Testament* (Grand Rapids: Eerdmans, 1987).

31. Roland H. Bainton, *Christian Attitudes toward War and Peace: A Historical Survey and Critical Re-evaluation* (Nashville: Abingdon, 1960), 52; cf. 111.

32. Susan Niditch, *War in the Hebrew Bible: A Study in the Ethics of Violence* (New York: Oxford University Press, 1993), 4.

33. Bainton, *Christian Attitudes*, 112–13.

34. Douglas S. Earl, *Reading Joshua as Christian Scripture* (Winona Lake, IN: Eisenbrauns, 2010).

35. This passage from C. T. Maier, "The Bible Moralisée and the Crusades," in *The Experience of Crusading*, vol. 1, *Western Approaches*, ed. Marcus Bull and Norman Housley (Cambridge: Cambridge University Press, 2003), 211, is cited in Douglas Earl, *Holy War in the Bible: Christian Morality and an Old Testament Problem*, ed. Heath A. Thomas, Jeremy Evans, and Paul Copan (Downers Grove, IL: IVP Academic, 2013), 24.

36. Earl, *Holy War in the Bible*, 25.

37. Ibid., 28.

38. Douglas S. Earl, *The Joshua Delusion? Rethinking Genocide in the Bible* (Eugene, OR: Cascade, 2011), 7.

39. Earl, "Joshua and the Crusades," in *Holy War in the Bible*, 35.

40. Bat Ye'or, *Islam and Dhimmitude: Where Civilizations Collide* (Teaneck, NJ: Fairleigh Dickinson University Press, 2002), 285.

41. Madden, "Inventing the Crusades."

Chapter 23: Turning the Other Cheek, Pacifism, and Just War

1. Joel S. Kaminsky, review of Susan Niditch, *War in the Hebrew Bible*, in *The Journal of Religion* 17, no. 3 (July 1994): 381.

2. N.T. Wright affirmed this in response to my (Paul's) paper "Evil and the Justice of God: A Response to N.T. Wright" at the American Academy of Religion in Washington DC (November 2006). For further discussion of Wright's views on the legitimate use of force, see Paul Copan, "A Friendly Response to N.T. Wright: Comments and Questions on *Evil and the Justice of God*." *Philosophia Christi* n.s. 10, no. 2 (2008): 451–60.

3. N. T. Wright, "N. T. Wright Wants to Save the Best Worship Psalms," interview with Andrew Byers, *Christianity Today* 57, no. 7 (September 2013): 79.

4. Miroslav Volf, "Faith and Reconciliation: A Personal Journey," in *God's Advocates: Christian Thinkers in Conversation* (Grand Rapids: Eerdmans, 2005), 222.

5. This chapter summarizes several portions of Robertson McQuilkin and Paul Copan, *Introduction to Biblical Ethics: Walking in the Way of Wisdom* (Downers Grove, IL: InterVarsity, 2014).

6. D. A. Carson, *Love in Hard Places* (Wheaton, IL: Crossway, 2002), 44.

7. Ibid., 72.

8. See Glen Stassen and David Gushee, *Kingdom Ethics: Following Jesus in Contemporary Context* (Downers Grove, IL: InterVarsity, 2006).

9. E. Randolph Richards, "An Honor/Shame Argument for Two Temple Clearings," *Trinity Journal* 29, no. 1 (2008): 19–43.

10. John R. W. Stott, *Christian Counter-Culture: The Message of the Sermon on the Mount* (Downers Grove, IL: InterVarsity, 1978), 113.

11. Richard Hays made this point at a panel discussion sponsored by the Evangelical Philosophical Society at the American Academy of Religion, Nashville, November 2000. See also the comments of James Skillen and Keith Pavlischek, "Political Responsibility and the Use of Force: A Critique of Richard Hays," *Philosophia Christi* 3, no. 2 (2001): 427 and note.

12. John Stott, *Involvement: Being a Responsible Christian in a Non-Christian Society*, vol. 1 (Old Tappan, NJ: Revell, 1985), 126.

13. Doris Kearns Goodwin, *Team of Rivals: The Political Genius of Abraham Lincoln* (New York: Simon & Schuster, 2012).

14. For documentation on Lincoln's faith, see Ronald C. White Jr., *A. Lincoln: A Biography* (New York: Random House, 2010).